HOUSES IN HERCULANEUM

CIRCUMVESUVIANA

EDITED BY

J.A.K.E. DE WAELE & E.M. MOORMANN

VOLUME 1

RICHARD E.L.B. DE KIND

HOUSES IN HERCULANEUM

A NEW VIEW ON THE TOWN PLANNING AND THE BUILDING OF INSULAE III AND IV

J.C. GIEBEN, PUBLISHER

AMSTERDAM 1998

© by R.E.L.B. de Kind, 1998 / Printed in The Netherlands / ISBN 90 5063 517 2

CONTENTS

PREFACE

This study of the houses in *insulae* III and IV at Herculaneum was begun in 1985, when the Department of Classical Archaeology at the Catholic University of Nijmegen carried out an extensive survey in Herculaneum, as part of the research programme 'Formal and functional analysis of ancient buildings'. The research on which this study is based was concluded around the middle of 1991. It was then submitted in 1992 in Dutch as my Ph.D. thesis. It was possible to insert references to some publications which appeared later, but several others are mentioned only in footnotes.

Professor Jos de Waele, whose involvement both as the initiator of the project and as the supervisor of my study was indispensable, must come first in the list of acknowledgements. I also owe a debt of gratitude to those who participated in the survey of 1985, without whose efforts this study could not have been realised, and to all those who assisted in the fieldwork between 1987 and 1990. I would like to express my thanks to Jeroen Bons, Paul Leunissen, Stephan Mols, Kees Peterse, Louis Swinkels and Ludwich Verberne for their invaluable comments on various parts of the text, and to Adam Haarhuis and Gemma Jansen for their great dedication during the 1988 expedition. I am also grateful to the late Ted Meijer, to Thea Heres, and to the staff of the Dutch Institute in Rome, for their hospitality during my two visits in 1988 and 1990. The Soprintendente Archeologico of Pompeii, Baldassare Conticello, the directors of the excavations at Ercolano, Umberto Pappalardo, Tommasina Budetta and Mario Pagano, and the staff involved in the excavations, granted permission for my work and provided assistance. My research was financially supported by the Faculty of Arts of the Catholic University of Nijmegen, the Dutch Institute in Rome, and the Netherlands Organisation for Scientific Research (NWO), which also gave a grant for the translation of this book.

The English translation of my book was done by Brigitte Planken and Ruth Westgate, to whom I am greatly indebted, both for this and for many useful comments.

Finally, three people deserve special acknowledgement for their contributions to the making of this book: Thomas Ganschow, who allowed me to use his unpublished material on the structure of walls in Herculaneum; draughtsman Ernst Ponten, who always created a good atmosphere and who drew the illustrations for this publication; and, last but not least, Saskia van den Boomen, who has provided constant support, not only during a number of expeditions, but even more so at other times.

INTRODUCTION

The way in which houses were built, furnished and inhabited in antiquity is a popular subject for archaeological research. One of the richest sources of archaeological evidence is the area round Vesuvius, where material remains have been preserved, frozen in time, following the volcanic eruption of 79 AD. The ancient houses here have been studied in numerous specialist and non-specialist publications. Recent examples of this interest include the series 'Häuser in Pompeji', a large-scale project under the supervision of the Deutsches Archäologisches Institut,[1] as well as special issues of non-specialist magazines such as the Italian *ARCHEO* (1991, no. 76) and the Dutch *Kunstschrift* (1991, no. 4). On closer examination of these publications, a number of remarkable similarities can be observed. First of all, many studies focus almost exclusively on houses in Pompeii; Herculaneum is often only mentioned to point out parallel features.[2] Moreover, often only those houses with traditional atrium plans are discussed; there are very few studies of other types of house.[3] Finally, the furnishing and interior of the houses is examined at great length, but their layout and embedding in blocks are rarely discussed.[4]

This study of the houses in *insulae* III and IV at Herculaneum will focus on the aspects neglected in the majority of recent publications. Herculaneum will be studied in its own right, and not to provide material for comparison with Pompeii. Thus this study will try to do justice to the archaeological remains at Herculaneum, which are of high quality. Furthermore, the houses in Herculaneum will not be considered as separate entities, but as elements within an urban context. Three levels will be distinguished. The highest level, the 'macro-level', is that of urban planning, the city plan. This determines the shape and the size of the 'meso-level', made up of blocks of houses. These blocks in turn constitute the framework within which we will consider the houses, which together comprise the 'micro-level'. All three levels will be dealt with in hierarchical order, since a proper analysis of the design of the houses (the micro-level) requires a study of the way the houses are interconnected (the meso-level) and of the connections between the frameworks within which they are situated (the macro-level). Because this study does not apply formal criteria but is confined to geographical units (two blocks of houses), it focuses on several types of house, and not just a single one, when the micro-level is examined. The advantage of this approach is that less common types of building are also discussed.

---

[1]   See among others Strocka 1984; Ehrhardt 1988; Michel 1990; Strocka 1991; Seiler 1992. Cf. also Strocka/Ehrhardt 1987.

[2]   Exceptions include Maiuri 1958; Cerulli Irelli 1974; Packer 1975; Deiss 1985; Tran Tam Tinh 1988; Ganschow 1989; Van Binnebeke 1991; Jansen 1991.

[3]   But see Packer 1975; Hoffmann 1979; Evans 1978; Evans 1980.

[4]   Exceptions include Peterse 1984; Peterse 1985; Ling 1983; Carocci / De Albentiis / Gargiulo / Pesando 1990.

This study will pay special attention to an analysis of units of measurement and the design of the houses. An analysis of the units of measurement used in building a house will make it possible to draw conclusions about its design and original appearance, both of which are essential for establishing a typology of the houses. An understanding of the designs used increases our knowledge of house-building in Herculaneum and the rest of Campania, because it enables us to point out basic concepts actually used by the architects. However, an analysis of the units of measurement used can only be made in combination with research into the history of the construction of the houses. A study of the wall and floor decoration and of the wall structures will give us an idea of the changes in a house from the design stage onward. Since an analysis of the wall structures is especially important in this, a full account of this type of research as undertaken in Herculaneum and its place in the present study will be given below. First, however, a survey of metrological research into ancient buildings will be presented, to indicate to which school of thought the metrological analysis here belongs.

Metrological research into ancient buildings

Research into the units of measurement used in antiquity was started in the nineteenth century by Hultsch (1882) and Nissen (1877; 1892). As far as Campania is concerned, these early studies of linear and square measures concentrate especially on two foot measures, the Oscan and the Roman foot. The Oscan foot was used before the Romans took possession of the region, that is until the 1st century BC; its name is derived from a tribe, the Oscans or Opici, who are thought to have been among the earliest inhabitants of Pompeii (see § 1.2 below). It was gradually replaced by the Roman foot, which was the official unit of measurement after 29 BC (Cassius Dio, LII 30,9). Nissen (1877) in particular takes great pains to determine the exact length of the Oscan foot. He finally arrives at a length of 27.50 cm, based on the writings of the Roman *agrimensores*, which say that 10,000 square Oscan feet (= 1 *versus*) are equal to 8,640 square Roman feet (Nissen 1877: 75; Nissen 1892: 884). W. Dörpfeld (1885: 290-293) is of the opinion that the foot was somewhat longer, i.e. 27.8 cm.

A study by U. Bracker-Wester (1980) shows that the Oscan foot is equal to the foot used in the construction of a pre-Roman tower at Cologne. A study of all possible sources, including the measuring-rods found in the area, leads her to the following conclusion: 'Der Fuß von 27.5 cm scheint demnach ein in Gallien/Germanien und angrenzenden Gebieten weit verbreitetes Maß gewesen zu sein' (Bracker-Wester 1980: 506). Textual sources indicate that another foot measure was also used in the north-western part of the Roman Empire, the *pes Drusianus*, which was derived from the official Roman foot, and measured approximately 33.3 cm. This foot is mentioned frequently in studies of the length units used in the towns in this region, especially those conducted by British archaeologists, which in some respects are very close to the present study.[5]

This brings us to the length of the Roman foot (the *pes monetalis*). This, too, has been the subject of debate, focusing especially on the degree of accuracy, i.e. the number of decimal places, to which the Roman foot can be defined in the metric system.[6] Nissen only uses a single decimal place, arriving at 29.6 cm (Nissen 1877: 86; Nissen 1892: 888); Hultsch, on the other hand, prefers a somewhat more precise figure, namely 29.57 cm (Hultsch 1882: 94). Fifty years later, A. von Gerkan pursued the matter again (Von Gerkan 1940: 143-144), claiming that the Roman foot was equal to the Attic foot, and putting it at 29.4192 cm, which can be rounded off to 29.42 cm.

Many studies of the units of measurement used in the Greek world are based on the work of W. Dörpfeld, who published his theories about ancient units of measurement in a number of articles in Athenische Mitteilungen (Dörpfeld 1882; 1883; 1885; 1890). Dörpfeld says that the ancient Greeks used only three foot measures: the Attic foot (29.4-29.6 cm), the Doric foot (32.5-32.8 cm) and the 'Samian' foot (34.7-34.9 cm). His theories were never disputed. On the contrary, the metric values of the 'unumstrittende Fußmaße' were calculated with an ever-increasing degree of precision.[7] Even if we leave aside the question of whether it is at all possible to determine a foot measure to more than two decimal places, these precise determinations of Greek foot measures create the impression that research into the units of measurement used in ancient architecture is a matter of irrefutable absolutes. They suggest a degree of accuracy which could not be attained in real life, and they disregard the innumerable examples of Greek architecture in which foot measures other than the three accepted by Dörpfeld were used. These two points were challenged by J. de Waele.[8] In his view, the foot measure used in the construction of a building should be deduced from the dimensions of the building itself and not *a priori* from the three foot measures accepted by tradition. Furthermore, he assumes a greater tolerance in the units of measurement used in construction than the scholars who adhere to Dörpfeld's theories. Both of De Waele's views are based on the building practices of the ancient Greeks, who used less sophisticated precision tools than are used in modern architecture. Weights and measures were not controlled as accurately as they are now, and there were not only regional but also local differences in the length of the foot measure (so there might be a difference between the measure used at the building site and that used in the quarry). Both factors influenced the length of the foot measure used. The clearest indication of the existence and use of foot measures other than the ones which have been generally accepted by scholars is provided by the metrological relief which was recently discovered on Salamis, which

---

[5]   See for instance Frere 1977; Walthew 1978; Walthew 1987; Duncan-Jones 1980; Bridger 1984; Buijtendorp 1987; Buijtendorp 1993; Smith 1987.

[6]   See especially the survey of the widely varying results in Hultsch (1882: 88-98).

[7]   See the studies by Büsing (1982) and Bankel (1983), among others. Koenigs 1990 presents a survey of present-day theories on measures and proportions used in Greek architecture.

[8]   See, for example, De Waele 1980A; 1980B; 1988; 1990A; 1990B. Cf. Mertens's criticism of De Waele in Mertens 1981.

shows a foot of 30.1 cm (De Waele 1990B: vi). The accuracy of calculations will be limited by errors made during construction (when the ground plan was marked out or when the blocks were put into position), changes in the condition of the building, and errors made in modern archaeological surveys. This down-to-earth approach to Greek architecture has produced important, convincing analyses of the plans of many well-known buildings.[9]

De Waele's approach is supported by the fact that it can also be applied to Roman architecture. After Von Gerkan's analysis of the Roman foot, mentioned above, research in this field took the same course as that into the length of Greek foot measures. The Roman foot too was defined with an increasing degree of accuracy, usually by converting the dimensions of one monument (for example, the height of the column of Trajan = 100 Roman feet). A striking example of this approach can be found in the study by K. Bauer (1983: 136 n.33). Working from the length of the sides of the base of the pyramid of Cestius, he concludes that the Roman foot equalled 27.47 cm. Bauer most probably was not acquainted with K. Hecht's study, published in 1979, which makes it clear that the various attempts at calculating a foot measure in this way have not yielded identical results. In addition, Hecht mentions three important points, comparable to what has been said above in relation to De Waele's theories: 1. there was no mathematical accuracy in Roman construction; 2. comparatively speaking, the level of inaccuracy was lowest in the case of large measurements; 3. mistakes and irregularities could already have occurred when the measurements of a building were determined in antiquity (Hecht 1979: 109). Hecht too arrives at a method whereby the foot measure used is derived from the dimensions of the building itself. He shows that to establish foot measures in this way, one should start with the smaller dimensions, because it is easier to derive the number of units to which they correspond. The accuracy of determination of the unit measure can then be refined by applying the provisional value to larger measurements. The unit of measurement that was used is calculated by adding together all the dimensions and dividing these by the estimated total number of feet (Hecht 1979: 110).

The fact that the journal in which Hecht's study appeared is not very well known probably explains why it took quite a long time for his ideas to evoke the response they deserve. This is clearly shown by various contributions to *Bauplanung und Bautheorie in der Antike*, the proceedings of a colloquium held at Berlin in 1983 and published the following year. What is perhaps most striking in this respect is the contrast of opinions which is apparent in the introductory articles by W. Hoepfner (Hoepfner 1984) and E.-L. Schwandner (Schwandner 1984). Hoepfner clearly seems to adhere to the three well-known, undisputed foot measures already mentioned above, although he mentions a number of exceptions and refers to the problems related to such a fixed system. Schwandner, on the other hand, lists a number of points indicating innovations in the way ancient measurements are regarded. For example, he

---

[9]   Cf. also the elucidating remarks in Höcker 1993 about the main issues in the 'Bauforschung': the precision of the building process (25-36), the building unit (36-49), the calculation of the unit (49-59), and the proportions (59-67).

contrasts the (very fine) tolerances considered acceptable in the analysis of ancient buildings with the modern tolerances accepted by the German Department of Weights and Measures, which permit a deviation of 4 mm in a total length of 2 metres. He also rejects the supposed 'Normierung' of units of measurements in the Greek *poleis*; in his view, they could determine their own units of measurement independently.

Among the contributions to *Bauplanung und Bautheorie in der Antike* which may be relevant to this discussion are two further articles which express diametrically opposed views: E. Buchner's contribution, which expresses the conventional view (Buchner 1984), and F. Rakob's, which puts forward ideas similar to those of Hecht (Rakob 1984).[10] Buchner's article begins with the following words: 'Es ist verlockend, von der Sonnenuhr des Augustus die genaue Länge des römischen Fußes ableiten zu wollen.' (Buchner 1984: 215). Eventually, he comes to the conclusion that the pattern of lines on the Sundial of Augustus is not quite precise enough to enable us to determine the exact length of the Roman foot. It is clear that Buchner has not taken Hecht's remarks to heart. Rakob, on the other hand, has taken heed of Hecht's comments, and has added a number of very important observations. First of all, he distances himself from attempts 'das (stadtrömische) Fußmaß 'in genere' auf Bruchteile von Dezimillimetern festzulegen' (Rakob 1984: 220). Instead, he argues that one should allow for a tolerance of approximately 2 mm in the length of the foot. Perhaps more important is Rakob's observation that in measuring Roman buildings one should take into account the fact that these buildings usually had concrete walls with double facings, which have broad foundations and which were covered with a thick layer of plaster. This means that it is not clear whether the lines forming the original plan indicated the inside of the walls, the outside of the walls, or the centre (the axis) of the walls (Rakob 1984: 220). Rakob assumes that in the actual process of construction, modules based on multiples of the Roman foot were often used. These modules were sometimes used in pairs with a lowest common denominator, so as to simplify construction practices, such as putting working drawings in proportion. 'Für einfache, orthogonal definierte Grundrisse hätten auch Kataloge mit Angaben zu Maß und Zahl, ergänzt durch Detailzeichnungen genügen können.' (Rakob 1984: 221). These conclusions are of vital importance to metrological research into Roman buildings.

In 1984, two articles appeared in the journal *BABesch* which make important contributions to the study of Roman and Oscan foot measures in general and to the metrological study of monuments in Pompeii in particular. The first article is J. de Waele's study of the Temple of Jupiter Capitolinus at Pompeii (De Waele 1984). In this he applies the method he used previously in relation to Greek architecture to the Pompeian Capitoline temple, and also discusses the Roman foot measure. The second article was written by C. Peterse and deals with the Oscan foot in a number of atrium houses at Pompeii (Peterse 1984). Independently, Peterse arrives at virtually the same

---

[10] Also valuable for the study of Roman house planning are the article by H. von Hesberg about Roman plans carved in marble (Von Hesberg 1984) and that by G. Zimmer about (depictions of) measuring-rods used by Roman architects (Zimmer 1984).

conclusions as Hecht and Rakob. He bases his metrological analyses on the sum of the measurements of a building, the way in which these measurements relate to each other and the state of the building. He points out inaccuracies and deficiencies in measuring a building's dimensions which make it impossible to assign an absolute value to a particular foot measure. This leads him to allow a greater margin of error in converting the value measured into a theoretical value than is generally considered acceptable in the literature. According to Mau and Nissen the measured value should not deviate more than 2 cm from the theoretical value. Peterse regards this deviation as an axiom, based on a degree of precision in the actual construction of a building which cannot be proved (Peterse 1984: 11). Thus he concludes 'daß man bei der Verwendung des oskischen Fußes mit Toleranzen rechnen muß und daß in Bezug auf die Größe der noch zulässigen Korrekturen keine Einzelnormen aufgestellt werden können.' (Peterse 1984: 12). In an article published in 1985 (Peterse 1985), Peterse again successfully applies his method, this time to one of the largest houses in Pompeii, the Casa di Pansa (VI 6, 1). In this study, the correct length of the foot measure used is once again determined in a clear, logical fashion (Peterse 1985: 42; Peterse 1984: 12). From a limited number of metric measurements, a provisional, hypothetical foot measure is deduced, which is checked against the other measurements made; if the hypothetical unit of measurement also appears to fit these data, it may be assumed that this unit of measurement is a close approximation of the foot measure that was actually used. The method Hecht suggests for determining the correct foot measure, i.e. adding up all the metric measurements and dividing these by the estimated total number of feet (Hecht 1979: 110), is also used by Peterse; he calls the result 'the weighted average foot measure'.

The type of research carried out by Peterse and De Waele was rejected by V. Kockel in his survey of archaeological research in Pompeii and the surrounding area (Kockel 1986: 455, 462, 548). Some of De Waele's very strongly worded ideas may indeed be queried, but in general Kockel's criticism of Peterse's and De Waele's method is too extreme. This criticism seems to be rooted in a number of axioms formulated in the past, mentioned above, to which Kockel adheres tenaciously, and it ignores the remarkable, demonstrable results produced by this new method.

Peterse's research is important for the study of houses in Pompeii and Herculaneum, because it adds a new dimension to the traditional way of examining these houses, which consists of surveying their decoration and the various phases of their construction. An analysis of the units of measurement used enables us to gain an insight into the way an architect planned a house or the way in which a house was built according to logical and coherent principles.[11] An insight into the design of a house and the coherent division of the space may be relevant not only to a study of the typology of houses and a further analysis of the use of space in a house, but also to research into the various phases of construction. However, as far as research into the history of a building is concerned, an analysis of the measurements used can only provide additional information; it can only play a limited role as evidence to support a

---

[11]   See also Van Binnebeke/De Kind 1996: 198-199.

8

chronology which was established on other grounds (construction materials, floors, wall decoration). Only when it is completely or nearly impossible to establish such a chronology in other ways can an attempt be made to formulate hypotheses about the various stages in the history of the building on the basis of an analysis of the measurements used.

The present state of research into walling materials

A study of wall construction is essential to research into the houses in *insulae* III and IV in Herculaneum. A knowledge of the structures used in building a house may lead to a greater insight into the relative or sometimes the absolute age of the walls. Naturally, this is also important for the metrological analysis of a house. If nothing is known about the wall structures, an analysis may degenerate into a fanciful enumeration of figures which has little to do with reality.

Until recently, the only study examining wall construction in Herculaneum in any depth was Maiuri's study of Herculaneum (Maiuri 1958). In writing this, Maiuri mainly used his own survey of walling materials in Pompeii (Maiuri 1942A) as a guide, although he himself had noticed a divergence in the development of wall construction at Pompeii and at Herculaneum. In addition, reference is often made to the dating of types of construction in buildings in Rome and Latium by Lugli (Lugli 1957), which, however, scholars including Lugli himself do not consider to be universally applicable.

Fortunately, an excellent new survey of wall construction in Herculaneum by Ganschow (1989) is now available, which provides a detailed typology of ancient structures as well as of the reconstructions made during nineteenth- and twentieth-century excavations.[12] Each type is described very conscientiously and where possible a relative dating is given, based on information provided by the walls themselves, which means that it is possible to say which type occurs at the same time as, before, or after another type. This has resulted in a division of the types into three groups, for which the author is able to provide a more absolute chronology by making use of external criteria, such as historical facts and wall paintings.

In brief, Ganschow distinguishes the following types.
- The oldest type of construction in Herculaneum is *opus incertum*, which Ganschow divides into five types: A, B (with subtypes a, b, c), C, D and C/D. The division into types A, B and C was already used by Maiuri, but Ganschow has subdivided Maiuri's type B into Ba, Bb, Bc, D and C/D.
- Four types of *opus reticulatum* are found: *opus quasi-reticulatum* (only a single wall in Herculaneum), *opus reticulatum* A, *polychrome opus reticulatum* A and *opus reticulatum* B. Maiuri distinguished only two types of *opus reticulatum*: A and B.
- *Opus quadratum* and stone frame construction used for entire walls, as found in Pompeii, have not been found in Herculaneum; however, *opus quadratum* was used

---

[12]   For a detailed discussion of this book, see De Kind 1991A. Cf. also Ganschow 1993.

to reinforce corners and for doorposts, as was *opus vittatum*. As far as the latter is concerned, Ganschow distinguishes an *opus vittatum variant* and *opus vittatum mixtum*, in addition to the ordinary type. Similarly, *opus testaceum* (and its variant with larger bricks) was only used to reinforce corners, for doorposts and columns/pillars.

- *Opus craticium*, half-timbering, was sometimes used for entire walls in Herculaneum.[13]

Each type can be briefly characterised as follows:

Opus incertum A: rather coarse masonry of various kinds of volcanic rock.

Opus incertum B: the smooth side of the volcanic rocks faces outwards; *Ba* = ashygrey, slightly porous lava; *Bb* = more *schiuma*, especially red/violet; *Bc* = large redbrown tufa blocks.

Opus incertum C: regular lines of small geometrically shaped, yellow tufa blocks.

Opus incertum D: made in the same way as *opus caementicium*, with all kinds of material, but with smaller pieces of stone than *opus incertum A* and *B*.

Opus incertum C/D: like *opus incertum D*, but with a preference for yellow tufa.

Opus quasi-reticulatum: small yellow tufa blocks set in irregular diagonal rows. The only example is: IV 19-20, room 2.

Opus reticulatum A: a lattice pattern of small pyramidal yellow tufa blocks.

Polychrome opus reticulatum A: like *opus reticulatum A*, but also including small red *schiuma* blocks.

Opus reticulatum B: a less regular lattice pattern, made with slightly larger and more irregular yellow tufa blocks than *opus reticulatum A*.

Opus quadratum: rectangular red-brown tufa blocks (often 0.40 m x 0.60/0.70 m).

Opus vittatum: small, rectangular yellow tufa blocks.

Opus vittatum variant: slightly larger blocks than in *opus vittatum*.

Opus vittatum mixtum: small, rectangular yellow tufa blocks, alternating with 1 or, more usually, 2 or 3 courses of brick.

Opus testaceum: bricks, often 0.02/0.03 m high and 0.18-0.25 m wide.

Opus testaceum variant: bricks, 0.05/0.07 m high and 0.15-0.30 m wide.

Opus craticium: wooden framework filled in with small yellow tufa blocks, *schiuma* and other material.

Ganschow distinguishes the following groups, which he arranges in chronological order:

- Group 1 (*opus incertum A, opus incertum Ba, opus quadratum*) and group 1a (*opus incertum Bb, opus incertum Bc*) consist of the oldest types, which were used side by side; these are to be dated to the Samnite period, down to c. 80 BC.

- Group 2 (*opus incertum B, opus reticulatum A, opus reticulatum B, opus vittatum, opus vittatum mixtum*) follows group 1 and dates from c. 80 BC to AD 79. Ganschow conjectures that the succession of types in this period was roughly as follows. Originally, the yellow Neapolitan tufa, which replaced the local stone used for *opus incertum A* and *B*, was laid in the old *incertum* way (*opus incertum C*). This period more

---

[13]   Cf. Papaccio 1993.

or less coincides with that of the Second Style of wall painting (c. 90-15 BC). The introduction of the *opus reticulatum* technique from Rome brought about a change, leading to the development of *opus reticulatum B*, which was later refined further and became *opus reticulatum A*. However, *opus incertum C* and *opus reticulatum B* continued to be used: *opus incertum C* was still used for alterations, while *opus reticulatum B* was used especially between AD 62 and 79. Group 2a (*opus testaceum, opus vittatum mixtum variants*), dating from the same period as group 2, is not found very often in Herculaneum; these types are mainly used to reinforce corners.

- Group 3 (*opus incertum D, opus incertum C/D, opus vittatum/testaceum variants*) belongs to the last period in the town's history. As the nature of the materials and the types of walling point to a method of construction in which speed had precedence over beauty, it seems logical to conclude that the types in this group are to be considered as makeshift solutions used to repair the damage caused by the earthquake that took place in 62.

Ganschow applies this classification of walling materials to seven houses in Herculaneum, two of which, the Casa dello Scheletro (III 3) and the Casa dei Cervi (IV 21), are in the *insulae* to be discussed in this book. The other five houses are in the south part of *insula* V: Casa Sannitica (V 1-2), Casa del Telaio (V 3-4), Casa del Mobilio Carbonizzato (V 5), Casa con Giardino (V 32-33) and Casa del Gran Portale (V 34-35). Ganschow has also studied the construction of all the other buildings in Herculaneum, but he has not yet published his findings. The present study will make frequent use of this unpublished material, which was kindly made available by Dr Ganschow. Because of the high quality of the analyses and typologies that have already been published and because of our long association, I have decided to use his unpublished findings instead of carrying out my own analysis of the wall structures, which would be time-consuming, expensive and probably superfluous.

The history of several of the buildings described in the unpublished study can easily be analysed using the same method as Ganschow applies to the seven houses in Herculaneum (Ganschow 1989). However, there are also houses where the type of construction cannot be used to determine the period in which the building was constructed or altered. A case in point is the Casa dell'Atrio Corinzio (V 30), where the walls are either not original or are hidden behind plaster. There are only a few minor clues as to the possible development of this house, which was severely damaged either by the eruption in 79 or by the 18th-century excavations (see § 2.2 below). It has proved possible to carry out a metrological analysis on the basis of these clues.[14] This example shows that wall structures are certainly not the only kind of evidence on which a metrological analysis can be based. Even if only a few general conclusions can be drawn from an analysis of the wall construction, it is sometimes justified to formulate a hypothesis about the design on the basis of the metrological data. In such cases, the minimum requirements should be that the metrological analysis is given a provisional status, is at least not inconsistent with the data about the wall structures, and, if

---

[14]   For a functional analysis of the house, see Van Binnebeke 1993 and for a discussion of its history and design, see De Kind 1993. Exhaustive: Van Binnebeke/De Kind 1996.

possible, is supported by information from other sources (floors, walls, etc.). In other words, an analysis of the wall construction is certainly important, but it should not be the only criterion.

Arrangement of this study

We can conclude our preliminary remarks with a survey of the present study. Part I focuses on Herculaneum in general and discusses the sources on which our knowledge of the city is based. Chapter 1 mainly deals with the written sources and what these can teach us about the location, the history and the end of the city. Chapter 2 describes on the history of the archaeological excavation of its remains. These chapters are intended to form the basis of the analysis of the houses that follows, but at the same time they can be read as a self-contained, independent survey. When the present study was being prepared, it appeared that such a survey of the history of the city and the excavations, incorporating recent archaeological finds and new insights, was lacking. The survey in Part I aims in particular to present additions and corrections to articles in *RE* (Gall 1912) and *EAA* (Maiuri 1960; De Franciscis 1970), to the general part of the monumental study by Maiuri (1958), to the very readable but often inaccurate book by Deiss (1985), and to the vivid work about the excavations by Conte Corti (1942), which is littered with dubious anecdotes and incorrect information. References to most of the secondary literature, as well as an excellent list of all the known written, epigraphic and numismatic sources, can be found in two recent studies by McIlwaine (1988) and Scatozza Höricht (1989B). The bibliography in the present study therefore only includes the works cited in the various chapters.

The arrangement of the remaining parts of this study is determined by the three levels of urban development and design discussed above. The form of the city plan and its place in the history of urban development (the macro-level) are discussed in Chapter 3. The information gathered from the written and archaeological sources described in Part I will play an important part in this chapter. Chapter 4, which ends Part II, focuses on the 'meso-level', the blocks of houses or *insulae*. This chapter will also examine the constructional and judicial problems which were caused by the use of shared walls.

Part III centres on the 'micro-level', the houses themselves. First, all the houses of *insulae* III and IV are discussed individually in Chapter 5. In this discussion, published material about the wall and floor decoration, inscriptions, archaeological finds and architecture is used as much as possible. However, the main part of each section consists of a consideration of the building history of the house on the basis of its decoration and wall construction, and an extensive analysis of its measurements, the combination of which often leads to an understanding of the design of the house. Chapter 6 starts with a short introduction about our present knowledge of Roman houses. This subject has been studied frequently and does not require extensive treatment. This is followed by a section presenting a new typology of the houses in Herculaneum, not only of those in *insulae* III and IV, but of all the houses in the city, based partly on the observations in Chapter 5. This typology is then compared with the general survey of the layout of Roman houses presented earlier.[15]

Finally, two remarks of a practical nature need to be made: 1) in many cases, the word *foot* has been replaced by the sign ′, sometimes followed by either the letter *O* or *R*. On its own, or if the letter *O* is added, ′ is used to refer to the Oscan foot. The Roman foot is referred to as ′*R*. 2) When the orientation of a building is indicated, the conventional designation of north, derived from Maiuri (1958), is used.[16]

---

[15]   Previews of this book have been published as: De Kind 1992A; 1992B; 1993B.

[16]   In fact, Maiuri's north arrow points slightly to the east of north, but it is generally accepted as standard. In Ganschow 1989 the side indicated as west in the present study is used as north. See also Ward-Perkins 1979: 38 n. 5 and De Vos/De Vos 1982: 265.

PART I

THE CITY OF HERCULANEUM

1. HISTORY OF THE CITY

1.1. Location

The number of references to Herculaneum in classical writings is not very large.[17] In a few instances the city is referred to in prose and poems that describe Campania; it is sometimes included in historical surveys and mentioned in correspondence. The earliest reference is often said to be in a passage from the *Historia Plantarum* by Theophrastus of Eresos (approx. 370-285 BC). In this book, which dates from 314 BC, Theophrastus writes about a number of poisonous herbs and natural antidotes, the effects of which were said to have been carefully ascertained by the 'Tyrrhenians in Herakleia':

Ταῦτα δὲ ἐξακριβωθῆναι μάλιστα παρὰ τοῖς Τυρρηνοῖς τοῖς ἐν Ἡρακλείᾳ
('and that these matters were carefully ascertained by the Tyrrhenians of Herakleia') (XI, 16, 6).

Many people assume that 'Herakleia' here refers to Herculaneum near Naples, providing written evidence that Herculaneum existed as early as the 4th century BC. This interpretation, however, should be regarded with scepticism.[18]

The Greek historiographer Dionysius of Halicarnassus (1st century BC), provides us with a mythological version of the founding of the city. In his *Antiquitates Romanae* he tells how Hercules, on his way home after successfully completing his tenth labour, the theft of the cattle of Geryon, founded a small town at the place where he moored his fleet. He then describes what this place, named after Hercules, looked like in his time: he writes that it is inhabited by Romans, lies between Naples and Pompeii, and provides safe harbours at all times:

πολίχνην ἐπώνυμον αὐτοῦ κτίσας, ἔνθα ὁ στόλος αὐτῷ ἐναυλοχεῖτο. ἢ καὶ νῦν ὑπὸ Ῥωμαίων οἰκουμένη Νέας Πόλεως καὶ Πομπηίας ἐν μέσῳ κεῖται λιμένας ἐν παντὶ καιρῷ βεβαίους ἔχουσα.

('and he built a small town which was named after him, at the place where his fleet was moored; to this day it is still inhabited by Romans and, situated between Naples and Pompeii, it always provides safe harbours'). (I, 44) - ed. C. Jacoby (1885).

---

[17] Cf. also comments on this subject by E. Lepore (1955: p. 423-429) which are still valid. Waldstein/Shoobridge (1908) provide a clear overview of passages written by classical authors in Appendix II (p. 255-270). See also Scatozza Höricht (1989B). The text editions used are those from the Loeb series, except Cicero, *Ad fam.*, Florus, Mela, Suetonius and Varro (Budé series), Frontinus and Hyginus (ed. Blume/Lachmann/Rudorff 1848), Sisenna (ed. Peter 1914) and Velleius Paterculus (ed. Portalupi 1967).

[18] See Lepore 1955: p. 425 and § 1.2.1. of the present study.

An important point which may contribute to our knowledge about Herculaneum is that there must have been at least two harbours, which appear to have been sheltered. It is not clear whether Dionysius, in referring to the legendary settlement of Hercules as a 'small town', intended to give an indication of the town's size in his own time.

This would correspond to the information contained in the short but striking description provided by L. Cornelius Sisenna, who lived a number of decades before Dionysius.[19] In a historical work which is only partly preserved, he tells us that Herculaneum was a town with less than impressive walls, situated at the foot of Vesuvius, on a hill by the sea, between two rivers:

'*Quod oppidum tumulo in excelso [loco] propter mare parvis moenibus inter duas fluvias infra Vessuvium conlocatum*'
('which city, with less than strong walls, is situated on a high hill by the sea, between two small rivers at the foot of Vesuvius'). (fr. 53, ed. Peter 1914).

We have to imagine the settlement as having been a small, walled town on a spit of land, bordered by rivers on both sides which flowed out into the sea. The good harbours that Dionysius speaks of may well have been situated at the mouths of these rivers, where shelter could be found.

Strabo, the geographer and historian who lived at the beginning of our era, and who deals with the environs of Vesuvius in book V of his *Geographica*, adds to this description:

Ἐχόμενον δὲ φρούριόν ἐστιν Ἡράκλειον, ἐκκειμένην εἰς τὴν θάλατταν ἄκραν ἔχον, καταπνεομένην Λιβὶ θαυμαστῶς, ὥσθ' ὑγιεινὴν ποιεῖν τὴν κατοικίαν.
('Next we come upon the Heraclean fort, with a spit of land which reaches out into the sea and meets the south-westerly winds wondrously well so that the settlement becomes a healthy place to live in'.) (V, 4.8, C 247).

Here, the spit of land is mentioned explicitly, as well as the climatic advantage which results from it, namely that the area was prone to south-westerly winds, making it a very pleasant and, in Strabo's opinion, healthy place to stay in. It is remarkable that there is mention of a fortified place, a 'φρούριόν'. This seems to correspond to the information provided by Sisenna. We can also deduce Herculaneum's size from the description given by Seneca; in his eyes Herculaneum is a mere *oppidum*, while the larger settlement of Pompeii is referred to as an *urbs* (*Nat. Quaest.* VI, 1; 2). The small town features in the journey of the snake of Aesculapius (in 291 BC), which is described by Ovid in the *Metamorphoses* (in which, incidentally, the town is referred to as *urbs*) and in Pomponius Mela's *Chorographia*:

'*inde legit Capreas promunturiumque Minervae et Surrentino generosos palmite colles Herculeamque urbem Stabiasque*'
('From that place he passed Capreae, the Cape of Minerva and the hills of Surrentum, rich in grapevines, past Herculaneum and Stabiae') (Ovid, *Metamorph.*, XV 709-711)
'*...Herculaneum, Vesuvii montis adspectus, Pompei, ...*'

---

[19]   Sisenna was praetor in 78 BC and fought for Pompey against the pirates in 67 BC. See Niese 1901.

('Herculaneum, which looks out on Vesuvius, Pompeii') (Pomponius Mela, *Chorogr.*, II, 70).

Before discussing the history of the town in detail, it should be noted that the area surrounding Vesuvius, including Herculaneum, is praised frequently for its beautiful landscape, its delicious wine and its favourable location[20]. L. Junius Moderatus Columella adds that there is a lagoon between Pompeii and Herculaneum, and salt-pans nearby:

'*dulcis Pompeia palus vicina salinis Herculeis*'
('the sweet lagoon of Pompeii near the salt-pans of Herculaneum') (*De Re Rustica* X, 135-136).

These accounts provide us with an idea of what the area around Herculaneum looked like before it was altered by the eruption of Vesuvius in AD 79 and by subsequent eruptions.

1.2. History

1.2.1. The period leading up to the earthquake

At a later point in his description Strabo gives a brief chronological overview of the inhabitants of Herculaneum and Pompeii. Before the arrival of the Romans, these cities were inhabited by the Oscans, the Tyrrhenians, the Pelasgians and the Samnites successively:

Ὄσκοι δ' εἶχον καὶ ταύτην καὶ τὴν ἐφεξῆς Πομπαίαν, ἥν παραρρεῖ ὁ Σάρνος ποταμός, εἶτα Τυρρηνοὶ καὶ Πελασγοί, μετὰ ταῦτα δὲ Σαυνῖται.

('This place and the next, Pompaia, along which the Sarnus river runs, were inhabited by Oscans, and subsequently by Tyrrhenians and Pelasgians and after that by the Samnites'). (V, 4.8, C 247).

As a result, Herculaneum is thought to have been subject to a similar sequence of events to Pompeii and other places in Campania, where the native Oscan tribe was driven out by the expansion of the Greeks, who in turn had to make way for the Etruscans. When the Etruscans lost supremacy over Campania after their defeat at the battle of Cumae in 474 BC, the subsequent vacuum was filled by the Samnites.

Greek supremacy over the Gulf of Naples was practically certain after the Greeks from Cumae founded Parthenope in about 650 BC and Neapolis after 474 BC. Their control of the area will no doubt have entailed annexation of the settlements or the formation of far-reaching alliances. It is possible that Herculaneum may have been occupied by the Greeks and used as a fort, to ensure control of the coastal road and

---

[20]   Cicero, *De lege agr.* II, XIV, 36; XXXV, 95. Pliny, *N.H.* III, 5, 60-62. Ovid, *Metamorphoses* XV, 710-712.

the Bay of Naples itself. The great influence of Neapolis is supposed on the basis of, among other things, similarities in the construction of both cities, which will be discussed below.

Strabo's mention of Tyrrhenians (Etruscans) is consistent with the information in the passage from Theophrastus referred to above, in which he speaks of the 'Tyrrhenians in Herakleia' (*Hist. Plant.*, IX, 16, 6). However, Lepore (1955: 425) rightly questioned whether this is really a reference to Herculaneum. It is possible that there may be another Herakleia at issue here.[21] The town was small and dependent on the large neighbouring town of Neapolis and there are no clues which may lead us to conclude that it was an important centre for the Etruscans.

There is also little evidence to support a Samnite period in the construction of the town. It is assumed that Herculaneum, like Pompeii, was a member of the League of Nuceria after the Samnites conquered Campania in the middle of the 5th century BC. The Campanians, as the Samnite inhabitants of the plain called themselves in order to be distinguished from the Samnites who lived in the mountains, were organised in small-scale alliances between towns. Nuceria formed an alliance with towns in the Sarnus valley (Stabiae, Surrentum, Pompeii and, supposedly, also Herculaneum); Capua was allied with Atella, Calatia, Casilinum and other cities. A *meddiss túvtíks*, or *meddix tuticus* in Latin, was put in charge of each of these districts. A reference to this functionary occurs in an inscription from Herculaneum.[22] Each district town had its own *meddix*: the *meddís Kapuans* for Capua and the *medikeís Púmpaiianeís* for Pompeii.[23] In addition there were a number of *quaestors* for each district and town (the *kvaísstur*), as well as a type of senate (*kombenniom*), and every settlement had its *aedilis* (Beloch 1890: 11, 243; Vetter 1953: nos 9-20). During the Second Samnite War, in 307 BC, the Romans must have gained supremacy over Herculaneum, as well as the other towns in the League of Nuceria. The passage in Livy (X, 45, 25) about the capture of Velia, Palumbinum and Herculaneum in 293 BC by the consul Carvilius during the Third Samnite War presumably refers to another town named Herculaneum, in Samnium (Beloch 1890: 219; Gall 1912: 534):

'*Iam Carvilius Veliam et Palumbinum et Herculaneum ex Samnitibus ceperat*'
('Carvilius had already captured Velia, Palumbinum and Herculaneum from the Samnites').

All the towns in Campania around Herculaneum had, by 293 BC, already been allied to Rome for a decade, so the city could never have survived on its own.

During this period of Roman domination the districts and the towns within them, including Herculaneum, retained their political systems and also continued to use Oscan as their official language (Sironen 1993). It is not known whether the Second Punic

---

[21]   The same applies to Phainias of Eresos's passage about tyrants in Herakleia, 'a city in Southern Italy', which is referred to by Deiss 1985: 6. This story (fr. 16 in the Wehrli edition 1969) pertains to events in Herakleia near Metapontum (Lucania) - cf. Wehrli 1969: 32.

[22]   Beloch 1890: 11, 221, 225 n.302, 419; Vetter 1953: no. 107. Cf. Livy, 23.35; 24.19; 26.6.

[23]   Beloch 1890 is unclear about the find-spot of the inscription referred to: Porta di Nola (11) or Porta di Sarno (243). In contrast, Vetter 1953: 47-49, no. 8 mentions Porta di Stabia.

War had any noteworthy effect on the town. The Social War (91-89 BC) did bring about substantial changes. Initially, Herculaneum sided with Rome but in 90 BC it chose to join the Italian ranks. The leader of the Samnite army, C. Papius Mutilus, was responsible for this action because it was during the same year that he terrorised the allied towns with violent military action against Nuceria (Münzer 1949). We learn from Velleius Paterculus how the town was subsequently taken in 89 BC; he describes how his ancestor Minatius Magius, under the leadership of the Roman legate Titus Didius, had been involved in the action:

'quippe multum Minatii Magii, atavi mei, Aeculanensis, tribuendum est memoriae (....) tantam hoc bello fidem Romanis praestitit, ut cum legione, quam ipse in Hirpinis conscripserat, Herculaneum simul cum T. Didio caperet'.

('After all much can be attributed to the memory of my ancestor Minatius Magius, from Aesculum, (...) who took up such a loyal position with respect to the Romans, that he took Herculaneum together with T. Didius, with the legion that he himself had recruited from among the Hirpini') (*Historia romana*, II, 16).

Fragment 54 of Sisenna's history presumably refers to the capture of Herculaneum, during which a river, maybe even one of the two mentioned earlier in this chapter, must have been traversed:

'...transgressus fluviam, quae secundum Herculaneum ad mare perfluebat...'

('crossed the river, which runs past Herculaneum to the sea') (frg. 54, ed. Peter 1914).[24]

From 89 BC Herculaneum became a Roman *municipium* and belonged to the tribe Menenia, as did the other towns in the League of Nuceria. It is unclear whether a colony of veterans was established, as in Pompeii and Nola (Beloch 1890: 13; 219). We cannot refer to the classical writers to determine what happened between 89 BC and AD 62. There is a reference in a letter written by Cicero (*Ad fam.* IX, 25, 3) to a *Herculanensis fundus*, a rural estate that belonged to Q. Fabius. Seneca also tells of a villa on the coast near Herculaneum, which belonged to Tiberius, and which was destroyed on the orders of the emperor Caligula, in order to put an end to defamatory rumours claiming that his mother had been imprisoned there:

'C. enim Caesar villam in Herculanensi pulcherrimam, quia mater sua aliquando in illa custodita erat, diruit fecitque eius per hoc notabilem fortunam; stantem enim praenavigabamus...'

('Because C. Caesar had a very beautiful villa near Herculaneum destroyed, because his mother had once been imprisoned there and thus her fate became public knowledge; because when the villa was still intact, we used to simply sail past it...') (*De ira* III, 21, 5).

This passage, together with the popularity of the region, which Pliny the Younger mentions in his letter to Tacitus (*Epist.* VI, 16), indicates that many Romans had discovered the beauty of the area around Herculaneum and had had country houses built

---

[24]   Sisenna's *Historiae* presumably contained the most extensive account of the Social War in antiquity. Velleius provides a summary. Cf. Portalupi 1967: 71.

there.[25] The famous 'Villa dei Papiri', just outside the town, must be one of these.[26] On one of the papyrus scrolls containing the writings of the philosopher Philodemus of Gadara (*PHerc.* 312), which were found there, the name *Hèrklaneon* is mentioned together with the city of *Neapolis* and *Siron* the philosopher. M. Gigante (1983: 32-37) deduces from this information that the villa housed meetings for people who moved in philosophical circles; these were chaired by Philodemus who maintained contacts with similar groups in Naples - Siron's for example. Virgil might possibly have been included in the list of members. According to Gigante (1983: 38-39), Virgil's '*vicina Vesaevo / ora iugo*' ('the region near the mountains of Vesuvius'; *Georgica* II 224-225) can be regarded as a poetic description of the coast near Herculaneum, where the poet had once stayed himself.

Herculaneum clearly remained secondary to Pompeii, or so it would seem from the aforementioned description by Seneca: Pompeii is an *urbs*, Herculaneum a mere *oppidum* (*Nat. Quaest.* VI, 1; 2). According to H. Solin (1973a), this lag in development can also be deduced from the fact that graffiti and election slogans, which form such a rich source for prosopographic and socio-economic research at Pompeii, are totally lacking at Herculaneum.[27] However, an election slogan for the office of *quaestor*, inscribed by M. Caecilius Potitus, has now been found (Pagano 1987), and a more carefully considered conclusion is called for.[28] Presumably the town must have run elections for public office, but this has not as yet been proved; to date only the least busy area of the town has been excavated. Elections might conceivably have been on a smaller scale here than in Pompeii. The political structure of the *municipium* of Herculaneum, which can be reconstructed on the basis of various inscriptions found over the years, is in any case comparable to that of Pompeii. In addition to the quaestor(s), whose existence is confirmed by the appeal for votes referred to above, there was also a city council of *decuriones* (CIL X 1414; 1422). There are also references to *duumviri* (CIL X 1441; 1453), to the normal *iure dicundo* (CIL X 1457), who was elected every year - sometimes for a second term (*iterum*) (Schumacher 1976: 169) - as well as the special *quinquennales*, who acted as *censor* every five years (CIL X 1442-1444; 1461). As there were normal administrative departments such as these, it is plausible to assume that Herculaneum was an 'average' *municipium*.

The honorary title of *patronus* (known from Pompeii through, among others, M. Holconius Rufus (CIL X 830), who, as *patronus coloniae*, acted as an intermediary between Rome and the colony[29]) was also bestowed in Herculaneum. We learn from a decree inscribed on an altar in front of the entrance to the Suburban Baths (*AE* 1976,

---

[25] See also D'Arms 1970; Scatozza Höricht 1985 (143-144: written sources).
[26] See especially Wojcik 1986, with an extensive bibliography (289-317).
[27] For a political and social history of Pompeii: Castrén 1975; Jongman 1988; Mouritsen 1988.
[28] However cf. Mouritsen 1988: n. 3. Also significant for our view of Herculaneum is the recently published inscription on the outer wall of the bar on the so-called *decumanus maximus* (VI 14), which announces the gladiatorial games - see Pagano 1988B: 210-211.
[29] Castrén 1975: 56, 97, 176 (M. Holconius Rufus); for the portrait of Holconius Rufus: Zanker 1981.

144)[30] that this title was given to M. Nonius Balbus. The decree provides interesting information about the political situation in Herculaneum in the 1st century AD. In inscriptions found in Herculaneum, there are frequent references to M. Nonius Balbus, who had been praetor and proconsul, and to his family. Numerous statues were erected in honour of Balbus and his relatives, which is why we are so well-informed about the Nonii Balbi.[31]

Balbus originated from Nuceria (CIL X 1429), and was a member of the Senate as well as proconsul of Crete and Cyrene (CIL X 1430-1434), an office he held in Augustan times.[32] Following Amedeo Maiuri[33], many archaeologists are of the opinion that Balbus lived in the Flavian era. They draw this conclusion from the fact that a certain M. Nonius erected a statue in honour of Titus, which must be dated before July in the year AD 72 (CIL X 1420), and from an inscription which records that M. Nonius Balbus paid for the construction or renovation of the Basilica, gates and walls from his own pocket (CIL X 1425). According to these archaeologists, this generous gesture was prompted by the earthquake that struck Herculaneum in AD 62. L. Schumacher, however, has made a reasonable case for placing the proconsul M. Nonius Balbus in the Augustan period.[34] The most important arguments in support of this claim are: firstly, that there is no indication in the building inscription that the renovation was intended to repair damage caused by the earthquake (unlike, for example, CIL X 846, which relates to the Temple of Isis in Pompeii, and CIL X 1406, the Temple of Mater Deum at Herculaneum); secondly, that the style of the statues depicting female members of the Balbus family puts them in the Tiberian era; and thirdly, that the M. Nonius Balbus of CIL X 1420 could have been a freedman of the Nonii Balbi (Schumacher 1976: 166-167). Another argument in favour of the Augustan date is the fact that Balbus and one of his fellow senators, App. Claudius Pulcher, had honorific seats or boxes at the theatre (CIL X 1424 and 1427). Pulcher was *consul ordinarius* in AD 38 and patron of the theatre.[35] Schumacher assumes that in Augustan times when the theatre was under construction, seats were furnished for both Pulcher, who was already dead, and Balbus the 'benefactor', who were considered to be the most important citizens.[36]

---

[30] Maiuri 1942B; Sherk 1970: 32 no. 28; Schumacher 1976; Guadagno 1978: 152 no. 50; Frischer 1982: 75, 84-86; PIR[2] 5.3 (1987): no. 129.

[31] Allroggen-Bedel 1974: 101-104; Adamo Muscettola 1982: passim; Zanker 1983: 260-263.

[32] See also, for example, Thomasson 1984: 362 no. 8 ('sub Augusto').

[33] The basis for this theory is his article on the decree: Maiuri 1942B.

[34] Cf. the comments on CIL X 1425 (Th. Mommsen) and Swoboda 1936. Ganschow (1989: 82-84, 86) and Pagano (1988A: 238) also place Balbus in the early Imperial period. However, Tran Tam Tinh (1988: 126-129) sticks to the later date, namely the period from AD 62 to 79. Although he manages to undermine Schumacher's arguments to some extent, he nevertheless fails to take into account certain linguistic peculiarities of the decree (discussed below, n.20), as well as the fact that Balbus' portrait was identified by Zanker (1981: 358-359; 1983: 260-261) as unmistakably late Augustan.

[35] Cf. CIL X 1423; Münzer 1899. See also an extensive discussion of the problem by Ganschow 1989: 84-86; there, the theatre is dated to the mid-Augustan period.

[36] Schumacher 1976: 168, especially n. 15. The reason for dating the decree to the early Impe-

The decree outside the Suburban Baths mentions five posthumous tributes to Balbus from the inhabitants of Herculaneum:

1. the erection of an equestrian statue, in the busiest location, financed by the public and bearing a pre-determined inscription

('*placere decurionibus statuam equestrem ei poni quam celeberrimo loco ex pecunia publica inscribique: M(arco) Nonio M(arci) f(ilio) Men(enia tribu) Balbo pr(aetori) proco(n)s(uli) patrono universus ordo populi Herculaniessis ob merita eius*');

2. construction of a marble altar on the spot where Balbus was cremated; again the inscription was determined beforehand

('*item eo loco, quo cineres eius conlecti sunt, aram marmoream fieri et constitui inscribique publice: M(arco) Nonio M(arci) f(ilio) Balbo*');

3. an annual procession which was to depart from this location, on the festival of the Parentalia

('*exque eo loco parentalibu(s) pompam duci*');

4. an extension of the traditional gymnastic games by one day in honour of Balbus

('*ludisque gumnicis qui soliti erant fieri diem adici unum in honorem eius*');

5. whenever the theatre put on a production, a *sella curulis* (official seat) was to be reserved in his honour

('*et cum in theatro ludi fient sellam eius poni*').

It is impossible to find archaeological and epigraphic evidence to prove that the decree was ever put into force. The equestrian statue which is mentioned in the first tribute is often linked to the statue in the Museo Nazionale in Naples (inv. 6104), which was found in 1746 between the theatre and the so-called 'Basilica', together with its inscription CIL X 1426.[37] The counterpart of this statue, another equestrian statue of M. Nonius Balbus (and not his father as is often assumed[38]) was, judging from inscription CIL X 1429[39], most probably erected as a tribute by the citizens of Nuceria, Balbus' home town. Nowadays, it is generally assumed that both statues were located in the forum at Herculaneum. It is only too tempting to identify the forum as the 'celeberrimus locus' referred to in the decree, and the first statue as the statue mentioned in the first tribute. However, the phrasing of CIL X 1426 is not consistent with that of the decree. Adamo Muscettola (1982: 5-6), supported by Allroggen-Bedel (1983: 154), refrains from linking the decree to the statue; in her opinion, the two statues depicting Balbus were erected at the same time, around AD 20. However, others (Maiuri 1942B: 273; Schumacher 1976: 171-172) are of the

---

rial period is the spelling of certain words, such as *praistiterit* and *gumnicis*. See Schumacher 1976: 170 to (2) and (3); De Vos/De Vos 1982: 278.

[37]   Schumacher 1976: 171-172; Allroggen-Bedel/Kammerer-Grothaus 1980:   102 n.44; Allroggen-Bedel 1983: 154.

[38]   Cf. Deiss 1985: 160-161.

[39]   Schumacher   1976:   172;   Allroggen-Bedel   1974:   102   n.   44-45;   Allroggen-Bedel   /
Kammerer-Grothaus 1980:   180; Adamo Muscettola 1982: passim; Allroggen-Bedel 1983:
154.

opinion that the inscription found with the statue is a simplified, less poignant version of the phrase in the decree. With regard to the altar, the second tribute to Nonius Balbus by the people of Herculaneum, Schumacher concludes that the altar on which the decree is inscribed must be the object in question, and that the square in front of the Porta Marina must have been the place where the body of Nonius Balbus was cremated.[40]

It is equally difficult to determine whether the remaining points in the decree were put into force. The last tribute, the honorific seat in the theatre, could be linked to the boxes reserved for Balbus and Claudius Pulcher which were mentioned above. The inscription that was found in Balbus' box (CIL X 1427) is the same as that on the base of the equestrian statue (CIL X 1426). In Pulcher's box there is an inscription which reads '*post mortem*' (CIL X 1424). It is assumed this could also have been applied in Balbus' case, but that the honorific decree which was issued would have made such an inscription redundant. The assumption that both inscriptions relate to the erection of *sellae curules* instead of statues does not seem probable.[41] Nevertheless, it is highly likely that the remnants of the two *sellae curules* which were found in the theatre (Museo Nazionale Naples, inv. 73152/73153) were the honorific seats reserved for Balbus and Pulcher.[42]

The contents of the decree are important if we are to form a picture of Herculanean society in the early Imperial period, as it gives us an indication of the inhabitants' attitude to the town's benefactor. It was typical of Roman society to pay tribute to the deceased for the good works he undertook for the town; these tributes typically consisted of statues and a *sella curulis* in the theatre. However, the annual *pompa* and the extra day for the games are not in keeping with Roman tradition. These ideas are clearly Greek-Hellenic in origin - they may possibly be explained by Herculaneum's location near the former Greek stronghold of Neapolis - and seem to indicate a type of hero cult. The location of the altar, in the exact place where Balbus was cremated, should be seen in a similar light: the construction of such altars was not uncommon as part of the Roman burial ritual, but was usually reserved for prominent members of society, linked in some way to the Imperial house.[43] The document shows us that, even in a small town such as Herculaneum, life could be influenced to a great extent by one man, who, judging by the many tributes, was subject to veritable hero-worship.

Finally, it should be mentioned that from the Augustan period onwards a college of

---

[40]   Schumacher 1976: 173. An important question remains unanswered: when was the square constructed? Maiuri dates the construction of the Suburban Baths to the early Flavian period, based, in part, on the assumed late date of the decree. Assuming that it originated in the Augustan period, the dates assigned to the baths and the other suburban buildings must be reconsidered. See § 3.1.2: The suburban buildings.

[41]   Schumacher 1976: 177; De Vos/De Vos 1982: 306; Schäfer 1979: 146.

[42]   Schäfer 1979: especially 146; Schäfer 1989: especially 46-47, 190-191, pls 14, 15.1.

[43]   Frischer 1982: 75; see further Schumacher 1976: 178-184.

Augustales was appointed in Herculaneum.[44] We know this from a list of members (CIL X 1403 and recent additions: Guadagno 1977) that has been found, as well as an inscription in the building where this college met, the Aedes Augustalium, at the corner of *insula* VI.[45] Herculaneum provides the most extensive material for the study of this order, which became popular in a very short time, particularly in Campania. The Augustales were a group of priests who together formed the college which was responsible for the cult of the deified emperor. The priests usually originated from the ranks of freedmen, because this was the only way in which rich freedmen could gain respect and manifest themselves at the socio-political level. A quid pro quo, in the form of generous donations to the town in which they lived, was gratefully received. The emperor too benefited from the smooth running of the colleges of Augustales, not only because they maintained and popularised the imperial cult, but also because they provided an antidote to possible social unrest and dissatisfaction among a growing group of prosperous freedmen.

1.2.2. The earthquake of AD 62

A momentous event in the history of Herculaneum, namely the earthquake which struck Campania on 5 February in the year AD 62, is recorded in passages by Seneca and Tacitus and can be illustrated further on the basis of epigraphical material.[46] In the *Naturales Quaestiones* (VI, 1, 1-2) Seneca mentions to his friend Lucilius that an earthquake has struck Pompeii and the surrounding area; he notes the exact date, as a result of which it was generally assumed that the earthquake took place on 5 February AD 63.

---

[44]   Overview of the *Augustales*, including explanations of the differences between the various organisations (seviri Augustales, magistri Augustales and Augustales) in Duthoy 1978: especially 1260-1265. Ostrow 1985 provides an excellent summary and clear arguments for the popularity of the colleges in Campania. See also Guadagno 1988.

[45]   AVGVSTO SACR(VM) / A. A. LVCII A. FILII MEN(ENIA) / PROCVLVS ET IVLIANVS / P(ECVNIA) S(VA) / DEDICATIONE DECVRIONIBVS ET / AVGVSTALIBVS CENAM DEDERVNT. Guadagno 1983: 170. There is some uncertainty about the exact findspot of the list of members (Albi), about both CIL X 1403, discovered in the Bourbon period, and the fragments that were uncovered in 1961. Allroggen-Bedel (1974: 104) assumes that the fragments are from a building on the corner of *insula* VII; Guadagno (1983: 173 n. 67) maintains that the fragments were found in the building that is situated opposite, in *insula* VI, which he identified as the 'Herculanensium Aedes Augustalium'. Since Guadagno's study, it would now seem to be an established and indisputable fact that this building was the seat of the college of Augustales. The importance of the discovery site of the list lies in the link between these fragments and the collection of statues and inscriptions of the Balbus family, which, according to Guadagno, should be situated in the same building (Guadagno 1982: 118 and n. 70; 1983: n. 67). But there is also a possibility that material from different buildings was carried by volcanic streams and thus ended up in the same location - see Adamo Muscettola 1982: 11, n. 129.

[46]   Onorato 1949; Andreau 1979; Adam 1986: 68 n. 9.

'Pompeios, celebrem Campaniae urbem, [....] consedisse terrae motu, vexatis quaecumque adiacebant regionibus, Lucili, virorum optime, audivimus...; Nonis Februariis hic fuit motus Regulo et Verginio consulibus.'

('Lucilius, my good friend, we have heard that Pompeii, the famous town in Campania, [...] has been struck by an earthquake and that the surrounding regions have also been laid waste ...; this earthquake took place on the Nones of February, during the consulship of Regulus and Verginius').

However, Tacitus indicates that the disaster occurred a year earlier:

'Et motu terrae celebre Campaniae oppidum Pompei magna ex parte proruit'

('And as the result of an earthquake the larger part of the renowned Campanian city of Pompeii has been destroyed'; *Ann.* XV, 22).

It is mentioned before the events which were recorded in the year 63 (*Ann.* XV, 23: *'Memmio Regulo et Verginio Rufo consulibus'* - 'During the consulship of Memmius Regulus and Verginius Rufus'). Another passage in Seneca's *Naturales Quaestiones* also points to this date (5 February 62). In VI, 1, 13 and VII, 28, 3, he states that the earthquake in Achaia and Macedonia took place during the consulship of Paterculus and Vopiscus (= AD 60), a year earlier than the one in Pompeii and the surrounding region:

'Anno priore Achaiam et Macedoniam quaecumque est ista vis mali quae incurrit nunc Campaniam laesit' (VI, 1, 13); *'Fecit hic cometes qui Paterculo et Vopisco consulibus apparuit, quae ab Aristotele Theophrastoque sunt praedicta: [...] at in Achaia Macedoniaque urbes terrarum motibus prorutae sunt'* (VII, 28, 3).

('Last year Achaia and Macedonia were struck by the same devastating force, whatever it is, that has now hit Campania'; 'The comet that appeared during the consulship of Paterculus and Vopiscus fulfilled the predictions of Aristotle and Theophrastus: [...] and in Achaia and Macedonia cities were destroyed by earthquakes').

The year 62 is now generally accepted as the year in which the earthquake took place. Seneca writes that Herculaneum also suffered considerable damage as a result of it; part of the city was destroyed, and buildings that were left relatively intact were declared unsafe:

'Nam et Herculanensis oppidi pars ruit dubieque stant etiam quae relicta sunt...'

('Because a part of the town of Herculaneum has collapsed and even the buildings that remain standing are unstable'- *Nat. Quaest.* VI, 1, 2).

The damage may have been less than in Pompeii, but presumably renovations took a long time to be carried out and were only partly finished when Vesuvius erupted in 79; a similar chain of events has also been shown to have taken place in Pompeii.[47] The activities undertaken to renovate public buildings were not financed exclusively from city funds or private donations, but were also supported by Rome. This is evident from CIL X 1406, which states that the emperor Vespasian rebuilt the temple of Mater Deum, which collapsed as a result of the earthquake: *terrae motu conlapsum*[48];

---

[47] For an overview of the consequences in Pompeii: Adam 1986.
[48] IMP. CAESAR VESPASIANVS AVG. PONTIF. MAX. TRIB. POT. VII IMP. XVII P. P.

the work was finished in AD 76. The inscription CIL X 1425 concerns the construction or renovation of the Basilica, the gates and the walls, financed by M. Nonius Balbus.[49] Many have assumed that this inscription was a reference to the building activities undertaken after 62 (Schumacher 1976: 166 n.5). Now that it seems to be proven satisfactorily that the proconsul Balbus lived in the Augustan period (see above), this link can no longer be maintained. Other inscriptions, CIL X 1457 (Macellum) and CIL X 925 (the Temple of Jupiter) for example, may relate to renovations after 62, but it has been difficult, as yet, to establish this with any certainty.

1.2.3. The eruption of Vesuvius (24 August 79)

In order to reconstruct the disaster that took place on that fateful day in August 79 and devastated Pompeii, Herculaneum, Oplontis and Stabiae, we may consult two sources of information: historical evidence (the letters of Pliny) and the stratification of the volcanic layers revealed by the excavations. Many theories have been proposed in the past regarding the manner in which Pompeii and Herculaneum in particular came to be buried. The most popular theory, put forward especially by A. Maiuri[50], is that Pompeii was snowed under with ash and lapilli which gradually covered the entire city, and that Herculaneum was flooded by thick layers of mud, which flowed down from the slopes of Vesuvius. These mud flows - an amalgam of ash, pumice stone and water - have, over the years, formed a thick layer of rock-hard, almost impenetrable material, nearly 20 metres thick; this is in contrast to the layers of ash and lapilli found in Pompeii, which can be shovelled up effortlessly. According to this theory, most people were killed as a result of the rapid accumulation of volcanic debris. As most of it fell on Pompeii, it is there that most lives are presumed to have been lost. In Herculaneum, where there was hardly any ash and pumice stone, it is assumed that nearly everyone had time to escape. Until recently, this had been the accepted theory. Research carried out by American volcanologists, however, has revealed that the disaster took place in different phases, which are reflected in both the volcanic stratification and the historical sources (Sigurdsson et al. 1982; Gore 1984).

The events which took place in Misenum can be reconstructed from information in letters written by Pliny the Younger to Tacitus, who was staying there at the time (VI 16 and VI 20); similarly, it is possible to reconstruct events in Stabiae, where eyewitnesses and members of Pliny the Elder's retinue survived the catastrophe. In VI 16 Pliny the Younger describes how his uncle saw the first signs of the natural disaster from Misenum at around one o'clock in the afternoon on 24 August: he saw a large

---

COS. VII DESIGN. VII TEMPLVM MATRIS DEVM TERRAE MOTV CONLAPSVM RES. Photograph in Andreau 1979: 43, fig. 13.

[49] M. NONIVS M. F. BALBVS PROCOS. BASILICAM PORTAS MVRVM PECVNIA SVA.

[50] For example, Maiuri 1941A; Maiuri 1977: 13.

cloud shaped like a pine tree rising from Mount Vesuvius. On seeing this, he decides to sail in that direction, initially intending only to watch; but later he receives a call for help from Rectina, wife of his friend Pomponianus Tascus, who is trapped.[51] As a result of falling ash and pumice stone he is forced to make a detour to Stabiae, where he meets Pomponianus. After a meal and a good night's rest, it appears that he is not safe there either, because the layer of ash and pumice stone is getting deeper and there are repeated earth tremors. Hereupon it is decided to move to the coast, but smothering sulphurous vapours prevent their passage; Pliny the Elder, described by his nephew as a corpulent man, cannot escape and dies.[52]

The second letter (VI 20) describes how Pliny observed the events in Misenum itself. At first he views the events fairly calmly, but repeated earth tremors make him and his mother decide to flee Misenum on the morning of August 25. A black cloud of ash covers Misenum and the surrounding area, and blots out the sun. It remains 'night' for some considerable time; when the cloud lifts, it becomes clear that everything is covered in a layer of ash. Pliny subsequently returns to Misenum.

The remaining evidence lies hidden in the layers of volcanic material. Volcanologists have distinguished three types (Sigurdsson et al. 1982; Pescatore-Sigurdsson 1993):

A. Air-fall pumice deposit: ash and pumice stone that were forced to the earth's surface during the eruption, then carried away by the wind. This is sometimes referred to as the 'Plinian' phase, after Pliny the Younger, who was the first to describe the phenomenon.

B. Deposits of pyroclastic flows (known as ignimbrites in their hardened form): hot, volcanic avalanches of pumice, ash and gases which flow down the volcano's slopes, following the lie of the land and filling up valleys, riverbeds and other depressions.

C. Ground surge deposit: a torrid, dense gaseous cloud of volcanic ash which sweeps across the land at speeds exceeding 100 km/hour. B preceded by C, mostly by only a few seconds, is also called *nuée ardente*, literally a 'glowing avalanche'. This type of volcanic activity is known as the 'Peléan' type after the eruption of Mt. Pelée on Martinique (1902).

These three types of deposit occur in most of the places around Vesuvius that were buried in 79; at the bottom can be seen a layer of pumice deposit, which is covered with a series of sedimentary deposits from the ground surges and pyroclastic flows. To the south of Vesuvius, in Pompeii and Stabiae, the layer of pumice is more than 200 cm thick (sometimes as much as 280 cm); to the west the layer is visibly thinner. In Oplontis it is 180 cm at most, and in Herculaneum it is less than 20 cm thick. At the time of the eruption, therefore, there must have been a north-westerly wind.[53]

The sedimentary deposits left by the ground surges and pyroclastic flows differ

---

[51] The reading of this passage is controversial: some editions prefer *Cascus* or *Bassus* (ed. Loeb) to *Tascus*. However, the argument put forward by Sherwin-White (1966: 373) is convincing. See also § 3.1.1.

[52] For an account of the skull in the Museo dell'Arte Sanitaria in Rome which is supposedly that of Pliny the Elder, see Waarsenburg 1991.

[53] See map fig. 1 in Sigurdsson et al. 1982.

from one area to the next. In Oplontis there is evidence of three ground surges amidst the accumulation of lumps of pumice, overlaid by evidence of yet another ground surge; evidence of this surge has also been found in Pompeii. On top of this, there is a layer of pyroclastic flows, which is between 60 and 180 cm thick. In Herculaneum about six layers of pyroclastic flows cover the modest layer of pumice; these layers, each about 2-3 m thick, together form one layer about 20 metres thick. Although it is difficult to distinguish between the mud deposits and the pyroclastic flows, the American researchers assume, as do fellow volcanologists, that most of the layers contain pyroclastic material and that maybe a single one consists of hardened mud.[54] Evidence which supports this particular theory is provided by, among other things, the presence of charcoal in the deposits, the carbonisation of wood in the houses (which must therefore have been heated to a temperature of 400 °C) and the vertical conduits in the layers, through which gas escaped from the deposits (Maury 1976: 297; Sigurdsson et al. 1982: 43 n. 18). It is now possible to give the following reconstruction of the events that took place.

The heavy earthquake that struck Campania in February of AD 62 is generally regarded as a sign of life from Vesuvius, after it had lain dormant for a long period of time - the last great eruption took place in the Bronze Age, around 1800 BC.[55] The earthquake was not seen by the local population as a bad portent indicating an impending eruption: earth tremors were not uncommon in this area and people might possibly have been unaware of the fact that Vesuvius was a volcano - although Strabo and Diodorus Siculus most certainly were aware of it.[56] The tremors that were felt repeatedly for some days before August 24 were a clear indication that pressure inside the volcano was increasing.[57] Its violent natural force erupted at around one o'clock in the afternoon on August 24: following a huge explosion, a column of pumice and ash was hurled 20 kilometres into the stratosphere. Within half an hour lapilli and ash began to rain down on Pompeii and the other towns to the south-east of Vesuvius; because the wind was north-westerly, Herculaneum suffered less.

This initial stage of the eruption is referred to as the Plinian phase. We may deduce from Pliny's letters that it must have lasted between 11 and 18 hours, from 1 o'clock in the afternoon (August 24) until 6 o'clock in the morning (dawn on August 25). The layer of pumice and ash increased by an average of 15 cm an hour. During this phase, Vesuvius hurled out the matter at the top of its crater, which contained much gaseous magma. However, around midnight the column began to collapse: the magma at the bottom of the crater, which contained less gas, was then able to flow over the edge in

---

[54]   It is remarkable that the theory of the mud flows was upheld by archeologists and historians (Maiuri; Conte Corti; Etienne; Mau) and that the theory of pyroclastic flows was favoured by volcanologists (Sparks; Walker; Helprin; Merill). See Sigurdsson et al. 1982: 43, n. 16-17.

[55]   For a chronological overview of the earlier eruptions of Vesuvius (Monte Somma): Albore Livadie/d'Alessio/Mastrolorenzo/Rolandi 1986: 57-62; Rosi/Santacroce 1986: 15, 22-26; Albore Livadie 1993. See also Cioffi 1993.

[56]   Strabo, *Geogr.* V, 4, 8; Diodorus Siculus, *Bibl. Hist.* IV, 21, 5. See also Beloch 1890: 215-218; 469.

[57]   Pliny, *Epist.* VI, 20, 3: '*per multos dies*'.

the form of a steaming hot pulp. This signalled the beginning of the second phase, the
Peléan phase. At this stage, *nuées ardentes* came down the mountainside, with a
force less violent than that which had created the initial column, but still powerful
enough - helped by gravitational forces - to reach speeds of 100 km/hour: first there
was a cloud of smothering gases, hot ash and dust, followed by a volcanic avalanche
of molten pumice stone and rock.[58] Pliny describes these phenomena as a black fiery
cloud, while his uncle and his companions saw fire and smelled sulphur:

> '*nubes atra et horrenda ignei spiritus tortis vibratisque discursibus rupta in
> longas flammarum figuras dehiscebat*' (VI, 20, 9); '*flammae flammarumque
> praenuntius odor sulpuris*' (VI, 16, 18-19).
>
> ('a fearful black cloud shot through with forked and quivering jets of fire, parted to
> reveal great sheets of flame'; 'flames and the predecessor of flames, the smell of
> sulphur').

The first *nuée ardente*, which raged across the land like a black sandstorm, was presumably enough to destroy all life: not because of its force, but because of the
smothering effect of the ash and the hot gases. The debris that followed buried practically all of the victims; at the same time, it ensured that they would be well-preserved.
The *nuée ardente* probably caused great damage to the buildings in Pompeii which
stuck out above the ashes and the layer of lapilli. The roofs would not have been able
to bear the weight of the lumps of pumice stone, but the walls were left intact. It must
have been rather different in Herculaneum. Here, the *nuées ardentes* swept across the
town, starting at midnight, and struck the town from the very start so that the number
of buildings that remained intact was considerably smaller. Wooden objects and
building materials have been better preserved, because they were carbonised instead
of burned.

The small number of victims at Herculaneum may be due to the fact that very little
ash and pumice stone landed there, which allowed people to escape. Recent excavations, however, have revealed that a number of the inhabitants thought they could
survive the disaster by taking shelter. Dozens of skeletons were found, well-preserved
in the volcanic mass, in a row of vaulted chambers (boathouses?) on the edge of the
town, near the ancient shore.[59] They were found in the same contorted postures as the
human remains in Pompeii, which have been preserved in plaster; the grouping of the
cluster of skeletons indicates that they sought protection with one another in much the
same way as inhabitants of Pompeii did. They were, without a doubt, overwhelmed by
the poisonous gases that descended from Vesuvius with the first *nuée ardente*.

It is strongly suspected that these people thought they could get away by ship. This
impression is confirmed by the passage in Pliny's letter (VI, 16, 8-9) in which he says
that his uncle intended to go to the aid of the inhabitants of the region in warships. A
Roman boat found near the skeletons seems to provide us with material evidence in
support of this theory.[60] What we may have here is a rescue vessel which capsized in

---

[58]   Cf. the extremely illustrative drawing by Gore 1984: 577.
[59]   Judge 1982; Pappalardo 1983: 345-346; Gore 1984; Deiss 1985: 10-23; Bisel 1987.
[60]   Judge 1982; Pappalardo 1983: 346-349; Gore 1984: 606-607; Steffy 1985; Deiss 1985: 19-20;

an attempt to get nearer to the coast, was swept onto the shore by the waves, and was subsequently buried under the volcanic layers.

However, because there was no evidence of woodworm (*Teredo*), it is likely that this boat had not been in use very long before the eruption. As considerable amounts of wood were also discovered in the vicinity, it seems more plausible to assume that there was a shipyard nearby, and that the boat was carried along from there and deposited dozens of metres further along (Gore 1984: 606-60).

A lamp discovered near a group of skeletons presumably indicates that Herculaneum was struck by the first *nuée ardente* in the night; that is to say, a considerable time before Pompeii was hit. The second and third *nuées ardentes* affected Herculaneum alone; the fourth, which appeared more than six hours later, around dawn, overwhelmed Pompeii and Oplontis. Many of the victims must have died at this stage (Sigurdsson et al. 1982: 49-50, n. 33). The fifth *nuée ardente* again only affected Herculaneum, and the sixth and final one swept over Oplontis and part of Herculaneum. No evidence of a *nuée ardente* was found in Stabiae. The eruption finally ended with some minor emissions of fine ash, which were carried on the wind and fell in the south-eastern area (Oplontis, Pompeii, Stabiae) only.

1.2.4. After the eruption of 79

Besides Pliny the Younger, Suetonius and Cassius Dio also reported on the eruption of Vesuvius in August 79 and the disastrous events that resulted:

'*Curatores restituendae Campaniae e consularium numero sorte duxit; bona oppressorum in Vesuvio, quorum heredes non extabant, restitutioni afflictarum civitatium attribuit*'

('He appointed supervisors for the restoration of Campania by lot from among the senior consuls; he assigned to the restoration of the stricken cities the possessions of those victims of the eruption of Vesuvius who had no surviving heirs') (Suetonius, *Titus*, VIII);

Ὁ δ' οὖν Τίτος τοῖς μὲν Καμπανοῖς δύο ἄνδρας ἐκ τῶν ὑπατευκότων οἰκιστὰς ἔπεμψε, καὶ χρήματα ἄλλα τε καὶ τὰ [χρήματα] τῶν ἄνευ κληρονόμων τεθνηκότων ἐδωρήσατο.

('Titus now sent two former consuls to the Campanians to restore the region and, in general, gave the inhabitants not only money but also property of those victims who had no surviving heirs') (Cassius Dio, LXVI, 24.3).

These authors tell us that after the disaster the emperor Titus sent envoys to the region to assess the damage and reimburse as much as possible; amongst other things, the property of victims of the disaster who had died without heirs was assigned to the

---

Budetta 1987; Budetta 1988; Ferroni/Meucci 1989. For the type, cf. also the boat found near Ginosar, at Lake Tiberias in Israel, Wachsmann 1990.

restoration of the towns.[61] Finally, Martial devotes an epigram (IV.44) to the changed state of the region surrounding Vesuvius - once fertile and hospitable - which, since that day in August 79, was a vision of sadness and dreariness:

'Hic est pampineis viridis modo Vesbius umbris
presserat hic madidos nobilis uva lacus
haec iuga, quam Nysae colles plus Bacchus amavit
hoc nuper Satyri monte dedere choros
haec Veneris sedes, Lacedaemone gratior illi
hic locus Herculeo numine clarus erat
cuncta iacent flammis et tristi mersa favilla
nec superi vellent hoc licuisse sibi.'

('This is Vesbius; yesterday it was still green from the shade of the vines; this is where the noble grape covered the dripping wine-vats; Bacchus loved these hills more than he did the hills of Nysa; not so long ago the satyrs danced here on this mountain; in this place, more dear to her than Sparta, lived Venus; this place was famous through Hercules' name. Everything is in flames and lies buried under horrible, glowing ash: even the gods of the heavens would rather this had not been allowed to them.')

After the disaster the cities were remembered for a considerable time, judging from passages by later writers and the place-names on the Tabula Peutingeriana. This map, which dates from the beginning of the 4th century but is thought to have been based on a map of the 1st century AD, shows a road branching off the Via Appia at *Neapoli*, then running down the coast to *Nuceria* and branching off to *Surrento*. The towns of *Herculanium*, *Oplontis*, *Stabios* and *Pompeis* lie along this road.[62]

The second-century historian P. Annius Florus also includes Herculaneum and Pompeii when he lists the coastal towns of Campania in his account of the Roman wars (which he based on earlier sources):

'Urbes ad mare Formiae, Cumae, Puteoli, Neapolis, Herculaneum, Pompei ...'

('The cities by the sea Formiae, Cumae, Puteoli, Neapolis, Herculaneum, Pompeii ...') (*Bellorum Romanorum*, I, 11, 6).

Tacitus, however, does not mention Herculaneum when he discusses the earthquake in 62 (*Ann*. 15, 22). The extent to which these towns appeal to the popular imagination is reflected in the meditations of the emperor Marcus Aurelius. To illustrate the transitoriness of life and the insignificance of mortal issues, he lists cities that are entirely 'dead', namely Helike (a city in Achaia which was entirely swallowed up by the sea in 373 BC)[63] and Pompeii and Herculaneum:

---

[61] For an overview of the economic damage caused by the eruption: Widemann 1986.

[62] Weber 1976: section VI; see also 32-36 for earlier literature (especially: Miller 1916; 1962); Bosio 1983; Scatozza Höricht 1985: 141-142; Dilke 1985: 112-120 (including recent literature in n. 3). Cf. also Stuart 1991 for the printed editions. According to Scatozza Höricht (1985: 142) this coastal road was also known as the *Via Herculea*.

[63] For Helike: see Bölte 1912.

πόσαι δὲ πόλεις ὅλαι, ἵν' οὕτως εἴπω, τεθνήκασιν, Ἑλίκη καὶ Πομπήϊοι καὶ Ἡρκλάνον καὶ ἄλλαι ἀναρίθμητοι.

('and how many cities are completely, if I may be allowed to use this expression, 'dead': Helike, Pompeii, Herculaneum and numerous others.') (*Meditations* IV, 48).

This region must have been reinhabited, in some form or other, soon after the eruption. This supposition is supported by the fact that the possessions of heirless victims were divided among the communities that had suffered, as mentioned by Suetonius (*Titus*, VIII). Archaeological discoveries such as milestones, burial grounds and villas from late antiquity support this picture (Pisapia 1981: 69-74; Scatozza Höricht 1985: 141-142, 164-165).

2. HISTORY OF THE EXCAVATIONS

2.1. The period 79-1738

The memory of the buried cities at the foot of Vesuvius survived until late Antiquity, but in the Middle Ages they came to be forgotten. The destructive pyroclastic flows had produced fertile land and new towns had been established in the region, often in the same locations as the settlements that had disappeared. This may be deduced from the location of the cemeteries (Scatozza Höricht 1985: 164-165), and also from the location of the city now known as Ercolano and previously known as Resina (until 1969), which is situated almost on top of the ancient city. In the Renaissance, study of the ancient sources led to renewed interest in the buried cities, whose exact location, however, remained unclear. As a result, it was assumed for some time that Herculaneum was located under Torre del Greco.[64] Presumably the confusion surrounding the exact location of Herculaneum was largely due to the reference on the Tabula Peuteringeriana (referred to above); this was probably also the reason why Pompeii was only identified with certainty as late as 1763, despite the fact that numerous pieces of evidence for its existence had been discovered in the past. As early as 1592, for example, parts of ancient Pompeii were unearthed during the construction of a canal. The name of the hill where this took place, Civita, had already attracted the attention of ancient historians, who assumed that the old city lay buried beneath it, but their comments were dismissed.[65]

At the beginning of the eighteenth century, however, this situation changed. Since the War of the Spanish Succession, the kingdom of Naples and its surrounding regions had been part of Austria, whose ruler, Prince Eugene of Savoy (1663-1736), was known as a powerful military leader and statesman. Emmanuel-Maurice de Lorraine (1677-1763), Prince D'Elbeuf, was a distant relative of his who commanded the cavalry and lived in Naples.[66] He bought a piece of land in the area around Portici, near the coast, with the intention of building a house there. The story goes that the merchant who sold him the marble to decorate his house referred him to the farmer

---

[64]   Scatozza Höricht 1985: 135 n. 25; McIlwaine 1988: 284-290 no. 3.40-68.
[65]   For example, De Jorio 1827: 13-17; Conte Corti 1946: 112-113, 116-119.
[66]   The most important study of the Prince D'Elbeuf is Brisson's article (1957: especially 24-29), in which he writes about the life of the 'prince' with somewhat cynical overtones: 'il est en effet difficile de rencontrer personnage moins recommandable et avonturier plus accompli' (Brisson 1957: 24). The prince was married twice, first to Maria Theresa, the Duke of Salsa's daughter (Gori 1752: 1), and after her death to Catherine de Rougé (Brisson 1957: 25, 28). No children resulted from either of these marriages. A brief biography of the prince can be found in La Grande Encyclopédie (1885: 735). The entry was written by L. Delavaud. See further De Jorio 1827: 18-21; Grell 1982: 45; Parslow 1995: 23-25, 327.

who had supplied it, one Nocerino, also known as Enzechetta. In the process of digging a well, Nocerino had discovered large amounts of precious stone (white marble, alabaster, *giallo antico*) on his property in Resina. Upon hearing this, D'Elbeuf decided to purchase the land from Enzechetta, and began to excavate it himself.[67] Although his activities can only be described as 'treasure-hunting', the prince did manage to reach the theatre in Herculaneum through a shaft; we may therefore consider this to be one of the first excavations carried out at Herculaneum.

His exploration of the terrain between 1711 and 1716 involved the area around the *scaenae frons*, in which a rich collection of statues was displayed.[68] Some of these, including the statue of Hercules, were discovered by D'Elbeuf. More statues and pieces of marble were brought to the surface, including three figures of women as well as a plaque bearing an inscription. The statues were secretly transported to Prince Eugene in Vienna, and were later acquired by Prince Frederick Augustus II for his palace in Dresden. Two of them are known as the 'large Herculanean woman' and the 'small Herculanean woman'.[69] The inscription (CIL X 1424) formed part of the decoration in consul App. Claudius Pulcher's honorific box (see above § 1.2.1).

However, it was still unclear what sort of building had been discovered, and where it was located. This state of affairs was to continue for some considerable time, because the prince's excavations did not produce any remarkable discoveries. In fact, the costs were disproportionate to the benefits of the entire exercise. They were so high that work ceased in 1716, possibly under pressure from the government, which is said to have prohibited any further excavations.[70] Shortly afterwards, in 1719, the prince left for France, where he died in 1763.[71]

Despite the discovery of a small number of exquisitely sculpted statuettes, the di-

---

[67]   De Jorio 1827: 20. It is sometimes assumed that it was D'Elbeuf who ordered the well to be dug (for example Gall 1912: 536). Gori's statement (1752: 2 n. 1) that the Neapolitan architect Giuseppe Stendardo led the excavations initiated by D'Elbeuf is contested by Francesco La Vega, who was head of the royal excavations at Pompeii and Herculaneum from 1780 onwards (see § 2.2). In a short note he writes that D'Elbeuf 'faceva dirigere il suo scavo da un certo M.ᵣ Tommaso la Marica, Napolitano' (Biblioteca della Società Napoletana di Storia Patria, Fondo Cuomo, ms. 2-6-2, doc. 5, c. 118 r; compare Guadagno 1986: 143). See also Pagano 1993A (especially 121-134) and Parslow 1995: 29-30.

[68]   It remains unclear when the prince initiated these excavations. De Jorio (1827: 18-19 n. 4) provides an overview of conflicting sources starting as early as the 18th century. He obtained information from the archives of the Monastery of the Alcanterini that D'Elbeuf did not officially buy the land to build his house on until 1711 and that he sold it again in 1716. The reference to D'Elbeuf's finds in part V of the Giornale de' Letterati d'Italia (Giornale 1711: 399-401) is an indication, however, that excavations were already being carried out in that period (January-March 1711). Compare also McIlwaine 1988: 298 no. 3.100.

[69]   Arneth 1864: III, 75 (especially 39). See also, for example, Bieber 1961: 22-23; Fuchs 1979: 219-221, figs 236-237. Other statues: Pagano 1993A: 123.

[70]   Gori 1752: 2; Gall 1912: 536.

[71]   Grande Encyclopédie 1885: 735. Grell (1982: 45) gives 1720 as the year in which the transfer to Vienna took place. In 1748, at the age of 71, the Prince received the title of Duke of Lorraine, as he was the only male in line to succeed his older brother Henri. He sold the dukedom to his nephew Louis-Charles in 1752, but retained his title (Brisson 1957: 24, 28).

rect results of D'Elbeuf's detective work were less than remarkable. The most important consequence was that people were made aware of the fact that the land in Resina contained ancient treasures. Some decades later this was to lead to the discovery of Herculaneum and subsequently to that of Pompeii and Stabiae.

2.2. The Bourbon period (1738-1828)

The twenty years that followed the end of the first 'campaign' saw a change in the structure of Italian politics. During the struggle in Europe over the Polish succession, the Austrians occupied Tuscany in 1733, but lost the Kingdom of Naples and Sicily to Charles of Bourbon (1716-1788), the son of King Philip V of Spain. The kingdom, with Naples as its capital, was exposed to French-Spanish influence after King Charles (1734-1759) ascended to the throne. Under his rule and that of his son, Ferdinand IV (1759-1825), the excavations in the region around Vesuvius became more systematic, and the 'treasure hunts' gradually came to be conducted in a more scientific and responsible manner. This period, named after the Royal House of Bourbon, has been the object of much attention from archaeologists in recent years; it has been found that the eighteenth-century archives can yield information for archaeological research in Pompeii, Herculaneum, Stabiae and other sites that were buried in 79, particularly with regard to urban development and the context of finds.[72] It would be impossible, and beyond the scope and context of the present study, to give an exhaustive account of the excavations that took place during the Bourbon period. However, to give a general impression of this very important period, I will discuss certain aspects of the exploration of Pompeii and Herculaneum and some of the people involved.

It appears from a study of the archives that the construction of the royal villa at Portici was not the result of Charles's interest in the possible presence of ancient treasures, but was inspired by a visit the monarch paid to Portici in May 1738, during which he realised that the region offered excellent opportunities to engage in his favourite pastimes, hunting and fishing. It was only later, in August of the same year, that the excavations were initiated, when the king heard of the Prince D'Elbeuf's discoveries from an engineer, Don Roque Joaquin de Alcubierre. He was conducting a survey in the area, and had been informed that there might be archaeological remains (Allroggen-Bedel/Kammerer-Grothaus 1980: 176-177; Parslow 1995: 24-29).

Alcubierre is one of the key figures in the Bourbon period.[73] This Spanish military

---

[72] By far the best survey of this period is Parslow 1995. However, the following studies in this area of research deserve also mention: Adamo Muscettola (1982); Allroggen-Bedel (1974; 1975 (A+B); 1976 (A+B); 1980 (with H. Kammerer-Grothaus); 1983; 1986); Guadagno (1981; 1982; 1983; 1986; 1987; 1988); Murga (1962; 1964); Pannuti (1983); Scatozza Höricht (1982; 1985); Strazullo (1980; 1982).

[73] Biographical details in Murga 1962 (where Alcubierre's conduct is sometimes too readily passed over) and especially Strazullo 1980; Murga 1964 was not available. Cf. also Parslow 1995: passim.

engineer, who was born in Zaragoza in 1704, had come to Italy as a member of the Count de Montemar's retinue and had gradually worked his way to the court of King Charles. In October 1738, he gained permission for a further investigation of the Prince D'Elbeuf's excavation. On 22 October 1738, Alcubierre started out, joined by a considerably larger number of workers than the 'dos o tres trabajores' which the court initially put at his disposal; 12 days later he gained his first success when he discovered a statue of Hercules. The king was enthusiastic about the find, and work was continued with great optimism. An inscription was uncovered on 13 January 1739, which immediately made it clear that this building was the theatre (CIL X 1443). Marcello De Venuti, who followed the excavations very closely, therefore concluded that the town being uncovered had to be Herculaneum (De Venuti 1748: XV-XVI; 57-62). From then onwards, the search continued for art treasures buried under Resina. The workers toiled in intolerable conditions, in narrow mine shafts which were draughty, damp and lit only by torches. In the early years, the excavations were directed on a day-to-day basis by Alcubierre, who was experienced in similar mining operations. Because of the unhealthy situation underground, however, he began to suffer increasingly from rheumatic pains and eye infections; on the advice of physicians he took a temporary break from work on 30 May 1741. Initially the Italian Francesco Rorro took his place, but he was replaced within a month by the French architect, Pierre Bardet de Villeneuve, who, judging by the drawings he made, must have been very competent.[74] Alcubierre returned to work, fully recovered, on 30 August 1745. In 1750 he was promoted and given additional duties in Naples, and the Swiss architect Karl Weber was appointed as his assistant. Weber served from 2 July 1750 until his death on 15 February 1764. He was replaced on 16 April 1764 by Francesco La Vega (1737-1804), a Spaniard born in Rome, who took over the excavations after Alcubierre died in 1780.[75]

Very soon after the start of the excavations, people were taken on to process the finds.[76] From May 1739, for example, the sculptor Giuseppe Canart was put in charge of the restoration of the marble statues and mosaics (Scatozza Höricht 1982). It was Canart who first suggested that the most beautiful parts of the wall paintings should be cut out and framed. In 1751, Camillo Paderni was taken on as draughtsman and curator of the royal gallery of antiquities, which housed a steadily growing collection. Together with Canart he was given more and more duties and was therefore able to exercise greater influence over the excavation process itself. In fact, these men determined whether or not objects were suitable to be included in the collection on display in the King's museum. In April 1761, incredible though it may seem, Paderni even gained permission from the minister in charge, Bernardo Tanucci, to destroy 'quelle tonache antiche colorite inutili' - in Paderni's judgement, of course; thankfully, this

---

[74] See for example the recently-published drawings of the *decumanus maximus* and the surrounding area made in 1743: Allroggen-Bedel 1983: figs 1 and 7; Guadagno 1983: figs 8 and 11. See also Ruggiero 1885: XIV and Parslow 1995: 38-41.

[75] For Weber, see now Parslow 1995.

[76] For this aspect of the Bourbon excavations, see especially Allroggen-Bedel/Kammerer-Grothaus 1980: 184-189 and Parslow 1995: passim.

licence to engage in archaeological vandalism was revoked in November 1763, following a number of protests.[77] After the discovery of the papyrus scrolls in the Villa dei Papiri, someone had to be found who could unroll, decipher and transcribe them. Father Antonio Piaggio, an expert from the Vatican, was eventually chosen to carry out this task. It would seem that not everyone was pleased with this choice: complaints about the slow pace at which Piaggio worked appear frequently in correspondence.[78] We know from 18th-century documents that these specialists worked within a well-defined administrative framework from the very beginning of the excavations. Alcubierre and his temporary replacements, Rorro and Bardet, all submitted weekly reports on new discoveries to the court, based either on their own observations or those of the foremen. From 1750 onwards, Alcubierre simply edited the reports that Weber or La Vega sent him, before they were passed on to the minister. In this way, he retained control and bore the final responsibility, and at the same time, of course, left himself the option of influencing the contents.[79]

Reports such as these were a necessity, because six months after the excavations in the theatre were started, new shafts were dug 150 metres away, and a few months after that further excavations were initiated at different sites in the area. Gradually, numerous new shafts were dug all over Herculaneum, in a far from systematic way. In order to limit the threat of buildings in Resina collapsing, old shafts were filled up with debris and closed off as soon as they were no longer in use. Although it may seem that these haphazard excavations ceased with the appointment of Karl Weber in 1750, they in fact continued in parts of Pompeii until 1763. Excavations were more methodical in Stabiae, where the villas of S. Marco and Varano were systematically stripped of their most important decorations (Ruggiero 1881; Allroggen-Bedel 1977). From 1750 onwards, work was carried out in only two places at Herculaneum: under the 'Masseria di Bisogno' (in the *decumanus maximus* region) and in the 'Pozzo de Ciceri', a shaft near the monastery of S. Agostino, which was used to climb down into the Villa dei Papiri between 1750 and 1765. The excavation of the Villa dei Papiri was Weber's life's work: it lasted through most of the period of his employment, from June 1750 until February 1761, when work was abandoned because of an escape of dangerous gas (a renewed attempt to investigate the site after Weber's death, between February 1764 and February 1765, did not produce any remarkable discoveries). The result was a masterpiece: the accuracy of his plans of the villa and his records of the finds is admirable (Parslow 1995). It was his documentation, for example, which enabled architects to build the John Paul Getty Museum in Los Angeles as an exact replica of the Villa dei Papiri (Neuerburg 1974), and which resulted in the recent discovery of the original shaft which was used in the 18th century to climb down to the villa (Knight/Jorio 1980); as a result, renewed investigation of the villa has been made

---

[77] Ruggiero 1885: XIV; Murga 1962: 26; Allroggen-Bedel 1976B: 153-157. See also Allroggen-Bedel 1986 for Tanucci.

[78] Murga 1962: 29, n. 94; Allroggen-Bedel/Kammerer-Grothaus 1980: 189, n. 69. More detailed information about Piaggio in Parslow 1995: 103-106.

[79] According to Murga (1962: 25), Alcubierre was very respectful of hierarchical relations: 'siempre tuvo un alto sentido del respeto a la jerarquía'.

possible.[80] In all, Weber left 45 drawings of Herculaneum, Pompeii, Stabiae and other sites, including 11 drawings of the theatre at Herculaneum and an axonometric plan of the Praedia Iuliae Felicis in Pompeii.[81]

We also have drawings of the theatre by Francesco La Vega; his greatest contribution, however, is the map which was published in the *Dissertatio isagogica* by Carlo Rosini in 1797 (Rosini 1797: tav. 2). La Vega incorporated all the information from the excavations at Herculaneum into a single map. As a result of his labours, we have an overview of part of the town plan, of the location of the Villa dei Papiri in relation to the town, and of a number of graves and what we presume to be the ancient coastline. This document, which is of inestimable value to anyone studying Herculaneum, will be dealt with below (3. Urban Development). Under La Vega's supervision, new excavations were initiated on a regular basis, starting in 1763 with the area around the theatre at Pompeii. La Vega also kept a diary in which he reported on sites in the *Insula Occidentalis* at Pompeii (Allroggen-Bedel 1976B: 146).

In order to assess the reliability of some of the 18th-century sources, it is necessary to study both the personal relationships at the court of Naples and the way in which the finds were treated. Extensive information about the excavations of the period is contained in the writings of Johann Joachim Winckelmann (1717-1768), especially in his open letters (Winckelmann 1762/1764), in which he gives detailed accounts of the archaeological discoveries in Campania, including the excavations in and around Herculaneum. He also relates events at the court of King Charles, and discusses the preservation and subsequent publication of the finds. In Portici, Winckelmann did not receive the co-operation he had expected, and the fact that he bore a grudge as a result is reflected in his letters, particularly when he lashes out at practices which he regarded as unscholarly. These stories, although amusing in themselves, have invariably been regarded as truthful accounts and have been used to illustrate the clumsy manner in which the Bourbon excavators are assumed to have worked.[82] Most of his information, however, originated from one single source: Camillo Paderni, curator of the royal museum, with whom Winckelmann got on well (Winckelmann 1762: 4, 34). It can be deduced from letters which have been preserved that Paderni wished to strengthen his own position at court and used every available means to achieve this aim, including bringing false accusations against Alcubierre and Weber. Winckelmann acted as his mouthpiece during this period.[83] One example of the anecdotes which may well have been circulated by Paderni, is the well-known incident related by Winckelmann (1762: 19) to show Alcubierre's ignorance of ancient history: Alcubierre is said to have had the bronze letters removed from an inscribed plaque, without having first noted down the actual text they made up. In fact, it seems that the

---

[80] Conticello 1987; De Simone 1987A; Longo Auricchio/Capasso 1987.

[81] Many of the plans are lost; see Parslow 1995: 274 and 277-280. Cf. Ruggiero 1885: XV, XIX, XXXIII-XXXIV (La Vega's comments on Weber's work). For the axonometric plan also: Parslow 1988; 1993.

[82] See for example Conte Corti 1946: 130-172; Deiss 1985: 27-28.

[83] Allroggen-Bedel/Kammerer-Grothaus 1980: 184; Murga 1962: 22-27. For Paderni see also De Vos 1993.

loose bronze letters of the inscription had already been removed from the original marble plaque, possibly in antiquity.[84]

Winckelmann also emphasises the poor relationship between Weber and Alcubierre, and the fact that the latter usually instigated their disputes. The clearest manifestation of their hostility is considered to be an attempt by Alcubierre to cause Weber's mine shafts to collapse (Conte Corti 1946: 144; Deiss 1985: 28). Murga (1962: 26) rectifies this misinterpretation: Weber had additional supporting beams put into place in the corridors under the 'Vico de Mare' in Resina to prevent subsidence of the houses above. During a visit to the corridors, Alcubierre had a number of supports removed, because he considered them to be of no use for the excavations. However, when Weber informed him why he had reinforced the corridors, Alcubierre realised that he had misjudged the situation and had the supports replaced (Ruggiero 1885: 375-378).

Winckelmann, then, cannot be regarded as a reliable source as far as events at the court of Naples are concerned. His sharp personal criticisms can be explained, however. Despite his reputation, Winckelmann was allowed little opportunity to study the objects that were discovered, because they were regarded as state secrets which were only put on view for a select audience. Initially they were simply stored away in the palace of Portici or displayed as decorations in the courtyards and gardens. From 1750 onwards, however, following the discovery of the Villa dei Papiri, more and more ancient objects were found, which resulted in part of the palace, the 'Museo Ercolanese', being set aside to house the expanding collection.[85] It was expressly forbidden to make drawings or notes, and it was presumably this restriction on scientific research that so offended Winckelmann. In this way, the king retained his rights over the finds and he made profitable use of them. The 'Accademia Ercolanese' was founded in 1755 to further the publication of the finds; earlier in the same year a catalogue of the museum was published (Bayardi 1755). In the eight volumes of the *Antichità di Ercolano*, which appeared between 1757 and 1792, members of the Accademia discuss the wall paintings and the bronze statues (Antichità 1757). This series of volumes were not sold, but were handed out as personal gifts by the king - a present which was, of course, much sought after! Luckily, German and English translations soon appeared, which made the unique finds more accessible to a larger audience (Bayardi/Martyn/Lettice 1773).

The Museo Ercolanese, at its largest, occupied 18 rooms, in which objects were displayed more or less thematically. The first six rooms contained household goods from Herculaneum - and later also from Pompeii - including objects such as tables, tripods, lamps, and musical and surgical instruments. The seventh room contained a reconstruction of a Pompeian kitchen, reminiscent of a modern museum display, complete with fireplace and cooking utensils. The remaining rooms were filled with

---

[84]   Murga 1962: 28-29; Ruggiero 1885: 23, 29; Allroggen-Bedel/Kammerer-Grothaus 1980: 184; Parslow 1995: 224. However, compare Conte Corti 1946: 138-139; Deiss 1985: 27.

[85]   For the establishment, function, history and an overview of the collection at the museum see Allroggen-Bedel/Kammerer-Grothaus 1980; compare also Scatozza Höricht 1982.

statues, mosaic floors and other *objets d'art*. Only the last room usually remained locked, because it housed material which was considered to be offensive. The steady supply of objects eventually resulted in a shortage of space in Portici, so the collection was gradually transferred to the much larger Museo Borbonico in Naples, the predecessor of what is now the Museo Nazionale Archaeologico. This operation was completed in 1827.[86] In the meantime, the Bourbons had already taken part of the collection to Palermo when they fled from the Napoleonic occupying force.

The evacuation of the collection to Palermo further increased the difficulty of determining the exact provenance of the objects. However, study of the eighteenth-century archive material has made it possible to reconstruct the context of many of the finds, including paintings and mosaics.[87] The continuation of this kind of research should eventually produce a general overview of the relationships between the objects, paintings and mosaics found in Herculaneum and Pompeii.[88]

2.3. The first excavation of the area (1828-1927)

After excavations in the theatre ceased in 1780, work in Herculaneum was not to be resumed for nearly fifty years. Attention was focused entirely on Pompeii, because of the valuable finds it yielded and the relative ease of uncovering them: the lapilli could simply be scooped up, allowing workers to uncover entire areas instead of searching for treasures in mine shafts. A scientific approach to the ancient finds became more and more vital, and it was with this in mind that an attempt was undertaken to excavate Herculaneum in its entirety. In 1827, the state purchased a piece of land where an old Bourbon shaft had been discovered some time earlier, and on 9 January 1828 an excavation was started under the direction of Carlo Bonucci. His detailed reports and lists of finds show that the work was carried out very thoroughly.[89] The new king, Francis I (1825-1830), showed his interest by paying a visit to the excavation site on 5 May 1828.

In the first year considerable progress was made, and two houses were almost completely uncovered, namely the 'Casa di Aristide' and the 'Casa d'Argo'. The following year saw the partial uncovering of the 'Casa del Genio'. In 1830, the excavations in this house continued, and workers chanced upon another house that became

---

[86]   The large procession of objects described by Jean-Louis Desprez, among others (Catalogue Pompeii 1973: no. 298) never actually took place - see De Franciscis 1963A: 42, fig. g; All-roggen-Bedel/Kammerer-Grothaus 1980: 183.

[87]   Allroggen-Bedel 1975A; 1975B; 1976A; 1983; Moormann 1984; 1986; De Kind 1991C.

[88]   Agnes Allroggen-Bedel has produced a study of this sort for the paintings in the Museo Nazionale in Naples: see Allroggen-Bedel 1991. Of course, the archive material published by, amongst others, Ruggiero (1881; 1885), Strazullo (1980; 1982) and Pannuti (1983) is also of equal importance.

[89]   See also the first guide to the excavations: Bonucci 1835. For an overview of Bonucci's life and work as an archeologist: Venditti 1970; Kockel 1988. Compare also below, n. 37.

known as the 'Casa dello Scheletro' after a skeleton that was found there on 10 February 1831 (Ruggiero 1885: 566). For the period 1832-1836 the only records are lists of finds; there are no detailed reports of the progress of the excavations, presumably because of the increasingly difficult nature of the work. The Bourbons had already removed a considerable amount of material from this part of the town, so subsequent finds were meagre. The transport and processing of large quantities of soil also presented a problem. Moreover, the annual budget of 2000 ducats allocated to the excavations was far from generous. This led to the work being halted in 1837 because, according to the Soprintendente Michele Arditi, 'esso però non ci ha dato che il più infelice risultamento' (Ruggiero 1885: 571). Fifteen years on, the excavations were resumed for a short period (until April 1855); work was carried out in the 'Casa dell'Albergo', and King Ferdinand II (1830-1859) visited the area in August 1852 in the company of a number of important guests (Ruggiero 1885: 577).

After Naples was annexed to the new kingdom of Italy, plans to continue excavations in Herculaneum were pursued with great zeal. The head of the Department of Archaeology at that time was the renowned Giuseppe Fiorelli (1823-1896), who had already shown his tremendous expertise in Pompeii. The purchase of an adjacent piece of land allowed the excavation to be extended; the new excavation was officially inaugurated on 8 February 1869, in the presence of King Victor Emmanuel II and numerous dignitaries.[90] The work was supervised at first by Niccola Pagano (replaced for a number of months in 1869 by Camillo Lembo), and subsequently, from October 1871, by Andrea Galella. Detailed records of the excavation were kept: activities and finds were recorded in on a daily basis in the 'giornale degli scavi', which provides a clear picture of the extremely laborious progress of the work (compare fig. 1).

In 1869 the excavation of the 'Casa dello Scheletro' and the 'Casa del Genio' was resumed; in addition, work was carried out on the west side of the 'Casa del Tramezzo di Legno' and in the shop on the street-corner opposite, to the north of the 'Casa del Genio' (Ruggiero 1885: 583-601). This work continued in 1870, but was soon abandoned because it was not producing any finds. However, later in the year further progress was made on the west side of the 'Casa del Tramezzo di Legno'; the *decumanus inferior* was reached in December (Ruggiero 1885: 602-616). Over the next few years (1872-1874) the *decumanus inferior* and *cardo* III to the north were uncovered as far as the extent of the excavation permitted, and the buildings at the intersection of the two streets were partially investigated (Ruggiero 1885: 627; 630-631).

In 1873 and 1874 work proceeded in the 'Casa di Galba', named after the silver portrait bust of the Emperor Galba found there on 11 September 1874 (Ruggiero 1885: 659). However, on 10 June 1874 rooms were discovered in an adjacent *insula* which were immediately identifiable as part of a bath, and thereafter the efforts of the excavators were devoted to uncovering the rest of the complex (Ruggiero 1885: 654). In fact, the workmen had already found part of the peristyle of the baths in the previous year, but the function of the building had not yet been recognised.

---

[90]   Ruggiero 1885: 583; Maiuri 1958: 3-5 (including illustration).

The excavation of the baths was completed in December 1875; after that, the excavation records simply note that 'si lavorò tutto il mese alle sole riparazioni che furono principalmente la sistemazione delle scarpe e alcuni muri di sostegno alle ripe soprastanti' (Ruggiero 1885: 674-676). This reinforcement work continued until 1877, but no attention was devoted to the buildings which had been exposed, which consequently began to fall into disrepair. Ruggiero (1885: XVI-XVII) criticises the 19th-century excavators for this neglect, as does Maiuri (1958: 4, 6).

The American archaeologist Charles Waldstein, who worked in England and later became known under the name Walston (1856-1927), was also concerned about this situation. At the beginning of this century, in collaboration with the Italian authorities, he launched a campaign to complete the excavation of Herculaneum; it was to be an international project, led by the Italians, but funded by contributions from abroad. The money to finance it was to be raised by national committees in Europe and America, chaired by the heads of state; each committee would be represented on an International Committee, chaired by the King of Italy, which would manage the funds and appoint the members of the international staff. In order to streamline the excavation process, Waldstein had already planned new working methods and schedules (Waldstein/Shoobridge 1908: 135-183).[91]

Waldstein's idea received much support in various countries. Initially the Italians were also very much in favour of it; but when the press voiced rumours that it was not the King of Italy but the President of the United States who would chair the International Committee, they began to have misgivings. The rumour was a blow to Italian chauvinism: public opinion swung against the plan and the government began to take a different stand. No matter how much Waldstein tried to defuse rumours about the chairmanship, the Italians continued to believe that their honour had been impugned, and eventually, in April 1907, they told Waldstein that they would not be able to accept any material aid or direct collaboration from other countries, and that they would continue the excavations at Herculaneum themselves (Waldstein/Shoobridge 1908: 52, 248-254; Maiuri 1958: 6).

A committee was set up to evaluate the implications of this decision; it concluded that the excavation of Herculaneum was not expedient, not only because of doubts about the quality of the material Waldstein expected to find, but also because it was believed that the project would endanger the progress of other excavations in Italy (Maiuri 1958: 7). As a result, no real action was ever taken, despite the promise made to Waldstein ('questi scavi saranno presto intrapresi' [92]), and only 'l'impegno solenne di iniziare e portare a compimento l'impresa' remained (Maiuri 1958: 7).

---

[91]   Waldstein sets out a number of arguments, many of them now outdated, to support the fact that Herculaneum was chosen as the most important excavation site (see Waldstein/Shoobridge 1908: 2-11). A brief overview of Waldstein's life can be found in Barnhart 1954: 4061.

[92]   Statement by the Ministero dell'Istruzione Pubblica, 24 April 1907 - see Waldstein/Shoobridge 1908: 254.

2.4. 1927-1961: Amedeo Maiuri

The Ministry's promise was eventually fulfilled under Amedeo Maiuri (1886-1963), who was Soprintendente of Naples and Campania for 37 years.[93] Maiuri, the son of a solicitor, was born in Veroli in 1886, grew up in the nearby village of Ceprano, and studied at the University of Rome. He was a student of the Italian School of Archaeology in Athens, gained experience doing fieldwork on Crete, and soon afterwards was appointed as supervisor to the Italian archaeological mission on Rhodes (1914). After the First World War, Italy was allowed to retain control of the Dodecanese, which it had annexed in 1912, and Maiuri was appointed Soprintendente of the monuments and excavations. In 1924 he was recalled to his native country and offered one of the highest offices in the world of archaeology, namely that of Soprintendente of Naples and Pompeii, an office he retained until 1961. In this period many archaeological projects were carried out in Campania: in Pompeii, large areas of the city walls and of regions I and II were uncovered[94]; in Capri the Villa Iovis, Tiberius' palace, was excavated (Maiuri 1956: 29-56); the cave of the Sibyl in Cumae was uncovered, and the baths were excavated in Baiae (Maiuri 1963: 72-86). Immediately after his appointment in 1924, Maiuri began work in Herculaneum, aiming to 'sollevare il velo di mistero che tuttora copriva la sepolta Ercolano' (Maiuri 1958: 8).

He proposed to extend the excavation to the north and east; the inhabitants of Resina who were affected by the expropriation of land were to be re-housed elsewhere[95]; and plans were made for processing the soil removed from the site. This programme was approved two months after Waldstein died, and on 16 May 1927 excavations began anew in Herculaneum, almost 100 years after the start of the first excavation. This time, however, the work was carried out with more sophisticated tools, and progress was made much faster. Nevertheless, there were still considerable difficulties, especially the mine shafts left over from Bourbon times, which riddled the area like a system of mole-tunnels. These had undermined many of the ancient structures, which forced Maiuri to have reconstruction and restoration work carried out as the excavation progressed (Maiuri 1958: 20-21). The new campaign began where the old excavations had left off: in *insula* III (see fig. 1).[96] From there, work proceeded as follows (Maiuri 1958: 10-18; 59):
1927-1929: *insula* III;
1928-1932: *insula* IV;

---

[93] See, amongst others, Caputo 1963; Romanelli 1963; Archeologi italiani 1965: 7-10; Maggi 1974; D'Amore 1983.

[94] Kockel 1986: 445-450 (Maiuri's policy on the excavations after 1948). See also, amongst others, Maiuri 1933.

[95] Maiuri admits that this part of the plan did not initially get off the ground (Maiuri 1958: 10).

[96] The numbering of the *insulae* and the names given to most of the houses are attributed to Maiuri, who based it on Francesco La Vega's map of 1797. See above (§ 2.2) and below (§ 3.1.1.).

1931-1932: the baths in *insula* VI;

1931-1934: the southern part of *insula* V;

1932-1941: *insula orientalis* I and II;

1937-1938: the northern part of *insula* V up to the so-called *decumanus maximus*;

1939-1940: *insula* VI, up to the area where the modern town begins;

1939-1942: suburban buildings (sanctuaries and baths).

For the rest of the Second World War work in Herculaneum was suspended. In contrast to Pompeii, damage due to bombings was minimal. Excavations were resumed in the Palaestra in 1952 (until 1954) and in the Suburban Baths, where the groundwater level caused many problems.

The great success of Maiuri's campaign was largely attributable to his organisational ability and his incessant drive. He avoided the mistakes made in the past, when the processing of excavated soil and the limited area of the site appeared to be insurmountable barriers. However, it should not be forgotten that he found himself in the right political climate to launch his plans. The Fascist government idolised the glorious Italian past and in consequence was willing to invest a large amount of money in the exploitation of ancient sites, including Herculaneum. It also seems probable that under a less totalitarian regime the large-scale expropriations would have been more difficult. Finally, the excavations must have benefited from the efficient administration in Italy at the time, however forcibly this may have been imposed.[97]

Maiuri succeeded in obtaining funds to continue his projects even after the Fascist era had come to an end. The most significant investments came from the 'Cassa per il Mezzogiorno', the emergency fund that was set up for the re-establishment and development of Southern Italy. As Maiuri writes (1958: 18), most of the grant from this fund went to the excavations in the Palaestra at Herculaneum. Part of the money was of necessity used for the maintenance and restoration of the excavated areas, a task which every archaeologist must surely set himself. Maiuri is often criticised for practically ignoring this aspect of the excavation in his eagerness to uncover new finds (Kockel 1986: 449). In Pompeii this neglect has resulted in parts of the 'nuovi scavi' along the Via dell'Abbondanza becoming very dilapidated; they are generally referred to as 'sconosciuti', because they are so inadequately published (Kockel 1986: 450, 472-487). Hopefully this situation will be remedied by new initiatives such as the 'Progetto Pompei', an extensive programme for the preservation of archaeological remains in Pompeii and the surrounding area, which includes provision for the restoration of the excavated *insulae*.[98]

Fortunately, Maiuri did publish the houses and public buildings of the 'nuovi scavi' in Herculaneum, although he failed to produce more than one volume (Maiuri 1958);

---

[97] For Maiuri's role in Fascist times see Manacorda 1982: 449; 454-455. Also, it is worth noting that Maiuri uses a quote from a speech by Mussolini in 1931 as the motto on the title page of his book on Ercolano (Maiuri 1932).

[98] Progetto Pompei 1988: 61, 63-68. A number of *insulae* (I 20, II 1, II 8-9) have been taken in hand since 1985 and were first made accessible to the general public in 1988. See Ciro Nappo 1988 (I, 20); Amadio 1987; 1988 (II, 1); De Simone 1987B; 1988 (II, 8); Sodo 1987; 1988 (II, 9).

the second part, which was to feature the wall paintings, floors, wood, finds and inscriptions (Maiuri 1958: VI), was never published because he died in 1963.

2.5. Discoveries after 1961

After Maiuri there was a change of policy on the part of the excavators of both Pompeii and Herculaneum: Maiuri's successors[99] pursued a more cautious policy, aimed more at preserving and restoring the area than extending it (Kockel 1986: 450, 523).

In Herculaneum, only the excavation of the so-called *decumanus maximus* (1960-1961) continued; the whole of *insula* VI was uncovered, including the building of the Augustales (Guadagno 1983) while on the other side of the *decumanus* the excavations proceeded as far as modern buildings permitted (see fig. 1). Here, a four-storey building was discovered, with shops at ground floor level; a shipment of glass from the workshop of P. Gessius Ampliatus, still packed, was found in one of these shops.[100] For a long time after this discovery, nothing new was found in Herculaneum, where the consolidation of existing excavations was of paramount importance.[101] It was only in 1980, when an earthquake caused damage to the monuments in Campania (to a lesser extent in Herculaneum than in Pompeii), that important discoveries were made in the suburban area. Here, work had been in progress for some years to remove areas of tufa and take measures to combat the groundwater level. It was discovered that there were vaulted chambers under the Suburban Baths, which contained numerous skeletons, the remains of people who had waited here in vain to be rescued in 79 (see § 1.2.3.). Another spectacular find was made in September 1982; archaeologists found a boat, which provided definitive evidence that the ancient coastline was much closer to the town than Maiuri had suspected (1958: 145-146).

Recent fieldwork in Herculaneum has tended to focus on the study of the existing remains[102], rather than trying to extend the excavations, although money has been reserved to fund soundings in Herculaneum and possibly the excavation of the Villa dei Papiri (Progetto Pompei 1988: 72-73; 126-127). However, the preservation of the town is equally urgent, because the repairs carried out under Maiuri's supervision are

---

[99] A. De Franciscis (1961-1977), F. Zevi (1977-1982), M.G. Cerulli Irelli (1982-1984), B. Conticello (1984-1994), P.G. Guzzo (1994-)

[100] De Franciscis 1963B; 1965; Deiss 1985: 4, 23; Kockel 1986: 528; Scatozza Höricht 1986.

[101] Accounts by De Franciscis (1961; 1965; 1966: 187; 1967A; 1967B: 237-238; 1969; 1975; 1977), Maggi (1976A; 1976B: 497-498; 1977; 1978; 1979; Zevi/Maggi 1978: 342-343), Zevi (1982) and Cerulli Irelli (1977: 757-758).

[102] See the progress reports written by Zevi (1982), Cerulli Irelli (1983; 1984), Pappalardo (1983; 1987), Conticello (1986), Budetta (1987; 1988; 1993). The imprint of the Flavian portrait in the ceiling of the corridor (compare Gore 1984: 568; Kockel 1986: 529) which was presented by Pappalardo (1983: 349, 351) as a new find, had already been recognised by Bonucci as a depiction of Vespasian, after a plaster cast had been made of it (reported 24 November 1828; Ruggiero 1885: 559).

in dire need of replacement. It is to be hoped that this type of restoration will form an important element in any future plans.[103]

---

[103] 'Progetto Pompei' only provides for the restoration of the part of the town that looked out over the sea: 'il recupero della visione antica' (Progetto Pompei 1988: 72).

PART II

URBAN DEVELOPMENT AND THE
DISTRIBUTION OF BUILDING PLOTS

3. URBAN DEVELOPMENT

3.1. The plan of Herculaneum

3.1.1. Sources of information about the city plan

Our knowledge of the city plan of Herculaneum is based on three sources, in addition to the ancient literary works discussed earlier. Each has its own particular relevance: 1. the information yielded by the exploration of the site in the 18th century: this is especially important because it revealed a large part of the plan of the city, as well as its location; 2. the excavations in the period 1827-1961: these have allowed a full study of the archaeological remains, which, while it has confirmed the basic accuracy of the 18th-century findings, has occasionally produced modifications or additional information; 3. the most recent discoveries since 1980: again, these have confirmed, qualified and, where necessary, further modified the picture that emerges from the first two sources of information.[104] One document from the time of the Bourbons is especially important for a general view of the city, namely the map mentioned earlier (§ 2.2), made by Francesco La Vega on the basis of the information then available, which had been obtained during the Bourbon excavations in the area around Resina. The map was drawn by Pietro La Vega, Francesco's brother, and was included as *tabula* 2 in the *Dissertatio isagogica* of 1797 (Rosini 1797: tab. 2), the historical introduction to Carlo Rosini's edition of the papyri found at Herculaneum (Rosini-Ciampitti 1793), which is based on a manuscript by A. Mazzocchi.

This map with its key, which has been reproduced many times,[105] depicts part of ancient Herculaneum and its original geographical situation, namely the ancient coastline between Portici and Torre del Greco, the peninsula on which the city was located, and the supposed course of the two small rivers on either side. It shows 8 rectangular *insulae*, in two rows of four, with a narrow strip of buildings on the west side, and on the east side a structure which is nowadays referred to as the Palaestra. Nearby La Vega locates a temple, near the continuation of the broad main street. This street, on which the 'Basilica' is situated, leads to the 'Forum', where we find another temple and the theatre. On the far side of the small river to the west is the Villa dei Papiri, and on the northeastern edge of the city are tombs. The name 'Retinae Portus' in front of the harbour of Herculaneum on the map is based on an erroneous interpretation of Pliny the Younger, *Epist.* VI.16, 8-9:

---

[104] See also Guadagno 1993 and especially Pagano 1996.
[105] For instance, Ruggiero 1885: tav. II; Waldstein/Shoobridge 1908: pl. II; Mau 1908: 532, fig. 294; Maiuri 1958: fig. 31; Maiuri 1977: fig. 2; Scatozza Höricht 1985: 134 fig. 3 (cf. also fig. 5).

instead of 'Rectina' (Tascus' wife), this was thought to read 'Retina', a toponym.[106]

A number of individual drawings of buildings and parts of the city from the early years of the 18th-century excavations can be fitted into La Vega's map without any difficulty. The way in which it represents the northwestern corner of the Palaestra, for example, seems to be based on a drawing by Pierre Bardet from 1743 depicting the area around the *decumanus maximus* (§ 2.2; Allroggen-Bedel 1983: 147, Abb. 1a+b). Another drawing by an anonymous artist, dating from 1749, shows the *insula occidentalis* of La Vega's map in detail (Ruggiero 1885: tav. II; Johannowsky 1982: 145-147, fig. 1). Undoubtedly La Vega had other smaller plans at his disposal, such as those of the theatre, the 'Basilica' and the Villa dei Papiri, which are still known to us.[107] It is remarkable that La Vega regularly corrects the plans he uses for making his map. In Bardet's plan, for instance, the orientation of the theatre is completely wrong, an error which is corrected on La Vega's general map. The drawing from 1749 was also incorporated in the city plan in an 'improved' version: La Vega extended *cardo* I to the south, although the original drawing shows *insula* I and the *insula occidentalis* as connected, closing off *cardo* I. The real situation is as yet impossible to determine. However, thanks to Maiuri's excavations, it is possible to judge the accuracy of the 18th-century plans on the other side of the city, in the *insula orientalis*. It appears that Bardet tended to 'improve on the original' in his drawings, that is, he made all the corners square and the walls straight. For example, he gave the Palaestra and *cardo* V the same orientation, although there is a difference of at least 10° between them. La Vega adopted this orientation, which has rightly led Allroggen-Bedel to conclude that he must only have had Bardet's plan at his disposal for this part of the city (Allroggen-Bedel 1983: 141). Her observations about the value of Bardet's drawing also seem justified: while individual details of the plan are correct, they are not put together correctly in relation to each other.[108]

3.1.2. The suburban buildings

It is remarkable that La Vega's map shows neither the buildings outside the city walls, nor the walls themselves; this has already been pointed out by Maiuri (1942B: 257). Neither the Suburban Baths, nor the small sanctuaries in the Area Sacra, nor the Casa del Rilievo di Telefo (*insula orientalis* I, 2-3) to the south of the Palaestra are shown on the map. There is no indication of excavations in this area in the reports of the 18th-century excavators, even though such excavations must certainly have been carried out, judging from the remains of shafts that have been found (Maiuri 1958: fig. 112). The high

---

[106] In the present version the passages read: '*accipit codicillos Rectinae Tasci imminenti periculo exterritae*'; '*ascendit ipse, non Rectinae modo, sed multis (...) laturus auxilium*' ('He accepted the letter from Rectina, wife of Tascus, who was terrified by the imminent danger'; 'he himself boarded the ship, not only to help Rectina, but also many others ...') Cf. Beloch 1890: 238 (old version) and 469-470 (corrected version). See also Sherwin-White 1966: 373.

[107] See Parslow 1995, especially 275-277.

[108] A detailed analysis of Bardet's plans is given in Parslow 1995: 49-60

groundwater level may have obstructed the work of the excavators even then.[109] Maiuri also corrected La Vega's map with regard to the geographical setting of the city. The map locates the buildings on some kind of plateau, with a very steep cliff facing the sea; this may explain the fact that the map does not show walls and extramural buildings. The excavations, however, have shown that the site is a gentle slope, gradually descending to the sea. This can be clearly observed in the differences in level within *insulae*, within houses, and even within parts of houses. Maiuri does agree with Rosini's and La Vega's conclusions regarding the ancient coastline. He estimated that it was about 150 to 200 metres from the southern walls (Maiuri 1942B: 259). He also assumed that a harbour had developed in the Imperial period, arising from simple constructions near the sheltered places where boats could be pulled up onto the beach (the 'eternally sheltered harbours' of Dionysius of Halicarnassus).

The recent discoveries on the outskirts of the city (see also § 1.2.3.) seem to confirm this hypothesis: the discovery of a boat together with a large quantity of pieces of timber may indicate the presence of a boatyard, and the vaulted chambers in which many victims of the eruption took refuge may have served as boathouses and warehouses. However, Maiuri locates this harbour in the wrong place. It was not about 150 metres from the city, where, according to him, the ancient coastline was, but at a lower level, where the suburban buildings were; the sea must only have been a few dozen metres away, much closer to the city than La Vega, Rosini and Maiuri assumed.[110]

It remains unclear in which period this part of the city was developed. Maiuri (1958: 151) dates the Suburban Baths to a rather late period (the Flavian period), on the basis of the freshness of the masonry bonds, the sophisticated details and the well-preserved stuccowork and wall decoration; in addition, the fact that building materials were found stored in one of the rooms suggests the building had not been fully completed in 79. The connection with Balbus' decree and the erection of his statue led Maiuri to opt for the Flavian period.

As we have seen, the last argument is unconvincing because Balbus' decree probably dates from the beginning of the 1st century AD. Although Maiuri's other arguments are not entirely convincing either - the decoration, the building materials and the wall structures may originate from alterations or repairs to the building - a late date would seem appropri-

---

[109] Cf. Maiuri 1958: 148. However, see also Guadagno 1987: 153-154, where Ruggiero's misinterpretation of a passage from the 'minute dei Dispacci' is corrected on the basis of Alcubierre's 'Giornale degli Scavi' (Pannuti 1983): instead of a single structure that was discovered between May and July 1743, two different buildings were found, the first 8 metres below the level of the ancient city ('se descubrió un edificio, trenta palm.s mas baja que el plano de la ciudad antigua' - Pannuti 1983: 213, 24 May 1743), which according to Guadagno was the level of the suburban area as it is known to us now. Recent finds in the 1980s disproved Maiuri's theory about an illegal excavation, during which, among other things, the torso of the statue of Marcus Nonius Balbus in the suburban square was stolen (Maiuri 1942B: 271). The torso and part of the dedicatory inscription were found outside the square, at a level which was 5 metres lower (Zevi 1982: 337; Maggi 1985: 37-42). See also Pagano 1988A for a reconstruction of the inscription.

[110] The coastline in L. Glanzman's reconstruction (in Gore 1984: 570-580), on the other hand, is too close to the city. Cf. also the remarks in Guadagno 1993: 86, pl. XVI, 2.

ate for the Suburban Baths, as compared to the Forum Baths. The Forum Baths are not as evolved as the Suburban Baths, as is clear from the form of the heating system and the less homogeneous overall design; they date from the Julio-Claudian period. The question remains whether the Suburban Baths and the square in front of them were constructed at the same time as the statue-base and altar of Balbus, and if so, when this was. In order to find the answer, it will be useful to examine the stipulations of the decree, and especially the second honour that was to be bestowed on Balbus.

This stipulated that an altar was to be erected at the place where Balbus' ashes were gathered, i.e. the place where he was cremated. Maiuri (1942B: 277) and Schumacher (1976: 173-174) do not consider whether the square where the altar was set up existed at the time of Balbus' cremation. In Maiuri's view the link is self-evident: the square and the baths belong to the early Flavian period and Balbus died some years before the eruption. Schumacher does not explain the discrepancy between an Augustan date for Balbus and a possible Flavian date for the square. It is possible that Balbus was cremated outside the city walls, at the place where the square with the altar and the Suburban Baths were subsequently constructed. However, the objection to this line of reasoning is that the altar is also dated to the early Imperial period, on the basis of the inscriptions, and therefore it must have been erected shortly after Balbus' death.

If we assume that the altar was erected in the same square where the statue is now, which is very plausible, we must conclude that the square, the cremation and the altar are contemporary and date from the beginning of the 1st century AD. The new layer of pounded earth put on top of the original *opus signinum* surface of the square (Maiuri 1958: 152) could be explained by the construction of the baths at a later stage, possibly only after 62. According to this hypothesis the suburban buildings date from two periods: the first at the beginning of the 1st century AD, when the square and the Area Sacra,[111] and the warehouses and boathouses beneath them, were constructed, and the second, in which the baths were built, probably after the earthquake. In accordance with this, Ganschow dates the Area Sacra, the square with the altar of Balbus and the construction of the Porta Marina near *cardo* V to the time shortly after Augustus at the latest (Ganschow 1989: 123-125). Pagano (1988A: 238) too assumes an Augustan date; he even suspects that one of the rooms in the Suburban Baths (Maiuri 1958: fig. 114, no. d) was a small mausoleum in honour of Balbus, before it was converted into a changing room or *cella ostiaria*.

Tran Tam Tinh (1988: 129-130), on the other hand, places Balbus in the Flavian period, and wonders whether it is a coincidence that all the activities in his honour (cremation, erection of an altar, the start of a procession) took place in the square directly below the luxurious Casa dei Cervi, which was probably the residence of a prominent citizen of Herculaneum. The connection between Balbus and the Casa dei Cervi implied by Tran Tam Tinh must be rejected on the basis of the arguments mentioned above. The relationship between the Casa del Rilievo di Telefo, which has often been referred to as Balbus' residence,[112] and the suburban area remains unclear. Maiuri (1958: 147-148) sees

---

[111]   Cf. the Third Style painting with a view of a garden in Sacello A - Maiuri 1958: fig. 149; Bastet/De Vos 1979: 139. See also the important remarks in Ganschow 1989: 101, 104, 123-125.

[112]   See, for example, De Vos/De Vos 1982: 276; Deiss 1985: 56; Catalano 1982: 960.

a connection between the house and the baths below; De Vos (1982: 277) dates it to the time of Augustus, with major renovations after 62; finally, Ganschow (1989: 98-100, 326) also suggests an Augustan date for the building as it stands, although he thinks some parts may date from the 1ˢᵗ century BC.

3.1.3 The location of the forum and the *decumanus maximus*

After these corrections and additions we can return to La Vega's map. In order to under-stand this map better and put it in a wider perspective, it is necessary to consider where in Herculaneum the forum was, since this was the most important square in a Roman town and functioned as its political, social and often economic centre - which does not mean that it was always the topographical centre of the town. La Vega's map is very clear about its location, situating it to the north of *insulae* VII and VIII, on the edge of the city (Rosini 1797: tab. 2, no. 3). Maiuri (1958: 85-87), on the other hand, thinks that the square cannot have been located there, because there are no indications of public buildings in the vicinity, the usual colonnades bordering such a square are lacking, and the area is too small for a forum. He suspects that the *decumanus maximus*, the broad main street, served as the forum and that Herculaneum did not have a real town square. He bases his assumption on the fact that the *decumanus* was closed to traffic and was used as a market; he points to the forum at Paestum as a parallel. This solution also fits very well with his view of the town plan of Herculaneum. In his opinion, the *decumanus maximus* was in the centre of the city, with a *decumanus* on the south side (the *decumanus inferior*), forming eight *insulae*, and another *decumanus* on the north side (the *decumanus superior*), which would mean that there were 16 *insulae* in all. According to Maiuri (1958: 30), such a division of the city with three *decumani* is comparable to that of nearby Neapolis. In that case, the main road from Naples to Pompeii would not have passed through Herculaneum, but would have gone around the city: the *decumanus maximus* was closed off and served as the forum, and, like the *decumanus inferior*, the *decumanus superior* was not wide enough to serve as a thoroughfare. Thus Herculaneum was bypassed by the road and saw very little in the way of trade.[113]

There is much evidence against Maiuri's hypothesis that the *decumanus maximus* served as the Forum. As Adamo Muscettola has shown convincingly (1982: 5-6), the 18ᵗʰ-century documents indicate that the forum was in the vicinity of the theatre, and as long as nothing more is known about the city it is better to accept this location. It is, however, possible that the broad *decumanus* may have served as a commercial centre - a parallel can

---

[113] Maiuri 1942B: 256; compare also the remarks by Lepore (1955), Solin (1973A) and Guadagno (1993: 87). The theory that the *decumanus maximus* was closed off and used as the forum is already found in Beloch 1890: 230. Spano (1937: 334-338) assumed that the main road was to the south of the city, that is, on the seaward side. This theory (which has been refuted by recent finds) contradicted Maiuri's earlier view that the city was intersected by the coastal road (Maiuri 1932: 47-48). Maiuri may have changed his mind in view of Spano's publication.

be found in Pompeii, where in the course of time the Via dell'Abbondanza assumed commercial functions previously fulfilled by the forum. The argument in favour of the theory that the *decumanus* was the forum, namely that three important buildings were situated on this street (Maiuri 1958: 86-87), does not carry much weight, for if the forum was really situated where La Vega places it, these buildings would still have been close to it. The buildings in question are the 'Basilica' and the two buildings opposite it in *insula* VI and *insula* VII. The functions of these buildings have been interpreted in many different ways. Before the excavation of the building in *insula* VI, which took place in 1960-61, Maiuri considered them to be municipal buildings: he thought that the 'Basilica' was the *curia* of the *ordo decurionum* and that the other two buildings were also *curiae*, analogous to the three buildings in the forum of Pompeii (Maiuri 1958: 90). Later, however, he realised that the building on the corner of *insula* VI had to be identified as the Aedes Augustalium, the seat of the college of Augustales, an interpretation which has been generally accepted.[114]

In connection with this, Allroggen-Bedel (1974: 105-109; 1983: 145-153) suggests that the three buildings on the *decumanus* constituted a religious centre, conceived in the Julio-Claudian period, which was associated with the imperial cult. According to this theory, the so-called Basilica was a roofless space where the deified emperors were worshipped, under the jurisdiction of the Augustales. They had their headquarters in the Aedes Augustalium opposite the 'Basilica', and also controlled the building on the corner of *insula* VII, which Allroggen-Bedel did not believe to be a basilica. However, since the statues of the *gens Nonia* were found here, erected in accordance with the decree of the decurions (*decreto decurionum*), Adamo Muscettola (1982: 10) argues that this was the Basilica of Herculaneum, the building restored at the expense of M. Nonius Balbus (CIL X 1425).[115] She assumes that La Vega located the forum correctly, and argues that the building is similar to the basilica at Pompeii, both in its form and its location in relation to the forum: it is of the eastern type, exemplified by the earliest basilica at Corinth; and, as at Pompeii, it is situated near the corner of the forum. These conclusions seem very plausible and enable us to reconstruct the town plan further, on the basis of analogies and logical deduction.

In Adamo Muscettola's reconstruction the *decumanus maximus*, the broad thoroughfare which ran through the city from east to west, should probably be situated further to the north. It may be identical with part of a street found under the 'Casa Savarese' on 28 April 1754.[116] This corresponds to the main road from Pompeii to Neapolis as indicated on the plan published by Ward-Perkins (1979: 26), which is further to the north than the street which is now referred to as the *decumanus maximus*. This would also be in accordance with the tombs found to the east of the city (referred to as *sepulcretum* by La Vega and indicated on the plan with the sign §§ - Rosini 1797: tab. 2). A description of such a

---

[114] Allroggen-Bedel 1974; Guadagno 1983. But see De Franciscis 1970: 311, who considers it to be the *curia*.

[115] See also § 1.2.1 above. Pagano 1990 provides a reconstruction of the eastern elevation of the building and a good survey of the remains of the wall paintings (scenes from the life of Hercules).

[116] Ruggiero 1885: 154; Allroggen-Bedel 1983: 154 n. 87; Scatozza Höricht 1985: 142.

tomb, discovered on 21 November 1750, can be found in Cochin/Bellicard (1757: 20-21, Pl. 6); Gori (1752: 134-135) includes a letter which mentions a tomb of the same type (a *columbarium*), discovered on 28 February 1750.[117] In the latter case, the cinerary urns in the niches of the vaulted space had names in red letters on them, not of the *gens Nonia*, as can be inferred from the text in CIL X 1473-1475, but probably of the *gens Pontia*; Alcubierre's diary (Pannuti 1983: 279) provides clearer and more comprehensive information on this (Guadagno 1981: 154-155 no 124).[118]

Gori's reference (1752: Dec. I, vol. I, 135; Schumacher 1976: 174 n. 39) to a tomb discovered near the theatre in 1739, decorated with paintings and provided with grave goods ('*prope Herculanei theatrum superius descriptum ante Augustum mensem, anno MDCCXXXIX detectum fuisse sepulcrum picturis variis ornatum et funebri supellectile instructum*') is based on an incorrect interpretation of the information available.[119]

No reference to this tomb can be found in Alcubierre's notes, nor is it indicated on La Vega's map. Yet it does not seem inconceivable that there were tombs to the west of the theatre, just outside the city. A similar situation is found in Pompeii, where several burial sites were located on the edge of the city, alongside the exit roads (near the Porta di Ercolano and the Porta di Nocera). Likewise, at Herculaneum there must have been tombs near the city boundaries, both to the east and to the west, along the main road from Neapolis to Pompeii, which ran through the city to the north of the present *decumanus*. This main road can be identified as the real *decumanus maximus*, which led to the forum and the theatre in the west of the city.

3.1.4 Summary

When we take into account all the revisions to the standard city-plan discussed in the

---

[117] See also De Jorio 1827: 41-43; Breton 1869: 329-330; Ruggiero 1885: XXXVII-XXXVIII, 526-527, pl. VIII, fig. 2a; Beloch 1890: 238; Mau 1908: 554, fig. 304; Schumacher 1976: 174 n. 39; Scatozza Höricht 1985: 142 + n. 50.

[118] The funerary inscription of M. Nonius Eutychus (CIL X 1471) had already been discovered on 2 February 1748 - Pannuti 1983: 257; Pagano 1996: 230.

[119] This passage is based on a letter by Rudolfino De Venuti to Gori, dated 8 August 1739 (Gori 1752: 46-47), which mentions a painted room, containing, among other things, a picture of Hermes taking the child Bacchus to Leukothea, and all kinds of pottery and small lamps. Venuti expresses his conviction that the room in question is 'un columbario' or a 'luogo che non ha correlazione col teatro'. Gori (1752: 135-136; 179-180) discusses this later and explains the paintings as typical of a sepulchral context. The picture of Hermes mentioned just now is the first in a list of 30 paintings provided by Alcubierre in 1739 (Ruggiero 1885: 52-54; Pannuti 1983: 180-181); it must have been discovered between the beginning of July 1739, when work was resumed near the theatre, and 21 July, when Marcello De Venuti was invited to visit the excavations to give advice about a coat of varnish for the wall paintings that were to be cut out. Rudolfino also writes about this in the letter to Gori mentioned above. Cf. also Allroggen-Bedel 1974: 102-104.

previous sections, the following picture emerges (see fig. 2).[120] Herculaneum was situated on a spit of land between two small rivers or streams; the area sloped down to the sea, which was a few dozen metres from the city. In pre-Roman times the city was a fortress surrounded by walls; later these were partly demolished and houses were built on them. In the course of the 1st century AD, a suburban quarter developed between the walls and the sea, with small temples, a square built in honour of Marcus Nonius Balbus, and baths. At sea level, in the vaulted substructures of this quarter, there were chambers for storing goods and boats; there may have been a boatyard, and it was possible to pull boats into shelters on the beach. The city itself was intersected by the road from Neapolis to Pompeii, which within the walls served as the *decumanus maximus*. This was presumably the starting-point from which the orthogonal network of streets with its *decumani* and *cardines* was plotted. In the southern part of the city 8 blocks of houses are known, rectangular in shape, flanked by two irregularly-shaped *insulae*; in the *insula* to the east the Palaestra was built later. A broad *decumanus* marks the transition from this residential area to the central part of the city, where several public buildings and squares were situated: the basilica, buildings associated with the imperial cult, the forum and the theatre. The latter two were on the western edge of the city, but bordering on the *decumanus maximus*. Just outside the walls on both sides of the city, tombs lined the main road. Because we do not know the size of the central area between the *decumanus maximus* and the *decumanus* that has been excavated, little can be said about the northern part of the city. If we assume that the city plan was symmetrical, there should be one or two additional *decumani* underneath the present city of Ercolano.[121]

Consequently, it is likely that Herculaneum had at least one *decumanus* more than the three proposed by Maiuri. His discussion of the city plan was probably strongly influenced by comparisons with Neapolis, where three *decumani* or *plateiai* are usually postulated in reconstructions. As Maiuri is not alone in comparing Herculaneum with Neapolis, it may be useful to take a brief look at the plan of this city and the background against which it is usually discussed.

3.2. The place of Herculaneum in the history of urban development

3.2.1 The city plan of Neapolis

The number of publications on the development of Neapolis has increased considerably

---

[120]   Our view is confirmed by Pagano's recent publication, which gives a fully detailed version of our fig. 2 (Pagano 1996: 229-238 , fig. 1).

[121]   However, it is also possible that the thoroughfare postulated here (the *decumanus maximus*) was situated away from the centre, just like the Forum. Incidentally, Catalano also assumes that the city was made up of 24 *insulae*, but he thinks there were three *decumani*; cf. Catalano 1953: figs 6 and 8; Catalano 1963: 214 n. 3.

over the last few years,[122] but there are hardly any essential differences between the interpretations of its general layout. Two periods are distinguished in the development of the city: the first period, in which the colony of Parthenope was founded from Cumae, started in c. 600 BC; the second period, during which the relatively small residential area of the colony was extended, began shortly after the battle of Cumae in 474 BC. The new city which developed in this second phase was called 'Neapolis', to distinguish it from the older settlement, which from then on was called 'Palaepolis'. Neapolis was founded on sloping terrain some distance from Palaepolis, which was situated on a rocky spit of land; according to Strabo (V, 4, 7) it was founded by Chalcidians from Cumae and by settlers from Ischia and Athens.

The plan of this new town can still be recognised to some extent in the present street plan and the modern layout of the centre of Naples. The street plan is rectilinear, with a small number of broad streets running from east to west, and a large number of small streets running from north to south. These streets are respectively referred to by the Greek terms *plateiai* and *stenopoi*, instead of the Etrusco-Roman terms *decumani* and *cardines*. Until recently, the number of *plateiai* in Neapolis was a point of contention: Castagnoli (1971: 35-39) argues that there were four, while Greco (1985; 1988), following Beloch (1890: 66) and others, suspects that there were only three, as the *plateia* that Castagnoli postulated in the south cannot be extended the full length of the town. In addition, Castagnoli assumes that there were 20 *stenopoi*, as against Beloch's 22. Greco identifies two squares in the street plan, one on either side of the large *plateia* that divides the city into two, which also marks a difference in level. In the northern *agora*, on the higher level, are the theatre, the *odeion* and the temple of the Dioscuri; in the lower, southern *agora*, there is a monumental building whose function is as yet unknown. Greco suggests that the northern *agora* served as the political centre of the city and the southern *agora* as the commercial centre or market-place (Greco 1988: 209).

This theory may be open to dispute, but there is a consensus about the dimensions of the *insulae* and the streets. The *stenopoi* were c. 3 metres wide, the *plateiai* 6 metres wide, except for the central one, which measured 13 metres; the *insulae* measured c. 35 by 180 metres. This corresponds to the following measurements in feet (one foot = c. 29.6 cm)[123]: the *stenopoi* are 10 to 12 feet wide; the *plateiai* are 20 and 50 feet wide; and the *insulae* or *strigae* measure 120 by 600-620 feet. This means that the blocks of houses were laid out in the proportion of 1 to 5, the width being equal to 1 *actus* (120') and the length being roughly equal to 1 *stadium* (600') (Castagnoli 1971: 35; Greco 1988: 202-203). Greco compares these oblong *insulae* with blocks of houses in Naxos (39 by 175 m), Himera (32 by 164 m), Paestum (35 by 273 m) and Agrigento. According to him, the layout of the houses in the *insulae* is analogous to those in Olynthos and Himera: each *insula* contains two rows of ten equal-sized houses, each c. 17 x 17 m square, of which 1 m at the back is reserved to form an alley between the rows (Greco 1988: 203; 213).

---

[122]   The studies by Greco (1985; 1988) and Baldassare (1985; 1988) are of particular importance.

[123]   R.P. Duncan-Jones (1980: 128) wrongly refers to this as a 'Roman' foot.

3.2.2. A brief survey of Greek urban development

These examples lead us to consider Greek urban development, a subject which has received a great deal of attention in recent years. A very important publication in this field is by W. Hoepfner and E.-L. Schwandner (1986), who try to unravel the Hippodamian system and to view it in the context of contemporary political and social structures. Hoepfner and Schwandner conclude that the Greek city in the Classical period was laid out according to systematic principles; they consider Hippodamus of Miletus to have 'invented' or at least perfected this system. His rules made it possible to apply the democratic principles of equal distribution to urban development and the construction of houses: they provided fixed, logical principles for planning a city, with standard measurements for every house and every street.

Long before Hippodamus, however, regular patterns of construction can be found in Greek cities, where the entire layout had been planned in advance; this is referred to as the 'neoteros tropos' or modern way of building, as opposed to the 'archaioteros tropos', the disorganised way of building in cities which developed organically, such as the old city of Smyrna. Because they are laid out *per strigas*, in oblong, parallel blocks of houses or *Streifen*, cities built according to this pattern are called *Streifenstädte* by Hoepfner and Schwandner. This pattern is found as early as the 8th - 7th century BC, especially in the Greek colonies of Sicily and southern Italy. The 'Streifen' are combinations of two rows of houses which are more or less identical in size, built back-to-back. From the 5th century BC the *Typenhaus* was used, a standardised type of house which enabled the development of an even more regular city plan. In this way, a greater degree of flexibility in planning a city was achieved; according to Hoepfner and Schwandner (1986: 250) the *Streifenstadt*, the best-known example of which was the city of Olynthos, founded in the Classical period, provided a 'beliebig variierbares, additives Häuser- und Insulasystem'.

Hoepfner and Schwandner consider Hippodamian town-planning to be characteristic of the Classical period and the democratic system. The Hippodamian method of building, which they believe was derived from the mathematical principles of Pythagoras of Samos, did not allow a city to be extended or reduced in size. The *insulae* are small, with a fixed number of houses, and are located in residential districts of set proportions. The streets are differentiated by size: there is one very broad main street, a few medium-sized ones, and many streets of normal width (3.5 - 5 m); some cities have a processional way which is twice as wide as the main street (c. 40 m). The city is divided into districts with distinct functions, with the *agorai* in the centre; the temples are located away from the main axis on different levels (the precursors of the terraced sanctuaries). The smallest unit of the city is the *Typenhaus*. Hoepfner and Schwandner regard it as characteristic of the system of Hippodamus and his successors that urban development is seen as a work of art, in which number theory plays a part (Hoepfner/Schwandner 1986: 255). The numbers 1-10 are used in various ratios, the ideal form being the hierarchical sequence 2:1, 3:2 and 4:3 (Hoepfner/Schwandner 1986: 255). Thus the Hippodamian-Pythagorean system of urban development is an expression of the democratic principles that were already found in the *Streifenstädte*.

Although Hoepfner and Schwandner's ideas often seem convincing, partly because of their splendid illustrations, several criticisms can be made. As far as the 'author' of the Hippodamian-Pythagorean city plan is concerned, for instance, they have ignored the observations of A. Burns (1976), who questions the link between Hippodamus and the foundation of Miletus in 476 BC. T. Lorenz expresses the same view in his recent study of Roman towns (Lorenz 1987: 54-55). Both authors consider Hippodamus to be the one who perfected the system, and not its inventor.[124] According to Lorenz, Aristotle's remark that Hippodamus invented cities with a regular layout is an ironic sentence, which should be seen in the context of the rest of the argument, in which he criticises Hippodamus. Equally weighty is the criticism made by H. Knell in his review of Hoepfner and Schwandner's book (Knell 1988): that they are not able to quote sources to support their theory that the *Typenhaus* is a reflection of *isonomia*, the equal rights of citizens in democratic states. This theory was presumably suggested by the fact that the development of the *Typenhaus* coincided with the appearance of the first democracies. Knell also points out that the impressive isometric drawings are sometimes based more on theory than on reality (Knell 1988: 561). The idea that the *Typenhaus* embodies democratic principles was also discussed at a symposium at Konstanz (Schuller 1989). Hoepfner and Schwandner's conclusions, and especially their interpretation of the political significance of the Hippodamian system, should therefore be treated with some caution.

The cities in Magna Graecia that Greco cites as parallels for Neapolis, are *Streifenstädte* rather than Hippodamian cities; this is a common form for Greek cities in the western Mediterranean, at least in the period up to the end of the 5th century BC. *Streifenstädte* have an orthogonal network of streets, forming narrow, oblong *insulae*; there are usually ten houses per block, sometimes more. In these cities the *agorai* are not in the centre, but on the periphery or on the edge of the grid of residential blocks.

Some Etruscan towns, such as Marzabotto, Bologna and Capua, also have orthogonal street plans (Lorenz 1987: 50-53). The orientation of these plans, however, adheres strictly to astronomical principles, with a broad street running from east to west (from sunrise to sunset) as the main axis, and another axis running at right angles from north to south; narrower streets run parallel to either axis, not always at regular intervals. In Marzabotto the length of the *insulae* is c. 160 metres, and the narrow streets are slightly less than 5 metres wide. This type of city-planning was probably connected with religious regulations, as later Latin writers note. It is remarkable, however, that orthogonal street-plans are not found in Etruscan cities until the 6th century BC. It seems likely that Etruscan town-planning was influenced by contact with the Greeks at that time.

3.2.3. Theories about the city plan of Herculaneum

The city plan of Herculaneum should be seen in the light of the two systems, Greek and

---

[124] See also the observations of H.-J. Gehrke in the proceedings of the symposium on *Demokratie und Architektur* (Gehrke 1989).

Etruscan, discussed in the previous section, as Campania had been exposed to both Greek and Etruscan influence for many years before the Samnite occupation. Theories about the city plan of Herculaneum reflect this. G. Spano, for instance, thinks that the regular network of streets was either constructed by the Etruscans, or added to an original Phoenician settlement at the time of the occupation by the Rhodians (Spano 1941: 146; 214-215). These ideas have not been accepted in the literature; neither has M. Coppa's suggestion that Herculaneum was of Oscan origin, which was supposed to explain the unusual orientation of the *insula orientalis* (Coppa 1968: 1040). His comparison of the *insulae* with those in Megara Hyblaea (Coppa 1968: 1041), however, is in accordance with current theories, which consider the plan of Herculaneum to be a Greek urban design or is at least based on Greek examples. Usually Neapolis is said to be the direct source of the orthogonal arrangement *per strigas* (i.e. three *plateiai/decumani* and several *stenopoi/cardines*).[125] However, it appears that the ratio used in the construction of the *strigae* in Neapolis is c. 1:5, that is, c. 120 by 600 feet, whereas the *insulae* in Herculaneum are much shorter, with a ratio closer to 1:2. This is a remarkable difference, as the other Greek cities that are comparable to Neapolis are also *Streifenstädte*, with long blocks of houses. The town plan of Herculaneum is thus significantly different from the usual plan, which makes it difficult to argue that it is Greek and that it was modelled on Neapolis. Lorenz, however, thinks it possible that the existing *insulae* in Herculaneum constitute a second phase in the development of the city, and originate from an earlier Greek plan with oblong *strigae*. He reconstructs this original plan by leaving out the *decumanus inferior* and joining up the *insulae* from north to south. He finds confirmation for his theory in the small atrium houses, whose regular, square plans can probably be traced back to the square houses of a regular city plan made under Greek influence. Subsequently when the *decumanus inferior* was built, the oblong *insulae* were cut in two, forming the present, more compact *insulae*.[126] This theory, however, is pure speculation and can only be accepted if concrete archaeological evidence is available.

Much more plausible is Lorenz's theory that the present city plan dates from the 4th -3rd century BC, when Campania was not dominated by the Greeks or the Etruscans (Lorenz 1987: 59). This means that Herculaneum is comparable to cities such as Fundi, Telesia, Nuceria, Surrentum and Pompeii, which have regular grid-plans of similar date. This link with a more native tradition of urban development is not new. F. Haverfield (1913: 100) had already considered the possibility that the city plan of Herculaneum - like those of Neapolis and Pompeii - followed an Italic tradition, although perhaps executed with Greek precision. A. von Gerkan (1924: 92-93, 156) also concluded that the plan was a mixture of Italic and Greek elements, not least because of the proportions of the *insulae* (1:2).

J. Boersma has made some significant observations on the subject. He argues that the first Roman *coloniae* in Italy had *insulae* which were narrow, like those of contemporary Greek settlements, but not as long (i.e., they measured 1 x 1 or 1 x 3 *actus*; Boersma 1982: 38). He concludes that the *insulae* at Herculaneum were not narrow, but were not

---

[125]   See, for example, Beloch 1890: 230; Pugliese Carratelli 1955: 419-420; Maiuri 1958: 28; Ward-Perkins 1979: 27.

[126]   Lorenz 1993. See also Lorenz 1987: 59.

as unusually broad as some contemporary (4th-century) *insulae* at Pompeii (e.g. I 2-4, I 6, I 10 and IX 1-6; Boersma 1982: 39-41), where increasingly large *insulae* were being built at that time.

The most important study of urban development in Herculaneum is that of W. Johannowsky (1982). He discusses the distribution of building plots in *insulae* III to VI, proposes a date for the city plan and points out the most important parallels (Johannowsky 1982: 148-149). First of all, he observes that the city plan, with *insulae* in the proportion of 1:2, represents a later stage of development than that of Neapolis. This means that the city was certainly built after the first half of the 5th century BC (when Neapolis was founded), and perhaps as late as the first half of the 4th century. Johannowsky justifies this date by pointing out that the houses measure c. 30 x 75 feet, a proportion of 2:5, which is characteristic of Etrusco-Italic houses with a *hortus* at the back; there are no parallels for houses of this shape in Greek settlements. According to this theory, the building plots within the *insulae* were arranged in two rows, back-to-back, except in *insulae* adjacent to the *decumanus maximus*, where the plots on the side next to the *decumanus* were arranged at right angles to the others, so that they faced onto the *decumanus*. He argues that the closest parallels for Herculaneum are Atella[127] and Acerrae, which, like the nearby Greek towns, had a less rigidly orientated street-plan than the astronomically-determined Etruscan model. Finally, Johannowsky (1982: 149) tries to show that the large peristyle house which he thinks can be detected in a plan dating from 1749 (see § 3.1.1 above) belongs to a different historical period from the belvedere houses Casa dei Cervi and Casa dell'Atrio a Mosaico, which probably date from the early Imperial period.

3.2.4. Conclusion

The following conclusions can be drawn about the place of the city plan of Herculaneum in the history of urban development. At present it is impossible to say what the origin of the settlement was - whether it was founded by the Oscans, the Phoenicians, or the Greeks - because the archaeological evidence is not conclusive. Apart from this, it seems that the city plan is best explained in connection with the city plan of Neapolis. The street plan of Herculaneum has the same general layout as Neapolis, which was founded shortly after 474 BC: 3 to 4 *plateiai* running parallel to the coast, several *stenopoi*, and a theatre situated near the forum (Bejor 1979: 132-134; Allroggen-Bedel 1983: 154). The fact that within this regular, orthogonal street plan the *insulae* are slightly wider and less long than in Neapolis suggests a later phase of urban development, in which Greek examples are less strictly followed. Following Lorenz (1987) and Johannowsky (1982), we can call this plan 'Campanian' or 'Italic'. Its date is still unclear, although it cannot be earlier than the late 5th - early 4th century, in view of the foundation date of Neapolis. This conclusion is not contradicted by the pottery found in sondages at Herculaneum: the oldest material is dated to the 4th century BC (Tran Tam Tinh 1977: 55; Pagano 1993B: 597-599). However, the

---

[127]   For Atella, see Castaldi 1908 and, most recently, Bencivenga Trillmich 1984: esp. 20-25.

walls of the buildings in the plan, as well as the material found in the sondages (Tran Tam Tinh 1977: 41; Pagano 1993B), point to a much later date, because the oldest type of construction that can be distinguished is a form of *opus incertum*, a type which was only in general use in Campania from the 2nd century BC.[128] These stone buildings were probably constructed at a later date to replace earlier structures in mud brick, which may have been damaged in the Second Punic War. However, it is not impossible that the stone buildings were the first structures on the site: the *insulae* may have been built up piecemeal, rather than all being filled with houses at one time; the four which have been fully excavated may not have been built over until the 2nd century BC. This was the case at Pompeii, where several *insulae* were still only partially built up at the time of the eruption (e.g. I 15, 20, 21 and II 8 and 9; cf. Castagnoli 1971: 30-31). A closer examination of the distribution of building plots within the *insulae* at Herculaneum may show whether all the houses were built at the same time and then rebuilt and repaired over the years, or whether the *insulae* were filled in one at a time, *insulae* III-VI being built at a relatively late stage.

---

[128]   Carrington 1933: 130; Adam 1984: 139-141. Maiuri (1958: 64) and Ganschow (1989: 120-122) date the oldest type of *opus incertum* at Herculaneum to the 'Samnite' phase.

4. THE DISTRIBUTION OF BUILDING PLOTS IN *INSULAE* III

AND IV AT HERCULANEUM

4.1. The overall dimensions of *insulae* III and IV

4.1.1. A general survey of *insulae* III-VI

Previous work on the town plan of Herculaneum and the distribution of building plots is not as valuable as it might have been, because it has not taken into account evidence from measurements and types of wall construction; neither Johannowsky (1982) nor Lorenz (1993) made sufficient use of this information. Conclusions drawn from existing town plans are likely to be unreliable if they are not supported by actual measurements and observation of the walling materials used. The following discussion of the distribution of building plots in *insulae* III and IV is based on measurements taken during several field trips between 1985 and 1989, as well as on a study of wall construction and wall and floor decoration. These allow more reliable conclusions to be drawn and must be the basis of any study of the history of the *insulae*.

The discussion will be restricted to these two *insulae* because the distribution of building plots in *insulae* V and VI are the subject of a study by H.M. Dresen.[129] According to her, *insula* III can be grouped with *insula* IV, and *insula* V with *insula* VI, on the basis of similarities in the shape of the *insulae* as a whole and the orientation of the building plots within the *insulae*. Dresen's conclusions about the building plots in *insulae* V and VI can be summarised briefly as follows: both *insulae* had three plots on the north side facing onto the *decumanus maximus*, each 50 feet wide and 80 feet deep. The remaining part of each *insula* was divided by a central north-south axis with plots on either side. The layout changed over the years, as in *insula* VI, where the Casa dei Due Atri was built across the axis, and the baths covered the entire southern part.

Insulae III and IV are both approximately 150 feet wide, as Johannowsky has already pointed out (1982: 148). He, however, assumes that an Attic foot measuring 29.6 cm (the same as the Roman foot) was employed, but in fact the *insulae* at Herculaneum were laid out in the Samnite period, after the presumed domination of the city by the Greeks and before the arrival of the Romans. In the Samnite period, the so-called Oscan foot of ca.

---

[129] Dresen is preparing this study in collaboration with M.C. van Binnebeke, which is to be part of the publication of a new plan of *insula* V. A short version of her results is included in De Kind 1993A. I would like to thank Leen Dresen for sharing and discussing her ideas with me.

27.5 cm was widely used (see Introduction). If it is assumed that this foot measurement was indeed used here, the design of the town plan and of *insulae* III and IV becomes clear. Before considering the dimensions of the blocks of houses, we will first consider the measurements of the streets. There is considerable variation in the width of the streets. The average measurements are:[130]

cardo III:	523 cm
cardo IV:	538 cm
cardo V:	615 cm (south: 523 cm; north: 661 cm)
decumanus inferior:	509 cm

The intended layout, at least of *cardines* III and IV, and probably also of the *decumanus inferior*, appears to have been:

pavement	5.5'
street	8'
pavement	5.5'
total	19'.

These are average measurements; in the southern part of *cardines* III and IV (and of *cardo* III), for instance, the width is approximately 20', and in the western part of the *decumanus inferior* it is 18'. Although the streets were probably not completely paved until Roman times, it may be assumed that the original measurements remained unchanged, except in the case of *cardo* V, which was widened at the north end because of the construction of the Palaestra (Maiuri 1958: 34, 39-40).

The widths of the *insulae* are as follows (see also fig. 4):

insula III:	4105 / 4124 cm
insula IV:	4363.5 cm
insula V:	4187.5 / 4358.5 cm
insula VI:	4234 / 4271 cm.

It is interesting to note that the widths of *insulae* III and IV differ considerably: 4105/4124 cm in the case of *insula* III and 4363.5 cm for *insula* IV. In terms of foot measurements, this means that *insula* III measures 150', assuming a foot of 27.37 or 27.49 cm (average 27.43 cm), and *insula* IV measures 160', with a slightly smaller foot of 27.28 cm.[131]

---

[130]   See also the measurements given by Beloch (1890: 231) and Maiuri (1958: 36, 38, 40, 42).

[131]   Note, however, that in *insula* IV only one width measurement is available to determine the foot measurement that was used, because of the disturbance of the original plan in the south. It seems that this *insula* is wider at the south end (cf. fig. 6).

4.1.2. The lengths of *insulae* III and IV

The original lengths of *insulae* III and IV can no longer be determined, because at a later stage the houses on the south side were built over the old city walls, across the boundaries of the *insulae*. However, it is still possible to make a hypothetical, rough estimate of the original length, taking as a starting point the line followed by the old city walls and the *decumanus inferior*, running parallel to it.

It is likely that *insula* III was twice as long as it was wide; *insulae* V and VI were also built in the proportion of two to one.[132] If we continue to reason along these lines, some surprising conclusions follow. On the west side, a distance of 4105 x 2 = 8210 cm, plotted from the northwest corner of the *insula*, brings us to a point just short of gate III and just north of the line formed by the south walls of rooms 24-26 in the Casa dell'Albergo (see fig. 3). This is the very point at which the orientation of the rooms in the house changes, presumably to follow the line of the city wall. On the east side of the *insula*, the north wall of corridor 57 is 8210 cm from the northeast corner. This wall is in the part of the Casa dell'Albergo that is built on the higher ground above gate IV. As this area was only built after the city wall had fallen into disuse, one might suppose that the southeast corner of *insula* III was originally further to the north, and that the length of the *insula* was not quite double its width. The only way to be certain about this is to reconstruct the original appearance of the southern part of the city near the walls, and in particular to work out the distance from the *insulae* to the wall and gates. This is less straightforward than it might seem, because several parts of the city wall are missing, such as the section adjacent to the Casa dell'Albergo, probably because there was a tower at this point which was demolished when the house was extended across the wall.

The distances can be worked out by considering the vaulted tunnel at the southern end of *cardo* IV, where the street slopes downwards towards gate IV. The total length of this tunnel is ca. 11 metres. According to Maiuri the walls were more than 2 metres thick, measured at the southern gates. Gate IV probably never had a large gatehouse, as no major roads entered the city on this side. The gate is therefore likely to have been about the same depth as the walls, i.e. 2-3 metres. The length of the tunnel from its mouth to the inner face of the gate is therefore about 8 metres. If we assume that there was a street of normal width (i.e. ca. 5.5 metres) between the *insulae* and the walls, and subtract the width of this street from the length of the tunnel inside the walls, the southeast corner of *insula* III would be ca. 2.5 metres south of the entrance to the tunnel. This is roughly the same point as we arrived at by measuring 8210 cm from the northeast corner of the *insula*. In other words, it is reasonable to conclude that *insula* III originally measured 150' x 300', and that it was extended to the south when the city wall was disused and the space behind the wall was filled in (see fig. 3).

Insula IV was slightly wider than *insula* III, i.e. 160 feet. The original length of the west

---

[132]   The length of *insula* V is 8111.5 cm on the east side and 8252 cm on the west side; the total length of *insula* VI, measured on the east side, is 8336 cm.

side was probably 300 feet, the same as *insula* III. If we measure inwards from the walls 8.5 metres, as above, assuming that there was a street between the walls and the block, the southwest corner of the *insula* would be on the line formed by the south walls of rooms 18, 17, 12 and 14 of the Casa dell'Atrio a Mosaico; this is ca. 8210 cm or 300 feet from the northwest corner. The east side of the *insula* was shorter than the west, because the southern edge of the block ran parallel to the city wall. Measuring inwards from the wall again, it seems that the original length of the east side was ca. 74 metres. This is equivalent to 270 Oscan feet, although it is likely that the length was simply determined by the line of the city wall. To summarise (see fig. 4):

insula III measures 150' x 300';

insula IV measures 160' x 300' (west side) or 270' (east side).

4.2. The distribution of building plots in *insula* III (fig. 5)

4.2.1. A survey of the building plots

Much of the original distribution of building plots in *insula* III can still be observed. With the exception of the southern part of the Casa dell'Albergo, which was made up of several earlier plots, there is a consistent pattern in the distribution of the building plots. In the northern half of the *insula*, the central axis that divides the plot into two equal parts can be clearly seen. On either side of this division, the building plots were orientated across the width of the *insula*, with the entrances facing onto the *cardines*. Although it is not possible to reconstruct the original arrangement of the southern half in detail, it seems likely that here too the houses were on either side of the central axis. It is unlikely that any of the plots were originally orientated towards the south because this would have meant that they faced the city walls. The same is true of the houses in the southern part of *insula* IV, as will be explained below (§ 4.3.1.).

The central axis divided the *insula* into two halves, each 75' wide; each house plot was therefore 75' long. In the northern half of the *insula* ten rectangular lots can be distinguished, plus one irregular strip; these will be referred to with the letters A to K (see fig. 5):

Lot A is the northwestern part of the Casa dell'Albergo, with entrance no. 2 (pl. I).

Lot B is the southern strip of rooms in the Casa dello Scheletro, reached through corridor 11. The original entrance on *cardo* III has disappeared (pl. II).

Lot C is the middle part of the Casa dello Scheletro, with entrance no. 3 (pl. II).

Lot D is the northern part of the Casa dello Scheletro (the *nymphaeum* and the *triclinium*), together with rooms 12/13 of the Casa a Graticcio; as in lot B, the entrance from the street no longer exists (pl. II).

Lot E consists of the rear part of the Casa del Tramezzo di Legno (the peristyle and rooms 11 to 17), with entrances no. 4 and 5 on *cardo* III (pl. III and fig. 9).

Lot F comprises the row of narrow, irregular rooms on the north side of the *insula* (entrances 6 to 10; pl. III); these rooms cannot really be regarded as a separate plot, but they are listed separately here because they function as a 'remainder', a strip of land which compensates for the difference in orientation between the short sides of the *insula*, which are parallel to the city walls, and the long sides, which conform to the overall grid-plan based on the *decumanus maximus*.

Lot G is the front part of the Casa del Tramezzo di Legno, with entrance no. 11, plus the shop next door, entrance no. 12 (pl. III).

Lot H is the Casa a Graticcio, with entrances 13 to 15, not including rooms 12/13 (pl. IV and fig. 10).

Lot I is the Casa dell'Erma di Bronzo (entrance 16; pl. V).

Lot J is the Casa dell'Ara Laterizia (entrance 17; pl. VI).

Lot K is the northeastern part of the Casa dell'Albergo, with entrance no. 18 (pl. I).

Lots E, H, I, J and K are ca. 2020 cm long; lots A, B, C, D and G are ca. 2065 cm long. These distances, measured from the facade to the back wall, are 73.5' and 75', assuming a foot of 27.5 cm. The difference in length is 1.5', which is the thickness of one wall. From this it can be deduced that there are two lot types in *insula* III: the so-called 'external' and 'internal' lots. 'External' lots are houses that are 75' long including the back wall (1.5' thick), while 'internal' lots are 75' long excluding the back wall. The division of space is considered in more detail in § 4.4.4.

4.2.2 The widths of the building plots; classification into groups

Three groups of building plots can be identified in *insula* III on the basis of width measurements:

1. narrow lots, 20' wide (ideally 550 cm; actual measurement 549.5 cm on average, with a range between 501.5 and 563 cm);

2. medium-sized lots, 27' wide (ideally 742.5 cm; average actual measurement 748.9 cm, with a range between 742.5 and 754 cm);

3. wide lots with a width of ca. 38' or 42' (ideally 1045 cm and 1155 cm; actual measurements average 1055.3 cm and 1159 cm respectively, with ranges of 1032-1082.5 cm, and 1156-1162 cm).

Group 1 comprises lots A, B, D, J and K (cf. fig. 5). The space in these houses was originally divided so that the central area, a hall, adjoins the *fauces* and has no rooms along its sides.

Group 2 includes two neighbouring lots, the Casa dell'Erma di Bronzo (lot I; cf. pl. VI) and the Casa a Graticcio (lot H; cf. fig. 10). Both are based (or were based) on the traditional *atrium* scheme, but there is no space for rooms along the sides of the *atrium*.

Group 3 consists of lots C, E and G (cf. pl. II, III). Lots C and E are 38.5 feet wide; in contrast G is 42 feet wide. Here there was enough space for a row of rooms along one side of the *atrium*.

The houses on lots E and G extend onto the irregular strip of land (lot F) left over on the north side of the *insula*. It is not clear whether this strip was taken into account in the original division into lots. If lot F is added to lots E and G, the result is two irregular house-plots which are narrower on the west side than on the east. The west side of lots E and F measures 1385 cm, which is 50', and the east side of lots G and F is 1789 cm or 65'; in other words, these dimensions appear to have been measured from the corners of the *insula* in multiples of 5'. On the other hand, the total width of lots C, D and E is the same as the total width of lots G, H and I (100'), which suggests that the initial division of land was measured out from the southern edge of lot F.[133]

The difference in width between lots E and G (38.5' as opposed to 42') may indicate that they were not planned at the same time, but this cannot be proved. Given the similarities in dimensions and the internal allocation of space, it seems reasonable to assume that lots A, B, J and K were built in the same period. This would also seem to be the case for lots H and I, where, although there is a difference of 5 cm in the average width of the plots (748 cm and 753 cm respectively), the original allocation of space is identical: this will be explained later (§ 5.4).

4.3. The division of space in *insula* IV (fig. 6)

4.3.1. Difference from *insula* III

Whereas the principle behind the division of space in *insula* III is clear, *insula* IV seems to be divided haphazardly. There seems to be no trace of a central axis, nor of the dividing line reconstructed by Johannowsky (1982: 148). Johannowsky extends the line formed by the back walls of the buildings at IV 8-9 and IV 10-11 to join the dividing wall between the houses in the south part of the *insula*, the Casa dell'Atrio a Mosaico (IV 1-2) and the Casa dei Cervi (IV 21). However, the two lots at the northwest corner are ca. 2065 cm deep, which is 75', but the Casa dell'Atrio a Mosaico is 77.5' (2130.5 cm) deep; moreover the wall dividing this house from the Casa dei Cervi appears to date from a later period. However, if the line proposed by Johannowsky is taken to reflect the original division of space in *insula* IV, we can at least determine that the dividing line was not down the centre of the *insula* because the lots on the east side were longer than those on the west. The *insula* is 160 feet wide and there is no line in the present layout that could have served as a central dividing line. The space in *insula* IV was divided in a different way from that in *insula* III, and this is reflected in their form and dimensions. All the lots were originally

---

[133]   The sum of the widths of G, H and I is 2739 cm: 404 cm (= width of room 2 + *fauces* of III 16) + 2018.5 cm (= distance from north wall of *fauces* III 16 to north wall of *fauces* III 4) + 306.5 cm (external width of room 2 in III 4). On the other side of the *insula* the sum of widths is ca. 2741 cm: lots C and D together are 1627 cm wide, lot E is 1073 cm wide, and the thickness of the wall between D and E is estimated at 41 cm.

70

orientated east-west.[134] The present arrangement in the south, where the houses face the sea, dates from the period after the city walls were demolished. The original buildings in this part of the *insula* had entrances onto the *cardines*, as Tran Tam Tinh found during excavations in the garden of the Casa dei Cervi.[135]

4.3.2. Description of the building plots

It is difficult to reconstruct the original divisions in *insula* IV or to determine which lots have remained in their original state. Looking at the existing houses, the following eleven old lots can be distinguished (see fig. 6).

Lot A is the northern part (orientated west-east) of the Casa dell'Atrio a Mosaico with entrance 2 on *cardo* IV (pl. VIII).

Lot B consists of the lower, southern half of the Casa dell'Alcova plus rooms 11-14 of the Casa dei Cervi; the original entrance has disappeared (pl. IX).

Lot C is the northern half of the Casa dell'Alcova, excluding room 16 (*triclinium*), with entrance 4.

Lot D is the Casa della Fullonica, IV 5-7 (pl. X).

Lot E is the Casa del Papiro Dipinto, IV 8-9 (pl. XI).

Lot F is made up of the shop and residence with entrances 10 and 11 on the *decumanus inferior*; it must have had an entrance on *cardo* IV originally (pl. XII).

Lot G is the northern part of the inn and residence, IV 12-16, which originally had a single entrance on *cardo* V (pl. XIII).

Lot H is the southern part of the same building; the entrance on *cardo* V has disappeared (pl. XIII).

Lot I is the irregularly shaped house with attached bar on *cardo* V, with entrances 17 and 18 (pl. XIV).

Lot J consists of the Casa della Stoffa (IV 19-20) and room 16 (*triclinium*) of the Casa dell'Alcova (pl. XV).

Lot K is the northern, east-west oriented part of the Casa dei Cervi (IV 21), not including rooms 11-14 (pl. XVI).

---

[134]   Ganschow (1989:323) arrives at the same conclusion. However, he claims that almost all of the houses at Herculaneum occupied half the width of an *insula*; he mentions the Casa Sannitica (V 1-2) and the Casa della Fullonica (IV 5-7) as exceptions.

[135]   See Tran Tam Tinh 1977. Unfortunately in the publication of the house the author barely discusses the results of this sounding - Tran Tam Tinh 1988: 21. Extensive building history: Ganschow 1989: 184-220 (Chap. II.1.2). See also De Kind 1991A.

4.3.3. The widths of the building plots; classification

The lots in *insula* IV can be divided into three groups on the basis of their widths, as follows:

Group a: narrow lots, 19' to 20' wide (ideally 536.3 cm; actual measurement 531.5 cm on average, with a range between 501 and 544 cm);

Group b: slightly wider lots, 28.5' to 30' (ideally 783.8 cm and 825 cm; actual measurements average 788.3 cm and 827.5 cm respectively, with ranges of 778-798 cm, and 816-845 cm);

Group c: wide lots, ca. 37' and 50' (ideally 1017.5 cm and 1375 cm; actual measurements 1016.5 cm and 1374/1381 cm).

Lots of group a are all found in the northern part of the *insula*, namely lots E, F, G and H. Group b consists of lots A, B, C, D and K; the two early houses on lots A and K, which have been incorporated into the grand houses on the terraces over the city walls, are 30' across, and the three remaining lots are 28.5'. It is possible that there are actually five lots of 30', of which two (A and K) have an 'internal' dimension of 30' and three (B, C and D) have an 'external' dimension of 30'. In lots A and K the internal width of the house was taken as 30', while it would appear that in the narrower ones a plot of 30' was measured out from an existing wall, which was used as one wall of the new house; the new house included the other side wall, and thus had an internal width of 28.5'. This could be an indication that lots B, C and D were filled in after the construction of houses on the north side of the *insula*. The order of construction and the length of the lots will be discussed further in connection with the wide lots that make up group c. This third group consists of the adjacent lots I and J on the east side of the *insula*. I is 50' wide, and J is 37', which might be an 'external' lot of 40', including two side walls.

4.3.4. The lengths of the lots: three possibilities

Because there is no central axis in the *insula*, the length of the lots differs considerably. The length of the two northern lots E and F is ca. 2065 cm or 75', the same as the lots in *insula* III. However, this appears to be fortuitous, as none of the other lots in *insula* IV is the same length; the nearest is lot A, which measures 2130.5 cm. Most of the other lots are longer than 75'. Lots G, H and K, on the east side opposite lots E, F and A, occupy more than half the width of the *insula*. Their length is about 83.5' - 84' (2295 - 2309 cm). Lots B, C and D on the west side extend across the middle of the *insula*, resulting in much shorter lots (I and J) in the east. It is unclear whether this has always been the case, or whether the allocation of space was once similar to that in *insula* III. An examination of the Casa della Fullonica might help to answer this question.[136]

---

[136] Ganschow (1989: 323 no. 12) also comments that the Casa della Fullonica extends over more than

The Casa della Fullonica (lot D) lies between the 'regular' lots E/F and the exceptionally long lots B/C; it is ca. 2618 cm long, and thus extends over the central axis. Considering the lots that surround it, there are three possible ways to determine the original length of the house (see fig. 7).

Option 1: The original back wall of lot D coincided with the back wall of E and F, and the house was thus 2065 cm deep. The dividing axis in the north of the *insula* was 75' from the west side.

To justify this explanation it must be assumed that the dividing walls between rooms 5 and 6 and rooms 7 and 8 of the Casa della Fullonica were originally an extension of the back wall of the Casa del Papiro Dipinto (lot E). This would seem to be a legitimate assumption if Maiuri's map of *insula* IV (1958: Pl. IV B) is used as a basis, but closer examination of the actual walls reveals that the back wall of lot E and the wall between rooms 5 and 6 in the Casa della Fullonica are not structurally connected. Remains of *opus incertum* B with doorposts in tufa, dating from the 2nd century BC, have been preserved in the walls between rooms 5 and 6 and 7 and 8 in the Casa della Fullonica. It is therefore improbable that this was the original back wall of the house. If there ever was such a wall, it must have been in existence before the 2nd century BC, but there are no remains from this period.

Option 2: The original back wall of lot D continued the line of the southern lots B and C (into what is now lot I); the length of the house would thus have been ca. 2955 cm, and the dividing line through the *insula* would have been approximately 107.5' from the west side.

This explanation is also produced by extending the lines on the plan of the *insula*. It is assumed that the back wall of lot C (the northern part of the Casa dell'Alcova) and the dividing walls between rooms 5 and 13 and 6 and 7 in the house with the bar (lot I) formed a continuous line. Rooms 5 and 6 in lot I would thus have been part of the Casa della Fullonica. Once again, however, scrutiny of the actual remains reveals that the east wall and the southern doorpost of room 5 are further east than Maiuri's map suggests (1958: fig. 382), and therefore are not aligned with the back wall of the Casa dell'Alcova.

Option 3: The present back wall of the Casa della Fullonica marks the original extent of the lot; if this is the case, there was never a clear dividing line in the *insula*.

The case for this option follows the same line of reasoning as option 2. It is likely that the rear strip of *taberna* IV 17-18 (lot I) was initially left unroofed to supply air/light. This can be deduced from the walls of rooms 6 and 7 of the Casa della Fullonica (lot D). Two blocked windows can be seen in the east wall of room 7 (the back wall) (Maiuri 1958: fig. 364). One is a semi-circular window in the lunette formed by the vaulted ceiling, the other is a window at eye level. Both openings originally looked out over what is now room 5 in lot I. Moreover in room 6 there is an infilled area, ca. 185 cm wide, in the southern part of the east wall. Unfortunately this infill is only preserved to a height of ca. 70 cm; above this,

---

half the *insula*.

73

the wall was restored at the time of the Maiuri excavations. At the north end of the infilled area is what looks like a remnant of a doorpost in *opus vittatum mixtum*. Presumably this is part of a doorway, ca. 225 cm in height, which has been closed off; there is a plaster rim at exactly that height. There is also a strip of floor, equal in width to the infill in the wall and ca. 60 cm deep, patched with loose pieces of *signinum*. This infill and the blocking of the door were undoubtedly part of the same building activity. Closing off a door at floor level does not usually entail altering the existing floor; the infill could therefore be an indication that there was a change in floor level here, and perhaps a small staircase. Presumably this door led to the lower part of the house on the east side. This part of the house was at the same level as the present room 6 of IV 17-18 (lot I).

The only possible conclusion from the above discussion is that there must have been a way through from the Casa della Fullonica to the area to the east. There are two possible times at which this access route may have been created. It may have been put in during the initial construction of the house. It is unclear what the function of the area behind the house was at that time: it may have been a *hortus*, perhaps occupying the same depth as rooms 5 and 6 in IV 17-18, but it is equally possible that the lot was not built on and that the doorway was a *posticum* or back door. The second possibility is that the door and steps were added later. Again, it is unclear whether there were any buildings on the lot to the rear at the time. In either case the door and the staircase were closed off at some later date, probably when rooms 5 and 6 in IV 17-18 were built. If there was a *hortus* at the back of the house when it was first built (which would mean that the depth of the house would have been the same as lots B and C), it is likely to have been on the same level as the other rooms. This was clearly not the case. Therefore it is more likely that the door led to an undeveloped lot behind the house, in which case it may either have been part of the original plan, or a later addition. The latter explanation is preferable, because there is *opus vittatum mixtum* in the wall; this type of construction is found almost exclusively in doorposts (Ganschow 1989: 55, 127). Clearly, then, the door must have been put in after the house was built; if it was put in at the time of construction, the posts would have been made of tufa, as in room 6.

On the basis of this explanation it can be presumed that the original length of the Casa della Fullonica (lot IV D) was the same as its present length. An analysis of the overall measurements of the house leads to a similar conclusion: the width is 28.5' and the length is 95' (see also § 5.9). This results in a width:length ratio of 1:3. At some time in its history the house was extended lengthways, but the extra space was later given up. This means that there was never a single division or 'central axis' in this *insula*.

As for the longer lots B and C (Casa dell'Alcova), although their original layout was changed over time, it seems that the outlines presented above produce a reasonably clear picture of the original situation. There is a further indication of this in Ganschow's analysis of the back wall of the north part of the house, behind rooms 12 and 13. He finds that the structure of this wall is almost entirely in *opus incertum* B, dating from the earliest period in Herculaneum; therefore 'muß es sich hier um eine Trennmauer zwischen zwei Häusern gehandelt haben' (Ganschow 1989: 208).

4.4. The division of the *insulae*

4.4.1. Ancient systems of land surveying

In order to understand the allocation of space in *insulae* III and IV better, it is important to consider whether the dimensions of the *insulae* can be related to units of measurement used in antiquity, and, if this is the case, whether the land in the *insulae* was divided in accordance with any of the known ancient traditions of land surveying. An increasing amount of literature on methods of allotment and the Roman system of *centuriatio* has appeared over the last few decades. The subject has been discussed in an article by U. Heimberg (1984), and K. Grewe (1984) has compiled a bibliography of the history of surveying, including many references to land surveying. Studies focusing specifically on Roman land surveying have been written by O. Dilke (1971), U. Heimberg (1977) and F.T. Hinrichs (1974), who pays particular attention to the legal aspects. Problems associated with the establishment of Roman cities come under discussion in a volume edited by F. Grew and B. Hobley (1985). Hultsch (1882) and Nissen (1892) discuss the units of measurement used for surveying in antiquity.

Possibly the most frequently used unit in Roman times was the *actus*, which measures 120 feet. The Greek equivalent is the *schoinos*, which was based on a smaller unit related to the Oscan foot, which features in the Herakleia tablets.[137] It is known from contemporary written sources that the unit used in Campania was the *vorsus* or *versus*, which was 100, rather than 120, feet; this name was also used for an area of 10,000 square feet. Varro writes that different units were used to measure land in different places: in Hispania the unit used was the *iugum*, while the Campanians used the *versus*, and the *iugerum* was used in Roman and Latin areas. *Iugum* refers to the area a team of oxen could plough in a single day; a *versus* is a square with sides of 100 feet.[138]

> '*Modos, quibus metirentur rura, alius aliter constituit. Nam in Hispania ulteriore metiuntur iugis, in Campania versibus, apud nos in agro Romano ac Latino iugeris. Iugum vocant, quod iuncti boves uno die exarare possint. Versum dicunt centum pedes quoquoversum quadratum*'.
>
> ('The units used to measure the land differ from place to place: in Hispania Ulterior it is measured in iuga, and in Campania in versus, while we use iugera in the Roman and Latin areas. A iugum is the name for the area a team of oxen can plough in a single day. A versus is a square with sides of 100 feet.') (Varro, *De R.R.*, I 10)

Frontinus also writes that the earliest unit was a square with sides of 100 feet. The Greeks referred to this as a *plethron*, while the Oscans and the Umbrians called it a *vorsus*:

> '*Primum agri modum fecerunt quattuor limitibus clausum, plerumque centenum*

---

[137]   Hultsch 1882: 668-669 provides a full explanation of this foot measure (27.77 cm). Cf. also Dilke 1971: 82. For the tablets from Herakleia and the allocation of land see Heimberg 1984: 284-287 (with earlier references in no. 24); Nicolet 1987.

[138]   Cf. Hultsch 1882: 671; Nissen 1892: 884; Dilke 1971: 83.

pedum in utraque parte (quod Graeci plethron appellant, Osci et Umbri vorsum)'.
('The first unit of measurement was an area marked off on four sides, usually 100 feet on each side (which the Greeks refer to as a plethron, and the Oscans and Umbrians as a vorsus)') (Frontinus, *De limitibus*, ed. Blume/Lachmann/Rudorff 1848, p. 30).
Actus and *versus* originally referred to the same distance, namely the distance covered by a team of oxen ploughing a field before they were made to turn round. The area of a square *actus*, which was also called an *actus*, was so large that it took half a day to plough. The double actus (240' x 120'), the area that took an entire day to plough, was called a *iugerum* in Roman surveying (Hultsch 1882: 83-84). Hyginus mentions that the *iugerum* was not used everywhere, and that other units were found in some areas: for example, the standard unit in Campania was the *versus*, which was 8640 (Roman) feet; conversely a single *iugerum* was 3 1/3 *versus*.

'Hoc quoque non praetermittam, quod plerisque locis inveni, ut modum agri non iugerum sed aliquo nomine appellarent, ut puta quo in Campania versus appellant. Idem versus habet p. VIII DCXL. Ita iugero sunt versus numero III SS.'
('I will therefore not leave out what I have discovered in many places, which is that the unit of land was not called a iugerum but something else; in Campania, for example, they call it a versus. This versus measures 8640 feet. Therefore 3 1/3 versus are equal to a iugerum.') (Hyginus, *De Condicionibus Agrorum*, ed. Blume/Lachmann/Rudorff 1848, p. 121-122).[139]
The length of the Oscan foot (ca. 27.5 cm) was derived from this information, and it was established that the proportion of the Oscan to the Roman foot was 93:100.

An examination of the dimensions of *insulae* III and IV leaves no doubt about the allotment of land in *insula* III: 150 x 300 feet is equal to 1.5 x 3 *versus*. In Roman units this would be 1.25 x 2.5 *actus*. *Insula* IV is more problematic. 160 feet is 1.6 *versus* or 1.33 *actus*, while 270 feet is 2.7 *versus* or 2.25 *actus*. At its smallest the area measures 160 x 270 feet = 43200 square feet or 3 square *actus*. If the east side had been 300' long, the *insula* would have measured 160 x 300 feet = 48000 square feet.

Insula III	*feet*	*versus*	*actus*
width	150	1.5	1.25
x	x	x	x
length	300	3	2.5
area	45000	4.5	3.125

[139] Blume/Lachmann/Rudorff (1848) read 'Dalmatia' rather than 'Campania', but the version preferred by Hultsch (1882: 671) is adopted here. Cf. also Nissen 1892: 884.

Insula IV	feet		versus		actus	
width	160		1.6		1.33	
x	x		x		x	
length	300	270	3	2.7	2.5	2.25
area	48000	43200	4.8	4.32	3.33	3

The idea that *insula* IV was laid out using a different method of land surveying from *insula* III (i.e. a Roman system based on the *actus*) is not tenable, because the layouts of *insulae* III and IV are clearly related. Both were designed as residential blocks with a length of 300 feet and a width of 150 feet, but because of its peripheral location, *insula* IV has become a 'leftover *insula*', which is wider (160 feet), but shorter (270 feet) on the east side. This was necessary because the city wall was not parallel to the *decumani*, but followed the line of the coast.

4.4.2. The Roman system of land and lot division

From actual measurements and contemporary written sources it can be established that the residential space in Herculaneum was divided up according to the Campanian system of land surveying. This was a decimal system, using the *versus* of 100 Oscan feet, which was a unit of both length and area. The Oscan foot (ca. 27.5 cm) was described by Nissen (1892: 885) as 'Träger eines besonderen italischen Systems'; this system was in use for a very long period, not only in Campania, but throughout southern Italy. Indeed it is remarkable that in Varro's time - the middle of the 1st century BC - Campania still had its own system of measurement, and that Frontinus, a century later, thinks it necessary to mention the Oscan and Umbrian unit of measurement. The Italian or Campanian system was used to lay out the city, as described above (§ 3.2.4). It is unclear how closely the Campanian system of land allotment is related to the Roman system, which is described in several sources and has been the subject of numerous studies. In order to get an idea of the relationship between the two systems, it will be necessary to discuss briefly a number of concepts and procedures from the Roman legal system that are connected with urban allotment. Next the layout of Herculaneum will be considered in the light of these regulations, in an attempt to determine whether any of these Roman rules were applied here.

In Hinrichs's study of Roman land surveyors (1974), the *gromatici*, there are several passages that throw light on the regulations for the division of land into building lots. Chapters II and III of Hinrichs's study (1974: 23-75) cover respectively the allotment of land *per strigas et scamna* (the *scamnatio*) and the *centuriatio*. The *scamnatio* is a regular division of land into adjoining lots, without the use of a crossroads as a basis. The *centuriatio* is a later and more strictly regulated version of the *scamnatio*, which starts from the crossing of a *cardo* and a *decumanus*, with streets 20 *actus* (2400') apart and lots of ca. 200 *iugera* (400 *actus*). This system uses Roman units of measurement and was clearly most suitable for the allotment of agricultural land outside the city. One example of land allotment that has been described in great detail in ancient written sources is the *centuriatio* in the area of Orange (Arausio). It has been possible to reconstruct the marble plaques showing the *centuriatio* which were put up in the land registry office. On these plaques, which date from the second half of the 1st century AD, there are three different systems of allotment.[140] Together with the tablets from Herakleia (see above) these plaques from Orange give an indication of the precision with which lots were staked out.[141] It is particularly relevant to the present study that in the *tabularium* at Orange there were records of certain urban lots, the so-called *merides* and *areae*. The *merides*, a Greek term, were parcels of land that were let out on long leases by the authorities. Usually these were *tabernae* in porticos and markets (Piganiol 1962: 329-336). The *areae* were larger areas in the city which could be rented more cheaply (Piganiol 1962: 343-385). This indicates that parcels of land in Orange, and perhaps in other cities, were not only sold but were also let out on long leases, and that a systematic record was kept of such transactions. Presumably most of the lots for residential buildings were sold.

In his discussion of the *actio finium regundorum* Hinrichs (1974: 171-223) considers the regulations for the division of land and the rights and duties of neighbours with respect to the boundaries between their building lots. He points out that as early as the Roman law-code of the Twelve Tables a distinction is made between rural and urban plots of land; Cicero (*Topica* 10, 43) also noted this (Hinrichs 1974: 174). One essential difference was that the boundary between two rural plots, the *confinium*, had to be 5 feet wide, while the area between two urban plots, the *ambitus*, only needed to be 2.5 feet.

J. Rainer (1987) has also published a study of the solutions offered by the Roman legal system to problems between neighbours. He discusses the public and civil building regulations, but does not consider town planning or land allotment. Nevertheless, his study is certainly relevant to the present investigation. From his discussion of the easements (the rights of a householder to make certain uses of his neighbour's land) it is clear that the regulations were designed to provide a sound basis for building and living in the city. More importantly, Rainer tries to establish links between building regulations and archaeological remains, using Herculaneum as a working example (Rainer 1987: 86-88). Although he is mostly concerned with regulations governing the supply of light to the houses, one of his observations is particularly relevant to the present investigation: 'daß offenbar in Herkulaneum keinerlei Bestimmungen über Abstände existieren, oder falls sie existierten, sie grundsätzlich nicht eingehalten wurden, was der Wertlosigkeit der Norm gleichkäme: der *paries communis* ist eine weitverbreitete, ja geradezu unentbehrliche Erscheinung' (Rainer 1987: 88). Indeed it would seem that the *ambitus* of the earlier legislation was not widespread in Herculaneum or elsewhere. Rainer briefly discusses the omission of the *ambitus* and its replacement by shared walls (Rainer 1987: 78-79). He suggests that the *ambitus* regulation became redundant in the 2nd century BC as a result of an increase in building

---

[140]   Piganiol 1962; Hinrichs 1974: 136-146; Heimberg 1977: 51-55.

[141]   Other examples of registers, from Greece and Egypt, are given by Heimberg (1984: 283-284) and Nicolet (1987: 23-24).

activity and lack of space in the cities. In a further study of the *paries communis* he repeats this opinion, adding that the *ambitus* was a relic of the original farming community of Rome, with its huts of mud and wood (Rainer 1988: 489).

In his discussion of this issue Rainer does not consider the extent to which Roman building regulations were applied in cities and areas which the Romans took over in later years. It is quite possible that in an area such as Campania, which had its own metrological system, city-planning and land allocation were subject to non-Roman regulations. So, for example, it is possible that the *paries communis* was not introduced as a result of a shortage of space, but had already been in general use for a very long time. However, because our only evidence relates to the Roman legal system, which probably reflects principles that were also in use in non-Roman areas, Rainer's work is relevant to the present study (Rainer 1987; 1988). His account of the legal implications of shared walls (i.e. single ownership with easements or joint ownership of a *paries communis*) is important because it may help to explain certain situations in Herculaneum.

4.4.3. Legal problems associated with allotment in the *insulae*

Studies of urban development in antiquity often devote attention to land-allocation, but rarely comment on the dimensions and boundaries of the individual plots of land. These aspects are covered in a number of articles on land distribution in Roman cities in the northwestern provinces of the empire.[142] However, most of these studies throw little light on land-allocation at Herculaneum, because they explain urban development in terms of the Roman system of measurement and surveying, which was developed after Herculaneum was laid out. Therefore the majority of these studies cannot be used for comparison. One exception is C.S. Sommer's paper (1991), in which he discusses the dimensions of houses and the system of land distribution in military *vici* in Germania Superior and Raetia.[143] Sommer (1991: 472) concludes that plots and houses were not of uniform sizes, but that there were groups of plots with identical dimensions. A large part of the article is concerned with the order of construction in the Ladenburg *vicus*, where there were shared walls between houses; this is similar to Herculaneum. Sommer (1991: 475) suspects that plots 'were assigned to individual camp-followers and were subsequently built up separately by them according to various 'building regulations''. What follows will focus on urban development in Campania and Latium, which has been the subject of a number of articles over the last few decades.

In the interim reports on the investigation of *insula* I 10 in Pompeii (the '*Insula* of the Menander'), Roger Ling gives a clear overview of the development of this residential block, starting in the 4th century BC (Ling 1982; 1983). The houses in the *insula* had common walls. Ling suspects that the depth of the earliest houses was determined as ca. 60' (1/2 *actus*), either by the city authorities or by the owner himself (Ling 1983: 41).

---

[142]   See Frere 1977; Walthew 1978; 1987; Duncan-Jones 1980; Bridger 1984; Buijtendorp 1987.
[143]   I would like to thank L. Swinkels for drawing my attention to this article.

Kockel (1986: 472) adopts this conclusion, and claims that this throws new light on 'die Besiedlung und die Besitzverhältnisse in der frühesten uns bekannten Bebauung der Stadt'. Unfortunately, it has to be concluded that the calculation on which Ling based his conclusions is incorrect. The earliest houses are mostly ca. 18.8 - 20 metres long. Given the early date of the initial development, it must have been the Oscan foot, rather than the Roman foot, that was used in Pompeii at the time, which gives a length of 68' - 73'. In view of the early date it is also unlikely that the *actus* was used as Ling and Kockel have assumed (see above, § 4.4.1).

Ling does not comment on the sizes and boundaries of the building plots. Boersma (1985) does discuss these aspects in his study of *insula* V ii in Ostia.[144] He demonstrates that the division of the *insula* into lots is based on a scheme of 8 x 4 units of 33' x 45', plus one row of half-units measuring 16' x 45'; the overall dimensions of the *insula* are thus 280' x 180', or 2 1/3 x 1 1/2 *actus* (Boersma 1985: 207-208; 1982: 48-50). In his chapter on the legal aspects (1985: 234-237), Boersma notes that the land in the *insula* was sold by the authorities in plots, often made up of 33' x 45' units, from the end of the 2nd century or beginning of the 1st century BC. The lots might be separated by a single, jointly-owned wall, or by two separately-owned ones. The shared walls and the similarities in the layout and wall construction of some of the buildings in the *insula* prompt Boersma to conclude that they may well have been built for the same patron.

If there are separate walls, with or without an *ambitus*, it is clear what the size of the plot was and whether it was bought including or excluding the walls. The builder bought the land and built his own walls, as can be seen in Ostia, for example, at the boundary between plots V ii, 2-5 and 11-14, or lot V ii, 13, which is completely separate from the lots that surround it (Boersma 1985: fig. 202). However, where there is a shared wall it is more difficult to determine the size of the lot. In a deed of purchase dating from the 2nd century AD, relating to half of a house in Dacia near what is now Alba Iulia (Pólay 1976), it is stated that the hedges, boundaries, entrances, locks and windows are included in the sale:

'*Eam domus partem dimidiam, q(ua) d(e) a(gitur), cum su[is s]aepibus, saepimentis, finibus, aditibus, claustris, finestris*'

('This half house, which is at issue here, including its hedges, fences, boundaries, entrances, locks, windows') (CIL III.2, 944-945 no. VIII).

Because this is a *domus partem dimidiam, interantibus partem dextram*, that is to say the right-hand half of the house, it presumably has common walls. However, it cannot be compared to the houses in Herculaneum because it is a house that already exists, not the first development on a plot of land. The regulations governing the building of a house can be deduced from Rainer's accounts of shared walls in general and the specific legal term *paries communis*.

The definition of a *paries communis* is that it is a shared wall belonging to two householders, who each have rights of ownership (Rainer 1988: 490). Examples show that it was possible to opt for a *paries communis* at the time of construction if both houses were

---

[144]   A brief, well-written account of Roman building regulations and their application in Ostia is provided by Hermansen 1982: 91-96.

built at the same time, but that a wall could also become common property through inheritance, or, as may have been the case in Dacia, as a result of the sale of a semi-detached house (Rainer 1988: 494-495). Alternatively, it was possible for the partition wall to belong to only one of the householders. This situation could result when someone had a house built and subsequently the owner of the adjoining lot used the existing dividing wall for the construction of his own house. According to Roman law three easements applied in such situations: the *servitus tigni immitendi*, the *servitus oneris ferendi* and the *servitus protegendi / proiecendi*. The first easement is the right to insert beams into the wall of the neighbouring house; the second gives the right to use that wall to bear loads; and the third is the right to build projecting roofs or overhanging floors over the neigh-bouring property (e.g. for a balcony).[145] The *servitus oneris ferendi* is clearly an extension of the *servitus tigni immittendi*, because it also governed liability for maintenance of the wall that supports the beams. Rainer (1987: 24) rightly points out that such an easement entailed a great imposition on the owner and that it must therefore have been more costly to introduce this service than to uphold the simple right to insert beams into the wall.

If the builder/owner of a house did not own the dividing wall himself (because it already existed, for example), it is clear that he could solve the problem in one of two ways. Both involved a financial transaction: either he paid the owner of the wall to allow him to take advantage of the easements without becoming an owner himself, or he bought joint ownership of the dividing wall, which then became a *paries communis*.

4.4.4. Explanation of the division of land in *insulae* III and IV

Let us now reconsider the allocation of land in *insulae* III and IV in Herculaneum, focus-ing on *insula* III in particular, where the land seems to have been divided up most sys-tematically. Here it seems that the common back walls of the houses in the northern area were not built exactly on the central axis of the *insula*, but to the west or east of the axis. This can be deduced from the lengths calculated above for the lots in the *insula*, which are not uniform, but fall into two types: an 'internal' type measuring 75' without the back wall, and an 'external' type, which is 75' long including the back wall. From these measurements it can be assumed that the length must initially have been determined at 75 feet, which is half the width of the *insula*.[146] Subsequent development of the area raised the following problem: where should the walls be placed and who would own them? There seem to be two possible solutions to the problem of ownership:

1. Building took place **simultaneously** on both sides of the *insula* and a *paries communis* was built between the houses. In such cases it would be expected that the

---

[145]   Rainer 1987: 19-26. See also Boersma 1975: 9-10; Russo 1984.
[146]   Strabo (XVII 1. 6) provides an interesting description of the procedure of staking out an area for urban development. He notes that in the initial staking out of Alexandria, the architects marked out the street plan with lines of chalk ('white earth') and, when they ran out of chalk, with flour. The same procedure is still used in southern Italy for the building of simple houses. I would like to thank M.C. van Binnebeke and J. de Mol for this information.

available width of the *insula* would be divided equally between both lots, with the *paries communis* exactly in the middle. However, this was not the case in *insula* III. Nevertheless, it is possible that a *paries communis* was built to one side of the central axis, producing plots of land of unequal sizes.

2. Building did **not** take place simultaneously but at different times, months or even years apart; initially one person owned the dividing wall at the back of the house.

In either case, the resulting houses were not of equal lengths, and it is not clear how it was decided which lot the dividing wall would be on. Were all the plots sold as 75' lots, or was the builder who built a *paries communis* on his land (in the case of simultaneous building) or who developed his lot first (where construction was not simultaneous) allowed to regard his lot as 75 feet 'internally' and thus acquire a larger area of land? If each buyer was allowed exactly 75', the person who built the back wall would have lost out, because he would thus have had a smaller living area than his neighbour, who had presumably paid the same price for his lot. His overall costs would be higher than his neighbour's, because he would have had to pay for the construction and maintenance of the wall. The income from easements would provide some compensation for this extra expense; alternatively the builder could sell his neighbour joint ownership of the wall, thus turning it into a *paries communis*. If, on the other hand, the builder of the back wall was allowed to buy a slightly longer plot, the advantages balance the disadvantages. His house would have been a full 75' deep internally, but he may have had to pay more for the extra 1.5' of land, as well as the cost for constructing the wall. The owner of the plot on the other side of the central axis may only have had 73.5' at his disposal, but he would not have had the expense of building a back wall. When he built his house he could either pay the owner of the wall to allow him to take advantage of one or more of the easements, or he could buy joint ownership of the wall, which would then become a *paries communis*, with all the associated rights and duties (Rainer 1988: 494-513).

The advantages and disadvantages can be summarised schematically as follows:

I. Different lot lengths

single ownership of the back wall, with easements

Lot length	Advantages	Disadvantages
76.5'	• larger living area • own wall • income from easement	• higher price for the lot • building expenses for wall • easement-obligation
73.5'	• one less wall to construct and pay for • lower price for a (smaller) lot	• smaller living area • easement costs

joint ownership of the back wall (*paries communis*)

Lot length	Advantages	Disadvantages
76.5'	• larger living area • proceeds from selling share in *paries communis*	• higher price for the lot • building expenses for wall
73.5'	• one less wall to construct and pay for • lower price for a (smaller) lot	• smaller living area • payment for buying share in *paries communis*

II. Equal lot lengths (75' each), with equal lot expenses

single ownership of the back wall, with easements

Lot of 75'	Advantages	Disadvantages
with back wall	• income from easements • own wall	• smaller living area • easement-obligation • construction costs of wall
without back wall	• larger living area • lower construction costs	• easement costs • no rights over wall

joint ownership of the back wall (*paries communis*)

Lot of 75'	Advantages	Disadvantages
with back wall	• income from selling share in *paries communis* • own wall	• smaller living area • construction costs of wall
without back wall	• larger living area • lower construction costs	• payment for buying share in *paries communis*

Although it was possible for a *paries communis* to be constructed between two lots of different length, it is more likely that the difference in length was the result of the lots being built at different times. In *insula* III there were probably lots of 76.5' long, on which houses were built with a back wall, and lots of 73.5' with houses that were built using existing back walls. The lots also have shared side walls, but these offer fewer clues to the order of construction on the lots. As shown above, the internal width of most houses is a round number of feet, so it may be assumed that the lots were large enough to allow for this width. The first builder needed a 23' lot to build a house 20' wide. If there was already a house on one side the lot needed to be 21.5' wide. Where there were buildings on both sides, a lot width of 20' was sufficient. The last two cases would involve easements or *parietes communes*. Consequently there were several lot sizes on which houses of 20' x

75' could be built.

For an actual living area of *1500 feet* the possibilities are:

- 23' x 76.5'   = build all walls
- 21.5' x 76.5'   = build facade, back wall and one side wall
- 20' x 76.5'   = only build facade and back wall.

For an actual living area of *1470 feet* (built against an existing house at the rear) the choices are:

- 23' x 73.5'   = build facade and both side walls
- 21.5' x 73.5'   = build facade and one side wall
- 20' x 73.5'   = only build facade.

The dimensions of some lots suggest that the width must originally have been a round figure, but that a single side wall had to be added. It is possible that these lots were developed later, when the builders had to make do with less width in return for lower construction costs, as in the case of the lengths of the houses. It is not clear whether any of the present widths are based on round figures minus twice the thickness of a wall. Theoretically the possibilities would then be as follows:

a) lots with an internal length of *75'*:

- 18.5' x 75'   = a single side wall on the lot   (actual living area 1387.5')
- 17' x 75'   = two side walls on the lot   (actual living area 1275').

b) lots with an internal length of *73.5'*:

- 18.5' x 73.5'   = a single side wall on the lot   (actual living area 1359.75')
- 17' x 73.5'   = two side walls on the lot   (actual living area 1249.5').

In *insula* III the houses on the west side have an internal length of 75 feet, while those on the east side have an external length of 75 feet. Only the original lengths of lots E and G (the back and front parts of the Casa del Tramezzo di Legno) are uncertain - the east lot may originally have been deeper than the west. Nevertheless it is likely that the houses on the west side of the *insula* were built first and those on the east were added later. The dimensions of lots A, B, J and K are so uniform that they were probably developed more or less simultaneously. It is likely that the remaining plots were not staked out at the same time, given the differences in their design and width. Lots C and E may have been intended as 40' x 75' originally, but ended up as 38.5' x 75' because a side wall had to be built.

Next the question arises as to how the *insula* was filled with buildings. It has been determined that the first houses were built on the west side of the *insula*, because these plots were 75 feet long internally. This is in keeping with the theory that building generally proceeded from the centre of the city to the perimeter. It cannot be determined with certainty which lots were built on first. If it is assumed that building proceeded from the centre to the periphery, the lots in the north corner were probably first to be developed. From here building continued southwards towards the city walls, first on the west side of the central axis, then on the east side. But it cannot be ruled out that the southern lots were developed soon after the lots in the north corner, and that construction continued from both ends towards the centre of the *insula*.

It is very likely that construction was piecemeal in *insula* IV too. This is suggested by the widths of lots B, C and D, which are 28.5' (see above § 4.3.3.). It is possible that these were based on an 'external' measurement of 30', including one side wall. In other words, construction started from an existing wall (on another plot). Because the Casa dell'Atrio a Mosaico (lot A) actually measures 30' internally, it is possible that building in the *insula* progressed from the corners towards the middle. If this was the case, lots B, C and D would have been developed relatively late and may have been allowed greater length to make up for their limited width. This was possible because the *insula* was wider than the usual 150', and because there was no need to start building on the east side of the *insula*: before the construction of the Palaestra, the Suburban Baths and the rich houses in *insula orientalis* I, this part was on the edge of town. Evidence of this can also be seen in the *insulae* on the edges of Pompeii (see above § 3.2.4). The development of lots I and J to fill up the unused space must have taken place before the construction of *insulae orientales* I and II. The fact that these *insulae* were built is an indication of a growing need for residential space; undoubtedly the existing area of the town will have been fully used before it was decided to allow building beyond its limits.

Ganschow (1989: 98-100) has demonstrated that the eastern part of the city walls was not abandoned in the Augustan period, as Maiuri assumed (1958: 113), but earlier, perhaps soon after the Social War (91-89 BC), when there was no longer need for a defensive wall. After this houses must have been built on terraces across the walls; traces can still be seen in *insula orientalis* I. The Palaestra (*insula orientalis* II) was built later, shortly after the death of Augustus at the latest: the variation in the width of *cardo* V would seem to support this. Large parts of the city wall and possibly houses on terraces like those in *insula orientalis* I were levelled for the construction of the Palaestra (Ganschow 1989: 100). Lots I and J would therefore seem to have been built no later than the first half of the 1st century BC.

PART III

THE HOUSES

5. THE HOUSES IN *INSULAE* III AND IV

Each of the following sections about the houses in *insulae* III and IV follows the same pattern. First, a short account is given of each house, including dates of excavation, overall dimensions, name etc., followed by a review of the most important literature (with comments). Next comes a description of the floor plan and the individual rooms, which is intended mainly to serve as a basis for the building history and typology; for a more extensive description the reader is referred to Maiuri's study (1958). The information presented in the sections about wall construction comes from various sources: Maiuri's publication, personal observations and, most important, from both published and unpublished material provided by Thomas Ganschow (Ganschow 1989; see also Introduction). The results of an extensive survey carried out in Herculaneum between 1987 and 1990 were used for the overview of the wall and floor decoration, with comments added where appropriate. In the discussion of the floors particular attention is paid to the use of materials, while the focus in the section on the walls is on the structural scheme and the use of colours. Next, published information about the inscriptions and finds in the house is listed. Such an overview has never been available before. In the discussion of the inscriptions the CIL version is nearly always used; there are no interpretations on the part of the author. Unless otherwise indicated the inscriptions refer to CIL, vol. IV (3,4), edited by P. Ciprotti. A more detailed study of the epigraphical material would be advisable, but falls outside the scope of the present study. Each section ends with a review of the building history, a metrological analysis and an outline of the design of the house. These final paragraphs are not intended to constitute a detailed account of the building phases based on the wall structures, but simply to indicate which phases can be distinguished on the basis of the wall structures and wall and floor decoration. The building history has been taken into account as far as possible in the metrological analysis. The method used is that of C. Peterse, which was described earlier (see *Introduction*). However, a precise calculation of the foot measure has proved to be difficult in some places, and it was therefore decided to express them not to the nearest 0.01 cm, but rounded off to multiples of 0.05 cm. Extensive lists of measurements have been included as appendices. The conclusions about the building history and metrology have been incorporated in the descriptions of the design.

5.1. Casa dell'Albergo (III 1-2, 18-19) (Pl. I)

This sizeable house, the largest in the excavated section of Herculaneum, covers the southern half of *insula* III and has four entrances: nos. 1 and 2 on *cardo* III, and nos. 18 and 19 on *cardo* IV. The house was partly excavated during the last century; in 1835 part of the portico with terrace was visible, as well as parts of the garden and peristyle, the north-west *taberna* and the subterranean rooms.[147] The rest of the house was unearthed under Maiuri's leadership between April 1927 and November 1929. The house was given its name in the last century by Bonucci, who assumed, wrongly, that it was a public building used as an inn. The portico and terrace play an important role in this theory, because Bonucci regarded this area as a place where carts could be unloaded.[148] The house is composed of various older properties, of which two have remained clearly visible: lot III A (entrance 2 = rooms 32-36) and lot III K (entrance 18 = rooms 37-44). The entire southern part consists of at least four, but more probably six or even eight old lots, equally divided on either side of the central axis of the *insula*. In all, the house has 68 rooms at ground floor level, including the garden. In addition, there is an underground floor, in the substructures under the panoramic rooms built out over the city walls; it was reached by way of a staircase at the end of corridor 53. Here we find 15 rooms, including corridors, of which three were clearly used as living accommodation. Above rooms 37-42 (lot III K) there was an upper storey, reached by a staircase in corridor 44; there was also an upper storey over rooms 19-21, which was accessible by way of a staircase in room 18 (Maiuri 1958: 330).

Select bibliography
Bonucci 1835: 43-44; Ruggiero 1885: 577 (5/8/1852; 11/9/1852); Van Aken 1943: 72, 77-79; Maiuri 1958: 323-335, figs 258-265; De Vos 1976: 63, fig. 45; Maiuri 1977: 25-27; Bisi Ingrassia 1977: 85, 94; Orr 1978: 195 no. 10; De Vos/De Vos 1982: 266; Bragantini/De Vos 1982: 50, 60, figs 43-44; Catalano 1982: 959; Barbet 1985A: 42, 262; Gassner 1986: 105 (table V), type B/2 (III, 2); McIlwaine 1988: 37, 3.288, 3.539-542, 4.32; Ganschow 1989: 37, 105-106, 125-127, 326-327; Wallace-Hadrill 1994: 82, 197.

An overview of the state of the house in the last century can be found in Bonucci (1835) and Ruggiero (1885). For an extensive description and plans, Maiuri's (1958) study is indispensable; it is summarised in Maiuri (1977) and De Vos (1982). The wall paintings in the bath suite are discussed in studies by De Vos (1976; with I. Bragantini: 1982), Barbet (1985A) and Ganschow (1989); in the latter work the wall structures in some parts of the house are also discussed. The shop with entrance no. 2 on *cardo* III is included in

---

[147] See Bonucci's description of the house (1835: 43-44) and a plan of the excavations by Ruggiero (1885: pl. XII).

[148] 'La seconda parte di quest'edifizio consiste in una larga piazza pel servizio dei carri fiancheggiata da forti e numerosi pilastri, che formavano degli archi coverti, ove poteano deporsi le merci, ed aversi il passaggio nelle stanze da dormire.' (Bonucci 1835: 44).

Gassner's overview (1986); a niche in the vestibule (50) is mentioned by Orr (1978). Chance finds are listed by Bisi Ingrassia (1977).

Plan and rooms (Pl. I)

Because large areas of the house are in a poor state of preservation, it is not always possible to determine precisely what the function of a particular room was. 'Clusters' of rooms can be distinguished: the old lot III K, for example, forms a separate suite of living quarters (37-44), as does a wing to the south of the *atrium* (1-11, 53-59); in addition, there is a bath area with service rooms (12-18, 46-47), and a number of living/sleeping rooms situated around the portico on the south side of the house (23-30, 60-63).

Entrance III 1 provides access to a very spacious peristyle (64-67) of 9 by 11 columns, enclosing a sunken garden (31). The discovery of the trunk of a pear tree suggests that the garden was used to grow fruit.[149] As well as rooms 23-26 in the south, the living quarters 34-36 in the north look out over this garden. Shop 32 (entrance III 2), the tiny connecting room 22 and the *atrium* (51) have doors into the peristyle.

The *atrium* can also be reached from the street, through entrance III 19 on *cardo* IV. To the south of the vestibule (49) that precedes the *atrium* there is a small chamber (50), which Maiuri (1958: 325) refers to as the *cella ostiaria*; it contains a small niche for a *lararium* and an alcove for a bed. On the north side of the *atrium*, there is a private bath, consisting of an *apodyterium* (12), a *tepidarium* (13) and a *caldarium* (14). The *praefurnium* (17), along with room 16 and a toilet (18), formed an annexe to the bath suite, which could be reached either through the bath, by way of corridor 15 and courtyard 47, or from the vestibule (49) via corridors 48 and 46. Corridor 48 gave access to another hall (45), where a number of washbasins were cemented to the south wall; around this are four living rooms (19-22). On the old lot III K (entrance III 18) there was a kitchen with latrine in room 38; the staircase was in corridor 44, and room 43 was the most luxurious living quarters, with extra light provided by a window opening onto the inner courtyard (11) of the Casa dell'Ara Laterizia (III 17). It is impossible to determine the exact function of the remaining rooms.

It is equally difficult to determine the function of the rooms to the south of the *atrium*. Rooms 1, 3 and 4 were luxurious living rooms, judging by their dimensions and floor decoration, while room 11 contained a large latrine with facilities for more than one person. On the south side of the garden are reception rooms (23-26), two opening only onto the peristyle (23 & 26), and two which open onto both the peristyle and the portico to the south (24 & 25). To the west of the portico (61) there were four smaller rooms (27-30), of which there is practically no evidence remaining now.

Wall construction

The house provides us with a number of clear examples of the types of wall construction that can be identified in Herculaneum. The oldest type, *opus incertum* A, can be found in the dividing wall with the Casa dello Scheletro, and *opus incertum* C can be seen in the private bath. Significantly, the bath is decorated in the Second Style, which helps to date

---

[149] See Maiuri 1958: 330, with a reference in note 125.

other examples of *opus incertum* C. The *opus incertum* C of the bath has been altered using the same technique (Ganschow 1989: 125-126). The annexe of the bath is also constructed in *opus incertum* C, while the southern wings which housed the living quarters (1-11, 23-30) were built at a later stage in *opus reticulatum* A and *opus vittatum*. Traces of old walls and reconstructions can also be found in rooms 37-44 (old lot III K). The dividing wall between rooms 37 and 39, for example, is of a later date, judging by its crooked form and its technique (*opus reticulatum* B). On the south side of rooms 42 and 43 is an arch of blocks of yellow tufa. Presumably this was once a doorway, which was later closed off, partly in *opus incertum* C. Along the bottom of the north wall of room 43 some evidence of *opus incertum* A or B can still be seen.

Floor and wall decoration
In several rooms of this house it has proved impossible to distinguish any ancient floors; this is the case in rooms 15, 17, 19, 48-52 and 65-67. There are stone tiles in the toilet (11). The remaining rooms have been paved very plainly. There is simple *opus signinum* in rooms 2, 4-10, 20-22, 25, 27-30, 32-34, 37-47 and 53-63; the slightly more luxurious version with bits of marble can be found in rooms 1 and 3. However, there are mosaic floors in some rooms. Plain white mosaic can be found in the more luxurious living rooms 35 and 36 in the northern area (lot III A), in the bath suite (12-14), and in the large rooms around the peristyle (23, 24 and 26). Presumably the colonnades of the peristyle also had mosaic floors, but now only a fragment of white mosaic with a black pattern survives, on the south side (64). Figurative motifs appear on the threshold mosaic between room 24 and portico 61 (a cock and a hen) and in the apse of the *caldarium* 14 (two dolphins flanking a plant).

It can be deduced from an overview of the wall decoration that the house was already in a bad state of repair when it was excavated. In 32 rooms (half the total number) not a single trace can be found of any wall paintings; the rooms are 2, 4-10, 16-17, 24, 27, 29, 30, 34, 45-48, 51, 54-58 and 61-67. In addition, the plaster in 29 rooms is so badly preserved that it is no longer possible to identify its style, type or colour. This is the case in rooms 1, 3, 11, 15, 18-23, 25, 26, 28, 32, 33, 36-42, 44, 49, 50, 52, 53, 59 and 60. Only five decorations can be considered in more detail here. Of these, the one in room 35 has faded; a Fourth Style scheme with elements of architecture on a red background is all that can be identified. The painting in room 43 has survived somewhat better: it is a 4th style panel decoration on red, with a socle, above which is an architectural scheme against a background of black and blue. The best-preserved wall decoration can be found in bath-rooms 12-14. The paintings are in the Second Style, with panels in the main zone and blocks in the upper zone. In room 12 the background is green, combined at the top with blue. The main colours used in the panels in room 13 are red and white, except for the socle, which is completely red. Finally, room 14 has white, red and blue panels in the top zone, and imitation marble on the plinth. Ganschow (1989: 105-106) dates the paintings to a fairly late period, between 30 and 20 BC However, a slightly earlier date, around 40 BC, cannot be ruled out.

Inscriptions

Della Corte reports the discovery of a number of inscriptions with dates under the staircase in the part of the house served by entrance III 18. Ciprotti was not able to find these inscriptions (CIL 10510 = Della Corte 1958: 252 no. 87). As usual, the toilet (room 11) was a popular place for writing graffiti; here, on the west wall, are the names 'ANICIAE FELICITER' and 'P. Quin(tilius)' ('IIII P QVIN'), as well as half of the Greek alpha bet.[150]

Published finds

The only relevant published finds are two small terracotta lamps.[151]

Building history

Although Maiuri does not provide a detailed history of the construction of the Casa dell'Albergo, we can form a reasonable impression of his ideas about the development of the house from a number of comments he made. He considers the bath suite and the adjoining *atrium* as belonging to the oldest parts of the house: 'la parte più signorile e più antica' (Maiuri 1958: 327). He regards the *atrium* as merely an entrance hall, rather than as the principal circulation area in the oldest living quarters. This was situated elsewhere in the house, as was the main entrance. Maiuri dates the bath area and several rooms to the south of the *atrium* (1-11) to the late Republican period. In his view, the peristyle dates from a later period, most probably the early Imperial period (Maiuri 1958: 330). The rooms off the south colonnade, which initially opened only to the north, were part of the original peristyle area, as were rooms 32-33 in the north range, which were later used as a separate *taberna*. The construction of the peristyle was eventually followed by an extension to the south, including a terrace which was partly built on the disused city wall and partly on a specially constructed substructure of arches and vaults which contained underground chambers. Maiuri does not provide a more precise date for this phase of construction.

In view of the bad state of the walls at the time of the excavation, Maiuri suspects that the house was badly damaged in the earthquake of 62 and may not have been inhabited in 79. The bath was certainly not in use in 79 (Maiuri 1958: 327). Perhaps renovations had just begun at the time of the eruption. Maiuri thinks that the house may possibly have been rebuilt, turning what had been a sizeable residence into a complex of rented houses and shops.

Ganschow (1989: 125-127) dates the paintings in the private bath to the period 30-20 BC. Because they were painted on walls in *opus incertum* type C, which were altered using the same technique, the bath suite itself must have been built earlier. Ganschow considers a date around 50 BC to be probable. The bath is one of the few surviving buildings in Herculaneum where *opus incertum* C was used as the principal technique.

---

[150] CIL 10511 = Della Corte 1958: 244 no. 15; CIL 10512 = Della Corte 1958: 245 no. 28; CIL 10707 = Della Corte 1958: 245 no. 28b. Catalano deduces from CIL 10512 (1982: 959) that 'Publius Quintilius' was the owner of the Casa dell'Albergo.

[151] Bisi Ingrassia 1977: 85 (type VIII E), 94 (type IX H_3).

Most houses that were built with this type of wall construction and decorated in the Second Style were later reconstructed using other techniques. In the Casa dell'Albergo only the rooms overlooking the garden and adjoining the terrace were rebuilt, in *opus reticulatum* A and *opus vittatum*. Ganschow (1989: 326) considers the house to be one of a group on the edge of the town which were probably built in the Augustan period. The Casa dell'Albergo is the only house that preserves traces of a major earlier construction period, in the middle of the 1st century BC.

We can distinguish the following main phases of construction on the site of the Casa dell'Albergo (minor renovations in individual rooms will not be considered in this discussion).

1. The original development (2nd century BC). On either side of the central axis of the *insula*, there were about four houses facing east-west. Remains from this period are still visible on the two lots on the north side of the house (III A and III K). The area between these two lots and the city wall was later completely rebuilt.

2. A major change took place in the middle of the 1st century BC, when the private bath and peristyle were built. The area of the *insula* to the south of the two lots mentioned above was levelled, and the entire area was used. In this period *opus incertum* C was used to build the walls, and the Second Style to decorate them.

3. As soon as the city wall could be used to support balconies and terraces (when it was no longer needed for defence purposes), the house was extended to the south. A large terrace was constructed, with a substructure built partly on the wall and partly to the south of the wall; in addition, a basement was built within this structure. Presumably it was during this period (in the Augustan era) that a small extension was added to the residential wing south of the *atrium*.

4. In 79 large areas of the house were in poor condition, probably as a result of the earthquake of 62. It is not clear how far repairs had progressed at the time of the eruption.

Metrological analysis (Pl. I)
The two original units in the northern part of the house (lots III A and III K) were of the same type as lots III B and III J. Both lots are 20' across, and it is possible, to some extent, to make out the original plan of III K. In III A only the broad outlines of the plan have survived. As lot III J is the best-preserved of the four examples mentioned above, the reader is referred to the discussion of this house (§ 5.6) for a detailed analysis of this particular type.

The old lot III A is 75' long (2072 cm) and 20' across (549-561 cm). Here the foot measure is 27.55 cm. The surviving rooms in III A give a fairly clear indication of the general plan of this type. The total length of rooms 32 and 33 together is 45' (1228/1238 cm). Room 32 was originally 32' long (869/870 cm), which corresponds with the 32' length of strip 1 (rooms on the side of the house adjoining the street) and strip 2 (*atriolo*) taken together. Room 33 is 13' long (359/368 cm) including its two dividing walls, which corresponds with the measurements of strip 3 on lots III B and J. The remaining length, 30' (834/836 cm), is divided more or less equally between rooms 34 and 35, each of which is 15' long (412/422 cm and 411.5/414 cm). In a later phase, room 36 was made wider

(160/164.5 cm).

Lot III K measures 20' (550-561.5 cm) across by 73.5' (2024/2028 cm). The foot measure is 27.65 cm. Lot III K must originally have had a similar layout to III J, although strips 1 and 2 were subsequently combined and re-divided along the axis of the lot into two rooms of equal width (ca 10' each). As in lot III A, the total length of strips 1 and 2 is 32' (872/873 cm). Rooms 40 and 41 correspond to the third strip in the plan of the lot; as in III A, its depth is 13' (356-365 cm). Room 40 has remained in its original state, except for the doorway at the back, and measures 7' by 10' (192/194 x 271/281 cm). The internal depth of room 41 is also 10' (273/274 cm), but here the north wall has been removed so that the corridor to the back (cf. layout of lot III J) no longer exists; only the post in the eastern corner remains. Little can be said about the floor plan of the back of the house. Its total depth is 28.5' (785/786 cm); rooms 42 and 43 were presumably constructed with dimensions of 9.5'R (275/283 cm) and 16'R (572.5/477 cm) long, by 13'R wide (382-396.5 cm). Here, a Roman foot measuring 29.45 cm was used.

The analysis of the rest of the house is difficult because it is impossible to determine precisely which foot measure was used in some areas. The study presented here is therefore limited to those parts where it is possible to determine the foot measure, and its aim will be to provide a general overview.

The width of the plot is divided into 100' for the peristyle (2730-2737 cm) and 50' for the rooms to the east (1387-1394 cm), assuming a foot measure of 27.4 cm. The length of the peristyle is 125', including the boundary wall on the south side (3420-3439 cm). However, it is also possible that the peristyle was once only 120' long (3283 cm). In fact the colonnades are all about 12.5' wide (340-350 cm; sometimes less: 323-335 cm), except on the south side, where they are 15'R wide (423-444 cm). If the south colonnade was originally the same width as the others, its rear wall would have been aligned with the north doorpost of entrance 54 and the south wall of room 1; this theory may be supported by the fact that there is a blocked door on the same alignment in the wall between portico 64 and corridor 53. On the east and west sides the columns of the peristyle are an average of 241.5 cm apart; on the north side they are about 251 cm apart. The average distance between cross-beams is therefore between 8.5' and 9'.

The widths of hall 45 and *atrium* 51 are half the total internal depth of the east range of the house, which is 47' (1307-1310 cm): the hall and the *atrium* are both 23.5' wide (650/665 cm and 640.5-646 cm respectively). Their lengths are 32' (875/875.5 cm) in the *atrium* and 33' (908-911.5 cm) in the hall[152]. In the bath area between the hall and the *atrium* it can be seen that 15' has been used as a basic module. Both the *apodyterium* (12) and the *tepidarium* (13) measure 15' x 12' (412/416.5 x 324/326 cm and 415/417 x 326/329 cm respectively). The *caldarium* (14) is 15' long without the *schola* (409 cm), and 23' including the *schola* and rectangular niche (635/637 cm); its width is 14.5' (396/402 cm). Finally, corridor 15 and room 16 together cover an area of 15' by 15' (413 x 417 cm); there is a possibility that they once formed a single room.

---

[152] These lengths may have been derived from their width, according to one of the formulae given by Vitruvius (VI, iii, 3).

To the south of the *atrium* (51), room 1 is 15' wide and 34' long (415/416 x 937/938 cm). Room 2 measures 12.5' x 13' (342.5/345.5 x 356.5/357 cm). North of hall 45, room 19 has internal dimensions of 12' by 20' (320/327.5 x 551/555 cm), and the original size of room 20 was presumably 12' x 12' (328 cm on the north and east sides, and less on the west and south sides: 307/320 cm).

The Roman foot (29.3 cm) was used in the area of the terrace on the south side of the house. The total width of the terrace on the north side is 60'R (1772 cm), of which 10'R (291.5 cm) was reserved for room 27. The terrace becomes wider towards the south, but the width of the portico remains practically the same (the extra width is taken up by the rooms along the west side). The pillars of the portico are arranged so that the colonnades are 10'R wide including the columns on the west and east sides (287.5-295 cm), and 10'R excluding the columns on the north (285-292 cm). The central intercolumniation on the north side is also 10'R (293.5 cm). The columns themselves are ca. 3'R in diameter (87-95 cm).

The rooms between the portico and the peristyle preserve traces of an earlier period when the Oscan foot was in use. For example, room 26 measures 14.5'O by 21'O (395/398.5 x 579.5/585 cm); the dimensions of room 24 are 13'O by 19'O (362.5/363.5 x 530.5 cm); and the starting-point for the construction of room 25 was probably a square whose sides measured 20'O (541-545 cm; north side 569 cm). Room 23 was rebuilt at some time, possibly when the portico was constructed. The total length of the room is 33'R (592/593 x 981/983 cm); its width is 20'R at the north end, but it narrows to 16'R in the southern part of the room, which is 20'R long (474 x 589.5/591.5 cm).

Design

We can reconstruct the main lines of the design of the two northern lots in the Casa dell'Albergo, lots III A and III K, because of their similarity to the two adjoining lots (III B and III J). Both pairs of lots were divided into strips, of which the two nearest the front, a row of rooms and a closed *atrium*, together occupied a length of 32'. The dividing walls between these chambers have disappeared or have been replaced. The next strip, 13' in length, comprised two small sleeping or living rooms on either side of a corridor leading to the back of the house. It is only on lot III K that part of this plan can still be made out. The broad outlines of the original floor plan of the back of the house can still be identified on lot III A; it was presumably divided into two equal areas measuring 15'. Completely new rooms were built on lot III K.

Not a single trace remains of the original construction to the south of lots III A and III K. This area was probably levelled to make room for a large residence with a peristyle and private bath. To this end, the available width of 150' (the entire width of the *insula*) was divided into 100' for the peristyle and 50' for the rooms, a ratio of 2:1. The peristyle was 120' or 125' long, so the ratio of length to width would have been 5:6 or 4:5; the colonnades were 12.5' wide, or 1/8 of the total width.

The widths of the two main circulation spaces in the residential area are half the internal width of the strip. Apart from this 1:2 ratio, other ratios were also applied. In the bath suite a measure of 15' served as the basic module for either a proportion of 4:5 (12' x 15' in rooms 12 and 13), or a square (a complete square in rooms 15 and 16; an almost complete square in room 14). Rooms 20 and 25 are also based on a square (12' x 12' and 20' x 20'). The ratio in room 19 was 3:5 (12' x 20').

For the construction of the terrace, round measures were used as a module: the total width (at the north end) was set at 60'R, of which 50'R was reserved for the portico including the dividing wall and 10'R for the rooms down the side. The floor plan allowed for the galleries to be 10'R wide, excluding the columns on the north side but including them along the others. The central opening between the north columns also measured 10'R. Finally, the reconstructed living room 23 was built with a width of 20'R, while the southern half of the room was constructed using a ratio of 4:5 (16'R x 20'R).

5.2. Casa dello Scheletro (III 3) (Pl. II; fig. 8)

This house is located on the west side of *insula* III, and can be entered by way of entrance no. 3 on *cardo* III. It was partly excavated in the 19[153] century, and completely unearthed by Maiuri in the period April 1927 - August 1929. The house was referred to as the 'Casa dello Scheletro' as early as the 19th century because of the skeleton found on the top floor on 10 February 1831. The house is almost square as a result of three original lots being put together (III B, III C, III D). Its irregular outline on the north-east side is explained by the fact that part of the earlier lot III D was not added to the house, but was acquired by the owner of the Casa a Graticcio. The total length of the house at its longest point is 2059 cm (measured on lot III C), and ca 1530 cm at its shortest (lot III D); its maximum width is ca 2213 cm (all lots taken together). The house has 28 rooms at ground level, most of them adjacent to one of the light wells or halls that are located around the house. Presumably an upper storey once covered the entire area of the house, reached by the staircase in 24 (Maiuri 1958: 268).

Select bibliography
Bonucci 1835: 43; Ruggiero 1885: 60 ('el nicho de mosaico', taken from *nymphaeum* 29), 564 (13/6/1830), 565 (7/9; 31/10/1830), 566 (10/2; 21/2; 18/4/1831), 567 (1831), 591 (28/5/1869), 595 (1/7/1831), 596 (3/7/1869?), 674 (17/2; 23/2/1876), 675 (31/5; 29/8/1876); Van Aken 1943: 39; Maiuri 1958: 265-275, figs 213-218, Pl. XXV; Tamm 1963: 165 no. 26, 203, figs 66 + 72; Neuerburg 1965: 50, 76, 89, 94, 135, fig. 154; Bisi Ingrassia 1977: 94; Maiuri 1977: 34-35; Sear 1977: 23, 24, 31, 37, 38, 40, 66-67 no. 26, 79, 80-81 no. 45, pls 13, 27; Orr 1978: 193 nos 1-3; Jashemski 1979: 61; De Vos/De Vos 1982: 267; Guidobaldi 1985: 186, 206, pl. 2.2, 12.3 (room 8); 196, 207, pl. 7.3 (*oecus* 10); Scatozza Höricht 1986: 60 Cat. 158, 62 Cat. 197, 64 Cat. 215; Moormann 1988: 104, Cat. 22/1, 22/2; McIlwaine 1988: 33, 34, 37, 50, 51, 54; 3.517, 3.520, 3.524, 3.530-532, 3.534, 3.537, 3.541-543, 3.548-549, 3.562, 3.575, 3.645, 3.831, 4.54, 4.116, 4.123, 9.314, 9.320; Conticello De Spagnolis/De Carolis 1988: 74 no. 66, 145 no. 116; Ganschow 1989: 147-183; De Kind 1991C; Mols 1994: 22, 39, 243, 250-251; Wallace-Hadrill 1994: 23, 24, 87, 199, figs 2.6-7.

The earliest description of the house dates from the 19th century (Bonucci 1835). Finds and discoveries from that period are reported in Ruggiero (1885). A general description of the whole house, together with its floor plan, is provided by Maiuri (1958) and in summary by Maiuri (1977), De Vos (1982), and Wallace-Hadrill (1994). The wall structures and construction history have been discussed by Ganschow (1989). Moormann (1988) chose to focus on the wall paintings, and the two nymphaea were investigated by Neuerburg (1965), Sear (1977) and De Kind (1991C). The *opus sectile* floors are the subject of a study by Guidobaldi (1985). Tamm (1963) studies the apsidal shape of room 10, while Orr

---

[153] Ruggiero's map shows an overview of the extent of the excavated area in the 19th century (1885: pl. XII).

(1978) examines a number of possible *lararium*-niches. Publications by Bisi Ingrassia (1977), Conticello De Spagnolis/De Carolis (1988) and Scatozza Höricht (1986) mention individual finds discovered in excavations in this century. Mols (1994) discusses the remains of furniture found in the house.

Plan and rooms (Pl. II)
The central circulation space of the house, the *atrium* (23), is entered from the only entrance to the house, the *fauces* in the central residential unit (1). This used to be an *atrium tuscanicum*, but after the addition of the upper storey it became a closed *atrium* (*atrium testudinatum* or *displuviatum*) (Maiuri 1958: 266). The windows that were put in on the upper storey to allow light into the *atrium* were still visible in the last century (Ruggiero 1885: 567, 17/5/1831). Every area of the house could be reached from the *atrium*. In the older lot III D, on the north side, was a *triclinium* (6), which looked out onto a *nymphaeum* (28/29). The 'traditional' plan of the *atrium* can still be identified in the central area of the house (lot III C): there is a *tablinum* (7) opposite the *fauces*, small living rooms or bedrooms (5, 9) at the side, and a large living room (4) at the front. A corridor (26) on the south side led to the small bedroom 8 (remnants of a niche for a bed), and from there to another living room (9). There is a large luxurious room (10) behind the *tablinum* on the east side of corridor 26. This may well have been an *oecus*, which, like *triclinium* 6, looked out onto a *nymphaeum* (27) - a rather smaller one than 28/29.

A number of smaller rooms in this part of the house were built later: rooms 2 and 3 were once a single room, as were staircase 24 and corridor 11. Presumably both rooms were originally living rooms opening off the *atrium*. The storage room 25 once served as a corridor to the back of the house, until the apse in room 10 was built. Corridor 11, which was built later, provided the only means of access to the southern area of the house (lot IIIB), as the original entrance on *cardo* III had been closed off. The state of rooms 12-16 and 22 is such that it is almost impossible to draw any conclusions about their function. Room 14 could have been a kitchen and latrine, accessed via corridor 13. Two small living rooms (15 and 16) are situated on either side of corridor 22, which leads to the back of the house. On the south side there is a room with washbasins; Maiuri (1958: 274) assumes that it had no roof, although traces of beams are visible. One step higher lies the anteroom (17), which gives access to the luxurious living rooms/bedrooms 18 and 19, lit from the inner courtyard 20.

Wall construction
The extensive treatment of the wall structures of the house by Ganschow (1989: 147-183) can be summarised as follows. The oldest types of construction (*opus incertum* A and B, with uprights in *opus quadratum*) are still visible on lot III B. Later alterations to this original unit were carried out in *opus reticulatum* B, *opus incertum* C and *opus vittatum*. In other parts of the house (lots III C and D) there are no visible traces of the older types of *opus incertum*. The main techniques here are *opus reticulatum* (A and B) and *opus vittatum*. The façade of these two original units is constructed in *opus reticulatum* A, with minor alterations in *opus incertum* C and *opus latericium*. Repairs were carried out

throughout the house in *opus incertum* D and C/D after the 62 earthquake.

Floor and wall decoration
Four rooms in the house had *opus sectile* floors (7, 8, 10, 26); it is remarkable that these are all in the central area (lot III C). In the *atrium* (23) the floor has disappeared almost completely, but remains of *opus sectile* are still visible along its edges.[154] The *fauces* (1) had pieces of *opus sectile* as decoration for a black mosaic floor. There are white mosaic floors in rooms 6, 9 and 17-19; the floor in 17 is patterned. *Signinum* floors are preserved in rooms 3-5, 21 and 27; little can be said about the floors in the remaining rooms, except that there was plain earth in the light well (20) and a marble gutter in the *nymphaeum* (29).

All of the rooms, except those excavated in the last century (11-16, 22, 24), were decorated with wall paintings, but only six can be described in detail. On the south wall of the small *nymphaeum* (27) is a painting of a garden, surrounding a niche framed by an aedicula and decorated with mosaics. The two living rooms 7 and 10 have Fourth Style paintings with architecture painted in perspective on a red background in the main zone. The panel decorations in the smaller living rooms 8, 18 and 19 are predominantly black. In room 19 the original ceiling is also preserved. The rear wall of the large *nymphaeum* (29) was decorated with a mosaic, which had courses of imitation masonry blocks on its lower half and a frieze with figured panels above it. Some of these were hacked out in the Bourbon period and later transferred to the National Museum in Naples (inv. 9989, 10009, 10011). A mosaic niche once stood in the centre; this was also removed from its original surroundings and is now in the museum in Naples (inv. 10008).[155]

Published finds
Several items were found on the upper storey: a skeleton was found on 10/2/1831, with a bronze vessel next to it; on 18/4/1831, in a room used for storage, were found a small terracotta vessel and lamp, bronze scales, a carafe and a small glass vase; finally, on 17/2/1871, a part of a bed was uncovered. In the last century the following items were found on the ground floor: bronze parts from a bed (room 6?, 28/5/1869; room 6, 1/7/1869); parts of the wall decoration of the *nymphaeum* 29 (plaster, shells, mosaic; room 6, 1/7/1869); a bronze cup without lugs and a bronze fitting with a ring (*nymphaeum* 29, 23/2/1876 and 29/8/1876 respectively).[156] Some small lamps were discovered during Maiuri's excavation: one was made of terracotta and two of bronze.[157] In addition, a

---

[154] Maiuri (1958: 268) notes that the original floor was black mosaic with white borders.
[155] An account of the method that was used as well as a reconstruction of the original wall are given in De Kind 1991C. See also fig. 8.
[156] See Ruggiero 1885: 566-567, 591, 595, 674-675; Mols 1994: 243. Ruggiero (1885: 596) assumes that the wooden chest containing silver and bronze coins and a silver ring shaped like a two-headed snake was found in room 4 on 3/7/1869, but in fact it was probably found in room 16 of the neighbouring house III 4-5. This may be deduced from the rest of the report filed in the excavation book for that year: the 'seconda casa a dritta della strada' is the house in which there is an 'arcuato della scalinata'; this can only be the section of the Casa del Tramezzo di Legno with entrances 4 and 5 on Cardo III.
[157] *Terracotta*: Bisi Ingrassia 1977: 94 (type IX H$_3$); *bronze*: found on 9/6/1927 (= E33) and on 13/6/1927 (= E38) - see Conticello De Spagnolis/De Carolis 1988: 74, 145.

number of glass objects were found in an *apotheca* on the top floor, and parts of a carbonised bed in room 16(?) on the ground floor. [158]

Inscriptions
In the apse of *oecus* 10 are a number of scratched characters, which presumably formed an addition sum: CIL 10495 (= Della Corte 1958: 245 no. 29).

Building history
Maiuri (1958: 265-267) dates the assimilation of the three pre-Roman units (lots III B, C and D) to the Julio-Claudian period, probably later than the earthquake in 62. In his view the walls date mostly from the Imperial Period (*opus reticulatum*), although there is also older *opus incertum* made up of various different types of material.

According to Ganschow (1989: 163-166, 176-177), the plan of lot III B was originally identical to that of the Casa dell'Ara Laterizia (lot III J); the entrance on *cardo* III was once located at the south-west corner of the house. Incidentally, it is not possible to reconstruct the rear part of either house. Lot III B was converted at a later date; exactly when cannot be ascertained. There may possibly have been a courtyard on the south side.

The original shape of lots III C and III D cannot be traced. Ganschow thinks that lot III C in its present state is an almost completely 'new' version (in *opus reticulatum* B) of the original plan. During this conversion lot III D was split up: the west part (which now comprises rooms 6, 28 and 29) was added to lot III C, while the east part (room 12/13) was incorporated into the Casa a Graticcio. Both lots were given a new façade in *opus reticulatum* A. Subsequently, the *triclinium* and the *nymphaeum* were built in lot III D, including a new back wall which was placed against the existing dividing wall (Ganschow 1989: 166-176).

The house acquired its present floor plan after the earthquake of 62. Ganschow (1989: 176-177) concludes that the earthquake damage was repaired before lot III B was added to the house. Once it had been assimilated, lot III B was subject to a number of minor alterations on the west side (in a coarse type of *opus reticulatum* B).

Metrological analysis (Pl. II)

1. Lot III B
Of the three original lots (III B, C and D), lot III B can be explained in the most detail and in its context. As Ganschow has already pointed out, this lot was originally the same as the house behind it, the Casa dell'Ara Laterizia. However, this layout was changed by later alterations, which did not always follow the original lines of the walls. The reader is referred to the analysis of the Casa dell'Ara Laterizia (§ 5.6) for a clearer description. The broad outlines of the design of the lot are as follows.

The house measured 552-558 cm across and 2065 cm in length. This corresponds with

---

[158]   *Glass:* E16 (14/5/1927), E21 and E31 (9/6/1927); see Scatozza Höricht 1986: 60, 62, 64. It is possible that the glass bottles E22 and E30 (Scatozza Höricht 1986: 61 Cat. 189, 50 Cat. 100 - 'mancano dati di scavo') belong to this group; compare the bronze lamp (E33) that was found on the same day in the same house (see previous note). *Bed:* Mols 1994: 251-252.

20' and 75' respectively, using an Oscan foot of 27.5 cm. The house is one of the 'internal' houses, which were possibly the first to be built in *insula* III (see § 4.4.4).

The length of corridor 13, including the wall of the façade, is equal to that of the *fauces* and the *atrium* in the Casa dell'Ara Laterizia, namely 875 cm or 32'. The width of the corridor is 147 cm (= 5'R?). Room 14 measures about the same as room 1 in the afore-mentioned house, namely 323 x 381 cm; this is roughly 12' x 14'. Presumably a strip 15' deep was marked off here, which produces an internal depth of 12'. Room 12 corresponds with the *atrium* of the Casa dell'Ara Laterizia. The dividing wall with corridor 13 is clearly older, and was built as economically as possible. The depth of room 12 is somewhat greater than that of the original *atrium*: 473 cm (= well over 17'). This may be the result of alterations made in this part of the house after it was added to the neighbouring units (see building history). The total width of rooms 12 and 13 taken together (once the breadth of the *atrium*) is equal to that of the house (20').

Two small rooms were situated on the east side of what used to be the *atrium*; a corridor between them led to the back of the house. To some extent its arrangement is evident from the corridor between rooms 15 and 16. The depth of this strip was once 357 cm (the length of corridor 22 plus the thickness of the east wall of room 12) which amounts to 13'. This corresponds to the original internal lengths of rooms 15 and 16, which measure 10'. Room 15 is 272-278 cm long, and room 16 276-282 cm; both are ca 203 cm (= 7.5') wide. Again, this is the same arrangement as in the Casa dell'Ara Laterizia.

As a result of later alterations it is difficult to determine the floor plan and function of the remaining rooms. There was 30' left at the back of the house after the allocation of 15' for strip 1 and 30' for strips 2 and 3. The length of the raised area of anteroom 17 is 10'R, the same as the external length of room 18. The width of the lot has been equally divided between them: the width of anteroom 17 is 10'O, the same as the external width of room 18. The internal dimensions of room 18 are 9'O x 9'R (248 x 269 cm). The internal depth of the rear strip has been increased to 10'R (291 cm.), judging from the measurements of courtyard 20. Room 19 is 12.5' (366 cm) wide, and courtyard 20 is 5.5' (157-165 cm) wide. The Roman foot which was applied in this area measures 29.3 cm.

2. Lot III C

According to Ganschow's analysis of the wall structures, lot III C was rebuilt on the basis of an old plan. The allocation of space is less simple than on lot III B because of a series of rooms along the side of the *atrium*. The lot measures 2059 cm in length. Presumably this was supposed to be 75', in which case the foot measure used was ca 27.5 cm. However, taking the internal allocation into account, it is more probable that a foot measure of 27.75 cm was used in the rest of the house, so that the width of 1051-1058 cm should be regarded as 38'.

At the front of the house is a strip with the *fauces* and the rooms on either side. The room on the north side was later divided into two separate rooms, while the one on the south has remained in its original state. The length of the *fauces* is 18.5', and the width 5.5' (146/152.5 x 507/512 cm). The internal length of room 4 is 15', the width 21' (412.5/413 x 580/585 cm). The room which was later converted into rooms 2 and 3 originally measured 8' (223.5/224.5 cm) by 15'; now the length of room 2 is 10'R

(287/291 cm), leaving 3'R (89/96 cm) for storage room 3.

It is likely that the central area of the house, the *atrium* with adjoining rooms, was divided up in the proportion of 13' (361-366 cm) for the rooms and 25' (687.5-693 cm) for the *atrium*. The west side of the *atrium* was divided into three sections measuring 10' - 5' - 10' (273/146/278 cm), and the east into 7.5' - 10' - 7.5' (211/272/210 cm). Lengthways the disposition of the *atrium* is probably not original; it was affected by the alterations at the back of the house when room 10 was built. The present length can therefore be regarded as 26'R (764-775.5 cm). A Roman foot measure was also used to measure out the rooms on the south side of the *atrium*, which are 11.5'O deep (311.5-318 cm): room 5 is 8.5'R long (252.5 cm), room 9 measures 9'R (267.5/270.5 cm) and room 8 is 7'R (202/202.5 cm). The Roman foot measures 29.6 cm.

The depth of the *tablinum* strip was affected by *oecus* 10, which was built later using a Roman foot measure. As a result, the *tablinum* is 10'R (295/297 cm) deep, with internal dimensions of 8.5'R by 13.5'O (254 x 370.5/372 cm). The narrow room (25) to the north of the *tablinum* measures 4'O by 10'O (113.5/118 x 273 cm), and corridor 26 measures 4'O by 11.5'R (111/120 x 339.5 cm).

The strip at the back of the house containing the *oecus* and the *nymphaeum* is 15'R deep (434-449 cm); the *oecus* is 20' R wide (583.5/591 cm), and the *nymphaeum* is about the same width as the rooms on the south side of the *atrium*: 11.5'O (319/320.5 cm).

3. Lot III D

The final form of lot III D can be deduced from its present state. It is more difficult to reconstruct the original shape of the lot. At one time, this plot of land measured 75' in length (up to the central axis of the *insula*) and presumably 20' across. The dividing wall between lots III C and III D, however, does not run exactly parallel to that between lots III D and III E, so the width varies from 18' (501.5 cm) on the side facing the street, to 19.5' at the back (537.5 cm). The length, excluding the façade, is 1384 cm, which is equal to 50'O or 47'R. However, when lot III D was divided up, the length would have been measured from the street up to and including the back wall of the *nymphaeum*, which was an extra wall placed up against the dividing wall with the Casa a Graticcio[159]; the owner of the Casa dello Scheletro would thus have acquired 50'R (the internal length plus twice the thickness of the walls) rather than 47'R. This distance is 50'R or twice the thickness of the wall (façade and *nymphaeum* wall) added to the interior length. Subsequently the internal length was divided equally to produce a *nymphaeum* area (rooms 28 and 29) measuring 23.5'R (689.5/691.5 cm) and a *triclinium* measuring 23.5'R (692.5/694.5 cm), including the dividing wall with the *nymphaeum*. The *triclinium* is 21.5'R long on the north side and 22'R on the south side (640.5/655.5 cm), because the dividing wall between it and the *nymphaeum* is not parallel to the façade or the back wall. The north side of the *nymphaeum* (29) measures 15'R, while the south is 15.5'R (446.5/456 cm). Conversely the anteroom (28) is longer on the north side than on the south (7.5'R against 7'R -

---

[159] This was because of the construction of the *nymphaeum*; it contained a niche about 60 cm deep, which could not have been placed in a normal single wall (usually 1.5' thick), and certainly not in a *paries communis* - see De Kind 1991C: 146-147. Compare also Ganschow 1989: 172; Rainer 1987: 122-123; Rainer 1988.

203.5/213 cm). The west side of the room is divided into 5' - 7' -5' (144/227/148.5 cm). The foot measure used in this area was 29.4 cm.

Design

Lot III B was built to the same design as lots III A, J and K. This means that the length was divided into three large strips: one measuring 15' at the front of the house and two additional strips of 30'. This produces a ratio of 1:2:2. The second strip was divided into unequal parts, 17' for the *atrium* and 13' for the rooms on the west side. The third strip was halved, producing two strips of 15' each. Evidence of this division has survived. In a later modification, a strip was laid out at the back of the house with an internal depth of 10'R, resulting in a ratio of 4:5 for room 19, which was 12.5'R wide.

The plan chosen for lot III C was an *atrium* with rooms at the side; the width of the *atrium* was 25'. The subdivision of the width into 10', 5' and 10' produces a proportion of 2:1:2. Room 4 was based on a ratio of 5:7 (15' x 21'). The most important rooms appear to have been proportioned carefully in later conversions. The measurements of the *tablinum* (7) are in the ratio of 4:5 (10' x 12.5'), while the large *oecus* (10) was laid out in the ratio of 3:4 (15' x 20').

After the owners of the Casa dello Scheletro and the Casa a Graticcio had divided the land, the available space on lot III D was 50'R. When the entrance to the *cardo* had been closed off and an additional rear wall had been constructed for the newly-planned *nymphaeum*, the remaining 47'R was divided into two equal parts (ratio 1:1), for a *nymphaeum* with an anteroom on the east side and a *triclinium* on the west.

5.3. Casa del Tramezzo di Legno (III 4-12) (Pl. III; fig. 9)

This house is on the north side of *insula* III and has two entrances on *cardo* III (4 and 5), several entrances on the *decumanus inferior* (6-10) and two more on *cardo* IV (11 and 12). The house is named after the panelled wooden partition that separated the *atrium* and the *tablinum*. Part of the house was excavated in the last century (between 1869 and 1875): the western area, up to and including the west wing of the peristyle, and the shops on the north side as far as entrance 9.[160] The remaining rooms were excavated during Maiuri's campaign, between January 1928 and December 1929. The house covers two original lots (III E and III G), as well as the irregularly shaped strip of land on the north side of the *insula* (lot III F). The total length of the house is equal to the width of the *insula*, ca. 4145 cm; its maximum width (on the side facing *cardo* IV) is 1789 cm. If the colonnades of the peristyle and the various *tabernae* are regarded as separate rooms, the total number of rooms on the ground floor is 32. These are grouped around the *atrium* at the end nearest *cardo* IV, or around the peristyle at the back; in addition there are several independent rooms, mostly shops, facing onto the street. The house had an upper storey over all the rooms except 6-8 and 20-24; it was reached by staircases in rooms 18, 26-30 and 32 (Maiuri 1958: 208).

Select Bibliography
Ruggiero 1885: 586 (21/4; 29/4/1869), 587-588 (13-15/5/1869), 590 (24/5/1869), 591 (28/5/1869), 592 (12/6; 14/6; 18/6/1869), 596 (3/7; 5-7/7; 9/7/1869), 596-597 (10/7/1869), 603 (6/2/1869), 604 (11/2; 13-17/2/1871), 605 (20-21/2; 23/2; 1/3/1871), 606 (6-7/3; 9-11/3; 13/3/1871), 607 (16-17/3; 21-23/3; 31/3; 1/4; 3/4/1871), 608 (4-6/4/1871), 614 (24-25/11; 27-28/11/1871), 615 (29-30/11/1871), 622-623 (23/5/1872?), 628 (26-27/9/1872?), 675 (13/3; 19/5/1876); Van Aken 1943: 6 no. 1, 40; Maiuri 1958: 207-222, figs 162-173, pl. XIX; Peters 1963: 150-151 (room 2); Tran Tam Tinh 1971: 92-93 Cat. 66, fig. 30; Packer 1971: 24; Tamm 1973: 59; McKay 1975: 49, pl. 17; Moeller 1976: 26, 113, pl. II; Maiuri 1977: 32-33; Bisi Ingrassia 1977: 88, 94, 96; Orr 1978: 193-194 nos 4-5; Jashemski 1979: 58-59; De Vos/De Vos 1982: 268-269; Adam 1984: 225, 323, 329, fig. 489, 681, 693-694; Barbet 1985A: 156-158, 265; Barbet 1985B: 104 (*tablinum* 7); Gassner 1986: 105 (table V), type B/1 (III, 10), B/2 (III, 4), B/4 (III 6), B/6 (III 8-9); Scatozza Höricht 1986: 54 Cat. 107-109, pls XVIII, XXXIII; McIlwaine 1988: 54, 439; 3.553-554, 3.558, 3.560, 4.14, 4.17, 4.31, 4.46, 4.48, 4.134; Ganschow 1989: 42, 168 no. 18, 322-323; Scatozza Höricht 1989A: Cat. 57; Ling 1991: 64, 69, fig. 65 (room 2); Mols 1994: 151-153 Cat. 1, 242-244, 252, figs 33-36; Wallace-Hadrill 1994: 83, 127, 199, fig. 4.12.

Ruggiero (1885) gives an account of the finds (see below) and the progress made

---

[160]   See the plan published by Ruggiero: pl. XII.

during the excavations in the 19th century. Maiuri (1958) gives a plan and describes the rooms; this information is summarised by Maiuri (1977), De Vos (1982), and Wallace-Hadrill (1994). The wall paintings in the house are discussed by Peters (1963), Jashemski (1979), Barbet (1985A; 1985B) and Ling (1991). Ganschow (1989) mentions the house in his discussion of wall construction. Gassner (1986) includes the shops around the house in her discussion, and Moeller (1976) briefly discusses the linen-press from *taberna* III 10. Orr (1978) mentions two niches for household gods. Individual finds are also referred to by Tran Tam Tinh (1971), Bisi Ingrassia (1977), Scatozza Höricht (1986; 1989A) and Mols (1994).

Plan and rooms (Pl. III)
The house has several entrances; the one on *cardo* IV (III 11) is the main entrance. This is the *fauces* (19) of an old *atrium* house, which has retained its original layout to a large extent. A peristyle was added at a later date. There is a room on either side of the *fauces* (1 and 2); room 2 has an entrance to the *atrium* (20). The *atrium*, of the Tuscan type, has two *cubicula* (3 and 4) and an *ala* (5) on the south side. On the west side are the large and luxurious room 6 (a *triclinium*?), the *tablinum* (7) with its wooden partition, and a passage to the back of the house (21). A small staircase leads down to shop 27 (III 8). The back of the house is centred around a garden (23) with colonnades on three sides (8, 22 and 24); the south colonnade (25) has been closed off. Opening off the colonnades are several living rooms, including one (12) which must have been a *cubiculum*, as there is a niche in one wall for a bed. The kitchen and the toilet were in room 14.

There are shops on three sides of the house, and two independent entrances to the upper storey, III 5 and III 7 (rooms 32 and 26). On the west side, entrance III 4 serves a group of rooms (16, 17 and 31) forming a shop; this was connected to the shop on the corner of the *insula* at entrance III 6 (room 15) which was also accessible from inside the house via room 13. At the other corner (III 10) there is a shop with an upper storey where the linen-press was found (room 30). Entrances III 8 and 9 give access to a shop with two rooms at the back (27-29), one of which is a kitchen and toilet (29); two flights of steps lead into the *atrium* (20) and the peristyle (8) of the house. Finally, III 12 (room 18) was a small shop with a staircase to the upper storey.

Wall construction
In his account of ancient wall construction in Herculaneum, Ganschow (1989: 42, 48) refers to two examples from the Casa del Tramezzo di Legno: the façade, which contains *polychrome opus reticulatum* A, and the north wall of room 25, which is constructed in *opus incertum* D. He also establishes that room 14 was largely built in *opus incertum* D, except the east wall (*opus incertum* A), and that *opus incertum* C is found in several walls at the back of the house.

A number of comments can be added. First of all, there are numerous tufa posts around the house. As Ganschow (1989: 64) has noted, some of these are the result of modern restorations, although presumably they are replacements for ancient posts. There are quoins at the corners of the *atrium* (20) and of rooms 11-14 and 17, and at entrances III 4, 5, 7 and 11. There are quoins set in the walls in rooms 11, 13 and 15. It cannot be established with certainty whether these are remains of an earlier construction period. There are doorposts in *opus latericium* in the façade near entrances 10 and 12 and at the back of the *tablinum* (7), among other places. In stair-case 26 the east and west walls were built up against the north and south walls without bounds; remains of an early type of *opus incertum* (A or B) can still be seen in the south wall.

Floor and wall decoration
None of the shops and related rooms around the house (15-18, 26-28 and 30) has an identifiable floor. The kitchen with toilet (29) had a floor of tiles. There was no pave-ment in the garden (23). The remaining rooms of the house are paved quite simply: there are plain *opus signinum* floors in rooms 1, 3, 4, 10, 13, 14 and 25, and deco-rated *opus signinum* with *crustae* of marble in rooms 5, 6, 8, 11, 12 and 19-22. The original floor of the *impluvium* was the same type of *signinum* as the rest of the *atrium*; later - in the Flavian period, according to Maiuri (1958: 212) - the bottom and the rim were covered with marble tiles. There is *opus signinum* with fragments of *opus sectile* in the eastern part of the peristyle. Finally, there are white mosaic floors in rooms 2, 7 and 9: the floors in rooms 7 and 9 are white with two black frames; in room 2 black coffer patterns cover the entire surface of the floor.

There are traces of wall decoration throughout the house, except in room 16. For the most part these are poorly preserved, as in rooms 1, 10-15, 17, 18, 21, 22 and 24-30. Of the remaining paintings, the one in the *viridarium* (23) is the most striking: a garden has been painted on a solid wall, which seems to suggest a continuation of the real garden. The background, however, is flat and black; it does not create a spatial illusion of the kind found in Second and Fourth Style paintings. The painting therefore fits in with the overall decorative style in the rest of the house, namely the Third Style.[161] In all the remaining rooms (2-9, 19, 20) are panel decorations on a black background, some with architectural elements; in some rooms black is combined with panels of other colours (red in rooms 5 & 6, red and blue in room 2). The socles are usually black, except in room 2, where yellow was used, and in the *atrium* (20), where the socle was divided into rectangular panels of various colours. In the upper zones there are traces of architectural schemes, either in a single colour (rooms 2-4 and 20) or in several colours (rooms 6-8 and 19).

Inscriptions
In *taberna* 15 (entrance 6) there is a *dolium* with the number LXXIIX (CIL 10871; Della Corte 1958: 251 no. 77). On the south wall of the *fauces* (29) there was a *graffito* which said that 'a denarius [was given] to Colonus': 'COL*ONO' (CIL 10497; Della Corte 1958: 246 no. 31). The wickedness of a certain 'MUS' is recorded in CIL 10498, which was found on the east part of the north wall of the

---

[161]   De Vos and De Vos agree (1982: 268). Maiuri (1958: 207), however, regards the decoration as Fourth Style.

peristyle (22): 'MVS NEQVA / ..S NEQVA / MVS / MMMMVS' (Della Corte 1958: 243 no. 9). The name of 'Remnius Rufus' - a family name known from several contexts at Herculaneum - is written on the west wall of room 16.[162]

Published finds

From Ruggiero's published reports (1885) of the 19th-century excavations, it can be deduced that several objects were discovered in the upper storey facing onto *cardo* III. For example, a sack containing carbonised flour was found on 13/5/1869. In a room where parts of the wooden doorposts had survived, there were a number of amphorae in a corner, and small terracotta cooking utensils on a wooden shelf (13/5/1869). Here the excavators also found an empty wooden cupboard (14/5/1869); a slate table with a marble base, on which were objects made of bronze, glass, terra-cotta, marble and bone (15/5/1869); a set of bronze scales, nails, shells, a lead weight, a small stone base, bread, a marble table-support, and the lock from a chest (14/6/1869). In a room to the left were found bronze kitchen utensils (13/5/1869) and objects made of glass, bronze, lead, marble, iron and terracotta (15/5/1869). On a mezzanine floor there was a portable set of wooden steps with five rungs (18/6/1869). An iron axe was found near some stone steps (24/5/1869), along with a small bronze lamp (28/5/1869) and an iron spade (12/6/1869). Presumably room 16 was the find-spot of a marble mortar and a small wooden chest (190 x 160 mm) with a limestone base, which contained a silver ring in the shape of a two-headed snake, four silver coins, and 162 bronze coins (3/7/1869).[163] The eastern area of the upper storey was excavated in 1871. There were numerous finds including: bronze kitchen utensils and small chains (6/2/1871); a mirror and several items of bronze kitchenware (13-14/2/1871); a small wooden cupboard with a lock, which contained several small terracotta lamps and some glassware (11/2, 15/2/1871); a mortar and a lead vase (16/2/1871); parts of a wooden easy chair (17/2/1871); and parts of a large bronze statue[164] (15/2, 17/2/1871). In one of the rooms behind the staircase (no. 11, 12 or 13) were found various foods: some bread in a bag (13/3/1871), garlic (11/3/1871), and olives in a bronze pot (16/3/1871). Other finds included kitchenware of bronze, glass and terracotta (7/3/1871), and iron furniture (17/3/1871). Finds in the portico included: a bronze bowl and pan, bread, and a small tufa altar with painted decoration in red (21/3/1871); a bronze fish hook (27/3/1871); remains of a straw broom (3/4/1871); and an iron hammer (6/4/1871). A small bronze bucket, a nail, a piece of marble, and some nuts and onions were found on 22/3/1871 in a side room (no. 10?); in room 9 were found parts of a human skeleton, as well as bronze kitchen utensils, remains of garlic, glass buttons, coins, and parts of bronze fittings from furniture

---

[162] CIL 10496; Della Corte 1958: 246 no. 35; Solin 1973B: 271-272. Cf. CIL X 1453, 1455, 1456. Catalano (1982: 959) regards Rufus as the owner of the Casa del Tramezzo di Legno.

[163] Ruggiero (1885: 596) indicates, probably wrongly, that these objects originated from room 4 of the Casa dello Scheletro. See the comments on the finds from that house (§ 5.2).

[164] Could these perhaps be the remains of the large bronze sculpture group of horses, many fragments of which were found between June and November 1871? (Compare Ruggiero 1885: 609-613).

(31/3, 1/4, 3-5/4/1871). The objects discovered in and around shop 15 were a *dolium*, parts of a headless skeleton, iron axes and a hammer (10/7/1869); a small onion (24/11/1871); scraps of fish in an amphora (25/11/1871); bronze kitchen utensils and a small terracotta lamp (27/11/1871); a bronze statue (28/11/1871); and parts of a set of scales (28-29/11/1871).

In addition to the wooden partition, two marble tables were discovered in the excavations in this century; one was in the *atrium*, while the other, a *trapezophoros* with a base in the form of a statue of Attis, was found in room 2 (Tran Tam Tinh 1971: 92-93 no. 66). There was a wooden bed in room 4, and a wooden shelf and linen-press in shop III 10 (= room 28). Other stray finds include a ring, three small terracotta lamps and three glass bottles (two from the garden and one from near the house).[165]

Building history
According to Maiuri (1958: 207), the house was created by amalgamating two existing houses; a spacious residence with an entrance on *cardo* IV (III 11) and a smaller house on *cardo* III (original entrance at III 5), which was subsequently rebuilt extensively. After the two houses were consolidated into one, several changes were made - the floors were raised, for example - which led Maiuri to conclude that the owner must have been one of the *nouveaux riches* of the merchant class who, around the middle of the 1st century AD, extended the old patrician houses to create space for commercial use.

At the front of the house (entrance III 11) Maiuri assumes that there must originally have been rooms and an *ala* on the north side of the *atrium*, which were later given over to commercial use and converted into shops with upper storeys. The floor level was raised for this purpose. Maiuri's next remarks must be taken into account when considering the history of the house (Maiuri 1958: 210-217). The *impluvium* was originally paved in *signinum*, like the *atrium* floor; the present marble paving dates from the Flavian period. The marble threshold blocks in the *atrium* were also later additions. In the *tablinum*, which faced the *atrium* before the creation of the garden, the tufa posts date from the earliest building period; the mosaic floor, on the other hand, is probably Augustan. Finally, there are paintings of the late Second Style in room 2.

According to Maiuri, the peristyle was originally open on all four sides, with brick columns plastered and painted in white and red, similar to the pilasters in the wall behind it. An upper storey was added after 62 to create more space. To this end the south colonnade was walled up (a garden scene was painted on the wall). A low parapet was added on the other three sides of the peristyle, with an opening on the west side facing *triclinium* 11; the columns on the north and west sides were replaced with brick pillars, and the columns on the east side with antae ending in engaged

---

[165] *Ring*: E199 - Scatozza Höricht 1989A: Cat. 57. *Lamps*: Bisi Ingrassia 1977: 88 (type IX A), 94 (type IX H₃), 96 (type X A). *Glass*: E94 (15/11/1927), E102 (9/12/1927) and E130 respectively (27/1/1928, on *cardo* IV) - Scatozza Höricht 1986: 54. See also Mols 1994: 151-153 for the bed and 242-244, 252 for other finds of furniture.

columns. All the rooms around the garden were built with relatively low ceilings to accommodate the upper storey (Maiuri 1958: 217-218). Shop 15 has retained its original floor level. The staircase (32) is simply a later conversion of the original *fauces* of the small house on *cardo* III; the benches on either side of the entrance are a further reminder of its former function. At the time, the house took up half the width of the *insula* (Maiuri 1958: 220-222).

Ganschow (1989: 326) also believes that the house consisted of two residences which originally occupied half the width of the *insula* each. However, he does not think that the staircase is an earlier entrance to the house on the west side of the *insula*; instead, he identifies entrance 4 as the original door. The tufa jambs flanking entrance 4 are, in his opinion, similar to the two tufa posts in the west wall of room 11; these four posts might well mark the corners of the original *fauces*. According to Ganschow, the tufa quoins in the walls in the rear part of the house (see above: wall construction) may be the remains of the earlier *atrium* house.

Finally, the dates given by De Vos (1982: 268-269) differ in some respects from those given by Maiuri. As mentioned above she regards the decoration of the front part of the house, as well as the garden painting, as Third Style. However, she also dates the mosaic in room 2 and the marble rim of the *impluvium* to the Julio-Claudian period.

Taking all these opinions into account, the architectural history of the Casa del Tramezzo di Legno falls into several phases. The earliest phase must date to the 2nd century BC. In this period there were two separate houses at the north end of *insula* III, on either side of the central axis. The *atrium* house on the east side is still clearly visible; there was also an *atrium* house on the west side, with a *fauces* at entrance III 4 or III 5. The external appearance of the latter house is difficult to reconstruct. For an impression of what it may have looked like, the reader is referred to the following section on the design of the house.

Maiuri believed that the shops along the north side of the eastern house (lot F) were originally rooms opening off the *atrium*. However, it is not necessary to assume that every house originally had rows of rooms on both sides of the *atrium*; this kind of symmetrical arrangement is the exception rather than the rule. On the other hand, as lot F is so small, the rooms in this strip cannot have formed an independent residence; furthermore, it is unlikely that independent shops would have been set up in this area before the construction of the Forum Baths. Initially, therefore, the rooms must have opened onto the *atrium*. If this was indeed the case, the dividing wall must have been in the same place as the present wall; this can be deduced from the position of the *impluvium* (see also Metrological analysis and Design).

The second phase of construction was when the two houses were combined into one. The house to the west was converted into a peristyle with colonnades on four sides and rooms on three sides. There is not enough evidence to determine precisely when these alterations were made, but it is unlikely that the assimilation and the final decoration of the houses took place at the same time. This is clear from Maiuri's meticulous account of the order of events in the peristyle area (see above). The only thing that needs to be changed in his account is the date: the latest paintings were not added after 62, but some decades earlier. It is obvious that the houses must have been made into one residence some time before the redecoration, so a date towards the end of the 1ˢᵗ century BC or at the beginning of the 1ˢᵗ century AD would seem more likely.

To the third building phase, presumably in the second quarter of the 1ˢᵗ century AD, belong not only the luxurious new decoration of to the eastern *atrium* house, but also an expansion of the living area by the addition of upper storeys in some parts of the house. Perhaps it was also in this period that the design of the shops on the north side of the house was conceived; they were built in a strategic location opposite the newly-built baths. However, it is not inconceivable that these rooms were separated off even earlier, at the same time as the conversion of the two houses into one.

Undoubtedly the earthquake of 62 caused damage in this house. Some of the walls were repaired in *opus incertum* D (14 and 25).

Metrological analysis (Pl. III)

The total depth of the front part of the house was 75' (2069/2077 cm), and its width, including the rooms on the north side, was 42' (1152-1162 cm). A foot measure of around 27.6 cm was used for this layout. However, the internal dimensions of the house are best analysed in terms of an Oscan foot which measures 27.4 cm. A Roman foot of 29.45 cm was used in the later alterations.

The depth of the *fauces* and the row of rooms facing the street is 17.5'O (474.5/476.5 cm); the *fauces* is 7'O wide (192/192 cm). The internal depth of the rooms is 14'O. Room 1 was altered at some stage, but originally measured 11' x 14'O (383.5/300 x 387 cm); room 2 has remained virtually unchanged and is 10' x 14'O (278.5/286 x 385/389 cm).

The *atrium* is 827.5 cm wide, which is 30'O, or 28'R. The position of the *impluvium*, which is related to the width of the *atrium*, has not changed, so it would seem that the width of the *atrium* has not been altered, and that the measurement was conceived as 30'O. The length of the *atrium* is twice the length of the *fauces*: 956 cm or 35'. The *atrium* was originally divided across its width into sections measuring 11' - 8' - 11' (295-301.5 cm; 224.5-227 cm). At a later date the basin of the *impluvium* was covered with marble, which may have changed the original layout slightly. The distance between the wall and sides of the *impluvium* is 10'R (295-299 cm), which is very close to 11'O. The *impluvium* is slightly west of the centre of the *atrium* and is 1.5' longer than it is wide: the length of the *atrium* is divided into sections of 12.5' - 9.5' - 13' (339/341 cm; 260/263 cm; 350/355 cm).

The external depth of the rooms on the south side of the *atrium* is 330-341 cm (341 cm on the east side of *ala* 5); this is equal to 12'O or 11.5'R. The internal depth is 10.5'O or 10'R (293-295 cm). The layout of the house is thus either 11.5'R + 28'R = 39.5'R, or 12'O + 30'O = 42'O. The second possibility is preferable, but it should be noted that the Oscan layout was modified in Roman feet when structural alterations were made in the second or third building phase. This only affected the depth of the rooms: their internal width is slightly greater than their depth (298-301 cm), and is best expressed as 11'O.

In the first building phase, 75' - (17.5' + 35') = 22.5' was left over for the rear area of the eastern house. This can be seen in room 6, which has an internal depth of 21' (577/587 cm) and width of 17' (458.5/464 cm). The *tablinum* is 16.5'R wide (486/488.5 cm) and 11.5'R (335/337 cm) deep. The length of corridor 21 is therefore 13'R (380/382 cm), and its width is around 4'R (115.5/126 cm). Room 8 measures 24'O across (659/659.5 cm), and its depth is determined by the space left over behind the *tablinum* (251.5-262 cm).

The rear area of the house is narrower: 39' not including the rooms to the north 1072.5/1075 cm). The external depth of the house is 75' (2068 cm) from the street up to and including the east wall of the peristyle. Originally, therefore, the available length amounted to 73.5'. In places it is difficult to determine which foot measure was used. It is assumed that the same Oscan foot measure (about 27.4 cm) was used in this house as in the eastern house, and that the Roman system (29.45 cm) was applied later when changes were made.

The peristyle is almost square. It measures 35'O on the north and south sides (950-961.5 cm), including the porticoes, and 33.5'O (914-917 cm) on the west, not including room 25. The intercolumniations on the north and west sides, which are of a later date, measure 4.5'R (130.5-135 cm), apart from the opening in front of room 11, which is 8.5'R (250 cm). Rooms 11 and 13 are the same size, 13'O x 18'O (355.5-364.5 x 490.5-495 cm). Room 14 has the same depth (493.5/494.5 cm). Rooms 17 and 12 are 10'O (279/280 cm) wide, and 9.5' (260 cm) and 11' (308 cm) long respectively. The western row of rooms (15, 16 and 32) has an external depth of 20'O (549 cm). Shop 15 therefore measures 17'O (467/473 cm) across internally; its length ranges from 22.5'O (616 cm) in the west to 23'O (638.5 cm) or more in the east. Room 16 is irregular in plan; it is ca. 12.5'O deep and 19.5'O long (348 x 534.5 cm).

The row of rooms on the north side of the *insula* widens from west to east, from 10'O (272.5 cm) on the west side of room 10 to 17'O (463 cm) in room 30. The length of room 10 is 15'O (413.5/417 cm); room 30 is basically a square of 17'/17.5'O (463-487 cm). Room 9 is 11'R long (326/329 cm); the shop (27) is 30'R in length (880/881 cm). Finally, rooms 28 and 29 are respectively 13.5'R (398 cm) and 5'R (147.5 cm) long on the south side.

Design (Pl. III)

1. Lot III G

The Casa del Tramezzo di Legno is made up of three lots (III E, F and G); the original design of lot III G (the front part of the house) can be best understood. When the land on the north side of the *insula* was first divided up, a straight line was drawn from east to west at right angles to the *cardines*. Thus the building-plots were rectilinear, despite the oblique angle of the north side of the *insula*, which followed the line of the city walls and the coast rather than the grid of *cardines* and *decumani*. This left a narrow wedge of land on the north side, which was not taken into account in the proportioning of the northern houses[166], although it did form part of them.

The starting-point for lot III G was therefore a rectangle of 42' x 75'. A 17.5' strip was constructed across the front of the house, creating 14' deep rooms. The width of the northern room (2) was 10', so that the ratio of width to length was 5:7. The *atrium* was made 30' across, so that 12' was left over for the southern rooms and the *ala* (a ratio of 2:5). These rooms are almost square internally; their depth is 10.5', exactly 1/4 of the total width of the house (42'). The length of the *atrium* is 35', twice the length of the *fauces*; thus the width-length ratio of the *atrium* is 6:7. The *impluvium* is almost in the middle of the room. It may have been intended to take up an area of 8' x 10' (4:5), which would result in a widthways division of 11' - 8' - 11' and a lengthways division of 12.5' - 10' - 12.5' (actually: 12.5' - 9.5' - 13'). Certainly the east side of the *impluvium* is exactly 30' from the street (cf. Casa dell'Atrio a Mosaico, § 5.7).

Thus 3/10 of the total length (22.5') was left at the rear of the house for the *tablinum* and the garden. The original layout of this part of the house was altered in a later building phase. It was linked to the plan of the new peristyle, which was the same depth as the *atrium* (35') and 33.5' wide. The rooms around it were constructed using the remaining space, which limited the possibilities for a coherent design.

2. Lot III E (fig. 9)
During this later construction phase the original *atrium* house on lot III E was almost completely obliterated by the peristyle and adjoining rooms. However, there is some evidence for the original appearance of the lot. The house had an entrance on the west side at III.5 in the same position as the present staircase (entrance 5); the old entrance was wider than entrance 5 is now (114 cm). There was a large room of ca. 12.5' x 15' to the south of the *fauces*; it covered the area of the present room 16. The *fauces*, which was about 16' long, led into an *atrium* that was 27' wide and ca. 32' long (twice the length of the *fauces*). The *atrium* would therefore have covered rooms 11 and 13 and a very small area to the west, and colonnade 24 of the peristyle. There was a row of rooms 11.5' deep along the south side of the *atrium*, giving an internal depth of 10' (now rooms 12 and 17). At the east end of this row of rooms, there was an *ala* ca. 8.5' wide, whose east wall coincided with the western colonnade of the later peristyle. On the north side of the *atrium* there were irregular rooms (now room 14), widening towards the east. The *ala* on this side was in the western part of room 10. In the rear area of the house - now occupied by the peristyle, part of room 10, and rooms 9 and 26 - there must have been a *tablinum*. Presumably this must have been ca. 13.5' deep with rooms on either side and a garden at the back; the arrangement at the rear of lot III G must have been similar.

---

[166] Cf. the same situation in Pompeii, in the Casa di Pansa (VI 6, 1) - see Peterse 1985: especially fig. 7.

5.4. Casa a Graticcio (III 13-15) (Pls IV, V; fig. 10)

This house was excavated between October 1927 and May 1929, and is on the east side of *insula* III, with entrances 13, 14 and 15 on *cardo* IV. The interior walls are mostly constructed in *opus craticium* (half-timbering), hence the name 'Casa a Graticcio'. The house consists of one original lot (III H), which extends to the middle of the *insula*, and part of lot III D, on the other side of the central axis, which was added later. This is one of the few houses whose upper storey is almost completely preserved. The upper storey will be considered separately in the metrological analysis below, in order to gain an insight into the layout and design of an upstairs living area. The house has a maximum length of 2613 cm including the back room, and is 756 cm wide. There are 15 rooms on the ground floor, including the courtyard which adjoins most of the remaining 14 rooms. There are also 15 rooms on the upper storey, of which 5 were only accessible by means of a staircase in hall 5 of the ground-floor residence. The other rooms in the upper storey were reached from a separate entrance at no. 13.

Select Bibliography
Ruggiero 1885: 61 (discovery of CIL 10478); Van Aken 1943: 13, 37, 45, 82, 87; Maiuri 1958: 407-420, figs 345-358, pls XXXIV-XXXV; Maiuri 1960: fig. 489; Tran Tam Tinh 1977: 56 no. 3 (figs 13, 14), 66 no. 17, 69 no. 24 (fig. 18), 92 no. 65; Packer 1971: 31, 43 (n. 62), 55-56, 62 (n. 74-75), pls CI-CII, figs 288-292; McKay 1975: 82-83, pls 28-29; Bisi Ingrassia 1977: 93; Maiuri 1977: 31-32; Orr 1978: 194 nos 6-7; De Vos/De Vos 1982: 268-270; Catalano 1982: 959; Gassner 1986: 88, 105 (table V), type C/3 (III 15); Scatozza Höricht 1986: 31 Cat. 12, 36 Cat. 44, 37 Cat. 52, 42 Cat. 72, 45-46 Cat. 77-80, 49 Cat. 97, 55 Cat. 117, 57 Cat. 128, 58 Cat. 132, 62 Cat. 199, pls IV.1, VIII.1, XIV, XVI, XXIV, XXVI, XXVII, XXIX, XXX, XXXI, XXXIV, XXXV; McIlwaine 1988: 37, 54; 3.558, 3.808, 4.9, 4.14, 4.16, 4.18, 4.28, 4.30; Budetta/Pagano 1988: 34-35, 100 (Cat. 8); 40-51 (Cat. 11-16); Conticello De Spagnolis/De Carolis 1988: 187 Cat. 125; Ganschow 1989: 50, 171-173; Scatozza Höricht 1989A: Cat. 11, 41, 139, 191-192; Clarke 1991: 257-263, figs 156-162; Mols 1994: 154-161 Cat. 2-5, 197-199 Cat. 27, 217-220 Cat. 35-36, 250-251, 253-255; Wallace-Hadrill 1994: 66, 97, 110, 112, 199, figs 5.2, 5.14-15.

Maiuri (1958) gives a description of the house with many illustrations and a plan. There are briefer versions of this account in Maiuri (1977) and De Vos (1982). In his study of wall construction at Herculaneum, Ganschow (1989) mentions the house only occasionally. The special character of the house (a multiple-family dwelling) is explored in several studies (Van Aken 1943, Packer 1971, McKay 1975, Clarke 1991, Wallace-Hadrill 1994). Other publications discuss the objects that were discovered in the house (Tran Tam Tinh 1971, Bisi Ingrassia 1977, Scatozza Höricht 1986; 1989A, Budetta/Pagano 1988, Conticello De Spagnolis/De Carolis 1988 and Mols 1994). The shop (III 15) is included in Gassner's account (Gassner 1986), and Orr (1978) mentions two *lararia* that were found in the house.

Plan and rooms (Pls IV, V)

The lot has three entrances: no. 13 gives access to the upper storey, no. 14 leads to the living quarters on the ground floor, and no. 15 is the wide opening at the front of *taberna* 10. On the ground floor there is an unlit room (1) to the right of the entrance, which extends under the wooden staircase (entrance 13) and was presumably used as a storage room. The long *fauces* (14) leads to a small hall (3) which is completely open on the west side facing the courtyard (4). Off the hall is a room (2) which must have been a *cubiculum*, judging from the wooden bed that was found there. On the south side of hall 3 is the entrance to room 8, which, together with the adjacent rooms 9 and 7, was one of the service rooms of *taberna* 10. The workshop (room 7), with its work-bench, was well lit by a large window in the north wall, looking out across courtyard 4. In this courtyard there is a basin for rain water and a well. In room 5, off the courtyard, there is an opening to the cistern that formed another part of this water-collecting system. Here there is also a staircase leading to part of the upper storey. The poorly-lit room 6 behind room 5 was presumably used for storage. There is a large living room (11) to the west of rooms 5 and 6. The long, narrow corridor 15 leads to a working area (12/13), which was partly roofed (room 12). In the northeast corner were the toilet and the drain from the upstairs toilet.

The upstairs rooms that formed part of the main house were on the west and south sides of the courtyard. The staircase in room 5 led to the landing (13), which gave access to bedrooms/living rooms 1 and 2. Room 1, in which there was a bed, was lit by a small window onto the *atrium* of the Casa dell'Erma di Bronzo (III 16). There were two beds and a large cupboard in room 2. Finally, a long corridor ran from the hall (14) to the latrine at the back of the house.

In the independent apartment at the front of the upper storey, there is a landing (12) at the top of the stairs from entrance 13, with a window looking out over the courtyard. In the southeast corner there is a built-in cupboard. A small vestibule (11), with a large west-facing window, gave access to living room 3. This room and the next room (4), were lit by small windows in the south wall looking out over the *atrium* of the Casa dell'Erma di Bronzo. To the north of this room there was a kitchen (10), with an oven in the southwest corner. Corridor 8 led to a balcony (7) over the street at the front of the house. Alongside the corridor was a small storage room (9). The balcony gave access to two more living rooms: room 6, on the north side, is relatively small, while the other room (5), on the west side, is the largest in the apartment. Two beds and a *lararium* were found here, so it may well have been the family's living room and bedroom.

Wall construction

Maiuri (1958: 408-410) has discussed in detail the fact that most of the interior walls in this house are in *opus craticium* (mostly in combination with posts in *opus latericium*). Half-timbering was a cheap and fast building method, which Vitruvius criticised because it was not stable or permanent (Vitruvius II, viii, 20). The reeds that can be seen on the west wall of the courtyard formed the bottom layer of the wall-plaster. Maiuri provides little information about the structure of the other walls: the exterior walls and several of the rooms are constructed in earlier techniques, but he does not identify them. Ganschow (1989: 115, 133) has found that *opus craticium* in Herculaneum occurs in combination with *opus latericium* and *opus incertum* types C, D and C/D. The only example he cites from the Casa a Graticcio is the pillars in *opus latericium* in the *fauces*. It has also been found that the pillars supporting the balcony were in *opus latericium*, and the pillars in the west wall of the courtyard were restored in *opus vittatum mixtum*.

Floor and wall decoration
The floors on the lower storey are all relatively plain. Five rooms (6, 8-10 and 15) have a floor of beaten earth, while rooms 1-3, 5 and 14 have floors of plain *opus signinum*. Only room 4 has a slightly more luxurious floor of *opus signinum* with marble *crustae*. In the remaining rooms (7, 11 and 12) the floors can no longer be identified. Less has survived on the upper storey. Practically the entire floor surface was put in during the restoration of the house after it was excavated. The original *opus signinum* seems to be preserved in rooms 1, 2 and 14 only.

Only two of the rooms on the ground floor (1 and 15) have no trace of wall plaster. In all the remaining rooms traces of wall decoration are still visible, but only in rooms 7, 9 and 11 can the paintings be analysed in any detail. These rooms have red areas in the main zone, which mostly form part of Fourth Style panel decorations, although Maiuri (1958: 414) suspects that the remains in room 11 are Third Style.

Upstairs, red was also the main colour on monochrome walls (rooms 1 and 4) or in panel decorations of the Fourth Style (rooms 2, 5 and 6). Rooms 9 and 10 are decorated with a simple scheme of red bands on a white ground, imitating stone blocks; in room 10 this layer has been applied on top of an older decoration of red lines on a white background.

Inscriptions
In the 18th century, on 9/1/1741, the following unintelligible text was discovered on the north wall of the courtyard: 'CAMPAN SPCVNDVS FVPLVS AXBVCIDSFRIOCAPHOXNEMI'. On 28/3/1928 it was recorded as: 'IPANSECVNI EVPI VS IXADSERIOETTIOINIML'.[167] On the upper storey, two inscriptions were found on the west wall of room 1: 'VASILEVS HABITAT / PVTELIS IN CASTRIS AVGVST../ SV.. VALERI..' (CIL 10502) and 'EX SE..TVCON / SVL..VVCA / ..E ICA / MANSI SOLVS' (CIL 10503).[168] CIL 10501, from the west wall of room 2, reads 'MANSI SOLVS X SC' and is probably related to the second inscription from room 1. The interpretation is that a certain Basilius lived in Puteoli in the Castra Augusta, while the writer himself had to remain in

---

[167]   CIL 10478 (= Della Corte 1958: 241 no. 3). For the 18th-century version see Ruggiero 1885: 61; Strazzullo 1982: 162; Pannuti 1983: 201.
[168]   Della Corte 1958: 242 nos 4-5; Solin 1973B: 272 (CIL 10502).

Herculaneum *ex senatus consulto* (Della Corte 1958: 242-243 no. 4, 5, 8). On the same wall of room 2 were the following inscriptions: 'LAGVNAS' (CIL 10500); and 'IDIBVS IANVARIVS / MYSTAGOGVS DOCENS / GEBEVM ET ETOEN / LVCIAN.. VICI..' (CIL 10499).[169] On an amphora found in the *taberna* (10: entrance 15), there was an indecipherable reference to the consul ('CAESAR..'); on another was the name 'MAXI(mus)', which occurs elsewhere in Herculaneum (CIL 10720, 10791; Della Corte 1958: 263 nos. 282-283, 281). Two jugs from the ground floor had 'M F' inscribed on them and an amphora was labelled 'NETV' (CIL 10748, 10861; Della Corte 1958: 246 no. 33-34). Finally, the name 'Philad(e)lp(hi)a Cn(aei) Octavi fili(a)' was inscribed on a block of black marble that was found in the apartment on the upper storey (III 13).[170]

Published finds
The house is particularly interesting because of the large collection of furniture that was preserved in it: a bed (room 2) and a wooden table or work-bench (room 7) were found on the ground floor, and seven beds, three marble tables and three wooden cupboards on the upper storey.[171] Upstairs there were also two wooden *lararia*, in rooms 2 and 5. The one in room 2 contained several statuettes, some of Oriental origin[172]. The other shrine contained a wooden ancestor-portrait (Maiuri 1960: fig. 489; Budetta/Pagano 1988: 34-35 no. 8). In addition to the jugs and amphorae, other finds on the ground floor included a windlass (room 4) and upper half of an *oscillum*.[173] Remains of lime were found in several basins in room 13. On the upper storey, there were three terracotta lamps and two spindles in room 3 (Bisi Ingrassia 1977: 93 type IX H₂), and a wooden cupboard in room 2 which contained several objects of bronze, terracotta and glass. More such objects were discovered throughout the house and the garden[174], including a bronze oil lamp[175]. Another of the wooden cupboards from the upper storey contained a chain. Inside a wall-cupboard

---

[169] Della Corte 1958: 242 nos 7 and 6; Tran Tam Tinh 1971: 92 no. 65; Solin 1973B: 276.

[170] See especially Maiuri 1958: 418 fig. 356; Guadagno 1978: 152 no. 51. Catalano (1982: 959) suspects that this 'Octavia Philadelphia' owned the entire house. A different interpretation is given by Della Corte (1958: 244 no. 18).

[171] Maiuri 1958: 407-420 gives a good account of the finds in this house. This section is based largely on his information. See, however, the more detailed description of Mols 1994: 154-161 Cat. 2-5, 197-199 Cat. 27, 217-220 Cat. 35-36, 250-251, 253-255.

[172] I.e. Harpocrates and Isis-Fortuna; see Tran Tam Tinh 1971: 69 no. 24, 56 no. 3, 66 no. 17, and especially Budetta/Pagano 1988: 40-49 no. 11-15.

[173] See Maiuri 1958: 352 for a picture of the windlass. Cf. also Jansen 1991: 151-152. The *oscillum* fragment was found on 20/10/1927 in room 13, not on the upper storey.

[174] Nos E147, 148, 148A, 151 (16/2/1928), 153, 157 (17/2/1928) and 174 (18/2/1928) were found on the upper storey - see Scatozza Höricht 1986: 31, 36, 37, 42, 49, 55, 57. Presumably E154 was also found here (Scatozza Höricht 1986: 56 Cat.124). E64-67 were found in the garden on 19/10/1927; E324 (3/10/1928) and E215 (17/4/1928) were discovered in other places in the house - see Scatozza Höricht 1986: 45-46, 58 and 62 respectively.

[175] E238 (25/4/1928) - Conticello De Spagnolis/De Carolis 1988: 187 no. 125.

were coins, beads and a gem, and more beads were found on the floor.[176]

Building history

Maiuri (1958: 414) reports that room 11 was unfinished at the time of the eruption: it was not roofed, but there were still remains of earlier wall decoration in the Third Style. The lime remains in the basins in room 13 and the unplastered layer of reeds on the courtyard wall also suggest that construction was not complete in 79. The room at the back (12/13) was a later addition to the house; according to Maiuri (1958: 58, 269) the back wall of this room was built against an existing partition. However, Ganschow (1989: 171-172) has shown convincingly that the wall in the Casa a Graticcio was the original partition, and the wall on the other side, in the Casa dello Scheletro, was added later when the *nymphaeum* was built (see above § 5.2). It is not known when this division of the original lot III D took place. In any case it must have occurred before 62, because there is evidence for repairs of earthquake damage.

Ganschow also modifies Maiuri's claim that the *opus craticium* and the changes to the Casa a Graticcio almost certainly date from after 62 (Maiuri 1958: 74). Certainly an analysis of the structures in which *opus craticium* is found suggests that it was used most extensively when repairs were being carried out after the earthquake; but the possibility cannot be excluded that it was also used before 62. The technique is described by Vitruvius, and therefore may have been in use as early as the Augustan period (Ganschow 1989: 133).

Although the building history of the house cannot be reconstructed in detail from the information above, it is possible to indicate provisionally three phases of building activity. In the first phase, presumably when the town was first being built, the house was built in its original form. The two houses on either side of the Casa a Graticcio, the Casa dell'Erma di Bronzo and the Casa del Tramezzo di Legno, also date from this period. However, they have not been subject to as many changes as the Casa a Graticcio. A reconstruction of the original appearance of the Casa a Graticcio will be given below. For the moment it is sufficient to note that it must have been very similar to the Casa dell'Erma di Bronzo.

In the second building phase part of lot III D, on the other side of the central axis of the *insula* (Pl. IV, no. 12/13), was added to the Casa a Graticcio. From the building history of the Casa dello Scheletro, and particularly the details of the construction and decoration of the *nymphaeum* (§ 5.2), it seems most likely that this change in ownership happened at some time in the first half of the 1st century AD. At the same time room 11 was made smaller to allow for the construction of corridor 15.

In the third building phase the layout of the house was dramatically changed by the construction of several new internal walls in *opus craticium*. At the same time an upper storey was added, creating two apartments, each with its own staircase. This remodelling must have taken place at some time after the acquisition of rooms 12 and

---

[176] E162; E177, E386; E359, E360, E353-357 respectively - Scatozza Höricht 1989A: Cat. 191; 139, 41; 192, 11.

13. This can be deduced from the fact that the toilet on both floors is in room 12/13: when the upper storey was added, the toilet was put directly above the toilet on the ground floor, so that a single drainage system would suffice. It is possible that this construction was part of the same phase as the work described above, which was still unfinished in 79. This, in turn, would mean that the upper storey was constructed and the entire ground floor renovated after 62. If this was indeed the case, the third building phase was not completed by 79. However, it is equally possible that the major changes to the house were made prior to the earthquake, and that the work being carried out in 79 was only repairs. Both these explanations are plausible. If the reconstruction took place before 62, four periods can be distinguished: 1) initial construction; 2) annexation of room 12/13; 3) reconstruction of the house in *opus craticium*; 4) repairs following the earthquake of 62. However, if the reconstruction occurred after 62, the last two periods can be regarded as one and the same.

Metrological analysis of the Lower Storey (Pl. IV)
The house is almost the same size as the Casa dell'Erma di Bronzo, 27' (746-756 cm) wide and 73.5' (2046.5 cm) long. On this side of the *insula* the 'external' length of the houses (including the back wall) is 75'. A metrological analysis of the house shows that the length was divided into several strips. Some of these are part of the original layout and others were created during the last construction phase. In the 'original' strips the Oscan foot (27.5 cm) was used, while a Roman foot of 29.6 cm was employed in the later ones.

The first strip, which includes *taberna* 10 and room 1, originates from the earliest building phase. The side walls of the *fauces* were later replaced by thinner walls in *opus craticium*, which changed the width of the rooms, but the depth of the strip remained unchanged at 13' (356-358 cm). The internal depth of the rooms is therefore 10'O (272-274 cm). The width of room 1 was 7'/7.5', and room 10 was 12'/13' wide. The *fauces* (14) is 5.5'O or 5'R (149 cm) wide.

The next strip includes rooms 2 and 9. Its internal depth is ca. 10'R (287-292 cm). The rooms are the same width as rooms 1 and 10: room 2 is 7.5'O (210/213 cm) and room 9 is 12.5'O (349.5 cm). The last strip before the courtyard, consisting of rooms 3 and 8, is 7.5'R (217-227 cm) deep. Room 8 is 13'O wide (359/362 cm) and room 3 is 13'R across (383.5/388 cm).

The second and third strips are not part of the original design of the house. It is highly likely that the space occupied by rooms 2, 3, 8 and 9, and the corridor between 2 and 9, was originally the *atrium*. It measured 20'O (551 cm) in length (= rooms 8 and 9 added together) and 27'O (752 cm) across (= the width of the house).

As in the neighbouring Casa dell'Erma di Bronzo (lot III I), there are three strips at the back of the house: the first includes workshop 7 and courtyard 4, the second is made up of rooms 5 and 6, and the last strip consists of the luxurious living room (11). These strips correspond respectively to the *tablinum* (4), room 7 and room 8 in the Casa dell'Erma di Bronzo.

The courtyard and room 7 are 12'O (331-335 cm) deep, not including the west wall. Room 7 is square: its width is also 12'O (331.5/332.5 cm). However, the basin in the courtyard is 7.5'R x 10'R (219/198 x 291/295 cm). Rooms 5 and 6 have internal depths of 10'O (269-281 cm) and are both 10'R across (289-301 cm). The largest living room (11) is 14'O (387/392.5 cm) deep and 21'R (620/623 cm) wide. This left ca. 3'R (83/85 cm) for the width of corridor 15.

The area at the back of the house (room 12/13), which was originally part of another lot, is 19'O (521/522 cm) deep. It is possible that this was the space left over after 50'R had been appropriated for the extension of the Casa dello Scheletro (including the back wall of the *nymphaeum*). The principles behind the internal division of 12/13 are unclear, except that the basins in the southwest corner were designed to occupy a square space (10'R x 10'R or 288/296 cm).

Design of the Lower Storey (Pl. IV and fig. 10)
It is still possible to reconstruct something of the original design of the Casa a Graticcio, which must have been virtually identical to that of the Casa dell'Erma di Bronzo (cf. Pl. VI). On the side nearest the street there was a strip with rooms on either side of a *fauces*, which had a total depth of 13'. Apart from the addition of *opus craticium* and a wooden staircase, this strip has changed very little over time; it was very similar to the present rooms 1 and 10.

In contrast, the *atrium* area was subject to major changes. It was divided into four rooms (2, 3, 8 and 9) and a corridor (western part of 14) by partitions in *opus craticium*. Originally the *atrium* measured 20' x 27'. The depth was divided into ca. 10'R for the eastern rooms and ca. 7.5'R for the western ones; the widths of the new rooms are based on the existing rooms along the street.

The strip containing the courtyard (4) and room 7 corresponds to the *tablinum* strip of the Casa dell'Erma di Bronzo. It is possible that the long corridor leading to the back of the house (15) is original and corresponds to corridor 6 next door. If this is the case, in the original layout of the Casa a Graticcio the *tablinum* would have covered the area of the courtyard and part of room 7, and the rest of room 7 would have been a side room next to it. However, the position of the well in the courtyard could be an indication that the side room was on the north side, rather than the south, as the side room in the Casa dell'Erma di Bronzo also has a well-head. In that case, the arrangement of the rooms in the *tablinum* strip may have been the same as in the neighbouring house. If so, the *tablinum* would have been where the courtyard is now, with a corridor to room 11 along the south side. The depth of the strip up to and including the back wall was presumably 15'.

Rooms 5 and 6 are similar to the room behind the *tablinum* in the Casa dell'Erma di Bronzo. The depth of this strip was 11.5', including the wall that divides it from room 11; its original width can no longer be determined. Finally, room 11 is comparable to the large room (*oecus* 8) at the back of the Casa dell'Erma di Bronzo. Room 11 is 14' long and was once 27' wide, before the construction of the corridor that led to 12/13.

Therefore the Casa a Graticcio was originally divided into strips as follows (see fig. 10):

I	(*fauces*)	13'
II	(*atrium*)	20'
III	(*tablinum*)	15'
IV	(room 5/6)	11.5'
V	(room 11)	14'
	total	73.5'

The sizes of the strips in the Casa a Graticcio and the house next door are slightly different (see § 5.5), but they still appear to be related. In strip I an internal depth of 10' was taken as a base unit, and twice this unit was taken as the depth of the *atrium* (strip II). 15' was reserved for the *tablinum* (strip III). The ratio of the depth of the *tablinum* to the depth of the *atrium* was therefore 3:4 (15' x 20'). The internal depth of strip IV is 10', while the width and length of the last strip (V) are almost in the ratio 1:2 (14' x 27').

Metrological analysis of the Upper Storey (Pl. V)
The dimensions of the back rooms on the upper storey are largely dependent on the layout of the ground floor.[177] Therefore room 1 is 10'O (278/282.5 cm) deep, the same as the room below it (6). Room 1 is 7'R/7.5'R (209/218 cm) wide. Room 2 is also very similar in size to the room below it (7): it is 12'O (332.5 cm) long on the north side (measured between pillars). The other sides, where the walls are in *opus craticium*, are slightly longer: 13'O (359.5/366.5 cm) in the south and west, and 12.5'O (342.5 cm) in the east. The landing (14) is 10'O wide (274/279 cm) and 5'R/5.5'R long (146.5/163 cm). Finally, corridor 13 is 2.5'R wide and slightly deeper than room 1 at 11'O (303/305 x 70/77.5 cm).

The apartment at the front of the house has a more independent layout; here too, however, the position of the supporting pillars was crucial to the allotment of space. As a result the widths of rooms 3 and 4 are the same as those of rooms 8 and 9 on the ground floor: room 3 is 7.5'R (219 cm) wide and room 4 is 10'R (286/292.5 cm). Rooms 3, 4 and 5 are all about 14.5'R (426 cm) long, which means that the internal length is 14'R (417-420 cm) in rooms 3 and 5, and 12'R (358.5/362.5 cm) in room 4. Room 5 is 10'R/11'R (288/317 cm) deep.

The balcony (7) is 6'R wide and 17.5'R long (175/186 x 520/521 cm). The remaining space on the north side is 7.5'R (220 cm), so it may be assumed that a width of 25'R was the starting-point for the construction of the upper storey. Room 6 was designed as a square (7.5'R x 7.5'R), but the southern dividing wall was put inside it, so that the available width was only ca. 7'R (213/218 x 220/225 cm). Corridor 8 is almost as long as the balcony (17'R or 508 cm), and ca. 3'R (85.5/94 cm) wide. The small storage space (9) is 3'R/3.5'R by 8.5'R (92.5/105 x 246.5/250 cm), and the kitchen (10) is 6'R by 9.5'R (171/175 x 283.5/285 cm). The module used for

---

[177] Because not all of the upper storey has been maintained properly, it was not possible to obtain measurements for the upstairs latrine and the corridor that led to it.

the length of the rooms on the south side (14'R) is repeated as the length of corridor 11 (up to and including the fireplace); the corridor is 3.5'R (96/103 x 409/412 cm) wide. The hall (12) is the same width on the west side as room 6, almost 7.5'R (216.5 cm), but on the east side the hall is a little wider (227.5 cm); it is 9'R long (257.5/263.5 cm).

Design of the Upper Storey

The fact that the design of the upper storey was heavily dependent on the design of the ground floor makes it less coherent in many places. Only in the apartment at the front was it possible to divide up the space more or less independently. Here it can be seen that the available width, determined at 25'R, has been divided on the basis of a ratio of 3:7, which works out at 17.5'R for the rooms and the connecting passageway on the south side, and 7.5'R for the strip on the north side. The width and length of the balcony are in the ratio of 1:3 (6'R x 17.5'R). In room 4 the ratio of width to length is 5:6 (10'R x 12'R), while it is 5:7 (10'R x 14'R) in room 5. Finally, a ratio of 1:1 (sides of 7.5'R) was taken as a starting-point for the small room (6) in the north-east corner.

5.5. Casa dell'Erma di Bronzo (III 16) (Pl. VI)

This house is on the east side of *insula* III, and has an entrance (16) on *cardo* IV; it was uncovered between October 1927 and May 1929. It takes its name from the bronze portrait-herm that was found on the upper storey. The house occupies a single building lot (III 1) with a rectangular plan (2020 cm long and 753 cm across), which is largely unchanged. It has 10 rooms, centred around a Tuscan *atrium*; most of the rooms adjoin the *atrium*, apart from a separate living room at the back of the house. The upper storey at the end nearest the street could be accessed by means of a wooden staircase in room 2; the living area above the back part of the house could be reached from room 5 by means of a staircase that was partly built in stone.

Select Bibliography
Van Aken 1943: 39 (*tablinum*); Maiuri 1958: 243-247, figs 190-192, pl. VIII; Peters 1963: 116 (corridor 6); Maiuri 1977: 29; Catalano 1982: 959; McIlwaine 1988: 3.822; Ganschow 1989: 44-46, 103, 168, 322, 326; Mols 1994: 53, 254; Wallace-Hadrill 1994: 199.

This house has received little attention in the literature. Maiuri (1958) provided a general account, a description and a plan; a short summary can be found in Maiuri 1977. Ganschow (1989) refers to the types of wall construction in the house and briefly mentions a number of wall decorations. Peters (1963) also discusses some of the wall paintings.

Plan and rooms (Pl. VI)
The plan is that of the 'classic' *atrium* house (with the *fauces-atrium-tablinum* line), but of the type that does not have side rooms off the *atrium*. The entrance-passage (1) to the house, which leads to the *atrium* (9), is off-centre. As a result the living rooms (2 and 3) on either side of the *fauces* are different sizes. Presumably the original residential character of room 2 was changed when the staircase to the upper storey was installed against the wall nearest the street. Most of the rooms at the front and the back of the house could be accessed from the *atrium*. The *impluvium* is in the centre of the room, and thus is to one side of the axis that runs from the *fauces* to the *tablinum* (4) opposite and room 7 beyond. Room 5 was a service room with an opening for a well or a cistern; it also contained another staircase, leading to the rooms at the back of the upper storey. On the other side of the *tablinum* is a corridor (6) to the back of the house. Directly behind the *tablinum* is room 7, entered from corridor 6. It is not clear what this room was used for. As there are no seams at the juncture of the wall and floor, this could have been an open-air room which could not be damaged by rainwater. In Maiuri's opinion (1958: 247) it was a light-well at one time and was later roofed. However, it seems unlikely that it was ever roofed, because it not only had a large opening for a window to the *tablinum*, but also a small skylight above the door to corridor 6. If it was a closed room, the position of the skylight

would be illogical. The room at the very back of the house (8) was also the largest; judging from its secluded position and the remains of rich decoration that were discovered there, it must have been an *oecus*.

Wall construction

Maiuri (1958: 243) points out that the house is very old: it has tufa posts, high doorways and a tufa *impluvium* in the Tuscan *atrium*, the most complete example preserved in Herculaneum. As well as additions and repairs in *opus latericium*, he distinguishes a rough type of *opus incertum* made of lava and tufa, and an *opus quasi-reticulatum* dating from the Republican period. In Ganschow's typology (1989: 44-46) these two techniques are the irregular *opus incertum* D generally found in repairs, and a coarse variant of *opus reticulatum* B or *opus incertum* C. Ganschow (1989: 322) regards this building as an example of one of the Samnite houses in Herculaneum which 'später mit jüngeren Mauerstrukturen größtenteils oder vollständig neu aufgebaut wurden'.

Floor and wall decoration

This house has very plain floors, mostly in *opus signinum*. The simplest type, without fragments of marble, is in rooms 7 and 9. The decorated type appears in rooms 3, 4, 6 and 8. The floor of room 2 is a layer of beaten earth; in the remaining rooms the floors can no longer be identified.

There are wall paintings in every room of the house, but in rooms 2 and 5 the paintings are too faded to be legible. The paintings in the remaining rooms have panel decorations in the main zone on red (room 6), blue (room 4), green (room 7) or black (room 9) backgrounds. In rooms 1 and 3 these are combined with architecture painted in perspective on a black or white ground. Remains of the ceiling-plaster can be seen in *tablinum* 4 (with relief mouldings) and corridor 6 (flat). In the upper zone in corridor 6 are painted small pastoral (sacro-idyllic) scenes (Peters 1963: 116). Finally, room 8 still contains parts of its original decoration of large landscapes with figures on a black background. Remains of this decoration are still visible on the west wall (Maiuri 1958: 246, fig. 192).

Maiuri regards the paintings as Third Style and dates them before AD 62. (Maiuri 1958: 244). However, it should be taken into account that the style of wall paintings in Herculaneum is often different from those in Pompeii and more archaistic.[178]

Inscriptions

There was a *titulus pictus* on the façade, an appeal to support the emperor (it is not known which emperor): '[Muni]cip[es, i]uvate / Caesarem' (CIL 10479); scratched underneath was CIL 10504: 'MOECIA CC' (Della Corte 1958: 248 no. 47, 48; Solin 1973B: 276 [10479]). The name 'ΚΟΓΙΤΑΤΟΥϹ Ϲ' was written on the north wall of

---

[178] Cf. Allroggen-Bedel 1979; Moormann 1987: 133-134; Strocka 1987: 36; Manni 1990: 139, 142. Ganschow (1989: 103) also regards the paintings as Third Style: in his opinion the decoration in room 4 is post-Augustan, applied on a wall in *opus incertum* C.

the *fauces* (CIL 10505; Della Corte 1958: 244 no. 16). On the southern *anta* of the *tablinum* there was an inscription that read 'SE(xtus) PORCIVS / S S' (CIL 10506) and 'IVSTAR' (CIL 10507).[179] Several more inscriptions have not yet been recorded in the CIL.[180]

Published finds
Few finds were made in the Casa dell'Erma di Bronzo. The most interesting are the bronze candelabrum and the herm with a bronze portrait, which was discovered upstairs in the room above room 3. The portrait clearly has Julio-Claudian character-istics; Maiuri (1958: 244) thinks it is a likeness of the owner. Mols (1994: 53, 254) reports also the find of a chair and a cupboard.

Building history and metrological analysis (Pl. VI)
Maiuri (1958: 244) regards the wall decoration as Third Style, but dates the pave-ments to the last phase of the Republican era: according to him there is coarse *opus signinum* in the *fauces* and *atrium*, and decorated *signinum* (so-called *opus segmen-tatum*) in rooms 3, 4, 7 and 8. As was mentioned above, Ganschow (1989: 322) regards this as one of the houses that were rebuilt on the old plan using new materials. Presumably the only changes to the original layout were in and around the *tablinum*.

The house can be divided up into five strips, on the same principle as the Casa a Graticcio (cf. fig. 10). The Oscan foot of 27.55 cm was used here. The house is 2021 cm, or 73.5' long. Like the neighbouring house, it has an 'external' length of 75'. The width of the house is 749-756 cm, or 27'.

The front strip of the house consists of the *fauces* (1) and living rooms 2 and 3. The depth of this strip is the same as the length of the *fauces*: 359/360 cm, or 13'. Because the walls to the west and east are 1.5' thick, room 2 is 10' x 8' (273.5/278 x 216/218 cm), while room 3 is 10' x 11' (273 x 310/320 cm). The *fauces* is 6' (162/168 cm) wide.

The second strip is the *atrium* (9), which has no side rooms and therefore occupies the whole width of the house, 27' (752-756 cm). The *impluvium* is in the exact centre of the room. The basin is 8.5' x 8.5' (233/235 x 236/239 cm), so rather over 9.25' (259-262 cm) is left over on either side. Of course, a division of 9' - 9' - 9' would have been ideal. The *atrium* is 21' long (576/578 cm) and once again, the *impluvium* is positioned as symmetrically as possible. The distance from the east wall to the basin is 6' (163/169.5 cm), and from the basin to the *tablinum* it is 6.5' (172.5/174 cm); the division of space thus works out as 6' - 8.5' - 6.5' (ideally: 6' - 9' - 6'). The east end of the *atrium* has been divided in multiples of 3' (from south to north): 3' - 6' - 6' - 9' - 3' (82/165/168/249/89 cm). The division of the west end would seem to be (from south to north): 4'- 4' - 10'R - 3.5'R - 4.5'R (114/109/294/105.5/130.5 cm).

---

[179] Della Corte 1958: 248 nos 49, 51. Catalano (1982: 959) takes Sextus Porcius to be the owner of the house.
[180] I.e. Della Corte 1958: 244 no. 17 (cf. Guadagno 1981: 161 no. 152); Della Corte 1958: 244 nos 19-20; Della Corte 1958: 245 no. 24.

The total depth of the two front strips is 34' (13' + 21'). The remaining 39.5' is divided into 3 strips of 14', 10.5' and 15'. The third strip is formed by the *tablinum*, which has a length of 14' (384.5 cm), and a width of 13' (355.5/359.5 cm). The *tablinum* originally had an open front, which was later narrowed to 10'R (294 cm) by the addition of a short wall in *opus latericium* on the south side.

Strip IV is occupied by room 7, behind the *tablinum*. This strip is 10.5' deep (289 cm), which is half the length of the *atrium*. The internal depth of the room is 8' (220/221 cm), and the width 13' (363 cm). Finally, the luxurious *oecus* (8) at the back of the house covers strip V. It is 15' (406/418 cm) deep and 27' (749/751 cm) wide.

Room 5 on the north side of the house and corridor 6 on the south side do not play a role in the allocation of space. It is not clear whether room 5 was always as long as it is now. It is possible that room 7 once extended right up to the north wall of the house. If this was the case, room 5 must have been part of the third strip, and must have been the same depth as the *tablinum*. As it is, now the room measures 7.5' x 21.5' (203/205 x 596/598 cm). Corridor 6 is 24.5' x 4' (666.5/674.5 x 114/118 cm).

Design

As in the neighbouring Casa a Graticcio, the area of the Casa dell'Erma di Bronzo can be divided into five strips:

I	(*fauces*)	13'
II	(*atrium*)	21'
III	(*tablinum*)	14'
IV	(room 7)	10.5'
V	(room 8)	15'
	total	73.5'

These strips all appear to be in simple ratios to one another, based on the length of the *atrium*, strip II. The ratio of strip I to II is 13:21, which are consecutive terms in the Fibonacci series.[181] The *atrium* and the *tablinum* (strips II and III) are in the ratio of 3:2 (21:14). Strip IV is half the depth of strip II (10.5:21) = 1:2. The ratio of strip V to strip II is 5:7 (15:21).

The dimensions of the rooms are also related to one another. In room 2, for example, the ratio is 4:5 (8' x 10'). In the *atrium* the principal dimensions are 21' x 27' (7:9); at the east end the division of space is based on multiples of 3'. In room 7 the Fibonacci series is reflected again in a ratio of 8:13. Finally, room 8 is 15' x 27', which is a proportion of 5:9.

---

[181]   The ratio of consecutive terms in this arithmetical series approximates the Golden Section in whole numbers. Cf. e.g. Peterse 1984: 16; Peterse 1985: 48 n. 36. For a more elaborate explanation see Käppel 1989: 90-91.

5.6. Casa dell'Ara Laterizia (III 17) (Pl. VII)

This house, which is on the east side of *insula* III and has an entrance on *cardo* IV, was uncovered between October 1927 and May 1929. It takes its name from a brick altar that was built into the back wall at the southwest corner. The house is narrow and rectangular, and consists of one original building lot (III J). Its total depth is 2019 cm, with a width of 550-555 cm. On the ground floor there are 11 rooms, grouped around the covered *atrium* or *atriolo* at the front of the house, and around the courtyard (11) at the back. A staircase in the narrow room 6 led to the upper rooms above the rear part of the house. There was also a living area above the rooms on the west side of the *atrium*, which may have been reached by means of a wooden staircase in the *atrium* (Maiuri 1958: 422).

Select bibliography
Maiuri 1941B: 406, 408, fig. 1; Maiuri 1958: 420-422; Packer 1971: 56, 61 (n. 69, 71), pl. CIII, figs 293-295; Orr 1978: 194 nos 8-9; Catalano 1982: 959; Tran Tam Tinh 1988: 125 n. 15; Ganschow 1989: 165, 166, 168, 173, 202 n. 10, 322; Mols 1994: 256; Wallace-Hadrill 1994: 199.

General overviews of the house, including a plan, can be found in Maiuri (1958) and Packer (1971). The wall construction and house type are discussed in Ganschow (1989). The altar is referred to in a study by Orr (1978), and is also used as a parallel for the 'Christian shrine' on the upper storey of the Casa del Bicentenario (V 15) (Maiuri 1941B).[182]

Plan and rooms (Pl. VII)
According to Maiuri (1958: 420) and Ganschow (1989: 165; Abb.10), the building is based on a simple design and has largely retained its original layout. The house is somewhat unusual because the *fauces* (10) is not in the centre of the façade, but at one side. It leads to an *atriolo* (9), a covered *atrium* or hall, lit by a skylight and a window in the north wall, which separates the house from the Casa dell'Erma di Bronzo. Next to the entrance there is a living room (1), which is fairly wide relative to the rest of the house because of the unusual position of the *fauces*. Given its location in the house, this could have been an *oecus*.[183] On the west side of the *atrium* there are two small rooms on either side of a corridor (8), which leads to the back of the house. The niche in the north wall of room 3 indicates that there was once a bed here. This is also the case in the room behind it (4). This *cubiculum* opens off the second hall (7), which provides access to the courtyard (11) in the southwest corner. Several rooms on the ground floor and the upper storey are lit from this courtyard. The upper storey could be accessed by way of a staircase (with a latrine underneath) in a narrow

---

[182] See also De Kind 1990: 201-202, 263.
[183] See the examples in *insula* V, summarised by Van Binnebeke (1991).

room (6) on the north side of the house. In the southwest corner, against the back wall, there is a brick altar under a lean-to roof. The room in the northwest corner (5) is lit by a window looking out onto the altar. On the other side of the court a window at eye level provides light and air to a room in the Casa dell'Albergo (III 18, room 43).[184]

Wall construction
Ganschow's fig. 10 (1989: 183) shows that there are still several old types of construction in the house (*opus incertum* A and B, posts in *opus quadratum*). The walls were all built in these older techniques apart from some parts of rooms 1, 5 and 6. This is an important observation, which could contribute to a reconstruction of the building history and the original design not only of this house, but also of the building lots to the west, southwest and south. Also worth noting are two tufa quoins in the façade, which presumably mark a doorway that has been closed off.

Floor and wall decoration
There are very few remains of floor and wall decoration in this house. The floors are very simple, paved in decorated or plain *opus signinum*. The *fauces* (10) is the most striking, because the *opus signinum* is decorated with fragments of marble, and the vaulted ceiling was stuccoed and painted. In the other rooms there are no remains of wall decoration (rooms 1, 5 and 6), or only sparse traces of plaster (rooms 3, 4, 7-9, and 11). Room 2 is the only place where parts of the original wall painting can still be observed, but they are too faded to determine the style.

Published finds
Several amphorae were discovered on the upper storey of the house (room above 3). A mortar was also found, which is now in room 2. Mols (1994: 256) reports the find of a carbonised bed in room 3.

Inscriptions
To the right of the entrance, above the bench for visiting clients, was an inscription: 'AMATA ALCIMVS' (CIL 10508 = Della Corte 1958: 241 no. 1). On the south wall of the *fauces* was found CIL 10509 (= Della Corte 1958: 252 no. 86) the name 'Q. VETIVS' (= Q. Vettius).[185] Another family name familiar from Pompeii was written on one of the amphorae found on the upper storey: 'CAECILIO IVCVNDO' (CIL 10768/10905 = Della Corte 1958: 247 no. 44). CIL nos 10760, 10797 and 10824 (= Della Corte 1958: 247 nos 42, 43, 41) are letters inscribed on the other amphorae that were found upstairs.

---

[184]   The opening of a well or cistern that is indicated on Maiuri's plan (1958: fig. 359) near the entrance to the courtyard could not be observed during our campaigns (1985-1990), because this part of the house is now used as a storage area for building materials.

[185]   From this V. Catalano (1982: 959) concludes that 'Quintus Vettius' was the last owner of the house.

Building history
Maiuri assumes that the house must once have been more luxurious than its present state would suggest: the roof overhung the street along the entire frontage of the house, the façade and podium had paintings on them, there was a stuccoed vault in the *fauces*, with a still life in the lunette, and at the back of the house there was a brick altar. Maiuri even goes so far as to suggest that the house was still being decorated at the time of the eruption. As was mentioned above, Ganschow also discusses the Casa dell'Ara Laterizia; he uses it primarily as a parallel for the southern part of the Casa dello Scheletro (Ganschow 1989: 165-166, 168, 173, 183 Fig. 10). He concludes that the design of both lots was the same; the layout of the Casa dell'Ara Laterizia has remained largely in its original state, except for the rear part of the house, which has been subject to a number of alterations.

Maiuri (1958: 420) compares the layout of the Casa dell'Ara Laterizia with that of the Casa del Sacello di Legno (V 31). This comparison is surprising: the only similarities between these houses are, first, that they both lack rooms along the sides of the *atrium*, which is not uncommon in houses at Herculaneum; and second, that they both have a corridor running between two living rooms. However, in the Casa del Sacello di Legno this corridor is a later addition.[186]

Metrological analysis (Pl. VII)
What the Casa dell'Ara Laterizia and the Casa del Sacello di Legno do have in common is the simplicity of their design and the fact that their layout was well thought out. The Casa dell'Ara Laterizia is relatively narrow (550-555 cm), and is one of the group of narrow lots mentioned above (§ 4.2). Lengthways, it is one of the so-called 'external' houses, on plots that only measure the full 75' if the thickness of the back wall is included. In Oscan feet (of 27.5 cm), the total depth of 2019 cm works out at 73.5' and the width is 20'.

Both the length and the width were divided systematically. First a strip of ca. 15' (404 cm) was staked out for the *fauces* and room 1; because the walls are 1.5' thick, the internal depth is 12' (here: 322 cm). Next, 17' (464-467 cm) was reserved for the depth of the *atrium*, and 13' (359.5-368 cm) was staked out for the row of rooms to the west; this produced a round figure of 10' (275-281 cm) for the internal depth of rooms 2 and 3. The total depth of the row of rooms and the *atrium* is 30', or double the depth of the *fauces* and room 1. A similar length was left over for the rear part of the house, including the rear wall; the internal length is 28.5' (30' - 1.5' for the wall). This was divided into 15' for hall 7 (413 cm) and 13.5' for courtyard 11 and room 5 (371 cm). In other words, the available area including the back wall was divided exactly in half.

The division of the house lengthways must have been roughly 15' - 30' - 30'(28.5'). The subdivision of these strips into smaller areas produces the scheme 15' - 17' - 13' - 15' - 15'(13.5'). This division will be discussed in detail below, along with the division of the width.

---

[186]   See De Kind 1993: 222; Van Binnebeke/De Kind 1996: 207.

Room 1, in the front strip, was ca. 12' x 14' (322 x 382/391 cm). The dimensions of the *atrium* (9) are 17' x 20' (464/467 x 550/555 cm). The east side is divided (from south to north) into 5' - 1.5' - 3.5' - 10', and the west into 3.5' - 3.5' - 1.5' - 3.5' - 1.5' - 3.5' - 3'. Room 2 has internal dimensions of 7.5' x 10' (205/210 x 277/281 cm), and room 3 is slightly narrower: 7' x 10' (189/196 x 275/279 cm). The width of corridor 8 decreases towards the west: ca. 3.5' x 13' (88.5/103 x 364/368 cm).

From his study of the wall construction, Ganschow concludes that the original layout of the rear part of the house was subject to a number of changes. The most important of these was the construction of the west wall of room 4, which was presumably put in to create room 6 (staircase/latrine) at the time when the upper storey was built at the back of the house. Originally room 4 must have extended as far as the east wall of room 5, where Ganschow found wall structures dating from the earliest building period in Herculaneum (1989: 183 fig. 10). The room with the altar may have been a closed room and hall 7 an open courtyard. In any case, if room 4 is reconstructed up to and including the east wall of room 5, it must have been 14.5' deep and ca. 6.5' wide (400 x 180.5/187 cm). Its present length is just over 10' (281/285 cm).

The hall (7) is 341 x 413 cm, which is 12.5' x 15'; the aim was a ratio of 5:6. Presumably room 5 was designed to be 10' x 13' (276/282 x 358 cm), but it must be noted that the room with the altar (11), like room 4, was not part of the original plan: the dividing wall with room 5 does not date from the earliest period. The present width and depth (255 x 365.5 cm) are best regarded as 9' x 13.5'. The original division of the width probably remained unchanged: each of the rooms takes up half the area, one without and the other with the dividing wall.

Design
On examination, the design of the house seems to be very logical and clear. The available length of 75' (external measurement, so including the back wall) was divided into 3 strips on the basis of the ratio 1:2:2. A strip of 15' was reserved for the *fauces* and the room at the front, and then two strips of 30' were staked out, one for the *atriolo* and the room behind it, and one for the rear part of the house around the hall. Both of the larger strips were divided further: the first strip was divided unequally into 17' for the *atriolo* and 13' for the living rooms, while the other was divided equally into two areas of 15', although only 13.5' remained for the rear part, because of the 'external' length of the house.

The width was also divided up logically. The front strip was divided on the basis of a ratio of 1:3; a width of 5' was staked out for the *fauces*, so that 15' remained for the living room. The rear strip was divided equally into 10' for one room, including the dividing wall, and 10' for the other, excluding the dividing wall. In the area between the last strip and the *atriolo* the ratio was 2:3. The width of the northern row of rooms is about 8'; the width of the hall measures 12'.

5.7. Casa dell'Atrio a Mosaico (IV 1-2) (Pl. VIII)

This house occupies the entire southwestern quarter of *insula* IV. It was excavated between June 1929 and August 1930. There are 2 entrances on *cardo* IV, a back door at no. 1 and the main entrance at no.2, which leads into the *atrium* with mosaic floor after which the house was named. This is a large house (maximum depth 5230 cm and maximum width 2435 cm); it is almost rectangular, but is slightly wider at the south end than at the north. In the north area, which includes the *atrium*, is an old rectangular building lot, oriented west-east (lot IV A). The rest of the house is at a lower level than the *atrium* area, and has a less traditional layout, oriented north-south. There is a garden with several living rooms around it. The house has a total of 30 rooms, including the garden and the *loggia*. There was an upper storey at the front of lot IV A (accessed by means of a staircase in room 2), above the north, east and west sides of the *cryptoporticus* (staircase in room 8)[187], above the southern rooms (staircase, part wooden, at the southwest corner of the *cryptoporticus*), and above room 15/16 (perhaps reached by a staircase in room 15).

Select bibliography
Van Aken 1943: 60, 77, 78, 91; Maiuri 1951B; Maiuri 1958: 280-302, figs 223-239, pls XXVII-XXVIII; Peters 1963;127 (*exedra* 9), 149 (room 14); Tamm 1963: 145, fig. 47 a, b; 203; Neuerburg 1965: 51 (*tablinum* 5); Cerulli Irelli 1971; Tamm 1973: 59; Scagliarini 1974: 22-24, fig. 20, 40; McKay 1975: 51-54, fig. 17-20; Elia 1976: 89-90; Maiuri 1977: 27-29; De Vos/De Vos 1982: 270-272; Catalano 1982: 959; Barbet 1985A: 261; Barbet 1985B: 80 (room 17), 127 (room 23), 198 (room 13), 226 (room 7); Guidobaldi 1985: 200, 211, pl. 9.3, 15.5 (*tablinum* 5); 207, pl. 12.5 (room 12); Scatozza Höricht 1986: 25 Cat. 1; Moormann 1988: 105-106, Cat. 025/1-025/5; McIlwaine 1988: 37, 55; 3.524, 3.637, 3.645, 3.651, 3.758, 4.18, 4.28, 4.31, 4.39, 4.48, 4.54, 4.62, 4.68a, 4.70, 4.77, 5.34, 9.135-136, 9.199, 9.309; Tran Tam Tinh 1988: especially 3, 22, 24, 92, 137, 147; Conticello de Spagnolis/De Carolis 1988: 143 No. 98-99, 144 No. 107, 203 No. 134, 219 No. 139; Ganschow 1989: 126 n. 17, 273, 298 n. 9, 326; Manni 1990: 134-135; Clarke 1991: 235-243, figs 141-146; De Kind 1991B (*exedra* 9); Mols 1994: 177-178 Cat. 14, 256-257 figs 94-96; Wallace-Hadrill 1994: 18, 19, 31, 51, 55, 56, 82, 127, 199, 204, figs 2.1-2, 3.23, Pl. 8.

The most elaborate and well-illustrated account is Maiuri's (1958). McKay (1975), Maiuri (1977) and De Vos (1982) have provided shorter descriptions. The architecture of the house is discussed by Maiuri (1951B), Tamm (1963; 1973), Neuerburg (1965), and Wallace-Hadrill (1994) among others. Tran Tam Tinh (1988) discusses the relationship between this house and the neighbouring Casa dei Cervi, and the original location of several fragments of wall paintings that were removed in the 18th century. A complete overview of the wall paintings, as well as a short summary of the

---

[187]   Maiuri (1958:282) only lists upper rooms above rooms 6 and 7.

building history, is given by Cerulli Irelli (1971). The wall paintings are also discussed in studies by Peters (1963), Scagliarini (1974), Elia (1976), Barbet (1985A; 1985B), Moormann (1988), Manni (1990), Clarke (1991), and De Kind (1991B). Ganschow (1989) deals briefly with the wall construction. A discussion of the *opus sectile* floors can be found in a study by Guidobaldi (1985). Several individual finds are mentioned by Scatozza Höricht (1986), Conticelli De Spagnolis/De Carolis (1988) and Mols (1994).

Plan and rooms

Lot IV A forms a separate area of the house, with a traditional layout at the front: the *fauces* (1), which has a room on either side (2 and 3), leads to an *atrium tuscanicum* (4) without side rooms. The original *tablinum* was converted into a so-called *oecus aegyptius* (5), a large reception room with a high central nave (with skylights) and two aisles (Maiuri 1951B).

The layout of the rest of the house was oriented north-south, and designed to take advantage of the views of the garden and the sea. The garden (30) is surrounded by a broad *cryptoporticus* (25-27) on 3 sides, with a narrower corridor on the east side (28-29), leading to the row of living and service rooms 6-11. Rooms 6, 7, 10 and 11 are more-or-less closed bedrooms, while room 9 is a luxurious open-fronted living room (*exedra*) facing the garden. To the north of this *exedra* there is a staircase (8) with storage space underneath. Presumably room 15 was also used as storage room and staircase. It is in the southernmost part of the house, which was built at a slight angle to the north-south axis of the garden area, following the line of the city wall, on which the *loggia* (21) and the terrace (22) were built. The central focus of this southern area is a large room (12), which is flanked by smaller living rooms (13, 14, 17 and 18). The back entrance (IV 1) gave access to corridors 19 and 20, which lead from the garden to the *loggia*. Presumably rooms 15 and 16 once formed a similar passage on the east side; later this passage was divided into two service rooms by a partition wall. At the east and west ends of the terrace there are small sheltered living rooms (23 and 24) of the type known as *diaetae*.

Wall construction

In his study of wall structures in Herculaneum, Ganschow (1989: 32) presents the Casa dell'Atrio a Mosaico as an example of a house where too many walls are covered with plaster to allow its building history to be completely reconstructed. Maiuri (1958: 282) also provides little relevant information about wall construction. In his opinion the wall construction is so homogeneous and coherent, apart from several repairs which he dates to the Claudian and early Flavian periods, that it is impossible to identify any changes or adaptations. In contrast, Cerulli Irelli (1971:12) lists several walls where earlier types of wall construction can be observed. There is *opus incertum* A, for example, in the podium between the columns of the *cryptoporticus* (an example of recycling). *Opus incertum* B can be observed in the north wall of *tablinum* 5, in a dividing wall between the *atrium* and the *cryptoporticus*, in the eastern outer wall (only in rooms 6 and 8), and in the remains of an earlier wall, which originally ran east-west, ca. 35 cm thick, just south of room 11. She finds it hard to explain the large area of *opus incertum* (she does not mention the exact type of construction) in the upper part of the dividing wall between room 13/14 and room 15, above 1.5-2 m of *opus reticulatum*.

Two walls in this house are in *opus craticium*: the dividing wall between rooms 13 and 14, and the partition wall mentioned above, between rooms 15 and 16. Both of these were put in to divide a single room into two smaller ones. Finally, the structure of the eastern wall of the house is interesting. One of the Bourbon tunnels, to the south of room 11, revealed that the wall is double for the entire length of room 15. It appears that an extra stretch of wall was built to the west of the existing wall, which was covered with black plaster. This double wall narrows towards the south, and ends opposite the doorway from room 14 to room 16.

Floor and wall decoration
Most of the rooms in the house have pavements, of various types, in a good state of preservation. There are only three exceptions: no original floor could be identified in room 2, while the garden area (30) did not have an artificial floor, and the floor in the staircase area (8) presumably consisted of a layer of beaten earth. Of the remaining rooms, eight have *opus signinum* floors. The more luxurious type of *signinum*, with marble *tesserae*, can be found on the terrace (22) and in rooms 3, 15 and 16; parts of an older floor in *opus signinum* are preserved in rooms 15 and 16, with two black mosaic bands around the edge. In the north and west corridors of the *cryptoporticus* (25 and 26), and in corridors 19 and 20, the *opus signinum* was decorated with panels in *opus sectile*. The floors of the various living rooms are even more luxurious. It is possible to identify a certain hierarchy of luxury in these rooms: the richest type of pavement (*opus sectile*) is found in the central salon-like rooms 9 and 12, while the rooms on either side have 'plain' white mosaic floors (6, 7, 10 and 11 in the east wing; 13, 14, 17 and 18 in the south). The two small *diaetae* in the south corners (23 and 24) have pavements in *opus sectile*. The most important circulation areas have floors of *opus sectile* combined with black mosaic: this type of floor is found in *loggia* 21, and in the east and south corridors of the *cryptoporticus* (27-29). Finally, the *fauces* (1) and the *atrium* (4) in the northern part of the house have white mosaic floors with various black patterns.[188]

G. Cerulli Irelli (1971) has discussed the wall decoration in detail, so a brief summary will suffice here. Like the floors, the wall decoration is well-preserved. Only in rooms 3 and 8 are no traces of wall paintings visible. In rooms 2, 15-17, 19, 21 and 22 there are only the remains of the lower layers of plaster. The other rooms all have Fourth Style wall decorations, with the usual scheme of panels and fields and architectural elements in the main zone. There are differences in colour as well as in refinement and detail. In the eastern living rooms (6, 7, 10 and 11), and in the *fauces* (1), the main colour is red. Side room 18 and *diaetae* 23 and 24 are predominantly

---

[188] For the distinction of systems in the floor and wall decoration see also Scagliarini 1974: fig. 40 and Clarke 1991: 235-243.

yellow, while white is the main colour in the *oecus aegyptius* (5) and in room 14, and black in rooms 12, 13, 25, 27 and 28. *Exedra* 9 deserves special mention, because here there is a richly decorative painting of mythical scenes in panels on a blue background and, probably, portraits on the east wall (De Kind 1991B). The highly elaborate decorations in room 14, *diaeta* 23, and the northern corridor of the *cryptoporticus* (25) are strikingly luxurious. Also of interest is room 7, where there is a painted ceiling (Cerulli Irelli 1971: fig. 7-8), and the east wall of the garden (30), where various panels with still lives and figured scenes are painted in the top zone.

Inscriptions

A graffito on the west wall of room 7 read 'ARA' (CIL 10518; Della Corte 1958: 250 no. 65a). Three inscriptions were recorded in corridor 15 (?): 'A EPICVRVS / SI ES VTICA', 'SAB(inus)' and 'Q.V.R.' (CIL 10515-10517).[189] In the northern part of this corridor, where it extends into the south wing of the peristyle, was the word 'FELICES' (CIL 10514; Della Corte 1958: 248 no. 52). An inscription in the eastern area of the peristyle (no. 25 or 28) read 'AM(andus?)/SVRVS/IANVA(ri) VA(LE)' (CIL 10513), while part of the Greek alphabet was written in the northern area (CIL 10708).[190] On an amphora found in the garden were the letters 'Q.B.EV' (CIL 10763; Della Corte 1958: 250 no. 68). Fish sauce (*garum*) was kept in an amphora from another part of the house: 'GAR.PRAI / A.LV' (CIL 10735; Della Corte 1958: 248 no. 53). There were also two jugs with inscriptions: one, from an upstairs room, was labelled 'LIQVAMEN OPTIMVM' (CIL 10744, 10746; Della Corte 1958: 271 no. 390, 249 no. 62). Two inscriptions on amphorae are important for establishing chronology: one (CIL 10718; Della Corte 1958: 250 no. 67) refers to the consulate of A. Vitellius and L. Vipstanus Poplicola in 48 ('VITELLIO VIPSTANO COS'); and the other (CIL 10719; Della Corte 1958: 250 no. 69) reads 'IMP III COS', which is probably part of the title given to Vespasian in his third year as consul (AD 71). Other texts on amphorae are recorded as CIL 10730, 10731 and 10776 (Della Corte 1958: 249 no. 60-61, 250 no. 66). The name 'Q. IVNIO SECVND(o)' (CIL 10780) was written on an amphora, and 'CLEME(n)S / PVTICVS' (CIL 10852) on a small lamp.[191] Not included in the CIL are the letters '..CH..' on a piece of white marble (Della Corte 1958: 249 no. 56; Guadagno 1981: 161-162 no. 152).

Published finds

In addition to the amphorae, jugs and terracotta lamp mentioned above, five bronze lamps were found in the house: four in the eastern part of the upper storey, and another in the peristyle.[192] In the kitchen (3) was a lead trunk. Furthermore a *mille-*

---

[189] Della Corte 1958: no. 249 no. 64a, 64; Solin 1973B: 276 (CIL 10515).

[190] CIL 10513: Della Corte 1958: 249 no. 63; Solin 1973B: 276. CIL 10708: Della Corte 1958: 250 no. 65.

[191] Della Corte 1958: 249 no. 59, 57. Catalano (1982: 959) regards Q. Iunius Secundus as the owner of the house.

[192] E485-488 (31/31930), E445 (13/8/1929): Conticello De Spagnolis/De Carolis 1988: respectively 144 No. 107, 143 Nos. 98-99, 219 No.139, 196 No. 127.

fiori glass is recorded, as well as a wooden table and fragments of beds.[193]

Building history
Maiuri (1958: 281) writes that the house was composed of two parts: an old *domus* with a traditional, closed plan (entrance no. 2, the old *fauces*) and a new, differently oriented and more open area (with a side entrance at no. 1). It was only later, perhaps after 62, that both parts were assimilated to make a single house. Because the considerable difference in floor level between the two areas was not adjusted, the house does not form a coherent whole. Cerulli Irelli (1971: 11-13) corrects Maiuri's claim that the house was made up of only two core areas. She points out that *opus incertum* can be seen in several different places throughout the house (see above) and thinks it possible that these are the remains of an older house, which may have extended from what is now the north boundary up to and including the *cryptoporticus*. If that is indeed the case, only the rooms that looked out across the sea were added later. But, according to Cerulli Irelli (1971: 12): 'il tutto mi sembra molto incerto'. In any case, the house in its present state is made up of several independent units: the *atrium/tablinum*; the *viridarium* with the *exedra* and the adjoining bedrooms; and the southern room around the terrace, including the large room and the *diaetae*. Ganschow (1989: 326) suspects that the house, like other large houses on the periphery of the town, was built in the Augustan period, when the empire was at peace and the economy was thriving.

From the existing architecture and the remains of the decoration, it is possible to form a somewhat impressionistic picture of the different phases in the development of the house, which necessarily excludes precise dates. During the first building phase, in the Samnite period, there were at least three houses, and probably four, on the site of the Casa dell'Atrio a Mosaico, oriented east-west. The only one of these houses surviving is on lot IV A, and forms the northern *atrium* area of the present house. This lot still remains in its original state as far as the back of the *atrium*; the rear part of the house was reconstructed in a later period. It is not clear exactly when the houses were demolished and the large north-south oriented complex was built, with the garden and *cryptoporticus*. The dimensions of this part of the house suggest that the remodelling took place before the Augustan period (see below).

Furthermore, it seems likely that the southern part of the house was built in two phases: the garden area was built first, perhaps at the same time as the *tablinum* on lot IV A was reconstructed; and in the second phase the house was extended further to the south, over the city wall, and rooms 12-24 were added. This is suggested by the different orientation of the rooms in the southernmost area, and the fact that different units of measurement were used in the two areas. As mentioned above, Cerulli Irelli also suspects that the southern rooms were built later than the rooms around the garden. Moreover, the rooms in the terrace area were altered at some time after their

---

[193] *Trunk*: Maiuri 1958: 284. *Glass*: E475 (5/12/1930) - Scatozza Höricht 1986: 25 Cat. 1. *Furniture*: Mols 1994: 177-178, fig. 94-96, 256-257.

initial construction. The floors in rooms 13-16 show clearly that the present layout is not original. The black borders of the mosaic floor in room 13 are not parallel to the walls. The *opus craticium* partition between rooms 13 and 14 and the difference in level between the rooms are further evidence of an alteration to the original plan; Maiuri (1958: 299) assumes that this took place in the Flavian period. It is even more difficult to reconstruct the original appearance of rooms 15 and 16. In the southern part of room 15 there are two black mosaic bands about 10 cm wide in total, framing a fine *signinum* floor made with a low proportion of crushed ceramic, but with many *tesserae* of white marble. On the north side these 2 bands extend across the entire width of the room and form a boundary with a coarser *signinum* floor at a higher level, which was made with a higher proportion of ceramic. The same bands emerge from under the extra wall built against the east wall of the lot halfway along the depth of the room. From this point they run south under the *opus craticium* wall, make a right-angled turn in room 16 at the point where the double east wall finishes, and end near the centre of the room. From this it may be concluded that rooms 15 and 16 once formed a single larger room with a pavement in *opus signinum* with black mosaic borders, which was largely obliterated by the west wall and the extra wall in the east. A plausible reason for the double wall is that the builders were planning to construct an upper storey, but would not, or could not, use the common outer wall as a foundation.

In sum: initially, there were three or four houses oriented east-west. In a second building period, two or three of the southern houses were reconstructed to form a garden area with rooms, and amalgamated with the northern house. Perhaps the *tablinum* in the northern lot was also altered at that time. Subsequently the terrace area was added, and changes to this area were made later, presumably when the upper storey was being built. It is highly likely that the second building phase took place in the Republican period, at the same time as the grand reconstruction of the Casa dell'Albergo (see section 5.1), and, if Ganschow's hypothesis is correct (1989: 216), the construction of the *viridarium* in the southern part of the Casa dei Cervi (see § 5.15). This assumption is supported by the dimensions of the *cryptoporticus*. The extension of the Casa dell'Atrio a Mosaico and its neighbour onto terraces over the city wall could then be dated several decades later, in the early Imperial period. Further alterations in this area must have taken place at some time in the 1st century AD.

Metrological analysis (Pl. VIII)

Lot IV A
The total depth of lot IV A is 77.5' (2130.5 cm), and it is 30' (824-828 cm) wide. The Oscan foot used here is 27.5 cm. As usual, it has a row of rooms along the street, whose depth equals the length of the *fauces* (19'; 520.5-527.5 cm). The internal depth of these rooms is 16' (room 3: 437.5/448 cm) or 15.5' (room 2: 422/428 cm), and they are 11' (300 cm) and 8' (219 cm) wide.

The *atrium* is 30' across (824-835 cm), with a length of 32' (870-875 cm). The *impluvium* is 10' (272 cm) long and is 11' (300-302 cm) away from the east and west walls; it is only 9' (248 cm) across, and presumably 10'R (281-295 cm) away from the north and south walls. As the *impluvium* is at a slant, its original disposition may have changed. Perhaps the basin was originally staked out with a width of 10', so that the dimensions would work out at 10' - 10' - 10'.

The *tablinum*, which was converted into an *oecus aegyptius*, has an internal length of 25' (685-696 cm). The central nave is 17.5' (474-482.5 cm) wide; the side-aisles are 5' (130-142 cm) across, and the intercolumniation is ca. 6.5' (173.5-188 cm).

The garden area

The total length of the *cryptoporticus* on the west side of the garden, up to the dividing wall with corridor 20, is 100' (2733 cm). The foot measure that was used here is 27.4 cm. On the east side, room 9 was built exactly in the centre of the row of rooms: the distance from the north wall of corridor 25 to the north wall of room 9 is 1010 cm, while the distance from the southernmost point of the room up to and including the south wall of corridor 27 is 1000 cm. The total internal width, including the row of rooms, works out at 76'O (2080 cm). The depth of the row of rooms is 14.5' (392-397.5 cm), so that their internal depth is 13' (359-366.5 cm). The dimensions of the rooms are as follows:

room 6: 13' x 15.5' (366/366.5 x 422/428.5 cm);
room 7: 13' x 15' (364.5/366.5 x 413/416.5 cm);
room 8: 14.5' x 4' (392/397.5 x 110/117 cm);
room 10: 13' x 12.5' (359.5/361 x 346/347.5 cm);
room 11: 13' x 13' (363-365.5 cm)

Room 9 has an external width of 21.5' (589 cm). Its internal design was probably a square, but it now actually measures 18' (500-503 cm) by 18.5' (512.5 cm). The length of the *cryptoporticus* is 61.5' (1681.5 cm) on the north side and 63.5' (1743 cm) on the south, as the house becomes wider towards the south. The width of the west corridor (26) varies significantly; at the north end it is 11.5' (315 cm) wide, the same as the north corridor (25); in the middle it is 10.5' (295-299 cm) across; and at the south end it is 12' (327 cm) wide. The width of corridor 27 diminishes towards the east, from 17.5' (489 cm) at the west end to 13.5' (376.5 cm) at the east end.

The terrace area

The theory that the terrace area was built at a later date than the garden area is supported by the units of measurement used: this part of the house was staked out using the Roman foot (29.8 cm). This is most obvious from the dimensions of room 12, which is 25'R (735/748.5 cm) across and 30'R (876/890 cm) deep. The large openings to the garden and the terrace were made 10'R (297.5 cm) and 12'R (357 cm) wide respectively. The total length of the *loggia* (21), from east to west, is 80'R (2353/2355.5 cm); the width is 11.5'R (331.5/337 cm). Rooms 17 and 18, to the west of room 12, together form a square with sides of 23'R (677-686.5 cm), divided into 8'R/9.5'R (240/280 cm) for room 17 and 12.5'R (371/379 cm) for room 18. The length of corridor 20 is the same as the side of the square (23'R), and its width is

4.5'R/5'R (137/148 cm). The dimensions of the remaining rooms are as follows:

room 13: 14.5'R x 13'R (425.5/428.5 x 377/386 cm);

room 14: 14.5'R x 16'R (425/425.5 x 452.5/475.5 cm);

room 15: 4.5'R/5.5'R x 27'R (133/159.5 x 794.5/796 cm);

room 16: was a space left over in the planning;

corridor 19: 4'O (110 cm), 11'R x 36'R/38'R (326 x 1063/1120.5 cm);

diaeta 23: 10'R/10.5'R x 10.5'R (289/307 x 312/313 cm);

diaeta 24: 10'R/10.5'R x 11'R/11.5'R (292/317 x 326/340 cm).

Finally, the terrace (22) is 83'R across on the south side, equal to the width of the house (2460 cm), and 57.5'R (1704 cm) on the north; its depth is 9.5'/10.5'R (283.5/308 cm).

Design

In each of the three areas of the house it is possible to reconstruct the principles which governed the design. In the *atrium* area the basic principles of the design are similar to those used elsewhere in Herculaneum for the layout of *atrium* houses without side rooms. The lot is divided into several strips; the strip at the front, with a *fauces* in the centre, is 19' deep. The *atrium* is 32' deep, and the *impluvium* is placed so that the space is divided symmetrically into 11' - 10' - 11'. As in the Casa del Tramezzo di Legno, the distance from the street to the edge of the *impluvium* is exactly 30', which forms a square area at the front of the house with sides of 30'. Presumably a width-ways division of space into 10' - 10' - 10' was intended but later changes to the house altered this layout. Several ratios were used in the construction of the new room that replaced the *tablinum*, the *oecus aegyptius*. Its total depth is 25', and its width 30', a proportion of 5:6. The ratio of the width and length of the central nave is 7:10 (17.5' x 25'), while the ratio of the width of the nave to that of the aisles is 7:2 (17.5' x 5'). For the aisles, the ratio of width to length is 1:5 (5' x 25').

An area of 76' x 100' (almost 3:4) was set aside for the garden area. About 1/5 of this area (14.5') was reserved for a row of rooms on the east side. The central room in this area, *exedra* 9, was exactly in the middle of the row of rooms and was deliber-ately built as a square of 18' x 18'.

The terrace area, which dates from a later period, was made wide enough in the south to allow for a *loggia* of exactly 80'R. The large reception room (12) was the central focus in this area, and measured 25'R x 30'R, a ratio of 5:6; its doorways were 10'R and 12'R wide.

5.8. Casa dell'Alcova (IV 3-4) (Pl. IX)

This fairly large house in *insula* IV has two entrances on *cardo* IV (3 and 4). No. 3 leads to part of the upper storey, while no. 4 is the entrance to the living quarters on the ground floor. According to Maiuri (1958: 59) the house was uncovered between November 1928 and December 1929[194], and it was named after the *alcova*, a bedroom with an *apsis* (24) at the back of the house. It is made up of two lots, IV B and IV C; at some stage room 16 of the Casa della Stoffa was added to IV C, while several rooms in IV B were incorporated into the Casa dei Cervi. The house is deepest in lot C: 2954.5 cm (3430 cm including room 16); in lot IV B the maximum depth is 2560 cm. Both lots were originally ca. 782 cm wide, so the total width of the house is 1604 cm. The house has 26 rooms on the ground floor. As was mentioned above, there was also an upper storey. The front part of the upper storey (above rooms 2, 5, 18 and 19) projected over the street, and had its own entrance at no.3. Another area at the front could be reached by a staircase in room 4. A staircase in room 9 gave access to the upstairs rooms at the back of the house.

Select bibliography
Van Aken 1943: 60; Maiuri 1958: 388-393, figs 320-329; Peters 1963: 156 (room 19); Tamm 1963: 163 no. 21, fig. 70 (room 24); Neuerburg 1965: 50 (room 24); Packer 1971: 56-57, 61 (n. 69-70), 62 (n. 75), Pls. CIII-CV, Fig. 296-300; Maiuri 1977: 30; De Vos/De Vos 1982: 272; Barbet 1985A: 226; Barbet 1985B: 33 + fig. 10 (room 19); Scatozza Höricht 1986: 36 Cat. 45, 43 Cat. 73, 60 Cat. 144, Pls XIII, XIV, XXVI, XXIX, XXXV; Moormann 1988: 106-107, Cat. 026 (room 19); McIlwaine 1988: 4.65, 4.68a, 4.117; Tran Tam Tinh 1988: 27, 30, 36, 137, 140; Conticello De Spagnolis/De Carolis 1988: 56 Cat. 21; Ganschow 1989: 38 n. 9, 47, 174 n. 33, 198 Fig. 12, 208-210, 216, 218 Fig. 14, 324; Mols 1994: 161-163 Cat. 6, figs 52-57, 256-257; Wallace-Hadrill 1994: 87, 199, 201.

A general account of the house, with a plan and illustrations, has been provided by Maiuri (1958) and later by Packer (1971). Summaries can be found in Maiuri (1977) and De Vos (1982). For the building history and architecture the following studies are indispensable: Tamm (1963), Neuerburg (1965), Tran Tam Tinh (1988) and Ganschow (1989). The wall decoration is the subject of articles by Peters (1963), Barbet (1985A; 1985B) and Moormann (1988), among others. Several of the finds are mentioned by Scatozza Höricht (1986) and Conticello De Spagnolis/De Carolis (1988). The *biclinium* is dealt with by Mols (1994).

Plan and rooms (Pl. IX)
The original division into lots is still reflected in the layout of the house: lot B is at a

---

[194] However, the dates on which some of the finds were discovered (in the spring of 1932) point to a different or longer period; see below under 'Published finds'.

lower level and consists of several large rooms, while lot C is at a higher level and consists of a succession of connected rooms. The two parts are linked by a large doorway, where the difference in level of ca. 40 cm is bridged by two steps. The rooms on the ground floor can be accessed via the *fauces* (25), which is flanked by four rooms. Rooms 1 and 2 are servants' quarters with low ceilings; room 4 is a plain living-room containing a wooden rack and a staircase, and room 5 was a kitchen, with a latrine for more than one person against the west wall. The latter two rooms could only be reached from the hall (3), which had relatively luxurious wall paintings. The southern part of the house could be reached from this hall, through the doorway mentioned above.

In the southern part of the house, the old lot IV B, there are two clearly separate living areas, one around hall 17, consisting of rooms 18-20, and the other off court-yard 22, with rooms 23 and 24. Room 18 is a living room whose exact function is not clear; it has a relatively low ceiling and a drain to the street. Barred windows looking out onto the street provide the room with light. Room 19 next door, with its luxurious wall decoration, has been built to much the same design. It contained the remains of wooden beds, and must have been a *biclinium*. The large room (20) on the other side of hall 17 was undoubtedly the most luxurious living room in the entire house, but almost all traces of decoration have now disappeared. The area at the back of the house, off courtyard 22, had a more intimate character. This area could only be accessed by means of the long corridor 21/28, which must have had a door, at the point where the corner of courtyard 22 projects into the corridor. Rooms 23 and 24 both have vaulted stuccoed ceilings and predominantly white wall decoration. Room 24 received light and air through a window to 22.

In the northern living area (lot IV C), hall 3 provided access to the open courtyard 26 and to *exedra* 6 on the north side of the courtyard. Further east there was a small *atrium* (7) with an *impluvium* against the north wall. Off this *atrium* is a living room (8) with two windows onto *exedra* 6; it had a lock on the door and luxurious wall decoration. To the east of this is a small room (9), which provided storage space and housed a staircase to the upper storey. Room 10 also opens off *atrium* 7; it contains the opening of a cistern, and was presumably a service room. A living area to the east of the *atrium* was reached via corridor 11 and portico 27. This area includes the living rooms 13 and 14, a store-room (15) on the north side, and a luxurious, secluded living room (16) to the east. All of these rooms received light and air from a small courtyard (12).

Wall construction

The following account of the wall construction in the Casa dell'Alcova is mainly derived from published analyses and unpublished observations by Ganschow. The facade was built in *opus reticulatum A*, and *opus incertum B* can be found in the dividing wall between the two original lots (Ganschow 1989: 47, 58). Many of the internal walls were built in *opus reticulatum B* and *opus incertum C*; some contain *opus reticulatum A* (e.g. between rooms 14 and 15) and have been repaired in *opus incertum D*. Blocked windows or doors can be seen in the west wall of court 26 and in the wall between room 10 and courtyard 12, among other places. The old *opus incertum type B* is still in evidence in several places, including the west wall of room 16, the south wall of room 13 and above the door from corridor 11 to *atrium* 7.

Floor and wall decoration

There are various types of floor in the Casa dell'Alcova. The southern part (lot B) contains the most luxurious pavements; in the northern part (lot C) there is only *opus signinum* and beaten earth. There were earth floors in rooms 2, 4, 5, 9 and 11; the simplest form of *signinum* can be found in rooms 1, 3, 6, 7, 10, 12, 14-16, 22 and 25-27, and a more luxurious version with small *tesserae* of marble in rooms 13 and 19. The richest form of *signinum*, with marble *crustae*, was used in rooms 18, 23 and 24. The long corridor in the south (21/28) has a white mosaic floor, and the hall (17) has a black mosaic with marble *crustae*. The luxurious room 20 was paved in *opus sectile*.

Throughout the house, except in rooms 1, 2, 11 and 21, there is evidence of plaster on all the walls. In most places there are only the remains of plaster, poorly preserved (rooms 5-7, 9, 10, 12-18, 20, 22 and 25-28). For rooms 23 and 24, which are relatively dark, a Fourth Style panel decoration on a white background was chosen, a simple scheme in room 23, and a more complex one with architectural elements in the alcove (24). The *biclinium* (19) is decorated with a similar scheme, but with a red background and rich detail. Part of it is now in the Museo Nazionale in Naples (Moormann 1988: 106). There are also Fourth Style decorations in the northern part of the house. In rooms 3 and 4 the main zone consists of red fields, alternating with architectural motifs. Room 8 received the richest decoration of fields with mythological paintings, alternated with architectural motifs, on a blue ground (Maiuri 1958: figs 324-325).

Inscriptions

On the west wall of room 3 was written the name 'PVRPVRA' (CIL 10480 = Della Corte 1958: 269 no. 368). On a fragment of pottery found in the *atrium* was the inscription 'VII' (CIL 10868). The words 'OLETI' and 'NETV' were written on amphorae found on the upper storey (CIL 10755, 10862 = Della Corte 1958: 268 no. 345, 251 no. 78). Finally, several names and letters were inscribed on amphorae that were discovered elsewhere in the house.[195]

Published finds

As well as the inscribed amphorae, three wooden beds, a bronze oil lamp and, probably, three glass vessels (two cups and a bottle) were also found in this house.[196]

---

[195]   CIL 10753, 10777 ('ICVCR'), 10792 ('MAXSI'), 10811 ('VETTIVS'), 10835, 10840, 10842; Della Corte 1958: 272 no. 395-396, 270 no. 381, 264 no. 293, 248 no. 50, 272 no. 394, 270 no. 382, 264 no. 292.

[196]   One bed was found in room 1 (Mols 1994: 257), the other two (the *biclinium*) are still in room 19 (Mols 1994: 161-163 cat. 6). The glass vessels E756, 761 and 788 were found in the house or its immediate surroundings on 22/2/1932 and 23/2/1932 - Scatozza Höricht 1986: 36, 43,

Building history (see also fig. 9)

As Maiuri has noted (1958: 388-389), the existing house is made up of two separate houses. One of these (IV B) lost a number of its rooms to the Casa dei Cervi; the other (IV C) gained an extra room from the Casa della Stoffa. The two houses differed greatly in character: the longer northern part, built on the axis of the *fauces*, was less richly furnished than the southern part, which was clearly rather grander. Because there are no rooms for commercial use, Maiuri suspects that the two halves of the house belonged to two related families.

More concrete evidence for the building history of the house can be derived from Ganschow's observations about rooms that were added to the Casa dei Cervi (1989: 208-210). First of all, he claims that rooms 11-14 in the Casa dei Cervi must have been part of the Casa dell'Alcova, rather than the Casa della Stoffa as Maiuri (1958: 310) and Tran Tam Tinh (1988: 12) have maintained. The wall between these rooms and the Casa della Stoffa is built in *opus incertum B*, and must date from the earliest building phase in this area of Herculaneum. It formed the original eastern boundary of the Casa dell'Alcova (see fig. 9). When these rooms formed part of the Casa dell'Alcova there was a door from room 12 (Casa dei Cervi) to room 23 (Casa dell'Alcova); corridor 21 (Casa dell'Alcova) continued into room 11 (Casa dei Cervi), and room 12 had a large window with a view of the small courtyard or garden 22 (Casa dell'Alcova). It is not clear how large room 12 was: it is possible that corridor 21-11 may originally have opened into a large single room (now rooms 12 and 28) - in which case the northern room 13/14 was perhaps an inner courtyard that provided light to rooms 12 and 23 -, but it is equally possible that the corridor continued along the east side of room 12 to room 13/14 (which may have had a window onto court 12 in the Casa dell'Alcova). In Ganschow's opinion either layout is possible (1989: 209).

More useful information about this area can be found in a study by Tran Tam Tinh (1988). He writes that the function of room 12 changed a number of times, but that it must originally have formed part of a bath suite, judging by the discoveries made during explorations in the 1970s (Tran Tam Tinh 1977: 46), which included a *tegula mammata* and an older floor equipped with a water drainage system with a terracotta pipe (Tran Tam Tinh 1988: 13-14).

The history of the house can be broadly reconstructed. First of all, two large plots of land were staked out and developed. These lots are referred to in the present study as lots IV B and C. The eastern boundary of both plots was on the line of the present back wall of the Casa della Stoffa. At this time, rooms 11-14 of the Casa dei Cervi formed part of the southern half (IV B) of the Casa dell'Alcova, and room 16 of the northern half (IV C) belonged to the Casa della Stoffa. As the technique used to build the walls was *opus incertum B*, this first building activity must have taken place in the 2nd century BC.

---

60. The bronze lamp is E805 (4/4/1932) - Conticello De Spagnolis/De Carolis 1988: 56 Cat. 21. The house number supplied by Bisi Ingrassia for some terracotta lamps is incorrect (Bisi Ingrassia 1977: 79 type V E, 83 type VII B , 94 type IX I); these came from IV 10-11.

The second phase in the building history of the Casa dell'Alcova presumably saw the construction of a bath suite at the rear of the southern part of the house. It is unlikely that this was part of the original design, as it is thought that bath suites were only built in Campanian houses after ca. 100 BC. There are several examples of bath suites with walls decorated in the Second Style, including the bath in the Casa dell'Albergo (see § 5.1). It is not unlikely that the mid-late 1st century BC. saw a vogue for the construction of bath suites[197], and so perhaps the bath in IV B was also built in this period. It is not clear which rooms were part of this complex or where the *praefurnium* was. The arrangement and design of rooms 22-24 in the Casa dell'Alcova and rooms 11-13 in the Casa dei Cervi are, however, very similar to other private bath suites known today.

It is possible that this bath suite was built after the two lots were combined into one house. However, it is most likely that the amalgamation took place at the same time as rooms 11-14 of lot IV B were added to the Casa dei Cervi and room 16 of the Casa della Stoffa to lot IV C. Ganschow (1989: 208-216) has demonstrated convincingly that the annexation of rooms 11-14 must have taken place in the early Imperial period, at the same time as the complete rebuilding of the rest of the Casa dei Cervi. The Casa della Stoffa was also rebuilt in this period. There seems to have been a major reorganisation of houses and land at this time, with some householders transferring ownership of rooms or possibly even whole properties. Perhaps further investigation of the wall construction will throw more light on this. If it is true that the amalgamation of lots IV B and C was the result of such a change in ownership, this stage in the development of the Casa dell'Alcova must have taken place in the Augustan period. The use of *opus reticulatum A* for the new facade required by the addition of the southern house seems to point to the same period (Ganschow 1989: 135-136).

In the next phase the available space was re-divided. Most of the alterations seem to have taken place in lot IV B, which thus acquired a rather more elegant character than the northern part of the house. In the northern area (lot IV C), on the other hand, the remains of older types of construction in the north walls of the connecting rooms 7 and 11 indicate that the existing structure was retained. A separate entrance from the street to the upper storey was built in one of the rooms next to the old *fauces*. Blocked windows and doors in lot IV C indicate that the available space was reorganised over the years. Finally, the fact that some walls were repaired in *opus incertum D* suggests that the Casa dell'Alcova was damaged in the earthquake of 62.

Metrological analysis (Pl. IX)
Originally lot IV B was as long as IV C (without room 16). The length, measured in IV C, is 2954.5 cm, or 107.5', based on an Oscan foot of 27.5 cm. Both lots are 28.5' across (771-788.5 cm). Like lot IV D (Casa della Fullonica), these may be 'external'

---

[197]   Nathalie de Haan (Department of Classical Archaeology - Catholic University of Nijmegen) is
         preparing a study of the private baths in Pompeii and Herculaneum. See De Haan 1993; 1995;
         1996.

lots measuring 30' across including one of the side walls (see also § 4.4.4). Because IV B was subject to drastic changes, its original layout can only be determined by comparison with lot IV C, where, despite later changes to the design which make a detailed analysis of subsequent divisions impossible, the basic pattern can still be seen, starting from the initial division into strips found in so many houses in Herculaneum.

Here too the first strip is made up of a *fauces* with rooms on both sides. The *fauces* (25) is 22.5' (618/628 cm) long and 6' (158.5/168.5 cm) across. The differences in dimensions between the rooms on the north and south sides probably have to do with the construction of the upper storey and the staircase on the south side. The rooms on both sides have an internal width of 10'. It was probably intended that the small rooms at the front would have an internal depth of 7.5' (9' including the front wall) and the larger rooms behind them an internal depth of 10.5' (13.5' including both walls or 12' including only the west wall). In room 1 this layout is still clearly visible: here the dimensions are 7.5' x 10' (200/205 x 270.5/271 cm). Room 4 also seems to have retained its original dimensions of 10' x 10.5'/12' (272/277.5 x 284.5/326.5 cm). Room 2 has been changed slightly and measures 7' x 10' (195 x 277 cm). The kitchen (5) was extended so that it is now 11.5' deep and 10.5' wide on the east side, although the width on the west side remained unchanged at 10' (276.5/286 x 308.5/313 cm).

The second strip comprises the hall (3) and the inner courtyard with *exedra* (26/6), which together measure 30' in depth, including the eastern dividing wall. The hall is 10' deep and is the same width as the house itself, namely 28.5' (271-281 x 782.5/789 cm). The inner courtyard 26 was presumably built in the shape of a square of ca. 17' x 17' (470 x 470 cm). The north side of the *exedra* (6) is 0.5' longer, so that its overall dimensions are 17'/17.5' x 11.5'O/11'R (470/478 x 312.5/324 cm). The entrance from inner courtyard 26 to *atrium* 7 is exactly in the middle of the east side.

Atrium 7 occupies the third strip in the design of lot IV C. Its internal depth is 25' (680.5/682 cm) and it is 17.5' (483 cm) wide. It is no longer possible to determine the original arrangement of the *impluvium*. Rooms 8 and 9 also form part of this strip. Room 8 is 9.5' x 16' (262.5/269 x 434 cm), while room 9 is 7.5' x 11' (209/214 x 302 cm).

The living quarters around courtyard 12 constitute the fourth and final strip. It is 30' deep, including the west wall. This is also the external length of corridor 11, which is 6' wide (831 x 162 cm). Room 13 is 9.5'O/9'R x 12' (268/268.5 x 327 cm), while room 14 measures 10' x 11' (276.5/280 x 300/301.5 cm) and store-room 15 is 4.5' x 9.5'O/9'R (126/127.5 x 268.5/269.5 cm). Courtyard 12 is on the south side alongside the service room 10, whose dimensions could perhaps be seen as 8' x 10.5' (217/225.5 x 286.5/294 cm); the courtyard is a square with sides of 11' (300-304.5 cm). The east portico (27) is 18' long and 6'/7.5' wide (491.5 x 170/204 cm). Finally, room 16, which is not part of the original design, probably measured 15' x 17.5' (417/422.5 x 472/481 cm).

Most of the rooms in lot IV B were probably staked out using a Roman foot of 29.5 cm. The hall (17) is the same width as the original house (28.5'), and is 14.5'R

(773/783.5 x 423/427 cm) deep. The two rooms on the west side occupy a strip of 17'R. This results in an internal depth of 15.5'R, so that room 19 was a square of 15.5 x 15.5'R (450-457.5 cm); although as its east wall does not run quite parallel to the facade, the south side is slightly longer (16'R = 468.5 cm). In room 18 the depth of 15.5'R was combined with a width of 10'R (455/461.5 x 291/295 cm). The large room 20 on the east side of hall 17 was staked out as 20'R wide with an external length of 30'R (591/592 x 888/889.5 cm). The long corridor to the back of the house has a total length of 51'R (1497/1498.5 cm) and is 4.5'R - 5'R wide (132/148 cm). Courtyard 22 was presumably designed in relation to corridor 21/28; the width of this courtyard is 8'R (238 cm), and its total length, including portico 28, is 19'R (558/563 cm). Living rooms 23 and 24 seem to have been designed using the Oscan foot, because room 23 is 11'O x 12.5'O (306/306.5 x 335.5/342 cm), while room 24 turns out to be 13'O x 12.5'O (359-369 x 340.5/344 cm).

Design
The original design of lot IV C is based on the well-known system of division into strips. The relationship between these strips is obvious:

strip I	(*fauces*)	22.5'
strip II	(hall + courtyard, including east wall)	30'
strip III	(*atrium* 7)	25'
strip IV	(corridor 11, including west wall)	30'
	total	107.5'

Strip I and strip II are in the ratio 3:4; strip III and strips II and IV are in the ratio 5:6. The dimensions of all these strips are based on multiples of 2.5', as is the total length of the house. Strip I is 9 x 2.5', strip III is 10 x 2.5', strips II and IV are each 12 x 2.5', and the total length of the plot is 43 x 2.5'. Simple ratios of length and width are also evident in the layout of the rooms, notably room 1 (7.5' x 10' = 3:4), room 4 (10' x 12' = 5:6), *atrium* 7 (17.5' x 25' = 7:10), corridor 11 (6' x 30' = 1:5) and room 16 (15' x 17.5' = 6:7).

When lot IV B was redesigned, it seems that space was initially reserved for a large room (20) measuring 20'R x 30'R (a ratio of 2:3). The available space at the front was divided to create two rooms, one with an internal depth and width of 15.5'R (*biclinium* 19) and another (18) measuring 15.5'R x 10'R.

5.9. Casa della Fullonica (IV 5-7) (Pl. X)

This house on the west side of *insula* IV, with entrances 5, 6 and 7 on *cardo* IV, was uncovered between April 1930 and August 1932. The main entrance is no. 6; the other two openings to the street were shops. The house owes its name to the fact that there must have been a *fullonica* here in the last years of the town's existence. It is not wide (788.5 cm), but it is deep (2618.5 cm), and it occupies a single original lot (IV D), which has probably remained intact. The house has 12 rooms on the ground floor including the shops, grouped around two central circulation areas: a covered *atrium* (9) at the front of the house and a Tuscan *atrium* at the back (8). Traces of an upper storey are still visible above rooms 2 and 12 (entrance 5); it probably extended above rooms 1-5 at the back of the house and rooms 10 - 12 at the front, partly projecting over the pavement. The rooms at the front were presumably reached by a wooden staircase in room 12, but it is not clear how the upper storey was accessed at the rear of the house; the most plausible assumption is that there was a second wooden staircase in the front *atrium*.

Select bibliography
Maiuri 1958: 422-423, fig. 362-364; Moeller 1976: 113; Maiuri 1977: 30-31; De Vos/De Vos 1982: 273; Gassner 1986: 105 (Table V), type C/1 (IV 7); Ganschow 1989: 39, 103, 121 no. 5, 126 no. 16, 272, 322, 323 no.12; Mols 1994: 153, 255; Wallace-Hadrill 1994: 201.

Maiuri (1958) gives a brief description and documentation for the house; De Vos (1982) provides a well-written summary. Gassner (1986) regards shop IV 7 as an example of type C/1, shops with direct access to a living room behind them. In his Appendix I on wool production in Herculaneum, Moeller (1976) mentions the small fulling installation in the *atrium*. Ganschow (1989) points out the significant fact that in this house the type of wall construction can be dated securely because it is covered by First Style paintings.

Plan and rooms (Pl. X)
At the front of the house are two shops, 10 and 12, which are both connected to the house; the *fauces* (11) leads between them to the covered *atrium* (9). The basins in the northwest corner of the *atrium testudinatum* suggest that it was later used as a work-room in the *fullonica* (Moeller 1976: 113). It gave access in turn to living room 1 (the former *tablinum*), room 2 (a store-room) and corridor 3, which leads to the back of the house. In the northeast corner of the *atrium*, above the entrance to service room 2, there is a niche (23 cm deep and 75 cm high) with white plaster and stuccoed pilasters on either side. Corridor 3 leads to the second *atrium* (8), an *atrium tuscanicum*. The *impluvium* is not exactly in the centre, but is positioned to leave more space on the south and west sides. Two cistern openings are still visible near the basin. Four living rooms open off this central room, two on the north side (rooms 4 and 5) and

two on the east (6 and 7). Room 4 was an *ala* or *exedra*, while room 5 was presumably a *cubiculum* (with a stuccoed ceiling - Maiuri 1958: 423). Both of the rooms on the east side (6 and 7) are luxurious living rooms, with stuccoed ceilings imitating coffers and early wall and floor decoration.

Wall construction
Most of the walls are in *opus incertum B*, which dates from the 2nd century BC.; various door-jambs and quoins are constructed in large blocks of tufa (*opus quadratum*). The doorjambs of the *fauces* (11) were clearly put in later: they are in *opus latericium* and *opus vittatum* (northern jamb adjacent to the street). At the back of the house, in the southeast corner of room 6, there is a repair, mainly in *opus vittatum mixtum*, which was described above in connection with the allotment of land in *insula* IV (§ 4.3).

Floor and wall decoration
Most of the rooms in the Casa della Fullonica have *opus signinum* floors. Two (in rooms 5 and 7) have stone *crustae* in them. The others are either plain (rooms 6 and 10), or decorated with small *tesserae* (rooms 1, 4 and 8). Beaten earth floors can be found in rooms 2, 3, 11 and 12. It is not known what the floor of room 9 was made of.
There are remains of plaster throughout the house, but most of it is not well-preserved and a detailed analysis is only possible in four rooms. There were First Style paintings throughout the house; some are still visible in rooms 1, 6 and 7. In room 6 imitation marble with white and yellow veining was painted on the socle, while in room 7 the socle was white. Finally, there is a very faded decoration in room 5, which was presumably a Fourth Style scheme of fields alternating with architecture in perspective.

Published finds
Several amphorae were found in room 12 and on the upper storey above it; some of these, judging by the inscriptions (see below), must have contained Falernian wine. Mols (1994: 255) mentions fragments of a bed, probably found on the upper storey of the house.

Inscriptions
On the facade, near entrance 5, there was a *graffito* 'SATVRNINA[E] MATR(I) VNCVS A.III' (CIL 10519 = Della Corte 1958: 265 no. 307). Inscriptions on three amphorae found on the upper storey describe their contents, namely Falernian wine (CIL 10723-10725 = Della Corte 1958: 265 no. 295-297). A fragment of an amphora that was discovered on the ground floor, in room 12, consists of the name M. Livius Alcimus (not otherwise known in Herculaneum): '(M. LIVI) ALCIMI [HERCL]ANI' (CIL 10787 = Della Corte 1958: 265 no. 298).[198] Another fragment of an amphora

---

[198]   Compare for example CIL 10722, 10784-10786, 10788.

from the same room had a number of indecipherable characters inscribed on it (CIL 10834 = Della Corte 1958: 265 no. 308).

Building history
Maiuri (1958: 422) and Ganschow (1989: 126) both regard the house as one of the oldest and most characteristic pre-Roman houses in Herculaneum. It is also important to note that the early type of *opus incertum* occurs here in combination with remains of First Style wall decoration. According to Maiuri the prestigious character of the house declined in the last years of the town's existence, when it came into the possession of a merchant family, who used the front part for commercial purposes and the rear part as a residence. Other traces of alterations may have been the result of such a change in ownership, including the addition of the upper storey, the construction of wide entrances from the street in rooms 10 and 11, the walling-up of the front of the *tablinum* (1), and the construction of additional doorposts in rooms 2 and 3.

The house is important evidence for the original allotment of land in *insula* IV. Together with lots IV B and IV C in the neighbouring Casa dell'Alcova (IV 3-4), the Casa della Fullonica (lot IV D) forms a group of very long lots that clearly extend across the central axis of the *insula* - if there was one. Ganschow has also commented on this (1989: 323).

It is likely that the house was once even longer: traces in the back wall of room 6 indicate that there was a doorway to a room at a lower level, in what is now *taberna* IV 17-18. Assuming that differences in level were neither necessary nor desirable in the initial construction of the house, it can be deduced that the connection with the room behind the house dates from a later period and was eventually closed off. The blocking of the windows in room 7 also suggests that there was once a second light source, which later went out of use (for more detail see § 4.3).

Metrological analysis (Pl. X)
The house is 784.5 cm wide, or 28.5', assuming a foot of 27.55 cm. As suggested above (§ 4.4.4), this should probably be regarded as an 'external' width of 30', including one outside wall. In its present form, which is a fairly close reflection of its original state, the house is 2618.5 cm, or 95', deep.

The length of the house can be divided into a number of distinct areas. First there is a strip of rooms along the street, whose depth is equal to that of the *fauces* (11), ca. 14' (375.5/381 cm). Because of the changes mentioned above, the rooms have not retained their original internal dimensions. It seems likely that a width of 10' and a depth of 11' was intended, but both rooms now measure 9.5'R x 10'R, using a foot of 29.5 cm (room 10: 280/283.5 x 290.5/295 cm; room 12: 274.5/283 x 295 cm). The *fauces* (11) is 6' across (160/166 cm).

A second strip consists of the *atrium* and *tablinum*. The total depth of these two rooms, including the east wall of the *tablinum*, is 30' (824/829 cm). The internal depth of this strip is equal to the width of the house; it is thus a square of 28.5' x 28.5'. This area is further divided into 17' for the *atrium* (467-470 cm) and 11.5' for the *tablinum* (319-322 cm). The *atrium* is therefore 17' x 28.5'. The west side is

148

subdivided into 11.5' - 5.75' - 11.25' (316/1160/312 cm); 11.5' - 5.5' - 11.5' was the original intention. The east side (with the *tablinum*) was most probably divided into 5' - 20' - 3.5' (132.5/555.5/97.5 cm). The *tablinum* strip, like the rooms along the street, was altered slightly at a later date, using a foot of 29.5 cm; the *tablinum* was intended to have an internal depth of 10'R (297/298 cm), and a width of 17.5'O (478/486 cm).[199] Room 2 was presumably staked out as 5' x 10' (133.5/136.5 x 280.5 cm), and corridor 3 as 3.5' x 13.5' (97.5/103 x 369 cm).

This left 51' for the rear area of the house, which was divided into 32' for the second *atrium* and 19' for the rooms to the east. The internal depth of the *atrium* is 32' (880 cm), measured on the north side, and ca. 0.5' less on the south side (867 cm). The space on the north side of the atrium was subdivided into 12' for room 4 (length: 328/333 cm) and 20' for room 5 (external length: 550 cm). The width of this part of the house was divided into 10' (276.5/277.5 cm) for rooms 4 and 5 and 18.5' (502-513 cm) for the *atrium*. Because the *impluvium* is not well preserved, it is not possible to explain its position in the *atrium*. It can only be assumed that the inner rim of the basin was 5'O (139/140 cm) from the north wall, ca. 8'O or 7.5'R (219-227.5 cm) from the south and east wall and ca. 15.5'O (422 cm) from the west wall. The area of the basin is presumably 5'R x 7.5'R (147/148 x 224 cm). As mentioned above, room 4 is 10' x 12'. Room 5 has an internal length of 19' (524 cm) and is 8.5' (233.5/242.5 cm) wide.

Finally, the last strip is occupied by rooms 6 and 7. The dividing wall between the rooms is not at a right angle to the rear wall, so their widths are not constant. Room 6 is 15.5' wide (425 cm) on the east side and 15' (410 cm) on the west, while room 7 is 12' (332.5 cm) wide on the east and 12.5' (341.5 cm) on the west. Both rooms have an internal depth of ca. 17.5' (475 cm).

Design
The layout of the house is based on a division into four strips:

I	(front strip)	14'
II	(*atrium* + *tablinum*)	30'
III	(second *atrium*)	32'
IV	(rear rooms)	19'
	total	95'.

The rooms in strip 1 (10 and 12) were presumably intended to have an internal depth of 11' and a width of 10'. Later changes to this part of the house make it difficult to ascertain whether this was actually the case.

The division of strip II into 17' for the *atrium* and 13' for the rooms is found else-

---

[199] Perhaps the width was intended to be 17'O, but the thickness of the walls turned out to be slightly less than the usual 1.5': 20' (external width of *tablinum*) - 3' (thickness of walls) = 17'. The width of the *tablinum* would then have been equal to the depth of the *atrium*.

where, for example, in the Casa dell'Ara Laterizia (lot III J). This strip seems to have been deliberately designed to form a square with equal internal depth and width (ratio 1:1). In room 2 the ratio of width to length is 1:2 (5' x 10'). The *tablinum* area has not retained its original layout.

In strip III the available space of 28.5' x 32' was divided between two rooms on the north side and an *atrium* on the south. The width of the rooms was determined at 10', and the *atrium* at 18.5'. Depthwise 12' was reserved for the west room (4) and 20' for the east room (5). This resulted in a ratio of 5:6 (10' x 12') in room 4, a ratio of 1:2 (10' x 20') in the external dimensions of room 5, and 3:5 (12':20') on the north side of the *atrium*. As far as can be determined, the position of the *impluvium* was based on an east-west division of 8' - 8' - 16' and a north-south division of 5' - 5.5' - 8'.

The last strip (IV) takes up 1/5 of the total depth of the house: 19':95' = 1:5. The internal depth of the rooms is 17.5', resulting in a ratio of 6:7 (15' x 17.5') for room 6 and 5:7 (12.5' x 17.5') for room 7.

Finally, it would seem that the choice of a basic rectangle of 28.5' x 95' for the house was not accidental. These figures reflect a ratio of 3:10. Some of the dimensions of the rooms and groups of rooms also seem to be related to the width or depth of the house. The frequent use of multiples of 9.5', such as 19' and 28.5', is particularly striking.

150

5.10. Casa del Papiro Dipinto (IV 8-9) (Pl. XI)

This house is on the west side of *insula* IV, with entrances 8 and 9 on *cardo* IV. It takes its name from the painting of an inscribed papyrus roll on the west wall of room 7. The house was excavated between June 1929 and April 1932. It is narrow and rectangular (width: 527 cm; depth: 2063 cm), and occupies a single original lot (IV E). Because of the elongated shape of the house, the 10 rooms on the ground floor were built one behind the other, with a long corridor on the south side. A separate entrance (9) led to the upper storey, which extended from the street to the inner courtyard (5).

Select bibliography
Maiuri 1958: 423-425, fig. 362, 365-367; Packer 1971: 57-58, 61 (nos. 69-70), Pl. CV, Figs. 301-302; Maiuri 1977: 31; De Vos/De Vos 1982: 273; Catalano 1982: 959; Budetta/Pagano 1988: 54-55 (Cat. 18); Ganschow 1989: 38 no. 9, 165 no. 11, 322; Wallace-Hadrill 1994: 201.

An account of the house, including a plan, is given by Maiuri (1958). Maiuri (1977) and De Vos (1982) have written brief descriptions of the house. It appears several times in Ganschow's study (1989) of wall construction in Herculaneum. Packer (1971) comments briefly on the form of the house and the functions of its rooms. A number of finds are mentioned in Budetta/Pagano's catalogue (1988).

Plan and rooms (Pl. XI)
The narrow, elongated shape of the lot is unusual, and has resulted in the rooms being arranged in a single row rather than grouped around a central space. There is a long corridor on the south side, running from the street to the rear room, which connects all the rooms in the house. The rooms at the front of the house, living room 1 and the kitchen (2) with latrine (10), were lit respectively by a window on the street and through the doorway of the *fauces*. The latrine was under the staircase to the upper storey, which had its own separate entrance (9) from the street. Room 3, east of the kitchen, was split in two by a small dividing wall, and must have been very dark, because there is no light source nearby. Maiuri (1958: 424) assumes that this was a store-room; the outlet pipe of the upstairs latrine came out in the northwest corner. Here, near the kitchen (2) and the latrine (10), there was probably a connection to the drainage system of the house. The more luxurious living rooms were at the rear of the house. The first room reached via corridor 8 was room 4, which received its light from a courtyard (5), with richly decorated walls and floor. This courtyard also provided light to the neighbouring house on the north side. Presumably there was another window into the large living room (6) at the very back of the house, which also had a window high up in the wall on the east side. In view of its location and fine decoration, this room may have been an *oecus*.

Wall construction

Maiuri (1958: 66) notes that one of the oldest types of construction in Herculaneum, *opus incertum B*, occurs in the Casa del Papiro Dipinto. This is confirmed by Ganschow (whose observations have not yet been published); he found that the entire south wall of the house (dividing it from the Casa della Fullonica) is built in *opus incertum B*. The same type was used in the north and west walls of room 4. Of a later period are the remains of *opus incertum C* in the east wall of the kitchen (2), and the *opus craticium* partitions between room 1 and the staircase, and room 6 and court 5.

Floor and wall decoration

The rooms in this house have relatively plain floors. The simplest, undecorated form of *opus signinum* can be found in rooms 1, 4 and 6-9; in room 5 the floor is made of *signinum* with stone *crustae*. The kitchen (2) and the toilet (10) have terracotta tiles, while room 3 presumably had a floor of beaten earth.

The house was decorated throughout with wall paintings. In rooms 1, 4, 6 and 10 remains of these paintings are still visible, but in the remaining rooms they are too poorly preserved to allow further analysis. However, some observations can be made. First, a papyrus was painted on the north wall of room 7 (see below: Inscriptions). Second, on the north wall of the toilet (10), there are two layers of paintings. The lower layer has been scored to receive the new plaster; it was white, with red bands in the middle zone and a white wave-pattern motif on a red background in the top zone. This layer is more richly decorated than the plaster laid over it, which was white with red bands. In room 1 the main zone consists of a panel decoration with red fields; in room 4 white fields are framed by architecture in perspective. Finally, room 6 has a red socle and a white and red upper zone, with painted architecture. Maiuri (1958: 424) mentions that remains of a 'garden'-painting could still be seen in court 5, but there is no trace of it now.

Inscriptions

There are a number of inscriptions in room 7, which are illustrated and discussed in detail by Maiuri (1958: 424-425, fig. 366-367), Della Corte (1958: 264 no. 288-290) and Ciprotti (CIL 10481, 10520, 10521). CIL 10481 (= Della Corte 1958: 264 no. 288; Maiuri 1958: 424-425, fig. 366), on the wall above the door into the court, is the name on the painted scroll mentioned above; it is inscribed here in Greek 'ΕΥΤΥΧΟϹ ΧΟΡΙΑ...', which is generally taken to be the name of a writer of choriambic poetry.[200] The second inscription, CIL 10520, was found on the south wall and is still reasonably clear; it refers to a corporation of *navicularii* from Herculaneum, who maintained contact with colleagues from Puteoli.[201] The last inscription in this room,

---

[200]   Maiuri (1958: 425) suggests the longest completion of this line: '.. Εὔτυχος χοριαμβικ[ὰ] σὺν μ[ο]υσυκαῖς..'. Catalano (1982: 959) is of the opinion that 'Eutychos' was the owner of the house (!).

[201]   '[ ]as[ ] conclavii Puteolis / [navic]ul(a)e convin(c)tores Herculane(n)ses nav(i)culae' - Della Corte 1958: 264 no. 288 bis, 289; Maiuri 1958: 425, fig. 367 gives a different reading

CIL 10521 (= Della Corte 1958: 264 no. 290), is on a pilaster, and reads 'MYRINII MARI'.

Published finds
Parts of a bronze fitting for furniture were found in this house on 18/3/1932 (Budetta/Pagano 1988: 54-55 Cat. 18).

Building history
Ganschow (1989: 322) regards the Casa del Papiro Dipinto as one of the oldest houses in Herculaneum and one of the few original Samnite houses. This conclusion seems to be justified, given the types of wall construction found in the house. Yet it is clear that the house was subject to a number of alterations, the most important being the addition of the upper storey, which extended from a balcony over the pavement to courtyard 5 at the back of the house. This extra storey needed independent access from the outside, because it was presumably rented out as an apartment, as Maiuri (1958: 424) rightly noted, and so a wooden staircase was built against the north wall of the house and the living room at the front (1) was made smaller. The original wall decoration of this room is still visible; it is the lower of the two layers of paintings on the north wall of the latrine (10), which is under the staircase.

Alterations also seem to have been made in room 6, at the back of the house, where the dividing wall with the courtyard (5) is in *opus craticium*. It is possible that this room was enlarged slightly when the upper storey was being constructed.

Metrological analysis (Pl. XI)
The house is even narrower than the examples of the 'narrow' type in *insula* III, and thus is one of the narrowest houses in Herculaneum. It is 527 cm wide, or 19'. The depth of the house is 2063 cm, which corresponds to 75', assuming a foot of 27.5 cm. The remaining dimensions in the house can best be analysed on the basis of a foot of 27.85 cm, which makes the depth 74'.

It can be seen that the length of the house has been divided into three. The first part consists of room 1 and kitchen 2, whose total depth is equal to that of *fauces* 9. This strip, excluding the dividing wall, is 20' deep (556 cm). Room 1 has retained its original internal depth of 10' (278 cm), but has been made narrower, as explained above, to make room for the additional entrance. In its original state the room was 12' wide (376.5 cm). The external depth of the room is probably 13', with 7' left over for the kitchen, but at present the space is divided into 12.75' (356 cm) and 7.25' (200 cm), possibly as a result of the later construction of the staircase and latrine, which also reduced the length of the west side of the kitchen to 10'R (294.5 cm). The *fauces* is 5.5' (151/151.5 cm) wide.

The second strip consists of rooms 3 and 4 on the north side and corridor 8 to the south. It is 30' deep (837 cm) including the west and east dividing walls. Half of the

---

of the first part of the second line: '*[navicular]ii consi(s)tont ..*'; Solin 1973B: 276 disagrees with the reading in CIL, without further explanation.

strip was reserved for room 3 (including the west wall), and the remaining 15' for room 4 (including both walls). Room 3 has an internal width of 13.5' (378/380 cm) and is 12.5' deep (350.5 cm), and room 4 is 12.5' wide and 13' deep (340/348 x 358 cm). The 0.5' difference in depth is because the north wall of corridor 8 is not parallel to the south wall of the lot and the corridor thus narrows from 143 cm (5') at the west end to 130.5 cm (just over 4.5') at the east.

The last strip takes up about 1/3 of the total depth of the house, and is composed of courtyard 5, anteroom 7 and the luxurious living room 6 at the back. The builders presumably intended a division of space in which 9' was reserved for rooms 5 and 7 and 15' for room 6. This layout is still reflected in some of the dimensions, although the execution is not very precise, probably as a result of the reconstruction mentioned above, when the partition in *opus craticium* was built in between rooms 5 and 6. It seems likely that the external depth of room 7 (including both dividing walls) was taken as a starting-point for this reconstruction (in which a foot of 29.5 cm was used) because it is 10'R (294 cm). Court 5 is 8.5' wide (236 cm) on the north side and 9' (249.5 cm) on the south, with a length of 9.5'R (283 cm). Room 6 is almost 15' deep (413 cm) on the south side and just over 14.5' (408 cm) on the north; it is 19' (527 cm) wide.

Design
The narrow area available to the architect was divided into three strips or blocks of 20', 30' and 24'. This means that strip I and strip II are in the ratio of 2:3, while strips II and III are in the ratio of 5:4. The blocks were then subdivided into:

    (I)   13' and 7'
    (II) 15' and 15'
    (III)9' and 15'.

In the front strip, no particular ratio was used as a starting-point; instead a practical solution was adopted. The external depth of a room was fixed at 13', creating an internal depth of 10', a round measurement which can easily be used to obtain a workable ratio. In room 1 this ratio is 5:6 (10' x 12'). In the middle and rear strips it is clear how the division of space was proportioned. Strip II is based on a ratio of 1:1; in strip III a ratio of 3:5 was used. The division of the width was also a practical one: 5' for the corridor and 14' for the rooms (5.5' - 13.5' at the front of the house).

5.11. Bottega (IV 10-11) (Pl. XII)

This house and shop is on the northwest corner of *insula* IV, and has two entrances on the *decumanus inferior*: 10 (*taberna*) and 11 (living quarters). The building was uncovered between June 1929 and April 1932. Originally this lot (IV F) must have had an entrance on *cardo* IV. The total length of the plot is 2061 cm (including the facade on *cardo* IV); its internal width ranges from 501 cm in the west to 542 cm in the east. There are 9 rooms on the ground floor. It is likely that there was once an upper storey, but it is not clear where the staircase was.

Select bibliography
Maiuri 1958: 432-433, fig. 375; Packer 1971: 58, 62 (n. 78), Pl. CVI, fig. 305; Bisi Ingrassia 1977: 79, 83, 94; Maiuri 1977: 58; Orr 1978: 195 no. 11; De Vos/De Vos 1982: 273; Catalano 1982: 959; Gassner 1986: 105 (Table V), type C/4 (IV, 10); Wallace-Hadrill 1994: 201.

An account of the rooms, together with a plan, can be found in Maiuri (1958) and Packer (1971). Maiuri (1977) and De Vos (1982) have provided summaries of this account. The *taberna* is featured in a study by Gassner (1986), and Orr (1978) discusses the *lararium* niche in room 1. Several individual finds are mentioned in a study by Bisi Ingrassia (1977).

Plan and rooms (Pl. XII)
Although the *taberna* and the living area are connected to one another, they are clearly distinct: the west part of the building (entrance 10), which consists of two rooms, had a commercial character, while the 7 rooms at the east (entrance 11) had a more private function. In the northwest corner of the *taberna* (1) was a counter with an inset of a *dolium*, which contained remains of wheat. There is a *lararium* niche with painted decoration on the east wall. Room 2 played an important role in the building's water supply: it contained a well or cistern shaft. Maiuri (1958: 432-433) assumes that the room housed a small domestic altar. According to Maiuri's plan (1958: fig.375), there was a dividing wall in room 3 of the living area, which is no longer visible. This room may have served both as a private room and as the back room of the shop. The actual living rooms are further to the east. From room 3 there is a small doorway into anteroom 5, which leads to a small living room (4). Traces of a bed-niche in the east wall indicate that this was a *cubiculum*. The second entrance to the house (11) led into anteroom 9, which gave access to the latrine (7) on the east side and an area (6) to the south, which was probably unroofed. There is a small *lararium* niche in the south wall of this area. The large living room 8 is located to the east, and is richly decorated with frescoes. Two windows provide it with light; one of them, high up in the south wall, looks out across the courtyard (5) of the neighbouring house. Judging by its location, size and decoration, this was the most important living room in the building.

Wall construction

At present little can be said about the wall construction in this lot. *Opus incertum B* was found in the dividing wall with the neighbouring Casa del Papiro Dipinto. The internal walls were repaired in many places, in antiquity as well as more recently (during this century); examination of these walls therefore provides no more than a rough impression of the original structure.

Floor and wall decoration

The floors in this lot are all of the plainest types: there is beaten earth in rooms 1, 2, 5, 6 and 9, and simple *opus signinum* floors in rooms 4 and 8. It is not known what kind of flooring rooms 3 and 7 had.

The wall decoration in this house is not particularly impressive either. Although traces of plaster can be found in all the rooms except room 7, the general state of preservation is such that only the decoration in room 8 can be studied in any detail. It was a Fourth Style painting with red fields and architecture in perspective, on a white background.

Inscriptions

There were several graffiti on the east wall of the *taberna*, near the *lararium* niche, including CIL 10522-10525. CIL 10522 is difficult to identify; Della Corte gives two different readings. The first version, copied shortly after its discovery (30/9/1929), appears to include a reference to an easement (*ius luminum*).[202] Fragments of names and customers are noted in CIL 10523 ('SPI', 'OCEANVS', 'ON', 'ASSIS IIIIHIINII CCCXXX') and 10524 ('IANV').[203] CIL 10525 (Della Corte 1958: 247 no. 40) records a visitor's name: 'HYACINTHVS HIC FVIT / VERGINIAE SVAE S(alutem)'. CIL 10526 (Della Corte 1958: 258 no. 154), inscribed on the outside of the house to the left of entrance 11, is the name 'PROCVLVS' next to a drawing of a man. CIL 10836 (Della Corte 1958: 247 no. 46) consists of the numbers 'SXI/VI', found on an amphora in the shop.

Published finds

Grains of wheat were found in the *dolium* set in the counter and elsewhere in the shop; it is therefore likely that cereal products were the principal merchandise (Maiuri 1958: 432). In addition to the inscribed amphora mentioned above, three small terracotta lamps were found in the building; these are mentioned in an article by Bisi

---

[202] '*qu[aesi]vi hic facias - re[s s]erva omnes res tuas - ... quem nol[i...] nobi[s iu]nge neque - servabo / ne [qui]s ius lum[inum] salvum (obstruat?)*' (Della Corte 1958: 247 no. 45, Pl. I); the second reading was made on 10/1/1934 and contains few coherent letters or words (Della Corte 1958: 273 no. 419). Solin (1973B: 276) has doubts about this reading.

[203] Della Corte 1958: 246 no. 36-39. In CIL 10523 (a), Ciprotti prefers 'Spi(culus)' to 'Spes', which Della Corte suggested, because Spiculus and Oceanus are the names of gladiators who are frequently mentioned in graffiti. 'Ianu(arius)' in CIL 10524 suggested to Catalano (1982: 959) that the owner of the house was 'M. Livius Ianuarius'.

Ingrassia (1977), although the house is identified there only as 'casa n. 3' in *insula* IV.[204]

Building history and metrological analysis (Pl. XII)

It is clear that this building underwent great changes over the years, but as both Maiuri and Ganschow have neglected to comment on the less than homogeneous wall construction in this lot, it is impossible, at present, to determine the precise order and extent of these changes. Maiuri does give some indication of what the lot must have looked like. Luxurious living room 8, at the back of the house, plays a particularly important role in his account. Maiuri claims that in the original layout, when the entrance to the house was still on *cardo* IV, this room was on the axis of the *fauces*. In the original plan the arrangement of the rooms was the same as in the neighbouring Casa del Papiro Dipinto (Maiuri 1958: 432-433). This theory is clearly supported by the metrological analysis.

The house is slightly narrower at the front than the neighbouring house IV 8-9 (501 cm, as opposed to 527.5 cm), but slightly wider at the back (541 cm wide, compared to 527 cm). The difference in width is the result of the fact that the south wall is perpendicular to *cardo* IV and the north wall is parallel to the *decumanus inferior*, which is not exactly at a right angle to *cardo* IV. In terms of feet, the width ranges from 18' in the west to 19.5' in the east. The length is the same as the Casa del Papiro Dipinto, at 2061 cm, and seems to have been planned as 74', using a foot of 27.85 cm (as in the rest of the house), rather than 75', using the more standard foot of 27.5 cm.

Originally IV 10-11 had an entrance on the *cardo*, probably on the west side. This theory is supported by the dimensions of some parts of the house: the internal width of both room 2 and anteroom 5 is 151 cm, which is equal to the width of the *fauces* next door. As in IV 8-9, there must have been a long corridor which extended along the entire length of the house, leading into a luxurious living room (8) at the back. However, there are more parallels between the two houses. The length of the *taberna* (1) is 555 cm, measured from the street to the dividing wall with room 3. This is exactly 20', and is therefore equal to the depth of the first strip in the neighbouring house. In IV 10-11 this area (which is likely to have been a living room and *fauces* originally) was later converted for commercial use, with a *taberna* (1) and a small back room (2). The space in the *taberna* was probably divided up at a relatively late date: the western area with the counter measures 3.5'R (103.5 cm) x ca. 10'R (290 cm), and the space between the counter and the east wall is also 10'R (298 cm). Room 2 was made 8'R (236 cm) long and retained its original width of 5.5'O (151 cm).

The remaining length of the house is divided up in the same way as in IV 8-9. The middle area measures 30', from the dividing wall between rooms 1 and 3 up to and

---

[204]   It is clear enough from Bisi Ingrassia 1977: 94 that it refers to shop IV 10-11: 'casa n.3 all'angolo fra il *cardo* IV e il decumano inferiore (*insula* IV)'. The finds themselves: Bisi Ingrassia 1977: 79 type V E, 83 type VII B (pl. XLVI, 3), 94 type IX I (pl. XLVII).

including the east wall of room 4. Here traces of the original division of the width are still visible: anteroom 5 was part of the old corridor and room 4 was one of a row of rooms similar to that found in IV 8-9. Anteroom 5 is 5.5' (152 cm) across, and room 4 is 12.5' (343/346 cm). Because the original layout of this strip was presumably destroyed when the *taberna* was created, the width of room 4 is best expressed in terms of a Roman foot of 29.45 cm, which makes it 7.5'R (226 cm).[205] The same applies to room 3, which is 16.5'R (487 cm) long on the north side.

The rear strip in lot IV F, as in lot IV E, is 24' deep, but the size of the luxurious living rooms at the back is different. The back room (6) in IV E was probably 15' deep; the corresponding room (8) in IV F at present occupies the same depth as room 3, at 16.5'R (489 cm). It seems likely that the room originally took up the entire width of the house and was 15' deep, but it was altered when the second entrance on the *decumanus inferior* was constructed. A square was staked out, with sides equal to the maximum width of the house (541 cm), and subsequently a latrine was built on the north side, thus reducing the space available for the living room to the south. The latrine is 3.5'R (106 cm) wide and 19.5' (541 cm) long, leaving an internal width of 13.5'R (402 cm) for room 8. At present the external dimensions of this room are 435 cm x 522 cm (14.75'R x 17.75'R, or almost 15'R x 18'R). Finally, corridor 6 is ca. 5'R across (146.5 cm).

Design
Like lot IV E, lot IV F was once divided into three strips: a front strip of 20', a middle strip of 30', and a rear strip of 24'. The intention was a ratio of 2:3 for strips I and II, and 5:4 for strips II and III, as in IV E. Because of later alterations, the design of these strips can only be partially retraced, but it was very similar to the strips in IV E. These later building activities, in which the Roman foot was probably used, followed the broad lines of the original design; they mostly involved the removal of internal walls. A square based on the width of the house was the starting-point for the new layout at the back of the house (strip III). Within this square area the existing living room was adapted so that its dimensions reflected a ratio of 5:6.

---

[205] It is possible that room 4 was part of the original layout; if so, the available space was not divided into two areas of equal size, as in IV 8-9, but into three smaller rooms, two with a width of 8.5', and a smaller room (7') in between. Room 3 would then have been created by removing the partition between the two western rooms.

5.12. Grande Taberna (IV 12-13, 15-16); Taberna Vasaria (IV 14) (Pl. XIII)

This *taberna* and house occupies the northeast corner of *insula* IV, and has entrances 12, 13 and 15 on the *decumanus inferior* and 16 on *cardo* V; entrance 14 on the *decumanus* serves an independent shop. The entire corner was uncovered between September 1931 and October 1932. The *taberna*, including shop IV 14, is a regular rectangle occupying two old lots (IV G and IV H), which must originally have had entrances on *cardo* V. At present, the total internal width of the area is 1112 cm, and it is 2295 cm deep (including the east wall). In addition to the independent shop IV 14, the *taberna* and house have a total of 13 rooms on the ground floor, divided into three groups: a living area served by entrances 12 and 13, further living rooms around the *atrium*, and a *taberna* with back rooms using entrances 15 and 16. It is not clear how large the upper storey was or where the staircase was.

Select bibliography
Maiuri 1958: 433-436, fig. 376-381; Solin 1973B: 98 (Diogenes inscription in room 6); Maiuri 1977: 58-59; Orr 1978: 195 no. 12-13; De Vos/De Vos 1982: 273-274; Catalano 1982: 959; Gassner 1986: 105 (Table V) type B/1 (IV 14), C/1 (IV 12); Moormann 1988: 107-108, Cat. 027 (room 9); McIlwaine 1988: 12.41-46 (Diogenes inscription); Ganschow 1989: 91 n. 66, 126 n. 19; Mols 1994: 68, 140, 258; Wallace-Hadrill 1994: 201.

A general overview, with illustrations and a plan, is provided by Maiuri (1958). Short summaries of this account have been written by Maiuri (1977) and De Vos (1982). The shops are mentioned in Gassner's typology (1986), and the wall painting in room 9 is included in Moormann's catalogue (1988). The wall construction in this lot is not discussed extensively by Ganschow (1989). On the other hand, a Greek inscription found in room 6, quoting the philosopher Diogenes, has received much attention; relevant studies are listed in McIlwaine (1988). Mols (1994) refers to wooden racks in the shops. Finally, Orr (1978) has discussed the two *lararia*.

Plan and rooms (Pl. XIII)
In this rectangular area two original lots can be identified, which have been merged into a single unit, excluding the *taberna* IV 14, which remained independent from the rest. In the last years of the town's existence, this room had a toilet in the southwest corner, separated from the shop by a thin wall. There was a room above the shop, which Maiuri thought was a mezzanine floor (1958: 436). All the other parts of the building are connected with each other. They include a shop (12) and two small living rooms (1 and 2) in the northwest corner, opening off a spacious hallway (10). The presence of two wells, diagonally opposite one another, is notable; a windlass was

found near one of them.[206] Hall 10 led into a Tuscan *atrium* (3) at a slightly lower level, with an *impluvium* in the centre, whose cladding has now disappeared. There is a room (4) off the west side of the *atrium*, with niches in the walls indicating that it must have been a bedroom. Opposite, on the east side of the *atrium*, is another living room (5). To the north, at a lower level, is another hallway (11), giving access to the rooms in the *taberna* area. The *taberna* consists of a shop (13) and four back rooms, two on the north side (6 and 7) and two on the south (8 and 9). There was a latrine in the southeast corner of the *taberna*. Room 8 was used a kitchen, and the other three rooms were presumably used as private dining rooms. Maiuri (1958: 434) noted that the strategically-placed shop, on the corner of *cardo* V and the *decumanus inferior*, is the largest and richest in the excavated area of Herculaneum.

Wall construction
It is clear from Ganschow's published and unpublished notes that the south wall of the property contains traces of the oldest types of wall construction (*opus incertum A* and *opus incertum B*). The west wall of room 5 also seems to be built in *opus incertum B*. *Opus incertum C* is visible in the later dividing wall between rooms 8 and 9. *Opus reticulatum* is the only other type found throughout the property; sometimes it is the 'neat' version (type A) - as in the south wall of corridor 10, for example - but the less refined form (type B) is more usual. Examples of the latter technique can be seen in the wall between room 6 and shop 13, in the *taberna vasaria* IV 14, and in the western rooms 1, 2 and 12. *Opus vittatum* also occurs in this area (room 12).

Floor and wall decoration
The predominant type of floor in the *taberna* and house is *opus signinum*. Plain *signinum* can be found in rooms 4, 6, 10, 12 and 13, and *signinum* with chips of marble in rooms 8 and 9. The more luxurious variety decorated with stone *crustae* is found in no less than five rooms (2, 3, 5, 11 and 14). In room 1 the floor is beaten earth, while nothing is known about the floor of room 7; perhaps it was a simple type of *signinum*, as in room 6.
    All the rooms had wall paintings, but half of them are not well preserved (rooms 1, 2, 6, 7 and 11-13). On the west wall of room 6 the remains of a painted landscape with a small boat are still visible. The decoration in rooms 3, 4 and 14 (the *taberna vasaria*) is similar, consisting of rich Fourth Style paintings with fields of architecture in perspective. Panel decorations have survived in rooms 5 and 10; the decoration in room 5 consists of white and red fields, while in room 10 the Fourth Style decoration has red and black fields. In rooms 8 and 9, which once formed a single room, was a rich Third Style decoration with a black socle, red panels in the main zone, and architectural elements on a white background in the top zone.

Inscriptions

---

[206]   For an illustration, see Maiuri 1958: fig. 380. Compare also Jansen 1991: 150-152.

In room 4 (?)[207], on the south wall, was found the exclamation '[A]VE FELICIT(ER) / QVID / AGAMVS / AC CVPIAMVS (feliciter)' (CIL 10482 = Della Corte 1958: 264 no. 291; Solin 1973B: 276). The largest number of inscriptions, 19 in total, including the most important one in the house, were found in room 6, behind the *taberna*. On the east wall was CIL 10528 (= Della Corte 1958: 261 no. 247; Solin 1973B: 272): 'EVHODVS / ET SATVRA / PVTEOLANI', next to a drawing of fighting gladiators. A whole series of graffiti was found around the small landscape painting on the west wall; most of them were greetings and exclamations.[208] However, the one that has been discussed most frequently is a Greek text of four lines, quoting the philosopher Diogenes (CIL 10529):

Διογένης ὁ κυνικὸς φιλόσοφος ἰδὼν γυναῖκα ὑπὸ ποταμοῦ φερομένην, εἶπεν· ἄφες φέρεσθαι <το> κακὴν ὑπὸ κακοῦ<κιυς>.

('Diogenes the Cynic Philosopher, when he observed a woman being swept away by a river said: 'Allow one evil to be carried away by the other' ').[209]

The inscription CIL 10546 (= Della Corte 1958: 267 after no. 337) on the south wall of room 9 consisted of several numbers ('IIII; IX'). Amphorae discovered on the ground floor of the *taberna*, were labelled with various names, including 'ANNIORVM VETVS XXXV' and 'ZHNΩN----M' (CIL 10727)[210]; several others found on the upper storey of the house had the names 'M. Aemilius Maximus' inscribed on them: 'M. AEMIL' (CIL 10759) and 'MAXIMI' (CIL 10790).[211]

The word 'VASA' on the outside wall between entrances IV 14 and 15 could perhaps be interpreted as the remains of an advertisement for the products in shop IV 14 (CIL 10527; Della Corte 1958: 260 no. 241). Several amphorae with inscriptions were found in the shop itself. All but three were labelled with the name of the presumed owner of the shop 'K.K. Zosimus' ('K.K.ZΩCI') (CIL 10795, 10889 = Della Corte 1958: 260 no. 239-240).[212]

---

[207] The findspot was described by Della Corte (1/4/1932) as: 'IV, 13 - Parete S, in fondo alla casa' (Della Corte 1958: 264 no. 291). Alternatively, this could refer to the south wall of *fauces* 10 (entrance 13).

[208] CIL 10530-10545; Della Corte 1958: 262 nos. 265-280; Solin 1973B: 272 (10532), 276.

[209] Della Corte 1958: 262 no. 264, Pl. II; Maiuri 1958: 435, fig. 379. See also McIlwaine 1988: 12.41-46 for an extensive bibliography on this text.

[210] Della Corte 1958: 260 no. 244. Also: CIL 10757, 10820, 10884 (= 10727b); Della Corte 1958: 260 no. 244, 268 no. 347, 261 no. 248, 251-252, 263 no. 284.

[211] Della Corte 1958: 261 no. 248, 249 . See also CIL 10809, 10838, 10878, 10903; Della Corte 1958: 261 no. 250, 253, 259 no. 177, 261 no. 256, 254, 261 no. 255. Catalano (1982: 959) regards M. Aemilius Maximus as the owner of the house. Three fragments of amphorae with inscriptions were found on the upper storey of the house (Della Corte 1958: 258 no. 160-162). For CIL 10896 (= Della Corte 1958: no. 160) IV 15-16 is recorded as the findspot; IV 7-8 is said to be the provenance of the other inscriptions, which is certainly not correct. CIL 10896 was presumably also found in IV 17-18 (see § 5.13).

[212] CIL 10893-10894 (33 amphorae); Della Corte 1958: 260 nos. 185-238; Maiuri 1958: 436. A total of 36 amphorae were found instead of the 35 reported by Della Corte and Maiuri, as CIL 10889 appears on two amphorae.

Published finds

As mentioned above, several amphorae were found in the *taberna* and the house, on both the ground floor and the upper storey; still more, of similar shape and size, were discovered in the *taberna vasaria* (IV 14), which was equipped for the sale of amphorae and other pottery (Maiuri 1958: 436). Other notable discoveries included the windlass from corridor 10, the remains of grain or wheat and vegetables in the *dolia* of the shop-counter, writing tablets, and wooden racks for the shops (Mols 1994: 258).

Building history

Maiuri and Ganschow give almost no information about the building history of this lot. Maiuri (1958: 433) only writes that all of the north-east area of *insula* IV, except *bottega* IV 14, once formed a single unit. It is not clear whether this means that the living quarters and the *tabernae* had always been connected. Maiuri (1958: 435) and Ganschow (1989: 126 n. 19) both mention the fact that rooms 8 and 9 were once a single room, which was later divided by a wall in *opus incertum C* to create a service room (8) and a dining room/bedroom (9).

As said above, the building was probably made up of two long rectangular plots of land (lots IV G and IV H), each of which had an entrance on the east side on *cardo* V. The types of construction found in the southern part of lot IV H suggest that these plots were developed during the earliest phase of the development of the city. The amalgamation of the two lots dates from a later period, and is probably related to the conversion of several rooms into shops. It is possible that this change of function was connected with the construction of the Palaestra, but because the plots were conveniently situated near a crossroads, it must always have been an attractive prospect to open a bar or shop there. The types of wall construction used do not provide enough information to determine an exact date: *opus reticulatum B*, which is the main type found in this house, was used from the 1st century BC onwards. Possibly this building phase is part of what Ganschow (1989: 329) has distinguished as the second period in the development of Herculaneum, which he dates to the Republican period. The changes to room 8/9 can only have taken place in the 1st century AD because the partition was built against a wall painting in the Third Style.

Metrological analysis (Pl. XIII)

Lots IV G and H were about the same width as the corresponding lots on the west side (IV E and IV F), ca. 535 cm or 19.5'. There were differences in length between the two lots: IV G was 2257 cm long (on the north side), while IV H was 2295 cm (north side). This is equal to 82.5' and 83.5' (Oscan foot = 27.5 cm).[213] This difference is an indication of the considerable variations in length that could occur, usually as a result of two outer walls not being parallel.

Despite their greater length, the design of the eastern plots is comparable in some respects to that of the lots on the west side of the *insula*. The rooms along the *cardo*,

---

[213]   In fig. 6 a length of 83.5' is assumed for both lots.

where the original entrances were, are 20' deep: room 8/9 is 552 cm deep, and the south side of *taberna* 13 measures 553.5 cm. These are internal dimensions, excluding the front wall; the external length of this strip, measured from the street up to and including the dividing wall with corridor 11, is 23'/23.5' (637/646 cm).

The types of wall construction used suggest that lot IV G has probably not retained its original plan. Lot IV H is more promising in this respect. Here it can be seen that the total length of *atrium* 3 and corridor 11 is 40' (1099 cm), from the dividing wall with room 8/9 to the dividing wall with hallway 10. Room 5 and corridor 11 have an external length of 12.5' (341.5 cm), or an internal length of 11' (299.5/305 cm). The width of corridor 11 is ca. 5.5' (149 cm), while room 5 has an internal width of ca. 13' (363/365 cm). The *atrium* (3) is 19.5' wide and 27.5' long (542 and 758/762 cm). Because the *impluvium* is not well preserved, it can only be assumed that it was exactly in the centre of the room. At present the subdivision of the east side of the *atrium* is 4.25' - 6' - 4' - 5.25' (117/165/116/149 cm), while the west side is divided into 2.25' - 6.5' - 5.5' - 5.25' (65.5/176.5/155/145 cm).

In the rear part of the house, the total depth of rooms 2 and 10 is 20' (550 cm), including the dividing wall with *atrium* 3. The total length of the plot, measured from the east wall of room 8/9, therefore amounts to 60' (1649 cm). The internal width of room 4 is 9.5' (256-264 cm), and it is 19'/19.5' (526/536.5 cm) long. The Oscan foot was used for the subdivision of rooms 2 and 10, despite the fact that these rooms were constructed during the rearrangement of the house after the assimilation of the two lots. The two rooms form a strip 20' deep, half of which was reserved for the external length of room 2 (274 cm). The external width of this room is also 10' (277 cm). If the thickness of the wall is taken to have been 1.5', both room 2 and the southern end of hall 10 were squares of 8.5' x 8.5'.

The construction of the north end of hall 10 and rooms 1 and 12 used the existing division of the space, but with several modifications, presumably as a result of the use of the Roman foot (29.5 cm). For example, the width of room 12 is 10'R (293 cm), and its external length, including both walls, is 10'R (296 cm). Room 1 measures 8'R x 8'R (241 cm) or 8.5'R x 8.5'R (253/254 cm). The total internal width of hall 10 is 29.5'O (810 cm).

On the east side of the plot, it can be assumed that the *taberna* (13) was once the same size as room 8/9 in IV H, and was later altered slightly. The width is still that of the original lot, which ranges from 19' (526 cm) to 19.5' (544 cm). The depth of the room is 20'R (592 cm) on the south side and 21'R on the north side (622.5 cm). The southern measurement reflects the original division in Oscan feet: 21.5'O, including the west wall.

The width of rooms 6 and 7 is also 19'O (521 cm). It is notable that the total depth of both rooms, including the dividing wall with the *taberna* (measured on the south side), is equal to that of the *taberna*, at ca. 20'R (599.5 cm). It is possible that there was once a room here with an internal depth of 20'O. At present room 6 is 6.5'R (194/195 cm) deep, and room 7 is 11.5'R/12'R (340/358 cm). Finally, *taberna* IV 14 is 14.5'R wide (421-426 cm), and 19.5'O deep (533 cm).

Design

In lot IV H it appears that the architects originally had at their disposal a front strip with an internal depth of 20', a middle strip 40' deep, for the *atrium* and a living room, and a rear strip of 20'. This design produced an 'irregular' strip at the front (23.5'), but the middle and rear strips were based on a ratio of 1:2. The middle strip was divided into two areas in the proportion of 5:11 (12.5' x 27.5'). In room 4 the ratio of width to length is 1:2 (9.5' x 19').

5.13. Taberna (IV 17-18) (Pl. XIV)

This reasonably large house, with an attached *taberna*, is situated on the east side of *insula* IV, with entrances 17 (*taberna*) and 18 (residence) on *cardo* V. It was uncovered between September 1931 and October 1932. One original lot (IV I) can be identified in its irregular plan. It is possible that the house was once square and that the two northwestern rooms formed part of lot IV D, before they were added to this lot. The maximum depth of the house, on the north side, is now 1760 cm; in the south it is 1438 cm. The house is 1373 cm wide. Apart from the *taberna* with its back room and three rooms along the street (including the *fauces*), all 9 rooms on the ground floor are grouped around the tetrastyle *atrium* (13) at the back of the house. In addition, there was living space on an upper storey, which could be reached by staircases in the *fauces* (11) and in room 4.

Select bibliography
Maiuri 1958: 436-440, figs 382-386; Tran Tam Tinh 1971: 97 no. 68 bis; Maiuri 1977: 59-60; Bisi Ingrassia 1977: 94; De Vos/De Vos 1982: 273-274; Scatozza Höricht 1986: 64 Cat. 217; Moormann 1988: 108, Cat. 028 (room 15); Mols 1994: 258; Wallace-Hadrill 1994: 201.

An illustrated account, with a plan, is provided by Maiuri (1958). Shorter versions were written by Maiuri (1977) and De Vos (1982). The Priapus painting is mentioned in Moormann's study (1988) of representations of statues in Roman wall painting. A number of finds from the house are included in accounts by Tran Tam Tinh (1971), Bisi Ingrassia (1977), Scatozza Höricht (1986) and Mols (1994).

Plan and rooms (Pl. XIV)
The building consists of a commercial area on the north side (entrance 17), and a living area which takes up the remaining space (entrance 18). The shop consisted of a *taberna* (15), where foodstuffs were traded (including nuts), and a back room (14), which was presumably used as a *triclinium* and store-room, given the presence of a couch on three sides of the room and traces of shelves that Maiuri (1958: 437) discovered there. A narrow doorway connected the *taberna* to room 9. The entrance to the house is the *fauces* (11), which also contains the staircase to the front area of the upper storey. There is a living room (1) off the *fauces*, connected to a smaller living room (2). The central circulation area of the house, the tetrastyle *atrium* (13), was reached via a small passage (12). There was a low parapet between the columns in the *atrium*. This room supplied light and air to the living rooms around it: two on the south side (3 and 4), two on the west (5 and 6), two on the north (7 and 8), and one on the east (9). The upstairs rooms on this side of the house (reached by a staircase in room 4) were also dependent on the *atrium* for light. Finally, the luxurious living room (10) at the front of the house had windows onto room 9 and *taberna* 15. As the windows are at a low level, it is likely that there were once couches in this room and

that it was a *triclinium*.

Wall construction

The wall construction in this house is not discussed in the studies of Maiuri (1958) or Ganschow (1989). Because several Bourbon tunnels were dug through the walls of the house (Maiuri 1958: 440), there are modern repairs in several places. The ancient wall structures also show traces of repairs, and so are far from homogeneous. In the north and south walls of the house there are traces of *opus incertum A* and *B*. From an examination of the sounding on the north side of room 6 it is clear that the north wall of this room was built in *opus incertum A* or *B* and the east wall in *opus incertum D*, using any available materials. The west wall contains sections of *opus vittatum mixtum* and repairs in *opus latericium*, but most of it is built in an older type of construction that includes a large amount of red cruma (*opus incertum Bb?*). *Opus vittatum* is used for the quoins and the north wall of the *atrium* (13). *Opus incertum D*, the irregular type of construction made up of various materials, is found in many places throughout the house, for example in room 10, corridor 12 and the northwest corner of *atrium* 13.

Floor and wall decoration

Only two rooms in this house have decorated pavements: in living rooms 2 and 10 there are *opus signinum* floors with marble *crustae*. Plain *signinum*, without the fragments of marble, can be found in rooms 3, 5, 6, 14 and 15. The floors in rooms 4, 8, 9 and 11-13 are of the most basic type, beaten earth. The floors of rooms 1 and 7 are no longer identifiable.[214]

The wall decoration of room 1 is also totally lost. Some remains of plaster are visible in rooms 2-9 and 11-14, but they are not well preserved. In room 15, the painted socle is clearly visible (yellow and red panels); the figured scene in the main zone is slightly more faded, but an ithyphallic Priapus, a woman and a *dolium* can still be identified. Finally, the luxurious living room 10 had a Fourth Style painting in the main zone, with architectural elements on a white background. It can be deduced from Maiuri's account (1958: 440) that the decoration in this room also included still lives with sea creatures, and that a room on the upper storey above the *retrobottega* (14) had a beautifully decorated socle depicting plants.

Inscriptions

Two inscriptions were found in the *retrobottega* (14): 'RVFVLA PVS' (on the west wall) and 'EVENO' (CIL 10548-10549; Della Corte 1958: 261 no. 257, 267 no. 336). Next to the painting of Priapus in the *taberna*, the symbol for '50' was written three times, and on the west wall there was an inscription that read: 'CROCALE

---

[214]   Maiuri (1958: 438, 440) mentions that there were also *opus signinum* floors with marble *crustae* in rooms 1, 7 and 8.

BARBATA'.[215] A small lamp found in the *taberna* was inscribed with the name 'Hebuna' (CIL 10854; Della Corte 1958: 267 no. 337). In room 9, 'MERCVRIVS' was written on the south wall (CIL 10551; Della Corte 1958: 258 no. 159), and a number on the west wall; there were also numbers in room 10 (CIL 10550, 10552; Della Corte 1958: 257 nos. 152-153) and on the *dolium* in *taberna* 15 (CIL 10847; Della Corte 1958: 257 no. 151). Several amphorae with letters and symbols were found here and elsewhere on the ground floor. On these amphorae the name 'Claudius Exochus' occurs twice (CIL 10770; Della Corte 1958: 259-260 nos. 180-181, 261 no. 259).[216] A jug had the name 'ATIMETI' inscribed on it (CIL 10762; Della Corte 1958: 263 no. 285). An amphora and a jug with inscriptions were discovered on the upper storey.[217] Finally, it is suspected that several CIL-numbers, whose origin is unknown, were also found in the *taberna* (CIL 10766, 10767, 10822, 10866 and 10896).[218]

Published finds
In addition to several amphorae, *dolia* and jugs, of terracotta and bronze, a number of other objects were found in this house: two types of kitchen utensil, a mortar, some nuts in a *dolium*, writing tablets, two small lamps and a small glass bottle.[219]

Building history
Maiuri (1958: 438) regards the tetrastyle *atrium* with a parapet and windows in the upper zone as very similar to the *atrium* of VI 15, 9 at Pompeii and the peristyle of

---

[215]   CIL 10483; Della Corte 1958: 257 no. 150; Maiuri 1958: 438, fig. 383; Solin 1973B: 276. CIL 10547; Della Corte 1958: 258 no. 156.

[216]   See also CIL 10721, 10772, 10833, 10726 (Della Corte 1958: 258 nos. 157-158.1-4), CIL 10828 (Della Corte 1958: 261 no. 258).

[217]   *Jug*: CIL 10750; Della Corte 1958: 265 no. 299. *Amphora*: CIL 10816; Della Corte 1958: 265 no. 300.

[218]   Della Corte 1958: 258 no. 162 (= 259 no. 176), 258 no. 161, 259 nos. 174-175, 258 no. 160. Ciprotti notes that CIL 10766 and 10767 cannot have been found on the upper storey of IV 15-16, as Della Corte indicates (Della Corte 1958: 258 nos. 161-162). Instead he suggests IV 7-8, because number 176 in Della Corte's list was found here (Della Corte 1958: 259 no. 176); in Ciprotti's opinion this inscription should be identified with CIL 10766, and he suggests that Della Corte wrote down the same inscription twice, with different findspots. However, the location described by Ciprotti cannot be right, because there is no house with this number. In the case of the inscription that Della Corte listed together with CIL 10766 and 10767 (Della Corte 1958: 258 no. 160 = CIL 10896), Ciprotti sticks to his theory that the findspot was the upper storey of IV 15-16. It is suggested in the present study that IV 17-18 was the provenance of all five inscriptions, mainly on the basis of their discovery dates. One possible explanation of Ciprotti's incorrect location is that a 1 was lost in Della Corte's original note, and that he had actually noted IV 7-8 instead of 17-8. Another reason for the confusion is the fact that it was not always possible to identify property boundaries during the excavation of the upper storeys.

[219]   See Maiuri 1958: 437-438, figs 383-384; Mols 1994: 258. One lamp, with an image of Cybele and Attis, is also mentioned by Bisi Ingrassia 1977: 94 type IX I (= Tran Tam Tinh 1971: 97 no. 68bis). The glass bottle is E744 (found on 12/2/1932) - Scatozza Höricht 1986: 64.

the Casa degli Amanti (I 10, 11).

There is not enough information available to determine the different phases in the history of the house precisely, so that only the broad lines can be discussed here (see also fig. 9). The first construction phase presumably took place after the construction of lots IV D (Casa della Fullonica) and IV C (north side of the Casa dell'Alcova). The shape of lot IV I is irregular because the lengths of these plots are not equal. The possibility that rooms 5 and 6 did not originally belong to this lot but to lot IV D has been discussed at length above (see § 4.3). It was argued that the original eastern boundary of lot IV D is identical to the present boundary, and that all or part of the area now taken up by rooms 5 and 6 was probably connected to, or even part of, lot IV D at a later stage. Perhaps the strip behind the Casa della Fullonica was undeveloped land; there may have been a rear entrance to the house that could be reached by way of this piece of land. It is also possible that this was a garden area, which was later added to the house and subsequently sacrificed to make room for another house. An examination of the wall construction does not provide an answer to this problem. As noted above (§ 4.4.4), the earliest building phase cannot have taken place later than the first half of the 1st century BC. It is no longer possible to determine the original appearance of the lot. An attempt will be made below, on the basis of the metrological analysis of the house and a discussion of its design, to give an impression of the basic scheme that was used in its initial development.

From the abundance of *opus incertum D* in the walls, it can be assumed that at some time the house was rebuilt or repaired quickly and cheaply. Ganschow's study showed that this phase probably occurred in the last decades of Herculaneum's existence, to repair damage caused by the earthquake of 62.

Metrological analysis (Pl. XIV)

If rooms 5 and 6 are not included in this analysis, the lot can be regarded as almost square. The width of this 'square' lot is 50' (1373 cm) and its length is 52.5' (1438 cm), expressed in an Oscan foot of 27.4 cm. Including the west strip, the length of the house is ca. 1760 cm, which is equal to 64'.

Despite the irregular shape of the lot, the same patterns were used as a basis for the division of space as elsewhere in Herculaneum. For example, the strip of rooms at the front of the house (rooms 15, 10, 11 and 1), including both walls, is 20' deep (545.5-552 cm). A similar allotment of space is found elsewhere in *insula* IV (lots IV E-H). The internal depth of the rooms is usually 17'. *Taberna* 15 is a little longer, 17.5' (477/482 cm), with a width of 13'R (377/382 cm). *Triclinium* 10 is 17'O x 12.5'R (470/474 x 365/371.5 cm), while the length of the *fauces* (11) is 17'O (465/471 cm) and its width varies between 200-217 cm, which was probably intended to be 7'R. The dimensions of room 1 are also rather irregular: it is 297/314 cm wide (= 10'R/10.5'R?) and 458/471 cm long (= 17'O). Presumably the width of this room is related to the other rooms on the south side of the house (rooms 2-4). This strip is ca. 12'R wide (347.5-352.5 cm), so the rooms have an internal width of 10.5'R (307-314.5 cm). The Roman foot measure used here is 29.45 cm. Rooms 3 and 4 are 10'R (292.5-295 cm) deep, and room 2 is only 7.5'R (222.5/227.5 cm). It should be noted that the total width of *fauces* 11 and room 1 is 20'O (549.5 cm); the same dimension (555 cm) is found on the west side of the house, measured from the southwest corner of room 4 to the protruding southeast corner of room 5.

At the back of the house, it is notable that the length of the north side from the back wall of the rooms along the street to the back of the plot is twice the length and width of the *atrium*: the total distance is 1214 cm, while the atrium is ca. 605 cm square. Room 9 is also 606 cm long. Presumably these lengths are based on a module of 606 cm or half of that (303 cm), or 22'O and 11'O respectively. A measurement of 303 cm is found as the interaxial distance between the columns on the north and south sides of the *atrium*, the internal length of rooms 5 and 6, and the external length of room 9. The following picture therefore emerges. The *atrium* is 22' x 22' (603.5-615 cm; south side: 623.5 cm), and was subdivided into 11' for the distance between the centres of the columns and 5.5' for the porticoes. This ideal layout was not perfectly executed, because the southwest and northeast columns were positioned inaccurately. Its actual dimensions are: 5.5'O - 10'R - 6'O (155.5/294.5/165 cm) on the east side; 6'O - 10'R - 5.5'O (162.5/290/154 cm) on the west side; 5'R - 11'O - 5.5'O (147/303.5/153 cm) on the north side; 5'R - 11'O - 6'R (146/302/175.5 cm) on the south side.

On the west side of the *atrium*, the wall between rooms 5 and 6 was not built at a right angle to the west wall of the house, and as a result the widths of the rooms vary considerably. The dimensions on the east side of these rooms presumably reflect the correct division. For room 5 this is 8.5' x 11' (235/256 x 299.5/301 cm); room 6 measures 11' x 18.5' (298/302 x 496/507 cm). The rooms on the north side form a strip with an external width of 15'O (411 cm). Internally their dimensions are as follows: room 7 is 11.5' x 13.5' (316/318 x 374/385.5 cm), while room 8 measures 9' x 13.5' (247/248.5 x 371/371.5 cm).

The external depth of the strip consisting of corridor 12, room 9 and the *retrobottega* 14 is a single module of 11' (303-308 cm). The length of room 9 is twice this unit (606.5/608.5 cm = 22'); it has an internal depth of ca. 8.5' (227/232 cm). The *retrobottega* (14) is a square of 8' x 8' (217.5-225.5 cm).

Design
Despite the obscurity of the building history of the house, it is possible to observe the following principles in its layout. On the remaining land to the east of lots IV C and D, which formed a plot of land measuring 50' in width and 52.5' - 64' in depth, a strip of 20' was staked out, starting from the street. This layout occurs frequently in Herculaneum. Widthways a division of 20' and 30' (a ratio of 2:3) can be observed. In the *atrium* area the available area of 30' was then halved; the resulting 15' for the northern strip of rooms still exists today.

Presumably the design of the rear part of the house was changed in a later phase. The starting point for this reconstruction was the length of the north side of the house, excluding the row of rooms along the street. The available length of 44' was divided into 4 parts, creating a module of 11'. One module was taken as the depth of the second strip (room 9) and the rear strip (rooms 5 and 6), leaving 2 modules for the *atrium*.

The row of rooms on the south side of the *atrium* occupied the remaining space. Presumably these rooms were reconstructed at a later date; their width (10.5'R) was left unchanged, while their depth was fixed at a round figure of 10'R.

5.14. Casa della Stoffa (IV 19-20) (Pl. XV)

This house is on the east side of *insula* IV and has entrances 19 and 20 on *cardo* V. The house was named after the remains of fabric that were found during the excavation, which lasted from September 1931 to October 1932. One original lot, IV J, can be identified in the layout, although its shape is now irregular because some rooms or parts of rooms have been transferred to other houses. The maximum depth of the house is 1470 cm, and the maximum width is 1016 cm. Of the 9 rooms on the ground floor, two form a north 'wing'. A large hall at the front of the house provides access to two rooms and a corridor which leads to the back of the house, where a further three rooms are grouped around the inner courtyard. The house had three storeys: the first floor, which extended at least above the central part of the house, could be reached by a staircase and a gallery; a separate entrance (no. 20) gave access to a staircase that led to the second floor (Maiuri 1958: fig. 369).

Select bibliography
Maiuri 1958: 425-426, Fig. 368-369; Packer 1971: 51, 57, 62 (n. 78), Pl. CVI, Figs 303-304; Moeller 1976: 113; Maiuri 1977: 60; Bisi Ingrassia 1977: 92, 96; De Vos/De Vos 1982: 274; Catalano 1982: 959; Adam 1984: 217-219, figs 474-476; Gassner 1986: 88, 105 (Table V), type D (IV, 19); Scatozza Höricht 1986: 65 Cat. 235, 70 Cat. 253-254, Pl. XXII, XXXIX; Tran Tam Tinh 1988: 12, 29; Ganschow 1989: 44, 103, 201, 202 n. 13, 207-208, 218 Fig. 15; Scatozza Höricht 1989A: Cat. 147; Mols 1994: 99; Wallace-Hadrill 1994: 201.

An account of the house, with illustrations and a plan, is given by Maiuri (1958) and Packer (1971). Summaries of these accounts are found in Maiuri (1977) and De Vos (1982). Moeller (1976) regards the remains of fabric as insufficient evidence to identify the house as a shop where cloth was traded. The 'shop' is included in Gassner's account (1986), while Adam (1984) makes a detailed analysis of the construction of the double staircase. The wall construction and the relationship with the surrounding houses are the focus of Ganschow's study (1989). Finally, several objects found in the house are noted by Bisi Ingrassia (1977) and Scatozza Höricht (1986; 1989A).

Plan and rooms (Pl. XV)
Originally, when room 16 of the Casa dell'Alcova and part of latrine 14 of the Casa dei Cervi were still part of the house, this plot was rectangular in shape. At that time the house was not very deep (because of the unusual length of the Casa dell'Alcova), but this was compensated for by greater than average width. As a result the rooms are not in a single row, but side by side. The only central circulation area in the house is room 1 at the front. This room contained the staircase to the first floor, and gave access to two living rooms (2 and 3) and the corridor (9) to the back of the house. There is a living room (4) off the north side of this corridor, and it leads into an ante-

room (8). This anteroom provides access to another living room (5) on the south side, where the remains of a stuccoed ceiling can still be seen; the room looks out across courtyard 6 to the west, and was presumably a *cubiculum*. Finally, room 7, west of anteroom 8, housed the latrine, which was in the southwest corner, next to the latrine of the Casa dei Cervi.

Wall construction
Ganschow's study is the most important contribution to our knowledge of the wall construction in the Casa della Stoffa. He concludes (Ganschow 1989: 208) that the reconstruction of the house must have taken place at the same time as the building of the Casa dei Cervi. Most of the internal walls were constructed in *opus reticulatum* A, except in corridor 9, where *opus incertum* C was used, and the west wall of room 2, which is the only example of *opus quasi-reticulatum* in Herculaneum. For the dating of this wall, it is important to note that remains of a Third Style decoration are still preserved on it (Ganschow 1989: 44, 103). The dividing walls with the neighbouring houses all show traces of *opus incertum* B (south walls of rooms 1 and 6, west wall of room 6, north wall of room 4). This confirms that the plot divisions assumed above correspond to the original boundaries. *Opus incertum* B can also be found in the west wall of room 4 and the north wall of room 7. Finally, *opus incertum* D is found in the west walls of rooms 6 and 7 and elsewhere.

Floor and wall decoration
From the pavements it can be deduced that the only room with luxurious furnishings in the Casa della Stoffa was room 2. In this room there is an *opus signinum* floor which has had *opus sectile* added to it (according to Maiuri there was a polychrome *emblema* in the centre). The remaining rooms have plain floors of beaten earth (rooms 3, 4, 8 and 9), or are so badly damaged that the floor type can no longer be identified (1 and 5-7). An overview of the wall decoration confirms that room 2 must have been a reception room. This room, and room 5, contain the best preserved remains of plaster. Both have Third Style paintings, consisting of a panel decoration with black, red and yellow fields in the main zone, and architectural elements on a white ground in the upper zone. The remaining rooms, except room 9, also have traces of wall decoration, but they are too faded to allow closer scrutiny.

Inscriptions
On the north wall of room 1 was a collection of graffiti, barely legible in places; the clearest is CIL 10553 (Della Corte 1958: 269 no. 370): 'P SEPTVMIVS'.[220] On the first floor, in the room above room 3, the following phrases were written on the west wall: 'CERE APOLLIN' and 'CERES COSSVTIVS (?)' (CIL 10556).[221] Several

---

[220] Catalano (1982: 959) regards this 'P. Septumius' as the owner of the house. The remaining inscriptions are CIL 10554-10555 (Della Corte 1958: 269 no. 371-374; Solin 1973B: 272, 276).

[221] Della Corte 1958: 259 nos. 168-169; Solin 1973B: 272, 276.

amphorae and jugs from the upper storey also bore inscriptions.[222]

Published finds

As well as the amphorae and jugs mentioned above, more amphorae were found under the staircase. A mortar of volcanic stone and some lengths of fabric were discovered in room 3. A chain, two small terracotta lamps and three glass bottles were also found here.[223]

Building history

Maiuri (1958: 425-426) argues that the house was made up of several more luxurious rooms from an older house. Because the space was limited by the surrounding houses, extra floors, rather than extensions at ground level, were added to develop it further. Both upper storeys were situated above rooms 3-5, while courtyard 6 provided light. The drain from the upper storey was in the southwest corner of room 7, where the drainage systems of two houses came out (this house and the Casa dei Cervi).

It was indicated above, in the sections on the Casa dell'Alcova (see § 5.8), that Ganschow's observations (1989: 208-210) about rooms 11-14 of the Casa dei Cervi are of particular importance. It was Ganschow who determined that these rooms must originally have formed part of the Casa dell'Alcova, and not the Casa della Stoffa, as Maiuri (1958: 310) and Tran Tam Tinh (1988: 12) have maintained. The dividing wall between these rooms and the Casa della Stoffa must be regarded as part of the first building phase, and formed the original east boundary of the Casa dell'Alcova (see also fig. 9).

The history of the house is closely linked with that of the Casa dei Cervi, as Ganschow pointed out, but also with that of the Casa dell'Alcova, because room 16 in this house was once part of the Casa della Stoffa. It was assumed above (see § 5.8) that a reorganisation of this part of *insula* IV must have taken place at some time, during which several rooms changed owners. The Casa della Stoffa was included in this reorganisation. We can distinguish with some certainty the following phases in its building history.

The original development of the plot probably took place later than the construction of the Casa della Fullonica and the Casa dell'Alcova on the west side of *insula* IV. It has already been noted above (see § 4.4.4) that the division of space in this area took place no later than the early 1st century BC. On the basis of the technique that was used (*opus incertum* B), the most likely date is some time during the 2nd century BC.

Later, probably in the early Imperial period, the house was involved in a large scale reorganisation of lots, which meant that space was sacrificed in two places. The room

---

[222] *Amphorae*: CIL 10817, 10823 (= 10909), 10845, 10887; Della Corte 1958: 259 no. 170, 258-259 no. 164, 259 no. 165, 164a. *Jugs* (9 in total): CIL 10831-10832; Della Corte 1958: 259 no. 171.

[223] Maiuri 1958: 426. *Lamps*: Bisi Ingrassia 1977: 92 type IX G, 96 type X B. *Glass*: E595 (10/11/1930), 602 (12/11/1930), 635 (1/12/1930) - Scatozza Höricht 1986: 65, 70. *Chain*: E610 - Scatozza Höricht 1989A: Cat. 147.

on the northwest side was added to the Casa dell'Alcova and the north-west corner of room 7 was made into a toilet for the Casa dei Cervi. The rest of the house was completely renovated. The new walls were constructed in *opus reticulatum* A. It is possible that room 2 had already been extended to the west using *opus quasi-reticulatum* for the west wall. Finally, repairs in *opus incertum* D would seem to date from after the earthquake in AD 62.

Metrological analysis (Pl. XV)
The original rectangular plot was staked out at 53.5' (1470 cm) x 37' (1016 cm), using an Oscan foot of 27.55 cm. The depth is presumably not a round number because it was the space left over after the construction of the other houses (lots IV B and C). The following observations can be made about the house in its present form.

Widthways the house is divided into two areas: a strip of rooms on the north side, which continues into room 16 of the Casa dell'Alcova, and the actual residential core to the south with a long corridor leading to the back of the house. The area on the north side is 15' (414 cm) wide, while the south area is 20' (545.5-555 cm) across. The available space was already divided in this way in the original layout of the house, judging by the traces of *opus incertum* B in the dividing wall between room 7 and room 16 of the Casa dell'Alcova.

It is likely that the plan of room 1 has also remained unchanged. It has an internal depth of 17.5' (477-485 cm) and a width of 20' (545.5/555 cm). Rooms 2 and 4 are 15' (414 cm) deep, but they have not retained their original width: the west wall of room 2 was moved, making the room 22'R (652/654 cm) wide. Room 4 is 7.25'R (212.5/213 cm) wide, which is presumably a 'leftover' space again, because room 16 in the Casa dell'Alcova remained unchanged (17.5' x 15'). The dimensions of room 3 are less easy to analyse. Presumably it is 15'O (407/410 cm) wide and 8.5'O or 8'R (235/236 cm) deep.

Some changes were made to the original design of the back of the house, probably as a result of the construction of the two upper storeys. A Roman foot of 29.45 cm was used in this reconstruction. Room 5 and courtyard 6 are both squares of 10'R x 10'R (289.5-296 cm). Room 7, excluding the drain, is 7.5'R x 7.5'R (225-226.5 cm), and room 8 measures 7'R/7.5'R x 10'R (208/221 x 296.5 cm). The length of corridor 9 works out at 10.5'R (311 cm), and its width is 3.5'R (99/103 cm).

Design
It is clear from an examination of the design of the house - insofar as it can be reconstructed from its present state - that a balanced division of the width was considered more important than the 'usual' depthwise division of the house into strips. Without doubt this was because the architect could not determine the depth himself; it was already fixed when building began. The relatively small depth available will also have influenced the design. In any case the width was divided so as to create a ratio of 3:4 between the two areas, creating one strip of 20' and one of 15'. Subsequently room (1) was constructed in the southern area, with a proportion of 7:8 (17.5' x 20'). Later changes altered the original plan at the back of the house and on the north side. At the

back of the house the basic outlines of the reconstruction can still be deduced: in this area the rooms are based on squares. The sides of room 5 and court 6 measure 10'R; the sides of room 7 are 7.5'R. Room 8 was designed with a proportion of 3:4 (7.5'R x 10'R).

Finally, the following observations can be made about the original design. The dimensions of room 1 (17.5' x 20') are practically the same as those of the halls or circulation areas in lots III A, B, J and K, which are also 20' across. The depth of room 2 (15'), which is situated on one side of the house, corresponds with the depth of the front strip of rooms in these lots. Perhaps in this house the 'usual' first strip of 15' was staked out at the side of the house instead of the front because of the lack of space.

5.15. Casa dei Cervi (IV 21) (Pl. XVI)

The entire southeastern quarter of *insula* IV is taken up by this house, which has an entrance (21) on *cardo* V. It takes its name from two statue-groups found in the garden, depicting a fight between a deer and a pack of hounds. The house was excavated between October 1929 and April 1932. Leaving aside the rooms to the northwest, the house is rectangular; one old lot can still be identified clearly (lot IV K), and several more make up the southern part of the house. The total depth of the house, measured from the northern rooms up to and including the *loggia* in the south, is ca. 5150 cm. The maximum width, measured in the south, is 2430 cm. The house has a total of 36 rooms on the ground floor, including the garden and several corridors. In addition there was an upper storey above the northern rooms (accessible by the staircase in room 38) and above rooms 16 and 17 (reached by staircases 36 and 37).

Select Bibliography
Van Aken 1943: 39, 77, 78; Maiuri 1943; Maiuri 1958: 302-323, figs 240-257, Pl. XXX; Tamm 1963: 144, fig. 47 a+b, 203; Scagliarini 1974: 23-25, fig. 41; McKay 1975: 60, fig. 17, 20; Allroggen-Bedel 1975B; Maiuri 1977: 60-63; Tran Tam Tinh 1977; Sear 1977: 27, 33, 96 no. 72, Pl. 41.1; Bisi Ingrassia 1977: 79, 82, 93; Orr 1978: 195 no. 14; Jashemski 1979: 120; Guadagno 1981: 155 no. 126 (bread with inscription); De Vos/De Vos 1982: 274-275; Catalano 1982: 959; Barbet 1985A: 228, 266; Barbet 1985B: 91, 127, 129, 250; Clarke 1985: 96; Guidobaldi 1985: 186, Pl. 2.1 (room 17); 190, Pl. 5.3 (room 5); 193, Pl. 6.5 (room 23); 200, Pl. 9.5 (room 15); 207, Pl. 12.4 ('tabl. 15' = corridor 31); Scatozza Höricht 1986: 46 Cat. 82, 56 Cat. 125, 60 Cat. 168, 61 Cat. 186, 64 Cat. 214, Pl. VIII.1, XVIII, XXX, XXXV, XXXVI; Moormann 1988: 108-109, Cat. 029/1, 029/2; Conticello De Spagnolis/De Carolis 1988: 196 Cat. 127; McIlwaine 1988: 55, 438-439; 3.578, 3.590, 3.599, 3.681, 3.761, 3.784, 3.787, 3.802, 4.14, 4.18, 4.28, 4.31, 4.48-49, 4.54, 4.62, 4.115, 4.123, 4.133, 5.34, 9.319-320; Tran Tam Tinh 1988; Ganschow 1989: especially 184-219; Scatozza Höricht 1989A: Cat. 146; Manni 1990: 140-142; Clarke 1991: 243-250, figs 147-152; Ling 1991: 82; De Kind 1991A; Mols 1994: 51, 58, 257-258; Wallace-Hadrill 1994: 19, 20, 31, 36, 51-53, 82, 87, 127, 128, 201, figs 2.3, 3.18. 6.6-7, Pl. 1.

The most comprehensive and extensively illustrated publication of the house is by Tran Tam Tinh (1988).[224] Maiuri (1958) also devotes much attention to it. Brief accounts of the architecture and descriptions of the house can be found in Tamm (1963), McKay (1975), Maiuri (1977), De Vos (1982), and Wallace-Hadrill (1994). Ganschow (1989) has produced an important analysis of its building history. Tran Tam Tinh (1977) has also published a summarised report of the excavations carried out in the 1970s. Allroggen-Bedel (1975A) examines the frescoes, as well as the

---

[224] For a review of this work (and of Ganschow 1989), see De Kind 1991A.

bread that is said to have been found in the house; Guadagno (1981) has published a response to her article. Other finds are mentioned in Bisi Ingrassia (1977), Scatozza Höricht (1986; 1989A), Conticello De Spagnolis/De Carolis (1988) and Mols (1994). The wall and floor decoration of the house is discussed by Scagliarini (1974), Sear (1977), Barbet (1985A; 1985B), Clarke (1985; 1991), Guidobaldi (1985), Moormann (1988), Manni (1990) and Ling (1991).

Plan and rooms (Pl. XVI)
Because it is extremely difficult to determine the precise function of several rooms, only groups of rooms that can be identified will be described. Near the entrance (1), around the *atrium* (24), there are several plain living rooms on both the ground floor (rooms 2-4) and the upper storey. Beyond is a group of luxurious living rooms of various sizes (rooms 5-10), the largest of which (room 5) is situated exactly on the north-south axis of the house. To the north of these rooms is a group of service rooms (11-14 and 28) in an annexe, accessed via corridors 25-27; these rooms include the kitchen (13) and a toilet (14). In the southern part of the house, off terrace 18, there is another series of living rooms, including some large rooms (15-17) and some of a more modest size (22 and 23). The rooms were conveniently situated to take advantage of the view out to sea, and were separated by the large garden (33) from the group of living rooms near the entrance. Small *exedrae* in the garden created secluded corners (34 and 35) and housed the two staircases to the rooms above the southern area of the house (36 and 37). Long, wide, covered corridors (29-32) connected the two living areas. The service rooms for the terrace area were in an annexe at the south-east corner (rooms 19-21).

Wall construction
For a comprehensive account of the wall construction in this house the reader is referred to Ganschow (1989: 184-219). One of the most important findings to emerge from his study is that the wall construction in the house is not as homogeneous as Maiuri (1958: 302) and Tran Tam Tinh (1988: 29) had always assumed. It is true that much of it is built in *opus reticulatum* A, reinforced in places with *opus vittatum mixtum* and *opus latericium*, but the old *opus incertum* type B is found in many places, in particular in the northern dividing wall of lot IV K and in the rooms in this old lot. The same type is also found in the western dividing wall (with the Casa dell'Atrio a Mosaico). It was often used for the lowest courses of a wall, with several courses of bricks on top, and the rest in *opus reticulatum* A. From this evidence Ganschow deduced that the bricks were intended to level off the old remains of the wall in *opus incertum* B, so that building could continue in *opus reticulatum* A.

Floor and wall decoration
The decoration of this house has been discussed in detail by Tran Tam Tinh (1988), so only a brief account will be given in the present study. Despite the fact that the house is generally well preserved, it is not possible to identify the floor type in rooms 4, 11-13, 19-21, 27, 28, 33, 35, 36 and 38. The plainest types of paving can be found in

the least important rooms: there is beaten earth in rooms 2, 14, 34 and 37, and plain *opus signinum* in the *atrium* (24) and several rooms around it (3, 25, 26).[225] In the more prestigious living and circulation rooms there are mosaic or *opus sectile* floors, or combinations of both types. The simplest form of mosaic floor (white) occurs in the more modest living rooms 9 and 22 (here with a single black border). Mosaic with inlays of *opus sectile* was laid in the connecting rooms, the *fauces* (1) and the corridors of the *cryptoporticus* (29-32). The remaining living rooms (5-8, 10, 15-18 and 23) were luxuriously decorated with *opus sectile* floors. The diversity of patterns in these rooms has been discussed by Tran Tam Tinh (1988: 35-37, 137-147).[226]

In more than half of the rooms in the house only faded remains of the wall decoration can be seen (rooms 1, 3, 4, 8, 9, 11-14, 18-21, 28 and 33-37). Two rooms (2 and 38) do not contain any traces of the original plaster at all. In some rooms (22, 26 and 27) only the socle is still visible; in each case it is black. The best-preserved paintings are all in the Fourth Style; the scheme with alternate fields and architectural elements dominates. Simple panel decorations, without architecture, can be found in three corridors: the panels have a black background in corridor 25 and a red background in both the east and west *cryptoporticus* (30 and 32). The main zones of the remaining walls are dominated by the colours red (room 7, 10, 17, 31) and black (5, 6, 24, 29). A red background was also chosen for the richly detailed ceiling preserved in room 7. Blue was used as a background in luxurious living rooms 16 and 23, while the large room 15 has red, yellow and blue fields. This room must have been richly decorated, judging from the remains of the marble socle and figured panels that were found in it. The same was probably true of room 17 next door, which also had a marble socle. Furthermore, numerous figured scenes were painted in the *cryptoporticus*, in the form of small panels depicting cupids (Tran Tam Tinh 1988: 52-68). Finally, the mosaic decoration of the pediment over the entrance to the garden (33) is worthy of mention: it depicts the head of Oceanus surrounded by sea creatures.

Inscriptions
The CIL-numbers related to the Casa dei Cervi are the following: CIL (X) 8058,18; CIL (IV) 10557-10561, 10728, 10743, 10754, 10771, 10773, 10781, 10782, 10796, 10799, 10808, 10826, 10827, 10841, 10844, 10846, 10867, 10900. Most of these are mentioned by Tran Tam Tinh (1988: 114-116, 123), who discusses both the pottery objects with labels and names (with an indication of find date and findspot), and the graffiti on the walls.[227] He only omits the letters 'A L S' on a fragment of plaster from

---

[225] Tran Tam Tinh (1988: 33) assumes that nearly all the common rooms, even those in which the original floor could no longer be identified, had *opus signinum* floors.

[226] See also Scagliarini 1974: fig. 41 and Clarke 1991: 243-250 for a discussion of systems in the floor and wall decoration.

[227] In some of his notes the CIL-numbers are missing: n.28a should refer to CIL IV, 10771; n.28f to CIL IV, 10799; n.28g to CIL IV, 10796; n.31a to CIL IV, 10558-10559. N.28k should read CIL IV, 10827. For a discussion of the bread with the name 'Q. Granius Celer' on it (supposedly the name of the last owner; CIL X 8058,18) which was said to have been found in the Casa dei Cervi: Tran Tam Tinh 1988: 123-124; Allroggen-Bedel 1975B; Guadagno 1981:

'ambiente 44' (CIL IV, 10557; Della Corte 1958: 251 no. 85); taking into account the number assigned to this room and the date on which the fragment was found, it seems that the room must have been on the upper storey.

Published finds
The finds in this house have been described in great detail by Tran Tam Tinh (1988: 97-120). He starts with a discussion of the sculptures (11 in total), and then moves on to the bronze objects (9, including a bath tub, jugs and tripods). He goes on to discuss ceramic objects (20 pieces of kitchenware, as well as several complete and fragmentary amphorae and jugs with inscriptions), terracotta lamps (7 in total)[228], glass (two bottles) and finally miscellaneous objects (a necklace[229], objects made of bone, and several small weights). A remarkable find (excavated on 21-22/10/1930) was a wooden chest in room 4, containing 16 pieces of pottery, six small lamps and four bone objects (E545-568). In addition, Scatozza Höricht reports that further glass objects (a large bottle and four small ones) were discovered in this house, while Conticello De Spagnolis/De Carolis refer to an additional bronze lamp, and Mols to a wooden rack in room 3.[230]

Building history
Judging from the refinement and quality of the wall construction, which he regards as homogeneous, Maiuri (1958: 303) dates the house to the reign of Claudius. Furthermore, with regard to the history of specific areas and rooms, he reports the following: rooms 8 and 9 once formed a single room, judging by the floor; room 12 was once a light well for the part of the house which had its entrance on the 'vicolo orientale' (*cardo* V); the depth of room 15 was the same as the smaller living rooms 16 and 17, which Maiuri maintains can be deduced from the wall construction of the part that protrudes into the garden; initially the ceilings of rooms 16 and 17 were the same height as room 15, but they were lowered to allow for the construction of an upper storey, and at some time during this construction phase the windows were altered (Maiuri 1958: 308, 310, 317-319).

Tran Tam Tinh (1988: 21) has ascertained that there were once more (maybe two) east-west oriented houses in the garden area, judging from remains found under the present ground level and from the orientation of the southern area. He agrees with Maiuri that the northern rooms once belonged to the Casa della Stoffa. He suggests that there was some special connection between the two houses, either as a result of a

---

155 no. 126. On the basis of CIL IV, 10796 (Della Corte 1958: 251 no. 94) Catalano (1982: 959) deduces that 'Novius Laluscus' must have been the owner of the Casa dei Cervi.

[228] See also Bisi Ingrassia 1977: 79 type V D, type V E (2 ex.), 82 type VII A, 93 type IX H$_2$.

[229] See also Scatozza Höricht 1989A: Cat. 146.

[230] *Glass*: E509 (24/4/1930) was found in the 'peristyle', and nos. E572 (6/11/1930), E587-589 (8/11/1930) were found in the house itself- Scatozza Höricht 1986: 46, 56, 60, 61, 64. *Bronze lamp*: E484 (24/3/1930) - Conticello De Spagnolis/De Carolis 1988: 196 Cat. 127. *Wooden furniture*: Mols 1994: 257-258. From Maiuri (1943) it can be deduced that a statue of Eros must also have originated from this house, but Tran Tam Tinh (1988) does not mention it.

family relationship between the owners, or as a result of official regulations, because the drain from the latrine of the Casa dei Cervi came out in the Casa della Stoffa, and because courtyard 6 in the Casa della Stoffa provided light to corridor 26 in the Casa dei Cervi. There was also a connection to the Casa dell'Alcova via a door in room 12, which was later walled up. Tran Tam Tinh (1988: 84) thinks that the construction of the Casa dei Cervi took place after the earthquake of 62: this conclusion is based on the use of *opus vittatum mixtum* in the pillars, *antae* and doorposts, the use of *opus latericium* in the facade of room 5, the marble veneer of the socles in rooms 15 and 17, and the construction of a *cryptoporticus* with a tiled roof.

However, from Ganschow's exhaustive analysis of the wall construction (1989: 184-219), it seems that the dates given by Maiuri and Tran Tam Tinh cannot be upheld. The reinforcement of corners with *opus vittatum mixtum* and *opus latericium* was particularly common in the Augustan period, and it therefore cannot be dated exclusively to the last building period in Herculaneum. The lack of uniformity in the construction of this house has already been mentioned above. Ganschow (1989: 216-217) distinguishes five phases in the building history of the Casa dei Cervi (see also fig. 9).

In the Samnite period there was a long rectangular house in the northern area (rooms 1-10 = lot IV K); in Ganschow's opinion its plan was similar to that of other houses in the town, with an off-centre *fauces* and a single row of rooms along the side of the *atrium*. This theory will be discussed in connection with the metrological analysis of the house. It is possible that in the earliest period of the town's history there were three houses in the garden area with entrances on *cardo* V. Traces of older buildings under the mosaics, finds from the excavations of the 1970s, and the appearance of *opus incertum* B in the facade would seem to support this theory. In that early period rooms 11-14 belonged to the Casa dell'Alcova, and not to the Casa della Stoffa as Maiuri and Tran Tam Tinh thought. The reader is referred to § 5.8 for a more detailed analysis of the history of this area.

The next stage in the development of the house is difficult to reconstruct; Ganschow (1989: 216) places this phase - with some reservations - in the Republican era. It is presumed that several north-south oriented walls were built in the garden area, which formed at least three rooms; corridors 30 and 32 of the *cryptoporticus* had already been constructed. In Ganschow's opinion this may have been the initial construction phase of either a *viridarium* or a neighbouring house, for which the older houses on the site were pulled down or assimilated.

The major reconstruction of the house, which constitutes the third building phase, presumably took place in the early Imperial period. At this time rooms 11-14 and the garden were annexed to the original lot IV K, a *loggia* was built on the city wall, and a modest upper storey was added above room 17. Staircase 36, which led to the upper storey above room 17, was positioned so that the existing drainage system (gutter to cistern opening) in the northwest corner of the garden remained intact. This observation is important not only for determining dates, but also because the gutter that led to the cistern was not taken into account when the upper storey was later extended, when staircase 37 was put in. Ganschow concludes that this reconstruction, the fourth phase in the history of the house, must have taken place at the same time as the cistern went out of use or some time afterwards. On the basis of information in Tran Tam Tinh (1977: 55), this phase must have begun in the first half of the 1st century AD. The more extensive reconstruction must have taken place before then. In any case, both phases must be earlier than the earthquake of 62, which caused damage to this house. Traces of the repairs that were carried out after the earthquake, the last building phase, have remained visible in several places to this day.

Metrological analysis (Pl. XVI)
The old core of the house (lot IV K) was a *domus* measuring more than 30' (842 cm: width) x 84' (2309 cm: depth); it is deeper than the corresponding area in the Casa dell'Atrio a Mosaico, which is only 77.5 feet long. Here a foot measure of 27.5 cm was used. There is little evidence for the original layout of the house. The *atrium* area may have retained its original plan, with rooms on the north and east sides, as Ganschow suggested. The strip at the front of the house is the same depth as the *fauces* (1) (13', 353 cm), so that the internal depth of room 2 works out at 10' (277/287 cm). The *fauces* is 6' (159/169.5 cm) wide, while the external width of room 2 is 10'R (296 cm). The division of the width in the *atrium* strip is more difficult to analyse. The width of the *atrium* (24) itself is 20'O (543.5-550 cm), but the external width of room 4 is 10'R (296/299.5 cm). The use of different units may indicate that the area was completely reconstructed at some time; the original layout of 10' for the rooms and 20' for the *atrium* was retained to some extent, but the width of the rooms was staked out using the new Roman foot of 29.4 cm. If this was the case, the width of the *atrium* should be regarded as 18.5'R instead of 20'O. It was indicated above that there was probably no *impluvium* in the original *atrium*. From an overview of *atrium* widths in Herculaneum (De Kind 1991A: 184) it would appear that an *atrium* with *impluvium* at the front of a house usually had a width of at least 25 feet. In this house the width of the northern area (30' in total) would mean that there was either no *impluvium* or no side rooms, as in the Casa dell'Atrio a Mosaico. As traces of the old type of construction *opus incertum* B were found in the walls of room 3, the first explanation would appear to be the most likely. Finally, room 4 has an internal depth of 8.5'O (232.5/233 cm) and is 8.5'R across (256/257 cm).

The present depth of the *atrium* (506 cm) is not original, because it was changed when the large room 5 was constructed. This room was built in the exact centre of the northern area: the distance between the west wall of the house and the west wall of room 5 (ca. 800 cm) is the same as the distance from the east wall of the room to the east wall of the house (internal dimensions). It forms a square, not including the passage to the south: it measures 19'R x 19'R (555-558.5 cm). If the corridor is included, the room is 23.5'R (694/696 cm) wide.

It cannot always be determined with certainty which of the rooms at the back of the house were original, which ones consisted partly of older remains, and which were rebuilt to totally new designs. The dimensions of the rooms are given below, together with the most likely equivalents in feet:

Room 6: 9'R x 10'O (263.5/267.5 x 276/277 cm);
Room 7: 13.5'O x 17.5'O (376/377 x 479.5/482 cm);
Room 8: 6'R x 7.5'R (177/178 x 217/225 cm);
Room 9: 8.5'R/9'R x 10.5'R (253/263.5 x 316/316.5 cm);
Room 10: 10.5'R x 13.5'O (308.5/312.5 x 374.5/383 cm).

In the northern area rooms 11, 12 and 28 formed a square with sides of ca. 15'R (432.5 cm x 444 cm). The dimensions of the rooms are as follows:
Room 11: 3.5'R/4'O x 9'R/11'R (102/110 x 265.5/322 cm);
Room 12: 8.5'R x 7.5'R/9'R (253/258 x 229/266.5 cm);
Kitchen 13: 10.5'R x 11.5'R (309 x 340 cm);
Latrine 14: 5'R x 5.5'R (145 x 156/158 cm);
Room 28: 6'R x 13.5'R (171.5/177.5 x 396 cm).

In the southern part of the house, in the area of the garden and *cryptoporticus*, traces of walls found under the mosaic floors seem to belong to the earliest building phase. It is possible that there were three houses with entrances on *cardo* V. The northernmost house may have been 40' O (1100 cm) across, judging from the traces in the west corridor of the *cryptoporticus* (32), while the total width of the other two houses may have been 60'O (1642 cm). It is striking that the garden area of the house measures exactly 100 Oscan feet (2728-2742 cm) from north to south, from the north wall of corridor 29 up to and including the north wall of corridor 31. This may support Ganschow's theory of a building phase in the Republican era, in which the north-south corridors 30 and 32 were built, some time before the large-scale reconstruction of the house.

At present the dimensions of the *cryptoporticus* are 77'R x 105'R (2277 x 3081.5/3088 cm), with a minor deviation on the south side, where it measures 76'R (2245.5 cm). The south corridor (31) is wider than the others: 12'R (355/356 cm) as opposed to 9'R (265-268.5 cm). The external width of the garden works out at 59'R (1733.5/1743 cm). The large room 15 is designed so that its north wall is on the east-west axis of the *cryptoporticus* area: the distance from this wall to the north wall of corridor 29 is the same as the distance to the south wall of corridor 31 (53'R = 1560/1565 cm). The internal dimensions of room 15 are 24'R x 36.5'R (703.5/704 x 1070/1073.5 cm); the northern area of the room has windows onto the garden, and the enclosed southern area forms a square with sides of 24'R (701/702.5 cm). The large central openings onto the garden and the corridor are 10'R wide (289/295 cm). The living rooms on either side (16 and 17) are 19.5'R (579-582.5 cm) deep and 14.5'R-15'R (431-460 cm) across. Presumably the two *exedrae* in the garden (34 and 35) measured 15'R x 17.5'R (439.5/444 x 509/513.5 cm) before the staircases were put in. In the southeastern annexe areas of 4.5'R x 10'R (127-136 x 292-296 cm) were staked out for rooms 19 and 20; room 21 has the same depth but greater length: 4.5'R x ca. 11.5'R (132-134 x 332.5 cm). The gazebo (18) on the terrace is 12.5'R x 17'R (366-371.5 x 496/506 cm). Finally, the small living rooms 22 and 23 measure 7'R x 12'R (207/210 x 345/348.5 cm) and 9.5'R x 11'R (285 x 321/333.5 cm) respectively.

Design

We can only put together a partial picture of the original design of the northern part of the house from the arrangement of the rooms around the *atrium* (24). It is likely that there was a strip of rooms on one side of this area (north side). This strip occupied a width of 10' and the *atrium* 20'. The *fauces* strip was 13' deep, so that the rooms along the street had an internal depth of 10'. The area of land to the south of this lot was 100' long, and it is likely that the original east-west oriented houses were replaced by other buildings at some time before the major reconstruction of the Casa dei Cervi.

The entire plot of land was redeveloped in the early Imperial period. Although some rooms were not based on exact ratios, it seems that most of the area was systematically designed. For example, there was a large luxurious living room (5), in the exact centre of the northern part of the house, centred on the newly created north-south axis; it formed a square with sides of 19'R, and it looked out across the garden and the sea to the south. The garden area, with rooms on the south side and a *cryptoporticus* surrounding it, occupied a rectangle of 77'R x 105'R, a ratio of 11:15. In this area the architect tried as far as possible to achieve symmetry on either side of the north-south axis. This axis runs through the exact centre of the large living room 15, which corresponds to room 5 at the other end of the garden. The depth of room 15 is closely related to the overall division of space because its north wall lies on the east-west axis of the southern part of the house. The internal dimensions of room 15 are 24'R x 36.5'R, which nearly makes for a ratio of 2:3. The width and depth of the *exedrae* on either side of room 15 (34 and 35) are in the ratio 6:7 (15'R x 17.5'R).

183

6. CLASSIFICATION AND TYPOLOGY OF THE HOUSES

In order to classify the houses in *insulae* III and IV, it is first necessary to consider earlier typologies of Roman houses in general and houses at Herculaneum in particular. As considerable attention has already been focused on the Roman house, the following overview will simply provide the reader with a summary of the most important theories of classification proposed in the past. The floor and wall decoration, which can be a useful tool for classification purposes, will not be considered in this chapter. Although these aspects of design have been systematically researched at Herculaneum, it is clear that their survival is very uneven, for various reasons: namely, the amount of attention that the Bourbon excavators devoted to each house, the state in which the individual houses were found, and the extent to which they were subsequently restored and maintained. From this point on, therefore, only the layout of the houses will be taken into account.

6.1. Classifications and typologies of the Roman house

For a long time theories about the development and design of the Roman house were based on information from Vitruvius and on the remains of Pompeii, Herculaneum and Ostia. From these sources it was concluded that the most common type was the *atrium* house, to which a peristyle was sometimes added at a later date. The 'standard' type of *atrium* house is illustrated by Mau (1908: figs 127-128): a square building with a central entrance at the front consisting of a vestibule (*vestibulum*) and a corridor (*fauces*), with spacious rooms on either side. The *fauces* led to the central hall (*atrium*), which had a hole in the roof (*compluvium*) and a corresponding basin in the floor (*impluvium*); adjoining it on both sides were rooms (*cubicula*) and open annexes (*alae*). Opposite the entrance was a large, open-fronted room (*tablinum*), which was also open to the rear of the house. There were rooms on both sides of the *tablinum*, including the dining room (*triclinium*), and on one side a passageway to the rear of the house, where the garden, and later the peristyle and adjoining rooms were situated. This type of house, with occasional deviations from the basic design, occurs frequently at Pompeii and has therefore been regarded as standard in surveys of Roman houses, for example, by Mau (1908), Maiuri (1951A) and McKay (1975).

Birgitta Tamm (1973) rightly argues that the prototype of the Roman house cannot be reconstructed by combining information from the description of Vitruvius, actual examples from Pompeii, and a theoretical reconstruction of the ancient Italian house. In her search for the typical Roman house she uses examples in Rome (on the Forma Urbis Romae) and in Ostia, which can be used as a source in combination with Vitruvius' text; she rightly rejects the houses in Pompeii, which were largely built during the Samnite period. However, Tamm continues to use Vitruvius as a starting-point, and offers few new ideas for a classification of houses in ancient Italy.

James Packer (1975) also fails to come up with a different classification of the material, but the virtue of his work is that it focuses on house types that deviate from the traditional *atrium* plan. Packer distinguishes a number of groups, depending on whether the living rooms open off a covered *atrium*, a peristyle or a corridor. He describes these non-traditional house types as 'middle- and lower-class houses'. However, this expression raises the question of whether it is appropriate to impose modern ideas of class-consciousness onto Roman society. In any case Packer showes that there were more types than the standard *atrium* house.

Another non-standard type is discussed in a study by Adolf Hoffmann (1979). In this short conference paper the writer points out the existence of 'terraced' houses in Pompeii. Hoffmann uses houses I 11, 12-15 as examples. These four houses, built side by side, had a different design from the usual *atrium* house. They each had a row of rooms along the street, opening off a closed *atrium* or hall, which was wider than it was long. Behind this there was another row of rooms and a garden or courtyard. The central hall presumably served two floors (Hoffmann 1979: fig. 1). Hoffmann points out that the introduction of the terraced house must have been an attempt to meet the ever-growing demand of the middle classes for living accommodation. An alternative to the *atrium* house was needed so that the available land could be used more economically. Light and air were supplied to this new type of house from the outside, rather than from the *atrium*.

Edith Evans' study (1978; 1980) of the layout of houses at Pompeii is the most systematic to date. She too opposes the established view that a study of domestic architecture in ancient Italy should use the 'typical' *atrium* house as a starting-point, and points out that this can sometimes lead to misinterpretations (Evans 1978: 175). Instead, she devised a system of analysis in which the houses at Pompeii are regarded as a series of 'ranges' or strips, which follow a number of different patterns. The 'front range' is the row of rooms between the street and the *atrium*; the 'side ranges' are the rooms on either side of the *atrium*; and the strip of rooms opposite the entrance, at the back of the *atrium*, is referred to as the '*tablinum* range'. However, her classification of *atrium* types seems to be somewhat contradictory to this line of reasoning: she uses the five established types distinguished by Vitruvius (*tuscanicum*, *tetrastylum*, *corinthium*, *displuviatum*, *testudinatum*). In another article Evans discusses 56 Pompeian houses without side-rooms off the *atrium* (Evans, 1978). From this, it can be deduced that a considerable number of houses, especially those built in the Samnite period, follow a plan that was far from 'ideal'. Instead, these houses were designed to use the available space as efficiently as possible. This meant, for example, that the front range was often used as a living space opening onto the *atrium*, instead of shops opening onto the street, and that many houses had upper floors (Evans 1978: 178-179). Perhaps the most important part of her study (Evans 1980) is her formal analysis of the *atrium* houses: she determined possible classifications for each range of rooms, so that each house could be regarded as one of various

186

combinations of range-types. For example, the Casa del Cenacolo (V 2, h) is a combination of front range type Aa (houses with one room on either side of the *fauces* and no side-rooms) and *tablinum* range type Ab (houses with the *tablinum* in the centre of the range, between a room and an *andron*). Evans (1980: 43) believes that the shape of the *atrium* depended on the preference of either the owner or the architect, who took as his starting-point the shape of the lot and the number of rooms that were needed. However, she thinks that it is impossible to propose a typology based on such information. This point of view is endorsed by the author of the present study: it would seem that it is not the *atrium* that determines the house-type, but the shape and size of the lot on which the house was built. We should therefore focus on the allocation of space in terms of width and length, and not on the 'completeness' of the *atrium*. The method proposed by Evans can be a very useful tool, as it is based on objective criteria. However, one possible objection to her conclusions is that she did not devote enough attention to wall construction at Pompeii, which was her main evidence for dates, after wall paintings and capitals. The analysis of this type of material is extremely difficult, particularly for the earliest building phases, and valid conclusions can only be drawn after a very thorough and extensive investigation.[231]

The same can be said of Carol Martin Watts' dissertation (Watts 1990), in which she tries to find a 'pattern language' in several houses in Pompeii and Herculaneum. Watts identifies geometric as well as decorative 'patterns'; in which squares form the basic units from which the layout of the house is built up. She argues that the main rooms in the house (*atrium, tablinum,* etc.) were located in these squares using geometric ratios such as the Golden Section. However, besides the fact that her solutions often seem rather contrived and bear little or no relation to actual building methods, her analyses of some houses in Herculaneum are totally invalid because she failed to take their building history into account. The Casa del Gran Portale (V 34-35), for example, is regarded as a systematically planned, pre-Roman house (Watts 1990: 96, 98), when in actual fact it was constructed very late in the history of Herculaneum, using parts of older houses (Ganschow 1989: 293-304). One merit of Watts' study is her approach to the decorative aspects of the houses: her surveys of the colours in the wall paintings and of the floors and ceilings allow for a more precise determination of the individual rooms.

In 1994 Andrew Wallace-Hadrill published an important study of the houses at Pompeii and Herculaneum (Wallace-Hadrill 1994). He discusses several interesting aspects of the Roman house, such as the organisation of space and the use of decoration to structure social differences, the spread of luxury down the social scale, and the relationship between working areas and living rooms. For the present study it is important to note that he also includes a brief review of all the houses at Herculaneum and a more detailed discussion of several of them. He also produces a rough typology for his sample of 234 houses in Pompeii and Herculaneum, by ranking them according to their size, and simply dividing them into four groups (Wallace-Hadrill 1994: 80-82). The smallest houses are in quartile 1, the largest in quartile 4. Each quartile is

---

[231]   Cf. Peterse 1993 for more information about the earliest building techniques in Pompeii.

then characterised according to the types of units they commonly represent. However, as Wallace Hadrill (1994: 80) states, 'this is not typology in an archaeological sense, but a guide to what, in the spectrum of possibilities, each quartile covers'. Type 1 (area: 10-45 m²) consists mainly of shops or workshops. Houses of type 2 (area: 50-170 m²) usually do not have a regular plan: some are shops, some have a central circulation space (sometimes an *atrium*). Type 3 (area: 175-345 m²) includes the more symmetrically planned, 'average' sized houses, many of which would be regarded as 'typical' Pompeian houses. Finally, type 4 (area: 350-3000 m²) contains the richest, largest, and most famous houses in the sample. This classification is adequate for Wallace-Hadrill's purposes, but it is too schematic to be of use in the present study.

6.2. The classification of the houses at Herculaneum

In his work on Herculaneum, Maiuri (1958: 197) classified the houses on the basis of their layout and the presumed wealth or status of the occupants. He arrived at the following typology:
1. Patrician houses built according to the traditional *domus* plan.
2. Middle-class houses built according to the *domus* plan.
3. The large villas in the southern residential quarter.
4. Houses which do not follow the traditional plan.
5. Middle-class houses with shops.
6. Houses with several separate living areas.
7. Houses owned by members of the merchant classes and shops with living quarters.
8. Shops and commercial premises in the *insula orientalis* II.[232]

Clearly this classification cannot be used as the basis for a typology of the Roman house. For a start, it is hard to determine the social status of the owner/occupant objectively. Too much information about household goods and individual objects was lost during the Bourbon excavations; and even when they were first excavated, the houses and their decoration were in varying states of preservation.. Furthermore the social stratification of Herculaneum has never been fully analysed, and it is still not clear, for example, whether the area that has been excavated so far was a residential

---

[232] *Group 1*: Casa Sannitica, Casa del Bicentenario, Casa del Salone Nero, Casa del Tramezzo di Legno. *Group 2*: Casa del Sacello di Legno, Casa V 11, Casa del Mobilio Carbonizzato, Casa dell'Atrio Corinzio, Casa dei Due Atri, Casa dell'Erma di Bronzo, Casa dello Scheletro. *Group 3*: Casa della Gemma, Casa di M. Pilus Primigenius Granianus, Casa del Rilievo di Telefo, Casa d'Argo, Casa di Aristide, Casa del Genio, Casa dell'Albergo, Casa dell'Atrio a Mosaico, Casa dei Cervi. *Group 4*: Casa del Gran Portale, Casa del Bel Cortile, Casa dell'Alcova. *Group 5*: Casa di Nettuno e d'Anfitrite, Casa di Galba. *Group 6*: Casa a Graticcio. *Group 7*: Casa del Telaio, Casa con Giardino, Casa della Fullonica, Casa della Stoffa, Casa dell'Ara Laterizia, Casa del Papiro Dipinto; the shops , IV 10-11, IV 12-16, IV 17-18, V 19-22, V 23-25, V 26-29, VII 1-1b.

quarter with a specific character, which may have determined what kind of people lived there.[233] A second reason for not adopting Maiuri's classification is that he took as his starting-point the *domus* with rooms on both sides of the *atrium*, and placed houses with different layouts more or less arbitrarily in five different categories, without any formal connection.

Van Binnebeke (1991) proposes an interesting, logical classification of the houses in *insula* V. Using similar principles to Packer (1975), she determines the function of a house and distinguishes three groups: houses that were used solely for living in, houses that were used for commercial purposes, and houses that combined both these functions. Her study shows that the internal allocation of space was different in each type. This classification is not suitable for the present study, because the formal aspects of the house-plans are not taken into consideration. It would be interesting, however, to compare the results of the functional analysis and the formal analysis of the houses and to integrate the findings in some way.

The best starting-point for a study of the formal aspects of the houses at Herculaneum is the typology proposed by Ganschow (1989). He concludes that in the Samnite period there were three types of houses, which were all half the width of an *insula* in length: 1) a wide type; 2) a medium type; 3) a narrow type (Ganschow 1989: 321-323, 329). In the wide type the *fauces* is on the central axis of the *atrium*, which is surrounded by rooms on three sides, with a *tablinum* at the back. The medium type is almost identical to the wide type, but has an *atrium* across the entire width of the house, with no rooms along the sides. Finally, in the narrow type the *fauces* is on one side of the house; there are no rooms along the sides of the *atrium*, and instead of a *tablinum* there is a corridor running along the central axis of the house, flanked by two rooms.[234]

This classification is still based on the *atrium*, but not on an 'ideal' *atrium*; instead Ganschow has looked at the way in which the available space was allocated. In this respect his method of categorising the earliest houses at Herculaneum is similar to Evans' approach at Pompeii (1978; 1980). The material presented in chapter 5 can be analysed further on the basis of both these studies.

6.3. Proposed typology of the houses in Herculaneum

The following typology of the houses in Herculaneum is based on the width of the

---

[233]   Cf. also the more detailed critique in Wallace-Hadrill 1994: 124-129. For comments on social stratification see § 1.2.1.

[234]   Examples of the wide type: the central part of the Casa dello Scheletro, the Casa Sannitica, Casa del Mobilio Carbonizzato, Casa del Tramezzo di Legno, Casa di Nettuno e d'Anfitrite, Casa dell'Atrio Corinzio. Examples of the medium type: Casa dell'Erma di Bronzo, Casa della Fullonica, Casa del Sacello di Legno. Examples of the narrow type: southern part of the Casa dello Scheletro, Casa dei Cervi, Casa del Papiro Dipinto, Casa dell'Ara Laterizia, north-eastern part of the Casa dell'Albergo (Ganschow 1989: 321-323).

houses and the internal allocation of space, using the original layout whenever possible. Shops with attached living areas are generally not taken into consideration, unless their building history is known. See also fig. 11.

TYPE 1.

Type 1 houses are wide enough to allow the construction of an *atrium* with two side ranges, or, in other words, the 'standard' *atrium* type. Their width is at least ca. 1375 cm (50'O). This type is represented by the Casa del Bicentenario (V 13-18), the Casa del Salone Nero (VI 11-13) and possibly, both the front and rear parts of the Casa del Tramezzo di Legno (III 4-12), lots III E and III G. The Casa del Bicentenario was rebuilt in the 1st century AD and is 60'R (ca. 1765 cm) wide. The Casa del Salone Nero has a width of ca. 1502 cm, which is 54'O. If it is indeed the case that the irregularly-shaped strip of land on the north side of *insula* III was originally part of lots III E and III G, the width of III E is 50'O (ca. 1389 cm) and the width of III G is 55'O - 61'O (1533-1683 cm).[235]

TYPE 2.

Type 2 corresponds to Ganschow's 'wide' type. These houses are ca. 40'O wide, providing room for an *atrium* with a single side range. The following houses fall into this category: lot III C (the middle part of the Casa dello Scheletro), the Casa Sannitica (V 1-2), the Casa del Telaio (V 3-4), the Casa del Mobilio Carbonizzato (V 5), the Casa di Nettuno e d'Anfitrite (V 6-7), Casa V 11 (V 9-12), the Casa dell'Atrio Corinzio (V 30) and the front areas of the Casa del Colonnato Tuscanico (VI 16-18), the Casa del Rilievo di Telefo (Ins.Or. I 2-3), and possibly also of the Casa della Gemma (Ins.Or. I 1).

Of the houses mentioned above, the front area of the Casa del Colonnato Tuscanico is the widest: 1346 cm, or 49'O. From its width alone this house could be classified as type 1, but as it only has a single strip of rooms along the side of the *atrium* it is classified here as type 2.[236] The entrance area of the Casa della Gemma is also fairly wide, around 1265 cm (46'O), but it is not certain whether the southern side range always belonged to this house; if it did not, the Casa della Gemma should be classified as type 3 (see below). Of the remaining type 2 houses, the Casa del Mobilio Carbonizzato, the Casa dell'Atrio Corinzio and the front part of the Casa del Rilievo di Telefo all have internal widths of 40'O (1113, 1122 and 1105 cm, respectively). The layout of the Casa del Rilievo di Telefo was probably altered at a later date. The Casa del Telaio and Casa V 11 are 40'O wide including one of their side

---

[235]   As mentioned above (§ 4.1.1), H.M. Dresen assumes, presumably correctly, that both *insulae* V and VI had three broad lots on the north side, each 50' wide and extending across the whole width of the *insula*. The only way of gaining any new insights into the extent and appearance of these houses would be to carry out a detailed examination of them, including small-scale excavations. These houses are therefore not considered in the discussion of type 1.

[236]   See also the comments in the previous footnote.

walls (1100 cm and 1096 cm); no traces have survived of the original layout of the former house.[237] It is possible that the middle part of the Casa dello Scheletro (lot III C), which is 1053-1058 cm wide, can also be regarded as a lot of 38.5'O. The Casa di Nettuno e d'Anfitrite is about the same width on the east side as the Casa dell'Atrio Corinzio, but is narrower on the street side (995 cm = 36'O). The Casa Sannitica, on the other hand, has an internal width of 41.5'O (1144 cm). Finally, both parts of the Casa del Tramezzo di Legno (lots III E and G) should be classified as type 2, if they did not originally include the northern strip of *insula* III, and therefore had only one side range. Lot III E is 39'O (1073 cm) wide without the northern strip and lot III G is 42'O (1152-1162 cm).

TYPE 3.

Houses of type 3 are narrower than those of type 2 and have an *atrium* with no side ranges; this type is similar to Ganschow's 'medium type'. The widths of the houses in this category range from 27' to 30'. In addition to the unusually long Casa della Fullonica (lot IV D) and Casa dei Due Atri (VI 28-29), examples of this type include the following houses of normal length: the Casa a Graticcio (lot III H), the Casa dell'Erma di Bronzo (lot III I), the Casa del Sacello di Legno (V 31), the entrance areas of the Casa dell'Atrio a Mosaico and the Casa dei Cervi (lots IV A and IV K), and possibly the Casa della Gemma and the northern part of the Casa con Giardino (V 32).

The two long houses both have two *atria*, one extending across the entire width of the house at the front, and another narrower *atrium* at the rear. Lot IV D is 28.5'O (788.5 cm) wide, or 30'O including one side wall, while the Casa dei Due Atri is 30'R (875 cm) wide. The Casa del Sacello di Legno (837.5 cm), lot IV A (824-835 cm) and lot IV K (842 cm) are also 30'O wide. The two lots in *insula* III (H and I) are slightly narrower. As indicated in § 5.4, the Casa a Graticcio originally had the same layout as the Casa dell'Erma di Bronzo (see also § 5.5); the width of these two houses is 27'O (756 cm for lot III H and 753 cm for lot III I). It is possible that the northern part of the Casa con Giardino was also originally staked out as 27'R (804.5 cm). Assuming that the southern side range of the Casa della Gemma does not belong to the original plan, this house should also be classified as type 3, with a width of 31'O (852 cm).

TYPE 4.

Type 4 houses comprise a very special group of houses in Herculaneum, with unique characteristics. They correspond broadly to Ganschow's 'narrow type', but he erroneously classified the Casa dei Cervi (lot IV K) and the Casa del Papiro Dipinto (lot

---

[237] See especially § 4.4.4, in which the issue of plot width and actual available living space is discussed. See Ganschow 1989: 239-260 for the wall construction and building history of the Casa del Telaio.

IV E) as belonging to this group. In actual fact, type 4 is made up of only four adjacent lots in *insula* III, namely III A, III B, III J and III K. These four lots are 20'O (ca. 550 cm) across; in the front range (15' deep) they have one fairly large living room and an entrance-passage at the side, then a covered *atrium* with no side rooms (17' deep); in the *tablinum* range (13' deep) is a corridor between two small living rooms; and at the back of the house are a courtyard and light well (each 15' deep), with adjoining rooms. A detailed analysis of this type is given in § 5.2 and § 5.6. Because these houses are on a series of adjoining lots, two on either side of the insula, they could be described as 'terraced' houses, which were most probably built at about the same time, if not simultaneously.

TYPE 5.

Type 5 covers a small group of simple houses, which can best be described as the 'narrow strip house', because its width is never more than 20'O. The narrow strip house is characterized by a layout in which several rooms are built behind one another (the house was divided into several 'living strips', as it were), connected by a long corridor along one side of the house. Examples of this type can be found in the northern half of *insula* IV, in the lots IV E (Casa del Papiro Dipinto), IV F (Bottega IV 10-11), and presumably also IV G and IV H (Taberna 12-16).[238] It was indicated in § 5.10 and § 5.11 that lots IV E and IV F were based on the same design: a narrow lot (ca. 527 cm = 19'O) with a succession of rooms, culminating in a luxurious living room at the back of the house. The lots on the other side of the central axis of the *insula*, IV G and IV H, are a little wider, ca. 535 cm (19.5'O). Their original layout is slightly different, assuming that lot IV G, which was later rebuilt, was originally the same size as lot IV H, which seems to have remained largely unaltered. The greater length of these lots meant that there was enough room for an *atrium* as well as rooms. In this respect these are more like type 6 houses, but their width places them in type 5.

TYPE 6.

Type 6 comprises the wide 'strip houses', which combine characteristics of type 3 and type 5 houses: they have a single row of rooms along the entire length of the house, like a type 5 house, but are the same width as a type 3 house (27'-30'). In contrast to type 3, and particularly the longer houses in that category, like the Casa della Fullonica and the Casa dei Due Atri, there is no *atrium* in the front part of the house. The only examples of type 6 are the two long lots IV B and IV C (Casa dell'Alcova); presumably lot IV B had a similar layout to lot IV C before it was rebuilt in its present layout (see § 5.8). Both lots are 28.5'O across (771-788.5 cm), or 30'O including one side wall.

---

[238] On the basis of its width, the narrow northern part of the Casa dello Scheletro (lot III D) could be classified as either type 5 or type 4. There is not enough information available about the original appearance of this lot to decide which category it belongs in.

TYPE 7.

Type 7 comprises the large houses with peristyles, which were created by merging more than one lot. These houses were built relatively late, and have a variety of dimensions and layouts. Most examples of this type are on the southern periphery of the town: the Casa d'Argo (II 2), the Casa dell'Albergo (III 1-2, 18-19), the Casa dell'Atrio a Mosaico (IV 1-2), the Casa dei Cervi (IV 21), the Casa della Gemma (Ins. Or. I 1) and the Casa del Rilievo di Telefo (Ins. Or. I 2-3). Some original lots that were subsequently incorporated into these houses have already been classified in the categories described above; the entire complex can be regarded as type 7. This applies to the the Casa del Colonnato Tuscanico, whose *atrium* area was referred to above in the discussion of type 3, and the Casa del Tramezzo di Legno, the Casa del Bicentenario and the Casa del Salone Nero, parts of which can be classified as type 1 on the basis of other characteristics. In the Casa del Genio (II 3) and the Casa di Galba (VII 2-3) the only part that has been excavated to date is the peristyle area. On the basis of this, both houses can be classified as type 7.

TYPE 8.

Finally, type 8 includes houses of various widths with irregular layouts. Some of these houses were built on plots of land that were 'left over', like lots IV I (Taberna IV 17-18) and IV J (Casa della Stoffa), which are 50'O (1373 cm) and 37'O (1016 cm) wide respectively. More often, however, houses of type 8 were created as a result of later alterations to the lots: for example the Casa di Aristide (II 1), the Casa del Bel Cortile (V 8), the entire Casa con Giardino (V 32-33), the Casa del Gran Portale (V 34-35) and the Casa di M. Pilus Primigenius Granianus (Ins. Or. I 1a).

6.4. Results and prospects

A number of conclusions may be drawn from the typology presented above (see fig. 11 and Table 1). Leaving aside the large peristyle houses (type 7), whose layout is less closely related to the original division in lots, it seems that half of the plots of land in Herculaneum were about 30'-40' wide (types 2, 3 and 6), about a quarter were no more than 20' (types 4 and 5), and only a very small proportion (four houses in total) were wider than 40' (type 1). It can therefore be concluded that the 'complete' *atrium* was certainly not standard in Herculaneum. It is more likely that the design used was related to the width of the lot, and that types with an *atrium* were preferred where possible. The type with a single side range (type 2) seems to have been particularly popular. It is striking that this type is most common in *insula* V. In the remaining *insulae*, as far as can be determined, other types and lot sizes occur more frequently than type 2: in *insula* III there are only three lots that are wider than 30', and in *insula*

IV there are no houses of the wider types at all.[239] It is not clear why the size of the original lots varied so much. The location of the *insulae* might account for it: *insula* V is nearer the centre of the town than *insulae* III and IV, and it might therefore have been more prestigious, and more attractive to the wealthier citizens, who could afford a larger plot of land. Another possibility is that *insulae* III and IV may have been divided up later than *insula* V, in a period when there was greater demand for living space, and the space was therefore divided into narrower plots, so that a greater number of people could acquire a piece of land.

In considering these results it should be borne in mind that this study is incomplete. As mentioned above (§ 3.1.4), the partly or totally excavated *insulae* constitute only part of the town of Herculaneum. Assuming that there were about 20 *insulae*, we have studied only a quarter or a fifth of the total area. It is obvious that general conclusions cannot be drawn on the basis of the material available. For the moment, however, the typology proposed above will suffice, because subjective criteria, such as the decoration of floors and walls or the social status of the owner, have not been taken into account. This makes it possible to compare the results of the present investigation with studies of houses elsewhere in the Roman Empire, and in particular at Pompeii. This chapter will therefore conclude with a brief consideration of the similarities between the typology proposed here and the classification proposed by Evans (1980).

The widest type, type 1, has room for two side ranges off the *atrium*, and also for the construction of a front range and a *tablinum* range. The houses identified as this type are reasonably uniform, and all of them can be classified as front range type Bb, i.e. with more than one room on either side of the *fauces*, with divisions that are contained within the limits of the *atrium* complex, and *tablinum* range Ac (the *tablinum* is in the centre of the range, with a room and the *andron* on one side, and another room on the other side).

Type 2 is more problematic, because the houses with one side range have too many different combinations of front and *tablinum* ranges, and it is therefore not possible to analyse them fully. For this reason only a single example will be cited here, namely lot III C, the middle part of the Casa dello Scheletro. This lot has a front range of type Ab (*fauces* between two rooms, centred on the axis of the *atrium* with a single side range) and a *tablinum* range of type Ag (*tablinum* in the centre of the range, with a closed *andron* on one side and an *andron* and a room on the other).

The examples of type 3 are reasonably uniform in their structure, although there are variations in the form of the *atrium*. In all cases there is a front range of type Aa (*fauces* between two rooms, and an *atrium* with no side ranges), in combination with a *tablinum* range of type Ab (*tablinum* in the centre of the range, between a room and an *andron*). This type, and specifically the Casa del Cenacolo in Pompeii, was referred

---

[239] It was suggested in § 5.15 that there might once have been a lot of 40' wide in the area that is now the garden of the Casa dei Cervi. This can only be determined for certain by extensive excavation.

to above in the discussion of Evans' work (§ 6.1). These two ranges are combined with an *atrium testudinatum* in the Casa della Fullonica, with an *atrium tetrastylum* in the Casa dei Due Atri, and with an *atrium tuscanicum* in the remaining houses.

Type 4 can also be classified clearly using Evans' typology. These houses have a front range of type Fa (*fauces* of a normal depth at one side of the range) which is not very common in Pompeii, and a *tablinum* range of type C (*andron* in the centre of the range). Front range type Fa also occurs in type 5 houses, which have no *atrium*, while the double front range (= Evans' category D) is found in type 6 houses.

It would be useful to carry out a detailed comparison of the types identified here and houses with similar combinations of ranges, as this might give us a better understanding of the distribution of building types. Similarly, it would be possible to establish more precise dates for the introduction of the different types by analysing the building history of the relevant lots in Pompeii. Finally, the material that is not discussed by Evans should also be studied, as her work is based on only about half (200) of the estimated total number of *atria* excavated in Pompeii (Evans 1978: 175).

TABLE 1.
Distribution of types across *insulae*

TYPE	1	2	3	4	5	6	7	8	TOTAL
INSULA II	0	0	0	0	0	0	2	1	3
III	2	1	2	4	1	0	2	0	12
IV	0	0	3	0	4	2	2	2	13
V	1	6	2	0	0	0	1	3	13
VI	1	1	1	0	0	0	2	0	5
VII	0	0	0	0	0	0	1	0	1
Or. 1	0	2	0	0	0	0	2	1	5
TOTAL	4	10	8	4	5	2	12	7	52

EPILOGUE

For our investigation into the architectural background of the town, the descriptions of a number of ancient authors, given in chapter 1, provide us with a clear picture of the appearance of the town in antiquity. The town, a fortified settlement in pre-Roman times, was situated on a spit of sand between two rivers or streams which flowed out into the sea. These estuaries provided Herculaneum with well-protected harbours. Furthermore, it can be established, with the aid of the Tabula Peutingeriana, that the town was situated on the coastal road which ran from Naples to Pompeii. The establishment of the town doubtless had something to do with the protection of this road and of the entire Gulf of Naples. It is highly likely that Herculaneum was built as a fortification either by the Greeks or by the Samnites (Campanians). Despite the fact that there were several important villas situated around the settlement, the town remained relatively small and its atmosphere fairly unexciting. In the Augustan period many building projects were made possible in the town with the support of Marcus Nonius Balbus, who was praetor and proconsul. In return for his generosity he was honoured lavishly after his death. Shortly after the town had recovered from a major earthquake in 62, which destroyed large areas of Campania, it was destroyed by the eruption of Vesuvius in 79. The disaster claimed many lives because the townspeople sought shelter in the harbour area just outside the town, where they waited for help to come from the sea. This has become clear from the discovery in 1980 and 1982 of victims and of a boat which was washed ashore. It shows also how close the ancient city must have been to the sea; it was probably only about 20 or 30 metres away.

This brings us to the history of the excavations (chapter 2). In the 18th century a systematic exploration of the buried area was started, mainly seeking for ancient treasures. It is clear that scientific excavations - such as we would have liked to have been conducted - never took place during the time of the Bourbons. However, the documentation from the early excavations is of great importance to the present study. In many instances it can be verified by reference to areas of the town which were exposed in later times. From 1828 onwards, excavators at Herculaneum started to excavate the ancient remains in their entirety, but it was only after 1927, when Amedeo Maiuri appeared on the scene, that the scientific study of Herculaneum really began in earnest. Most of the remains of the town which are visible today were uncovered (and published) under his supervision.

In chapter 3, by combining this information with data from the 18th-century sources, we are able to draw conclusions about the size of Herculaneum and the place of the city's plan in the history of ancient urban development. Herculaneum must have been a fortified settlement located on a spit overlooking the sea. After the advent of the Romans during the 1st century BC, the city walls, which had ceased to be used for defensive purposes, were partly demolished and used as terrace walls for the houses at the edge of the town. During the 1st century AD a suburban complex was established between the walls and the sea. Below that, at sea-level, was the harbour area, which provided shelter to pull boats onto dry land, where there were storage areas for goods and boats in the arched substructures of the suburban complex, and where the boat yard was also probably situated.

We are able to draw the following conclusions about the city plan (fig. 2). The road from Neapolis to Pompeii ran through the middle of the town and functioned as a *decumanus maximus* within the city walls. Just outside the walls, on both sides of the town, the road was lined with tombs. The rectangular street plan, probably derived from the city plan of Neapolis, which was established shortly before 474 BC, consists of about four *decumani* and various *cardines*. Herculaneum possibly had about 20 *insulae* in all, of which 8, containing residential units, are known in the southern part of the town. These are all rectangular in shape, and they are flanked by two irregularly shaped *insulae*: in the easternmost *insula* the Palaestra was later built. A fairly wide *decumanus*, interpreted by Maiuri as both *decumanus maximus* and forum, marks the division between this residential area and the central part of the town, containing public monuments such as the forum, the basilica, buildings for imperial worship and the theatre. As in Neapolis, the theatre and the forum are close to one another on the western side of the town, judging from the 18th-century documents. Furthermore, it is proposed in chapter 3 that the theatre and the forum bordered the *decumanus maximus*, which was further north than the street that Maiuri identified as the *decumanus maximus*. Because the dimensions of the central area between the *decumanus maximus* and the previously exposed *decumanus* are not altogether clear, little can be said about the northern part of the town. We suspect that the *decumanus maximus* marked the division between the central area of the town and the northern residential area, again consisting of 8 *insulae*. The city plan, with *insulae* which were slightly wider and much shorter than those of Neapolis, can be dated to 400 BC and forms part of a Campanian tradition of urban development. The earliest buildings that remain visible were built about two centuries later, and date from the end of the 3rd century or the beginning of the 2nd century BC.

In chapter 4 it is confirmed that the background to this urban development and the internal sub-divisions of the city plan are of a regional character. Judging from the measurements used, it appears that a decimal system was applied in Herculaneum, with a unit of measurement consisting of 100 'Oscan' or 'Italic' feet. The *insulae* measure about 150 x 300 feet, which constitutes a ratio of 1:2. *Insula* III, which was later extended to the south, had these dimensions, but the more peripheral *insula* IV is wider (160 feet) and must have been shorter on one side (270 feet). A study of the measurements also makes it clear that the allotment of land in *insula* III was much more regular than in *insula* IV. The *insula* has been divided into two halves, each measuring 75 feet, with the result that all the houses are the same length. This provides us with a problem: the partition walls are shared and the back walls of the houses are not exactly on the central axis of the *insula*. The solution to this problem seems to be that the person who was the first to build bought an area of land which was 1.5 feet (the width of a wall) longer than the 75 feet that was needed. The actual length of the house was thus 75 feet. As a consequence, the neighbour at the rear was left with 73.5 feet of potential residential space at his disposal, but there was no need for him to build a back wall. Other solutions to this problem are discussed in detail in chapter 4, but none of them would have provided the first builder with the relevant legal advantages. Much depends on the possible application of Roman law to civil disputes at Herculaneum. It is an established fact that, as the allotment of building plots took place within the framework of the Campanian tradition, the laws and rules of the Roman gromatici will not have been applied literally. However, it is possible that the Campanian system was very similar to the Roman system. In the matter of common walls, Roman law has been used to show that the owner of the wall had certain rights and duties - or advantages and disadvantages - when his neighbour wanted to use it for certain building projects. This enables us to give a convincing explanation of the situation in *insula* III. In the northern half of the *insula*, ten of the original lots may be identified (fig. 5). Five of these are so-called 'internal' lots which measure 75 feet excluding the back wall, and the other five are 'external' lots, that is to say lots with a length of 75 feet when the back wall is included in the measurement. From the widths we are able to conclude that there were three groups of lots in *insula* III, namely small lots which measure 20 feet, medium-sized lots which measure 27 feet, and large lots of about 40 feet. This regularity in measurements contrasts with the division of *insula* IV, where it seems that different principles were followed, presumably as a result of the greater width of the *insula* (fig. 6). Here there was no clear axis and as a result the lots were of different lengths. Some are very long, as in the case of the adjoining Casa dell'Alcova and Casa della Fullonica, which extend over more than half the total width of the *insula*. Additional research has shown that this situation was original and did not result from later conversions. In the northern part of the *insula* (as in *insula* III, the southern part was completely altered) eleven original lots may be identified. Working from the width of the lots we can again distinguish three groups: small lots of about 20 feet, slightly wider lots of about 30 feet, and finally a couple of very wide, but also very short lots, which measure 37 and 50 feet.

The houses in *insulae* III and IV are discussed separately in chapter 5, and the classification is refined in chapter 6 and combined with the typology of all the houses of Herculaneum. Using the widths of the lots and the method of allotment as a starting-point, we offer an overview of the building-plans of the individual houses. Eight types may be distinguished. It appears that the types used in *insula* III varied considerably, that most of the smaller types are represented in *insula* IV, and that the wider types prevail in *insula* V. When we look at the various types in *insulae* III and IV we may draw the following conclusions.

The wider type is represented by the Casa del Tramezzo di Legno, which consists of two lots (III E and G) to which the narrow strip on the north side (referred to by us as lot III F) has been added. This strip played no role in the original design of the other two lots; when the eventual design of the house took shape, however, the northern strip was incorporated into the *atrium* as one of the side ranges. The western house, lot III E, was added to the eastern house and converted to function as a peristyle. For this reason the entire house has been included under type 7. In § 5.3 a reconstruction is given of the original form of lot III E, which was smaller than lot III G. The width of this last lot is divided into 12' (without strip III F) for the side range and 30' for the *atrium*. Along its length, 17.5' was allowed for the front range, 35' for the *atrium* and 22.5' for the *tablinum* range and the garden. The joining together of the two lots may have taken place at the end of the 1st century BC, after which minor alterations and a major conversion were carried out in the first half of the 1st century AD. Finally, it is worth remarking that the excavations which took place during the last century in the peristyle area yielded large quantities of household goods.

Type 2 is found in *insula* III, in the middle section of the Casa dello Scheletro (lot III C). This lot has a side range which measures 13', and the width of the *atrium* is 25'; the front range measures 18.5'. The present length of the *atrium* and the *tablinum* range are not the original dimensions. The history of the construction of this house is well documented by Ganschow (1989). From his analysis it appears that three lots gradually coalesced into one house. Initially, lot III D was divided up between the owner of the Casa a Graticcio and the owner of lot III C. Subsequently a *nymphaeum* was built at the side of the Casa dello Scheletro, against an additional partition wall. In this way nothing remained of the original plan of lot III D. Judging by the house's wall and floor decoration and by the fact that another *nymphaeum* was built in the middle section, the owner must have been an affluent citizen.

After the earthquake in 62, lot III B was also added to the house. Initially this section was one of four 'terraced houses' which had been built on either side of the central axis. These houses, lots III A, B, J and K, represent type 4. This type makes an important contribution to our knowledge of Roman domestic architecture. First, it becomes clear that builders in Herculaneum preferred to use the available space for narrow, simple house types instead of the 'standard' *atrium* house. Second, these houses show that houses were sometimes built in series; they corroborate the examples described by Hoffmann (1979) as terraced houses in Pompeii. Finally, they seem to support the theory that Roman house-builders worked with plans designed according to very simple principles, which were easy to put into practice. The length, which measured 75', was divided up into ranges which were of equal proportions or could be expressed in round figures: a front range of 15' (= 1/5 of the length of the house), with an entrance on one side and one living room; a covered *atrium* which measured 17' in depth and a *tablinum* range, consisting of an *andron* between two rooms, which measured 13' (internally 10') - 30' in total (2/5 of the length of the house); and finally a second hall with a side range and a light well, which also measured a total of 30' (15' each). The Casa dell'Ara Laterizia, whose wall and floor decoration is not well preserved, provides the best example of this scheme.

The examples of type 3 also show how the architect who built more modest homes opted for practical schemes which were simple and capable of variation, but which all had as their main aim the most advantageous use of space. The two examples in *insula* III can also be regarded as terraced houses, because the neighbouring houses, the Casa a Graticcio (in its original state) and the Casa dell'Erma di Bronzo, were built according to the same plan. In the Casa dell'Erma di Bronzo, which must be regarded as one of the most authentic houses of the Samnite period, we see the

200

following ranges: front range 13', *atrium* without side range 21', *tablinum* range 14', intermediate room (light well) 10.5', and luxurious living quarters 15', all with a width of 27'. The measurements of the corresponding ranges in the Casa a Graticcio were respectively 13', 20', 15', 11.5' and 14'. Later, however, this house was considerably altered.

First a section of lot III D was added, and then, possibly only after AD 62, the upper floor with its separate apartments was constructed and the layout of the ground floor was completely changed. The house is important mainly because of the building technique that was used (*opus craticium*), because of the clear division of the space into several different living units, and because of the discovery of household goods and furniture which helps us to understand life in a family dwelling like this.

The Casa della Fullonica is another example of type 3. This house has an 'external' width of 30', which was perhaps regarded as small and was therefore combined with extra length. The width:length ratio is 3:10. Although the length of the house must, at one time, have been greater, its present length is probably the same as its original length. We may distinguish four strips here, measuring 14', 30', 32' and 19'. This is one of the few houses which contains an example of a First Style wall decoration. Another example of type 3 is lot IV K, the northern area of the Casa dei Cervi. Little can be said about the original layout of this lot. At a later stage, in early Imperial times, this layout was lost when the Casa dei Cervi was re-designed. The new design resulted in the central living room in the north wing being situated exactly on the north-south axis of the house, to take advantage of the view of the sea through the garden and the terrace. It is highly likely that a building of about 100' (probably a peristyle) had existed in the area of the garden as early as the Republican period. For a further discussion of the building history and the decoration of the house the reader is referred to the studies of Ganschow (1989) and Tran Tam Tinh (1988).

One section of the neighbouring house, the Casa dell'Atrio a Mosaico, is also an example of type 3. It comprises the northern entrance and the reception area (lot IV A), which was originally an *atrium* house consisting of a front range of 19', an *atrium* without side ranges of 32', and a *tablinum* range whose dimensions can not be precisely established; this was later replaced by an *oecus aegyptius*. The rest of the house, which is an example of type 7 (like the Casa dei Cervi), was built in different periods. It is presumed that some earlier houses facing east-west had to be demolished in the second half of the 1st century BC to make way for the garden complex with its adjoining rooms. Its dimensions were about 75 x 100 feet. After that, in the early Imperial period, the terrace area was built on the city wall, to be extended during the 1st century AD by the addition of an upper storey. With regard to the comparatively well-preserved decoration, it can be established that the pavements reflect a clear hierarchy of room-function: *opus sectile* is used in the most important living quarters, black mosaic with pieces of *opus sectile* in the passageways, white mosaic with patterns in the entrances, and plain white mosaic floors in the simpler rooms.

The Casa dell'Albergo, which is a further example of type 7, has a similar building history. Two lots of type 4 (III A and III K), already mentioned, form part of it, as does a large part of the southern half of *insula* III. Several houses on both sides of the central axis of the *insula* disappeared around the middle of the 1st century BC, to provide space for the peristyle, which measured 100' x 125', and for a private bathhouse (with adjoining rooms), which was decorated with Second Style wall paintings. In Augustan times the house was re-built and extended to the south with a terrace. The earthquake of 62 caused extensive damage which in many places had still not been restored by 79.

A vivid contrast to this enormous residential area are the narrow strip houses which are examples of type 5. The space in these houses - on the north side of *insula* IV - is so limited that the ranges could only be built one behind the other, in a row. The best example is the Casa del Papiro Dipinto (lot IV E), where strips of 20', 30' and 24' follow each other; these strips are subdivided into rooms of 13' and 7', 15' and 15', and 9' and 15'. Extra space was created at a later stage, when the upper storey, with a separate entrance, was constructed. The neighbouring house, lot IV F, had the same basic layout, but the exact subdivision of space cannot be established, as a result of a later reconstruction which converted the house into a shop with living-rooms. Of the corresponding lots on the other side of the *insula*, IV G and IV H, the first has undergone major alterations to convert it from residential to commercial use, probably because of its advantageous location on a crossroads near the Palaestra. Lot IV H shows that the longer version of type 5 provided the builder with an opportunity to incorporate an *atrium*. The resulting division was 23.5' (front range), 40' (*atrium* and intermediate range) and 20' (back of the house).

Houses of types 6 and 8 are located opposite each other in the *insula*: on the west side we find the long lots IV B and C (Casa dell'Alcova), and on the east, as a result of this extra length, there are very small and irregular lots, IV I (Taberna IV 17-18) and IV J (Casa della Stoffa). The longer lots were once probably identical. Lot IV B was completely altered by the construction of a private bath-house (probably in the mid-late 1st century BC) and by the change in layout after it was joined to lot IV C (in Augustan times). Lot IV C shows how the limited width (both lots are 28.5' wide) was compensated for in length: there is a succession of strips or living units with openings for light and air. Of the remaining lots, IV I has the largest area. The irregular shape of this lot, which is 50' wide and 64' long, is the result of the discrepancy in length between the Casa della Fullonica and the Casa dell'Alcova. The space behind the front range of 20' was later divided into modules of 11'. The Casa della Stoffa is even smaller: 37' by 53.5'. Furthermore, this house had to sacrifice one room to the Casa dell'Alcova, probably in the Augustan period, during a re-allocation of space in the middle of *insula* IV. The layout is similar to that of type 5, with rooms built behind each other in two separate blocks, 20' and 15' wide respectively.

After this résumé of the analytical chapters we can summarise the results of our study in relation to the general building history of Herculaneum. First, the design of the city plan: on the basis of its typological position in the history of urban development we conclude, as indicated above, that the town must have been laid out at the end of the 5th or the beginning of the 4th century BC. The earliest residents must have arrived in the course of the 4th century. This corresponds with the findings of the excavations

directed by Tran Tam Tinh (1977) and with the evidence of a passage of Theophrastus - assuming that this passage is applicable to 'our' Herculaneum. It is not clear
whether the present site of the town was also the site of an earlier settlement. At all
events, the settlement that was established shortly before or after 400 BC was
inhabited by Samnites. It was only about 200 years later, presumably soon after the
Second Punic War, that stone construction was introduced, initially in rough forms of
opus incertum (types A and B). For a considerable period, houses of various types
were built in this technique. It was actually the width of the lot that determined its
eventual plan. *Atrium* houses with only one side range were popular in some parts of
the town, while narrow, simple 'terraced houses' were built in other parts. Longer lots
of limited width were bought whenever possible, that is to say, when the *insula* was
not neatly divided into two equal halves. Herculaneum flourished in the period after
89 BC, when it became a Roman *municipium*, as suggested by a phase of intense
building activity around the middle of the 1st century BC. New elements were added
to existing houses, using new materials and building techniques. Usually this was
accompanied by the demolition of old houses, which were replaced by spacious
peristyles and gardens, with beautifully decorated living quarters or private baths.
Living space was sacrificed to luxury. The southern half of *insulae* III and IV was
changed completely: in place of the houses built back-to-back in an east-west direction, large town houses were built lengthways in the area which extended up to the
city wall. The Casa dell'Albergo was built in *insula* III, with a peristyle and a private
bath, and the Casa dell'Atrio a Mosaico, with a garden and associated rooms, in
insula IV, as well as part of the Casa dei Cervi - possibly a peristyle. Luxurious rooms
were also created in other parts of the town, for example in the southern part of the
Casa dell'Alcova, where a private bath was built at the end of the 1st century BC.

There was even greater activity in the early Imperial period. The appearance of the
town was completely changed, probably through the initiatives of the most important
resident at that time, M. Nonius Balbus. The theatre and the Aedes Augustalium are
two public buildings which were constructed during this period. The inscription CIL
X 1425 reports building activities - financed by Balbus - which were carried out on
the basilica, the walls and the gates. It is highly likely that this refers to the use of the
city walls as terrace walls for the houses on the southern edge of the town. As a result
of greater social stability, defensive walls were no longer necessary and could be used
for other purposes. This meant that the vacant strip of land between the *insulae* and
the walls was raised to the floor level of the existing houses on the southern edge of
the town, and the city wall was exploited for the construction of luxurious terrace
complexes: the Casa di Aristide, the Casa dell'Albergo, the Casa dell'Atrio a Mosaico, the Casa dei Cervi, the Casa della Gemma and the Casa del Rilievo di Telefo. At
the same time, just outside the town wall, a public complex was built, with temples
(the Area Sacra) and a large square, both supported by arched substructures, which in
turn functioned as storage rooms for the nearby harbour. Elsewhere in the town
various houses were re-decorated and altered: the Casa del Tramezzo di Legno, for
example, was created by joining together two lots, the western one of which (lot III
E) was converted into a peristyle. In the centre of *insula* IV, there was a re-allocation

of space between the Casa dell'Alcova, the Casa della Stoffa and the Casa dei Cervi.

The changes carried out in the course of the 1st century AD were minor. Examples are the division of lot III D between the Casa a Graticcio and the Casa dello Scheletro, and the re-decoration of the Casa del Tramezzo di Legno. More important was the period after 62, when the town had to repair the damage caused by the earthquake. Makeshift repairs were carried out in many houses, traces of which were still evident in 79. Most of the houses needed new wall decoration. There is also evidence of new housing development or complete reconstruction. Baths were built just outside the town, to increase the capacity of the 1st-century Forum Baths. Some houses, like the Casa a Graticcio, underwent a total metamorphosis. Here, as a result of a reconstruction which had probably started before 62, a residence for more than one family - something considered to be very 'modern' in those times - was created from a small Samnite *atrium* house without side rooms.

The phasing we have postulated is based on a combination of data obtained from the study of the decoration, from the wall construction and from analysis of the measurements, and is similar to the one proposed by Ganschow. Further research into the houses and public buildings, especially small-scale excavations to study the pre-79 levels, could clarify whether this chronology is correct.

WORKS CITED

Abbreviations for titles of journals follow those of the *Archäologische Bibliographie* 1992, XXV-XL, with the exception of the titles given below.

ANRW   Aufstieg und Niedergang der Römischen Welt, H. Temporini (ed.),
                Berlin 1972 -
CIL   Corpus Inscriptionum Latinarum, Berlin 1893 -
EAA   Enciclopedia dell'Arte Antica, Roma 1958 -
RE   Paulys Realencyclopädie der classischen Altertumswissenschaft, hg.
                von G. Wissowa, W. Kroll, K. Ziegler, Stuttgart 1894-1980.

Adam, J.-P., 1984: *La construction romaine. Matériaux et techniques*, Paris

Adam, J.-P., 1986: Observations techniques sur les suites du séisme de 62 à Pompéi, in: Albore Livadie 1986, 67-89

Adamo Muscettola, S., 1982: Nuove letture borboniche: i Nonii Balbi ed il Foro di Ercolano, *Prospettiva* 28, 2-16

Aken, A.R.A. van, 1943: *Nieuwe wegen in de Romeinsche woningbouw van Sulla tot Domitianus*, diss. Utrecht

Albore Livadie, C. (ed.), 1986: *Tremblements de terre, éruptions volcaniques et vie des hommes dans la Campanie antique*, Naples (Bibliothèque de l'Institut Français de Naples, 2ᵉ série, vol. VII)

Albore Livadie, C., D'Alessio, E., Mastrolorenzo, G., Rolandi, G., 1986: Le eruzioni del Somma-Vesuvio in epoca protostorica, in: Albore Livadie 1986, 55-66

Albore Livadie, C., 1993: Les plus anciennes éruptions pliniennes du Somma-Vésuve et la protohistoire de la Campanie, in: Franchi dell'Orto 1993, 439-448

Allroggen-Bedel, A., 1974: Das sogenannte Forum von Herculaneum und die borbonischen Grabungen von 1739, *CronErcol* 4, 97-109

Allroggen-Bedel, A., 1975A: Der Hausherr der 'Casa dei Cervi' in Herculaneum, *CronErcol* 5, 99-103

Allroggen-Bedel, A., 1975B: Herkunft und ursprünglicher Dekorationszusammenhang einiger in Essen ausgestellter Fragmente von Wandmalereien, in: Andreae/Kyrieleis 1975, 115-124

Allroggen-Bedel, A., 1976A: Ein Malerei-Fragment aus der Villa dei Papiri, *CronErcol* 6, 85-88

Allroggen-Bedel, A., 1976B: Die Malereien aus dem Haus Insula occidentalis, 10, *CronPomp* 2, 144-183

Allroggen-Bedel, A., 1977: Die Wandmalereien aus der Villa in Campo Varano

(Castellammare di Stabia), *RM* 84, 27-89

Allroggen-Bedel, A., 1979: Zur Eigenart der herculanischen Wandmalerei (resumé), in: Coldstream, J., Colledge, M.A.R. (eds.), *Greece and Italy in the Classical World. Acts of the IXth International Congress of Classical Archaeology*, London, 284

Allroggen-Bedel, A., 1983: Dokumente des 18. Jahrhunderts zur Topographie von Herculaneum, *CronErcol* 13, 139-158

Allroggen-Bedel, A., 1986: Tanucci e la cultura antiquaria del suo tempo, in: *Bernardo Tanucci. Statista, letterato, giurista*, Napoli, 521-536

Allroggen-Bedel, A., 1991: Lokalstile in der Campanischen Wandmalerei, *KölnJbVFrühGesch* 24, 35-41

Allroggen-Bedel, A., Kammerer-Grothaus, H., 1980: Das Museo Ercolanese in Portici, *CronErcol* 10, 175-218

Amadio, B., 1987: Regio II, ins. I, *RStPomp* 1, 154-156

Amadio, B., 1988: Le insulae su Via di Nocera. Regio II, ins. 1, *RStPomp* 2, 192-195

Andreae, B., Kyrieleis, H. (eds.), 1975: *Neue Forschungen in Pompeji*, Recklinghausen

Andréau, J., 1979: Il terremoto del 62, in: Zevi, F. (ed.), *Pompei 79*, Napoli, 40-44

Antichità 1757: *Le antichità di Ercolano esposte*, Napoli 1757-1792

Archeologi italiani 1965: *Gli archeologi italiani in onore di Amedeo Maiuri*, Cava dei Tirreni

Arneth, A. von, 1864: *Prinz Eugen von Savoyen*, Wien[2] I-III

Baldassarre, I., 1985: Problemi archeologici, in: Napoli antica 1985, 122-132

Baldassarre, I., 1988: Osservazioni sull'urbanistica di Neapolis in età romana, in: *Atti del XXV. Convegno di studi sulla Magna Grecia* (Taranto 1985), Taranto, 221-231

Bankel, H., 1983: Zum Fußmaß attischer Bauten des 5. Jahrhunderts v. Chr., *AM* 98, 65-99

Barbet, A., 1985A: *La peinture murale romaine. Les styles décoratifs pompiens*, Paris

Barbet, A., 1985B: *Fouilles de l'Ecole française de Rome à Bolsena (Poggio Moscini). 5. La maison aux salles souterraines. 2. Décors picturaux (murs, plafonds, voûtes)*, Rome (Ecole française de Rome. Mélanges d'archéologie et d'histoire, suppl. 6)

Barnhart, C.L. (ed.), 1954: *The New Century Cyclopedia of Names*, vol. III, New York

Bastet, F.L., Vos, M. de, 1979: *Proposta per una classificazione del terzo stile pompeiano*, 's-Gravenhage (Archeologische Studiën van het Nederlands Instituut te Rome, IV)

Bauer, H., 1983: Porticus Absidata, *RM* 90, 111-184

Bauplanung 1984: *Bauplanung und Bautheorie der Antike*, Berlin (DiskAB, 4)

Bayardi, O.A., 1755: *Catalogo degli antichi monumenti dissotterrati dalla discoperta città di Ercolano...*, Napoli

Bayardi, O.A., Martyn, T., Lettice, J., 1773: *The Antiquities of Herculaneum*, London

Bejor, G., 1979: L'edificio teatrale nell'urbanizzazione augustea, *Athenaeum* N.S. 57, 126-138

Beloch, J., 1890: *Campanien. Geschichte und Topographie des antiken Neapel und seiner Umgebung*, Breslau[2]

Bencivenga Trillmich, C., 1984: Risultati delle più recenti indagini archeologiche nell'area dell'antica Atella, *RendAccNap* LIX, 3-26

Bieber, M., 1961: *The Sculpture of the Hellenistic Age*, New York[2]

Binnebeke, M.C. van, 1991: Some Remarks on the Functions of Houses and Rooms in the Insula V at Herculaneum, *MededRom.Antiquity* 50, 136-144

Binnebeke, M.C. van, 1993: The Houses 'Dell'Atrio Corinzio' (V, 30) and 'Del Sacello di Legno' (V, 31) at Herculaneum: the Use of Space, in: Franchi dell'Orto 1993, 229-236

Binnebeke, M.C. van, Kind, R. de (eds.), 1996: The Casa dell'Atrio Corinzio and the Casa del Sacello di Legno at Herculaneum, *CronErcol* 26, 173-228

Bisel, S., 1987: Human Bones at Herculaneum, *RStPomp* 1, 123-129

Bisi Ingrassia, A.M., 1977: Le lucerne fittili dei nuovi scavi di Ercolano, in: Instrumentum domesticum 1977, 73-104

Blume, F., Lachmann, K., Rudorff, A., 1848: *Die Schriften der römischen Feldmesser*, I, Berlin

Bölte, F., 1912: Helike, in: *RE* VII, 2855-2858

Boersma, J.S., 1982: Large-sized Insulae in Italy and the Western Roman Provinces, *BABesch* 57, 38-51

Boersma, J.S., 1985: *Amoenissima Civitas*, Assen (Scrinium, I)

Bonucci, C., 1835: *Ercolano*, Napoli

Bosio, L., 1983: *La Tabula Peutingeriana. Una descrizione pittorica del mondo antico*, Rimini

Bracker-Wester, U., 1980: Das 'Ubiermonument' in Köln, *Gymnasium* 87, 496-534

Bragantini, I., Vos, M. de (eds.), 1982: *Museo Nazionale Romano. Le Pitture II, 1. Le decorazioni della Villa romana della Farnesina*, Roma

Breton, E., 1869: *Pompéia décrite et dessinée, suivie d'une notice sur Herculanum*, Paris

Bridger, C.J., 1984: The Pes Monetalis and the Pes Drusianus in Xanten, *Britannia* 15, 85-98

Brisson, C., 1957: La découverte d'Herculanum en 1713 par le 'Prince d'Elbeuf', *RevSocSavHauteNormandie* 6, 21-29

Buchner, E., 1984: Die Sonnenuhr des Augustus und römischer Fuß, in: Bauplanung 1984, 215-219

Budetta, T., 1987: Attività dell'Ufficio Scavi: 1985-1986, *RStPomp* 1, 194-198

Budetta, T., 1988: Ercolano. Attività dell'Ufficio Scavi: 1987-1988, *RStPomp* 2, 234-238

Budetta, T., 1993: I nuovi scavi nell'area suburbana di Ercolano, in: Franchi dell'Orto 1993, 677-690

Budetta, T., Pagano M., 1988: *Ercolano: Legni e Piccoli Bronzi*, exh.cat. Roma,

Castel S. Angelo (23/3-26/4/1988), Roma

Büsing, H., 1982: Metrologische Beiträge, *JdI* 97, 1-45

Buijtendorp, T., 1987: Romeinse landmeters in Forum Hadriani bij Voorburg, *Westerheem* 1987/3, 74-96

Buijtendorp, T., 1993: De winkelstraat van Forum Hadriani. Analyse en reconstructie, *Westerheem*, 110-119 (I), 230-240 (II)

Burns, A., 1976: Hippodamus and the Planned City, *Historia* 25, 414-428

Caputo, G., 1963: Amedeo Maiuri (1886-1963), *Atena e Roma* NS 8, 1-7

Carocci, F., Albentiis, E. De, Gargiullo, M., Pesando, F., 1990: *Le Insulae 3 e 4 della Regio VI di Pompei. Un'analisi storico-urbanistica*, Roma (Archeologica, 89)

Carrington, R.C., 1933: Notes on the Building Materials of Pompeii, *JRS* 23, 125-138

Castagnoli, F., 1971: *Orthogonal Town Planning in Antiquity*, Cambridge (Mass.)

Castaldi, G., 1908: Atella. Questioni di topografia storica della Campania, *AttRealAccNap* XXV, 65-93

Castrén, P., 1975: *Ordo populusque pompeianus. Polity and Society in Roman Pompeii*, Roma

Catalano, V., 1953: *Storia di Ercolano*, Napoli

Catalano, V., 1963: Case, abitanti e culti di Ercolano, *Annali S. Chiara* 13, 213-342

Catalano, V., 1982: Intervento, in: Regione sotterrata 1982, 957-960

Catalogus Pompeii 1973: *Catalogus Pompeii* (Exhibition Den Haag, Gemeentemuseum), Recklinghausen

Cerulli Irelli, G., 1971: *Le pitture della Casa dell'Atrio a Mosaico*, Roma (MonPittAnt III. Ercolano I)

Cerulli Irelli, G., 1974: *La Casa "del colonnato Tuscanico" ad Ercolano*, Napoli

Cerulli Irelli, G., 1977: L'attività archeologica nelle province di Napoli e Caserta, in: *Atti del XVI. Convegno di studi sulla Magna Grecia (Taranto 1976)*, Napoli, 755-816

Cerulli Irelli, G., 1983: L'attività archeologica a Pompei, Ercolano, Stabia, in: *Atti del XXII. Convegno di studi sulla Magna Grecia (Taranto 1982)*, Taranto, 411-419

Cerulli Irelli, G., 1984: Attività archeologica a Pompei, in: *Atti del XXIII. Convegno di studi sulla Magna Grecia (Taranto 1983)*, Taranto, 507-520

Cioffi, U., 1993: Prodotti vulcanici anteriori al 79 nell'area archeologica di Ercolano, in: Franchi dell'Orto 1993, 655-658

Clarke, J.R., 1985: Relationships between Floor, Wall, and Ceiling Decoration at Rome and Ostia Antica: Some Case Studies, *BulletinAIEMA* 10, 93-103

Clarke, J.R., 1991: *The houses of Roman Italy, 100 B.C. - A.D. 250: Ritual, Space, and Decoration*, Berkeley

Ciro Nappo, S., 1988: Le insulae su Via di Nocera. Regio I, ins. 20, *RStPomp* 2, 186-192

Cochin, C.N., Bellicard, J.C., 1754: *Observations sur les antiquités d'Herculanum*, Paris 1754, 1757[2] (repr. Genève 1972)

Conte Corti, E.C., 1942: *Pompeii en Herculaneum. Haar ondergang en herrijzenis*, Utrecht

Conticello, B., 1986: L'attività della soprintendenza archeologica di Pompei, in: *Atti del XXV. Convegno di studi sulla Magna Grecia (Taranto 1985)*, Taranto, 507-516

Conticello, B., 1987: Dopo 221 anni si rientra nella Villa dei Papiri, *CronErcol* 17, 9-13

Conticello De Spagnolis, M., Carolis, E. De, 1988: *Le lucerne di bronzo di Ercolano e Pompei*, Roma (Cataloghi SAP, 2)

Coppa, M., 1968: *Storia dell'urbanistica dalle origini all'ellenismo*, Torino

D'Amore, L., 1983: Amedeo Maiuri, *PompHercStab* 1, 353-361

D'Arms, J.H., 1970: *Romans on the Bay of Naples*, Cambridge, Mass.

Deiss, J. J., 1985: *Herculaneum. A City Returns to the Sun*, London[2]

Della Corte, M., 1958: Le iscrizioni di Ercolano, *RendAccNap* XXXIII, 239-308

Dilke, O.A.W., 1971: *The Roman Landsurveyors*, Newton Abbot

Dilke, O.A.W., 1985: *Greek and Roman Maps*, London

Dörpfeld, W., 1882: Beiträge zur antiken Metrologie. I. Das solonisch-attische System, *AM* 7, 277-312

Dörpfeld, W., 1883: Beiträge zur antiken Metrologie. II. Die aegyptischen Längenmaasse. III. Die königliche Elle des Herodot und der philetaerische Fuss, *AM* 8, 36-56, 342-358

Dörpfeld, W., 1885: Metrologische Beiträge. IV. Das italische Maass-System, *AM* 10, 289-312

Dörpfeld, W., 1890: Metrologische Beiträge. V. Das äginäisch-attische Mass-System. VI. Das griechische Stadion, *AM* 15, 167-187

Duncan-Jones, R.P., 1980: Length-units in Roman Town Planning, *Britannia* XI, 127-133

Duthoy, R., 1978: Les *Augustales, in: *ANRW* II, 16.2, Berlin, 1254-1309

Ehrhardt, W., 1988: *Casa dell'Orso (VII 2, 44-46)*, München (Häuser in Pompeji, 2)

Elia, O., 1976: Per la storia della pittura ercolanese, *CronErcol* 6, 89-91

Evans, E., 1978: A Group of Atrium Houses without Side Rooms in Pompeii, in: Blake, H., Potter, T., Whitehouse, D. (eds.), *Papers in Italian Archaeology* I, Oxford (BAR Suppl.41), 175-195

Evans, E., 1980: *The Atrium Complex in the Houses of Pompeii*, unpub. diss. Birmingham

Ferroni, A.M., Meucci, C., 1989: Prime osservazioni sulla Barca di Ercolano: il recupero e la costruzione navale, in: Tampone, G. (ed.), *Il restauro del legno* I, Firenze, 105-112 (Atti del 2° Congresso Nazionale Restauro del Legno)

Franchi dell'Orto, L. (ed.), 1993: *Ercolano 1738-1988. 250 anni di ricerca archeologica. Atti del Convegno Internazionale Ravello-Ercolano-Napoli-Pompei, 30 ottobre - 5 novembre 1988*, Roma (Monografie SAP, 6)

Franciscis, A. De, 1961: Herculaneum. Scavi e scoperte, *FA* 16, 4650, fig. 71

Franciscis, A. De, 1963A: *Il Museo Nazionale di Napoli*, Cava dei Tirreni

Franciscis, A. De, 1963B: Vetri antichi scoperti ad Ercolano, *Journal of Glass Studies* 5, 137-139

Franciscis, A. De, 1965: Herculaneum. Scavi e scoperte, *FA* 20, 4637

Franciscis, A. De, 1966: L'attività archeologica nelle province di Napoli e di Caserta, in: *Atti del V. Convegno di studi sulla Magna Grecia (Taranto 1965)*, Napoli, 173-191

Franciscis, A. De, 1967A: Herculaneum. Scavi e scoperte, *FA* 22, 4975

Franciscis, A. De, 1967B: L'attività archeologica nelle province di Napoli e di Caserta, in: *Atti del VI. Convegno di studi sulla Magna Grecia (Taranto 1966)*, Napoli, 233-242

Franciscis, A. De, 1969: Herculaneum. Grande Palestra, *FA* 24/25 (1969/1970) 8284

Franciscis, A. De, 1970: Ercolano, in: *EAA Suppl.*, Roma, 310-311

Franciscis, A. De, 1974: *Ercolano e Stabia*, Novara

Franciscis, A. De, 1975: Attività archeologica. Ercolano, *CronPomp* 1, 248-249

Franciscis, A. De, 1977: Herculaneum. Relazione di scavo della necropoli in via Doglie ad Ercolano, *FA* 32/33 (1977/1978) 10837

Frere, S.S., 1977: Town Planning in the Western Provinces, *Berichte der Römisch-Germanischen Kommission* 58, 87-103

Frischer, B., 1982: Monumenta et arae honoris virtutisque causa. Evidence of Memorials for Roman Civic Heroes, *BullCom* 88 (1982/1983) 51-86

Fuchs, W., 1979: *Die Skulptur der Griechen*, München[2]

Gall, R., 1912: Herculaneum, in: *RE* VIII, 532-548

Ganschow, Th., 1989: *Untersuchungen zur Baugeschichte in Herculaneum*, Bonn (Antiquitas 3, 30)

Ganschow, Th., 1993: Funktion und Stellenwert der Mauerstrukturen in Herculaneum, in: Franchi dell'Orto 1993, 161-164

Gassner, V., 1986: *Die Kaufläden in Pompeii*, Wien 1986 (Dissertationen der Universität Wien; 178)

Gehrke, H.-J., 1989: Bemerkungen zu Hippodamos von Milet, in: Schuller 1989, 58-63

Gerkan, A. von, 1924: *Griechische Städteanlagen. Untersuchungen zur Entwicklung des Städtebaus im Altertum*, Berlin/Leipzig

Gerkan, A. von, 1940: Der Tempel von Didyma und sein antikes Baumaß, *ÖJh* 32, 127-150

Gigante, M., 1983: Virgilio fra Ercolano e Pompei, *Atena e Roma* NS 28, 31-50

Giornale 1711: Novelle letterarie di Napoli (gennaio - marzo 1711), *Giornale de' Letterati d'Italia* V, Venezia, 399-401

Gore, R., 1984: The Dead Do Tell Tales at Vesuvius, *National Geographic* 165, nr.5, 557-613, m.n. 577, 606-610

Gori, A., 1752: *Symbolae litterariae opuscula varia*, (Decas I, Roma 1748-1753; Decas II, Roma 1751-1753), Dec.II, vol.II, Roma

Grande Encyclopédie 1885: *La Grande Encyclopédie. Inventaire raisonné des sciences, des lettres et des arts*, Paris (Societé anonyme de la grande encyclopédie) 1885-1901, T.15, 735 (art. 'Elbeuf', L. Delavaud)

Greco, E., 1985: Problemi urbanistici, in: Napoli antica 1985, 132-139

Greco, E., 1988: L'impianto urbano di Neapolis greca: aspetti e problemi, in: *Atti del XXV. Convegno di studi sulla Magna Grecia (Taranto 1985)*, Taranto, 187-219

Grell, C., 1982: *Herculanum et Pompéi dans les récits des voyageurs français du*

XVIIIe siècle, Naples

Grew, F., Hobley, F. (eds.), 1985: *Roman Urban Topography in Britain and the Western Empire*, London (CBA Research Report 59)

Grewe, K., 1984: *Bibliographie zur Geschichte des Vermessungswesen*, Stuttgart

Guadagno, G., 1977: Frammenti inediti di albi degli Augustali, *CronErcol* 7, 114-123

Guadagno, G., 1978: Supplemento epigrafico ercolanese, *CronErcol* 8, 132-155

Guadagno, G., 1981: Supplemento epigrafico ercolanese II, *CronErcol* 11, 129-164

Guadagno, G., 1982: Contributi epigrafici per la storia amministrativa e la topografia ercolanese, in: Regione sotterrata 1982, 193-210

Guadagno, G., 1983: Herculanensium Augustalium Aedes, *CronErcol* 13, 159-173

Guadagno, G., 1986: Nuovi documenti del XVIII secolo per la storia degli scavi di Ercolano, *CronErcol* 16, 135-148

Guadagno, G., 1987: Frustula herculanensia, *CronErcol* 17, 153-156

Guadagno, G., 1988: I graffiti della Aedes Augustalium: documenti sull'accesso all'augustalità, *CronErcol* 18, 199-203

Guadagno, G., 1993: Ercolano. Eredità di cultura e nuovi dati, in: Franchi dell'Orto 1993, 73-98

Guidobaldi, F., 1985: Pavimenti in 'opus sectile' di Roma e dell'area romana: proposte per una classificazione e criteri di datazione, in: Pensabene, P. (ed.), *Marmi antichi* (Studi miscellanei, 26), Roma, 171-233

Haan, N. de, 1993: Dekoration und Funktion in den Privatbädern von Pompeji und Herculaneum, in: Moormann, E.M. (ed.), *Functional and Spatial Analysis of Wall Painting* (Proceedings of the Fifth International Congress on Ancient Wall Painting, Amsterdam 8-12 September 1992), Leiden

Haan, N. de, 1995: Roman Private Baths, *Balnearia. Newsletter of the International Association for the Study of Ancient Baths* 2: 1994, 8-9

Haan. N. de, 1996: Die Wasserversorgung der Privatbäder in Pompeji, in: Haan, N. de, Jansen, G.C.M. (eds.), *Cura Aquarum in Campania* (Proceedings of the Ninth International Congress on the History of Water Management and Hydraulic Engineering in the Mediterranean Region, Pompeii 1-8 October 1994), Leiden

Haverfield, F., 1913: *Ancient Town Planning*, Oxford

Hecht, K., 1979: Zum römischen Fuß, *AbhBraunschWissGesellsch* 30, 107-137

Heimberg, U., 1977: *Römische Landvermessung. Limitatio*, Stuttgart

Heimberg, U., 1984: Griechische und römische Landvermessung, in: Bauplanung 1984, 277-296

Hermansen, G., 1982: *Ostia. Aspects of Roman City Life*, Edmonton

Hesberg, H. von, 1984: Römische Grundrißpläne auf Marmor, in: Bauplanung 1984, 120-133

Hinrichs, F.T., 1974: *Die Geschichte der gromatischen Institutionen. Untersuchungen zu Landverteilung, Landvermessung, Bodenverwaltung und Bodenrecht im römischen Recht*, Wiesbaden

Höcker, Ch., 1993: *Planung und Konzeption der klassischen Ringhallentempel von Agrigent*, Frankfurt am Main (Europäische Hochschulschriften: Reihe 38, Archäologie; 44)

Hoepfner, W., 1984: Einführung: Maße - Proportionen - Zeichnungen, in: Bauplanung 1984, 13-23

Hoepfner, W., Schwandner, E.-L., 1986: *Haus und Stadt im klassischen Griechenland*, München (Wohnen in der klassischen Polis, 1)

Hoffmann, A., 1979: Ein Beitrag zum Wohnen in Pompeji, in: Wohnungsbau im Altertum, Berlin (DiskAB, 3), 162-164

Hultsch, F., 1882: *Griechische und römische Metrologie*, Berlin[2] (repr. Graz 1971)

Instrumentum domesticum 1977: *L'instrumentum domesticum di Ercolano e Pompei nella prima età imperiale*, Roma

Jansen, G., 1991: Watersystems and Sanitation in the Houses of Herculaneum, *MededRom.Antiquity* 50, 151-173

Jashemski, W., 1979: *The Gardens of Pompeii, Herculaneum and the Villas Destroyed by Vesuvius*, New Rochelle NY

Johannowsky, W., 1982: Problemi urbanistici di Ercolano, *CronErcol* 12, 145-149

Jongman, W., 1988: *The Economy and the Society of Pompeii*, Amsterdam (diss. Leiden)

Jorio, A. de, 1827: *Notizie sugli scavi di Ercolano*, Napoli

Judge, J., 1982: A Buried Roman Town Gives Up Its Dead, *National Geographic* 162, 6 (Dec.), 687-693

Käppel, L., 1989: Das Theater von Epidauros, *JdI* 104, 83-106

Kind, R. de, 1990: Themis en Iusta voor vrouwe Justitia. Vondsten op een bovenverdieping in Herculaneum, *Hermeneus* 62, 196-202, 263

Kind, R. de, 1991A: The Study of Houses at Herculaneum, *BABesch* 66, 175-185

Kind, R. de, 1991B: Two Tondo-Heads in the Casa dell'Atrio a Mosaico (IV 1-2) at Herculaneum. Some Remarks on Portraits in Campanian Wall-Paintings, *KölnJbVFrühGesch* 24, 165-169

Kind, R. de, 1991C: Casa dello Scheletro at Herculaneum: the large Nymphaeum, *CronErcol* 21, 133-147

Kind, R. de, 1992A: *Huizen in Herculaneum. Een analyse van de stedebouw en de maatvoering in de huizenblokken III en IV*, diss. Nijmegen (Indagationes Noviomagenses Ad Res Antiquas Spectantes, VII)

Kind, R. de, 1992B: A new typology of the houses in Herculaneum, *MededRom.Antiquity* 51/52 (1992/1993), 62-75

Kind, R. de, 1993A: The Houses 'Dell'Atrio Corinzio' (V, 30) and 'Del Sacello di Legno' (V, 31) at Herculaneum. Metrological Analysis and Building History, in: Franchi dell'Orto 1993, 219-228

Kind, R. de, 1993B: Houses at Herculaneum. An Analysis of Town Planning and of Measurements in insulae III and IV, *CronErcol* 23, 161-167

Knell, H., 1988: Review of Hoepfner/Schwandner 1986, *BJb* 188, 560-562

Knight, C., Jorio, A., 1980: L'ubicazione della Villa ercolanese dei Papiri, *RendAccNap* LV, 51-65

Kockel, V., 1986: Archäologische Funde und Forschungen in den Vesuvstädten, II, *AA*, 443-569

Kockel, V., 1988: Ein unpublizierter Plan der Villa Sora von Carlo Bonucci, *CronEr-*

col 18, 205-208

Koenigs, W., 1990: Maße und Proportionen in der griechischen Baukunst, in: *Polyklet. Der Bildhauer der griechischen Klassik* (exh.. cat. Frankfurt a.M.), Mainz, 121-134

Lepore, E., 1955: Sul carattere economico sociale di Ercolano, *La Parola del Passato* 10, 423-439

Ling, R., 1982: The British Project at Pompeii, *CurrArch* VII, 2 (No.85), 55-61

Ling, R., 1983: The Insula of the Menander at Pompeii: Interim Report, *AntiqJourn* 63, 34-57

Ling, R., 1991: *Roman Painting*, Cambridge

Longo Auricchio, F., Capasso, M., 1987: I rotoli della Villa ercolanese. Dislocazione e ritrovamento, *CronErcol* 17, 37-46

Lorenz, T., 1987: *Römische Städte*, Darmstadt

Lorenz, T., 1993: Überlegungen zur Frage: basiert der Stadtplan von Herculaneum auf einer ursprünglich griechischen Anlage?, in: Franchi dell'Orto 1993, 421-428

Lugli, G., 1957: *La tecnica edilizia romana, con particolare riguardo a Roma e Lazio*, Roma

Maggi, G., 1974: *Archeologia magica di Amedeo Maiuri*, Napoli

Maggi, G., 1976A: Attività archeologica. Ercolano, *CronPomp* 2, 248-249

Maggi, G., 1976B: Ercolano e Oplonti, in: *Atti del XV. Convegno di studi sulla Magna Grecia (Taranto 1975)*, Napoli, 497-500

Maggi, G., 1977: Attività archeologica. Ercolano, *CronPomp* 3, 219-220

Maggi, G., 1978: Attività archeologica. Ercolano, *CronPomp* 4, 234

Maggi, G., 1979: Attività archeologica. Ercolano, *CronPomp* 5, 193-194

Maggi, G., 1985: *Ercolano, fine di una citta*, Napoli 1985

Maiuri, A., 1932: *Ercolano*, Novara

Maiuri, A., 1933: *La Casa del Menandro e il suo tesoro di argenteria*, Roma

Maiuri, A., 1941A: Nuovi studi e ricerche intorno al seppellimento di Ercolano, *RendAccLinc* VII, 2, 127-180

Maiuri, A., 1941B: Dissensi e consensi intorno alla croce di Ercolano, *Rivista dell'Istituto di Studi Romani* XIX, 399-413

Maiuri, A., 1942A: *L'ultima fase edilizia di Pompei*, Roma

Maiuri, A., 1942B: Un decreto onorario di M. Nonio Balbo scoperto recentemente ad Ercolano, *RendAccLinc* VII, 3, 253-278, tavv. I-II

Maiuri, A., 1943: Fanciullo Erote da Ercolano, *Le Arti* V, fasc. IV-V, 175-179

Maiuri, A., 1951A: *La casa a Pompei*, Napoli

Maiuri, A., 1951B: Oecus Aegyptius, in: Mylonas, G., (ed.), *Studies presented to David Moore Robinson*, St. Louis, I, 423-429

Maiuri, A., 1956: *Capri. Storia e monumenti*, Roma (Itinerari dei musei, gallerie e monumenti d'Italia, 93)

Maiuri, A., 1958: *Ercolano. I nuovi scavi (1927-1958)*, I, Roma

Maiuri, A., 1960: Ercolano, in: *EAA* III, Roma, 395-408

Maiuri, A., 1963: *I Campi Flegrei*, Roma[3] (Itinerari dei musei, gallerie e monumenti d'Italia, 32)

Maiuri, A., 1977: *Herculaneum*, Roma[7] (Itinerari dei musei, gallerie e monumenti d'Italia, 53)

Manacorda, D., 1982: Per un indagine sull'archeologia italiana durante il ventennio fascista, *Archeologia medievale* 9, 443-470

Manni, M., 1990: Per la storia della pittura ercolanese, *CronErcol* 20, 129-143

Mau, A., 1908: *Pompeji in Leben und Kunst*, Leipzig[2]

Maury, R.C., 1976: Evolution à haute température des materiaux organiques dans les formations volcaniques ou à leur contact, *BullCentreRechPau-SPNA* 10, 289-300

McIlwaine, I.C., 1988: *Herculaneum. A guide to printed sources*, Napoli

McKay, A., 1975: *Houses, Villas and Palaces in the Roman World*, London

Mertens, D., 1981: Entgegnung zu den Entwurfshypothesen von J. de Waele, AA 1980, *AA*, 426-430

Michel, D., 1990: *Casa dei Ceii (I 6, 15)*, München (Häuser in Pompeji, 3)

Miller, K., 1916: *Itineraria romana. Römische Reisewege an den Hand der Tabula Peutingeriana*, Stuttgart

Miller, K., 1962: *Die Peutingersche Tafel*, Stuttgart (repr.)

Moeller, W.O., 1976: *The Wool Trade of Ancient Pompeii*, Leiden (Studies of the Dutch Archaeological and Historical Society, III)

Mols, S.T.A.M., 1993: Osservazioni sulla forma e sulla tecnica del mobilio ligneo di Ercolano, in: Franchi dell'Orto 1993, 489-498

Mols, S.T.A.M., 1994: *Houten Meubels in Herculaneum. Vorm, Techniek en Functie*, diss. Nijmegen (Indagationes Noviomagenses Ad Res Antiquas Spectantes, X)

Moormann, E.M., 1984: Le pitture della Villa dei Papiri ad Ercolano, in: Atti del XVII Congresso Internazionale di Papirologia, Napoli, 637-674

Moormann, E.M., 1986: Un fior di giardino ed altri frammenti di pittura ercolanese, *CronErcol* 16, 123-133

Moormann, E.M., 1987: Die Wandmalereien in der Casa del Mobilio Carbonizzato in Herculaneum, in: *Pictores per provincias* (Cahiers d'Archéologie romande, 43), Avenches, 127-134

Moormann, E.M., 1988: *La pittura parietale romana come fonte di conoscenza per la scultura antica*, Assen/Maastricht (Scrinium, II)

Mouritsen, H., 1988: *Elections, Magistrates and Municipal Élite. Studies in Pompeian Epigraphy*, Roma (AnalRom - Suppl. XV)

Murga, F.F., 1962: Roque Joaquin de Alcubierre, Descubridor de Herculano, Pompeya y Estabia, *AEArq* 35, 3-35

Murga, F.F., 1964: *Los ingenieros espanoles Roque Joaquin de Alcubierre y Francesco La Vega, descubridores de Herculano, Pompeya y Estabia*, Madrid

Münzer, F., 1899: Ap. Claudius Pulcher, in: *RE* III, 2853-2854 (Nr. 298)

Münzer, F., 1949: C. Papius Mutilus, in: *RE* XVIII.3, 1078-1080

Napoli Antica, 1985: *Napoli Antica* (exh. cat. Museo Archeologico Nazionale), Napoli

Neuerburg, N., 1965: *L'architettura delle fontane e dei ninfei nell'Italia antica*, Napoli

214

Neuerburg, N., 1974: The New J. Paul Getty Museum, *Archaeology* 27, 175-181

Nicolet, C., 1987: La table d'Heraclée et les origines du cadastre romain, in: *L'Urbs*, Rome, 1-25

Niese, B., 1901: L. Cornelius Sisenna, in: *RE* IV, 1512-1513

Nissen, H., 1877: *Pompejanische Studien zur Städtekunde des Altertums*, Leipzig

Nissen, H., 1892: Griechische und römische Metrologie, in: Müller, I. von (ed.), *Handbuch der klassischen Altertumswissenschft. I. Einleitende und Hilfsdisziplinen*, München[2], 833-890

Onorato, G.O., 1949: La data del terremoto di Pompei: 5 febbraio 62 d.c., *Rend-AccLinc* VIII, 4, 644-661

Orr, D.G., 1979: *Roman Domestic Religion: A Study of the Roman Household Deities and Their Shrines at Pompeii and Herculaneum*, Ann Arbor (diss. Maryland 1972)

Ostrow, S., 1985: Augustales along the Bay of Naples: a case for their early growth, *Historia* 34, 64-101

Packer, J., 1971: *The Insulae of Imperial Ostia*, Roma (MAAR XXXI)

Packer, J., 1975: Middle and Lower Class Housing in Pompeii and Herculaneum, in: Andreae - Kyrieleis 1975, 133-146

Pagano, M., 1987: Una iscrizione elettorale da Ercolano, *CronErcol* 17, 151-152

Pagano, M., 1988A: Iscrizione della statua di Marco Nonio Balbo posta davanti alle Terme Suburbane, *RStPomp* 2, 238-239

Pagano, M., 1988B: Semo Sancus in una insegna di bottega a Ercolano, *CronErcol* 18, 209-214

Pagano, M., 1990: Un ciclo delle imprese di Ercole con iscrizioni greche ad Ercolano, *RM* 97, 153-161

Pagano, M., 1993A: Il teatro di Ercolano, *CronErcol* 23, 121-156

Pagano, M., 1993B: Ricerche sull'impianto urbano di Ercolano, in: Franchi dell'Orto 1993, 595-608

Pagano, M., 1996: La nuova pianta della città e di alcuni edifici pubblici di Ercolano, *CronErcol* 26, 229-262

Pannuti, U., 1983: Il 'Giornale degli Scavi' di Ercolano (1738-1756), *MemAccLinc* 26, 163-410

Papaccio, V., 1993: Il telaio ligneo (opus craticium) ercolanese: considerazioni e ricerche sui requisiti antisismici, in: Franchi dell'Orto 1993, 609-616

Pappalardo, U., 1983: Ercolano. Attività negli anni 1980-1983, *PompHercStab* 1, 344-353

Pappalardo, U., 1987: Attività dell'Ufficio Scavi: 1984-1985, *RStPomp* 1, 191-193

Parslow, C., 1988: Documents illustrating the excavations of the Praedia of Julia Felix in Pompeii, *RStPomp* 2, 37-48

Parslow, C., 1993: Karl Weber and Pompeian Archaeology, in: Franchi dell'Orto 1975, 51-56

Parslow, C., 1995: *Rediscovering Antiquity. Karl Weber and the Excavation of Herculaneum, Pompeii, and Stabiae*, Cambridge

Pescatore, T., Sigurdsson, H., 1993: L'eruzione del Vesuvio del 79 d.C., in: Franchi dell'Orto 1993, 449-458

Peter, H. (ed.), 1914: *Historicum Romanorum Reliquiae*, Leipzig[2] (vol. I, 276-297 = L. Cornelii Sisennae Historiae)

Peters, W.J.T., 1963: *Landscape in Romano-Campanian Mural Painting*, Assen

Peterse, C., 1984: Der oskische Fuß in pompejanischen Atrien, *BABesch* 59, 9-30

Peterse, C.L.J., 1985: Notes on the Design of the House of Pansa (VI, 6, 1), *MededRom* XLVI, NS 11, 35-55

Peterse, C.L.J., 1993: *Bouwkundige studies van huizen in Pompeii: muurwerk, maatvoering en ontwerp*, diss. Nijmegen (Indagationes Noviomagenses Ad Res Antiquas Spectantes, IX)

Piganiol, A., 1962: *Les documents cadastraux de la colonie romaine d'Orange*, Paris (Gallia Suppl. XVI)

Pisapia, M.S., 1981: L'area ercolanese dopo l'eruzione del 79. Evidenze archeologiche. La necropoli di Via Doglie ad Ercolano, *RendAccNap* 56, 63-74

Pólay, E., 1976: Hauskaufvertrag aus dem römischen Dakien. (Ein Beitrag zum provinzialen Bodeneigentum der Römer), *Oikumene* 1, 197-213

Portalupi, F. (ed.), 1967: *Velleio Patercolo, storia romana*, Torino (introduzione e commento di F. Portalupi)

Progetto Pompei 1988: *Progetto Pompei - primo stralcio. Un bilancio*, (exh. cat. Pompei, Casina dell'Aquila, 22/6-22/7/1988), Napoli

Pugliese Carratelli, G., 1955: Sulle origini di Ercolano, *La Parola del Passato* X, 417-422

Rainer, J.M., 1987: *Bau- und nachbarrechtliche Bestimmungen im klassischen römischen Recht*, Graz (Grazer Rechts- und Staatswissenschaftliche Studien, 4)

Rainer, J.M., 1988: Der Paries Communis im klassischen römischen Recht, *Zeitschr.Savigny Stift., Rom.Abt.*, 105, 488-513

Rakob, F., 1984: Metrologie und Planfiguren einer kaiserlichen Bauhütte, in: Bauforschung 1984, 220-237

Regione sotterrata 1982: *La regione sotterrata dal Vesuvio. Studi e prospettive (Atti del convegno 11-15/11/1979)*, Napoli

Romanelli, P., 1963: Amedeo Maiuri, *Studi Romani* 11, 317-319

Rosi, M., Santacroce, R., 1986: L'attività del Somma-Vesuvio precedente l'eruzione del 1631: dati stratigrafici e vulcanologici, in: Albore Livadie 1986, 15-33

Rosini, C., 1797: *Dissertationis isagogicae ad Herculanensium voluminum explanationem pars prima*, Napoli

Rosini, C.M., Ciampitti, N., e.a., 1793: *Herculanensium voluminum quae superstunt* ...., Napoli 1793-1850 (tomus 1-6, 8-10)

Ruggiero, M., 1881: *Degli Scavi di Stabia dal MDCCXLIX al MDCCLXXXII*, Napoli

Ruggiero, M., 1885: *Storia degli scavi di Ercolano ricomposta su' documenti superstiti*, Napoli

Russo, A., 1984: Servitú di appoggio e 'refectio parietis', *Labeo* 30, 71-79

Scagliarini, D.C., 1974: Spazio e decorazione nella pittura pompeiana, *Palladio* 23-25 (1974-1976), 3-44

Scatozza Höricht, L.A., 1982: Restauri alle collezioni del Museo Ercolanese di Portici alla luce di documenti inediti, *AttAccPont* XXXI, 495-540

Scatozza Höricht, L.A., 1985: Ville nel territorio ercolanese, *CronErcol* 15, 131-165

Scatozza Höricht, L.A., 1986: *I vetri romani di Ercolano*, Roma (Cataloghi SAP, 1)

Scatozza Höricht, L.A., 1989A: *I monili di Ercolano*, Roma (Cataloghi SAP, 3)

Scatozza Höricht, L.A., 1989B: Ercolano, in: Nenci, G., Vallet, G. (eds.), *Bibliografia topografica della colonizzazione greca in Italia e nelle isole tirreniche*, Pisa-Roma, vol. VII, 289-343

Schäfer, Th., 1979: Le 'sellae curules' del teatro di Ercolano, *CronErcol* 9, 143-151

Schäfer, Th., 1989: *Imperii Insignia: Sella Curulis und Fasces. Zur Repräsentation römischer Magistrate*, Mainz (29. *RM*-Erg.Heft)

Schuller, W. (ed.), 1989: *Demokratie und Architektur. Der hippodamische Städtebau und die Entstehung der Demokratie (Symposion Konstanz 1987)*, München (Wohnen in der klassischen Polis, II)

Schumacher, L., 1976: Das Ehrendekret für M. Nonius Balbus aus Herculaneum, *Chiron* 6, 165-184

Schwandner, E.-L., 1984: Zur Entschlüsselung antiker Baumaße, in: Bauplanung 1984, 24-25

Sear, F., 1977: *Roman Wall and Vault Mosaics*, Rome (23. *RM*-Erg.Heft)

Seiler, F., 1992: *Casa degli Amorini Dorati (VI 16, 7.38)*, München (Häuser in Pompeji, 5)

Sherk, R.K., 1970: *Municipal Decrees of the Roman West*, New York (Arethusa Monographs, 2)

Sherwin White, A.N., 1966: *The Letters of Pliny: A Historical and Social Commentary*, Oxford

Sigurdsson, H., Cashdollar, S., Sparks, S.R.J., 1982: The Eruption of Vesuvius in A.D. 79. Reconstruction from Historical and Vulcanological Evidence, *AJA* 86, 39-51, 315-316

Simone, A. De, 1987A: La Villa dei Papiri. Rapporto preliminare gennaio 1986 - marzo 1987, *CronErcol* 17, 15-36

Simone, A. De, 1987B: Regio II, ins. VIII, *RStPomp* 1, 156

Simone, A. De, 1988: Le insulae su Via di Nocera. Regio II, ins. 8, *RStPomp* 2, 184-186

Sironen, T., 1993: La documentazione epigrafica osca di Ercolano. Considerazioni e riletture, in: Franchi dell'Orto 1993, 537-541

Smith, R.F., 1987: Land-division and Property Boundaries in Roadside Settlements, in: *Roadside Settlements in Lowland Roman Britain*, Oxford (BAR, Int.Ser. 157), 22-58

Sodo, A.M., 1987: Regio II, ins. IX, *RStPomp* 1, 156-159

Sodo, A.M., 1988: Le insulae su Via di Nocera. Regio II, ins. 9, *RStPomp* 2, 195-202

Solin, H., 1973A: Die herkulanensischen Wandinschriften. Ein soziologischer Versuch, *CronErcol* 3, 97-103

Solin, H., 1973B: Review of CIL IV, Suppl. 3 en 4, *Gnomon* 45, 258-277

Sommer, C.S., 1991: Life beyond the Ditches: Housing and Planning of the Military Vici in Upper Germany and Raetia, in: Maxfield, V.A., Dobson, M.J. (eds.),

Roman Frontier Studies 1989. Proceedings of the XVth International Congress of Roman Frontier Studies, Exeter, 472-476

Spano, G., 1937: Porte e regioni pompeiane e vie campane, *RendAccNap* NS XVII, 267-360

Spano, G., 1941: *La Campania Felice nelle età più remote. Pompei dalle origini alla fase ellenistica*, Napoli

Steffy, J.R., 1985: The Herculaneum Boat: Preliminary Notes on Hull Details, *AJA* 89, 519-521

Strazullo, F., 1980: Documenti per l'Ing. Rocco Alcubierre scopritore di Ercolano, *AttAccPont* XXIX, 263-296

Strazullo, F., 1982: I primi anni dello scavo di Ercolano nel diario dell'ingegnere militare Rocco Gioacchino d'Alcubierre, in: Regione sotterrata 1982, 103-181

Strocka, V.M., 1975: Pompejanische Nebenzimmer, in: Andreae/Kyrieleis 1975, 101-114

Strocka, V.M., 1984: *Casa del Principe di Napoli (VI 15, 7.8)*, Tübingen (Häuser in Pompeji, 1)

Strocka, V.M., 1987: Die römische Wandmalerei von Tiberius bis Nero, in: *Pictores per provincias* (Cahiers d'Archéologie romande, 43), Avenches, 29-44

Strocka, V.M., 1991: *Casa del Labirinto (VI 11, 10)*, München (Häuser in Pompeji, 4)

Strocka, V.M., Ehrhardt, W., 1987: 'Case di Pompei': un progetto scientifico internazionale dell'Istituto Archeologico Germanico, *RStPomp* I, 203-208

Stuart, P., 1991: *De Tabula Peutingeriana*, Nijmegen (Museumstukken, II)

Swoboda, E., 1936: M. Nonius Balbus, in: *RE* XVII.1, 875 (Nr. 25-26)

Tamm, B., 1963: *Auditorium and Palatium. A Study on Assembly-rooms in Roman Palaces during the 1st Century B.C. and the 1st Century A.D.*, Stockholm (Acta Universitatis Stockholmiensis, 2)

Tamm, B., 1973: Some Notes on Roman Houses, *OpRom* 9, 53-60

Thomasson, B.E., 1984: *Laterculi Praesidum*. Vol. I, Göteborg

Tran Tam Tinh, V., 1971: *Le culte des divinités orientales à Herculanum*, Leiden (EPRO, 17)

Tran Tam Tinh, 1977: A la recherche d'Herculanum preromaine, *CronPomp* 3, 40-56

Tran Tam Tinh, 1988: *La Casa dei Cervi à Herculanum*, Roma (Archaeologica, 74)

Venditti, A., 1970: Bonucci, Carlo, in: *Dizionario Biografico degli Italiani*, XII, Roma, 455-456

Venuti, M. de, 1748: *Descrizione delle prime scoperte dell'antica città di Ercolano*, Roma

Vetter, E., 1953: *Handbuch der italischen Dialekten* I, Heidelberg

Vos, A. de, Vos, M. de, 1982: *Pompei, Ercolano, Stabia*, Roma/Bari (Guide archeologiche Laterza)

Vos, M. de, 1976: Scavi Nuovi sconosciuti (I 9, 13): pitture e pavimenti della Casa di Cerere a Pompei, *MededRom* XXXVIII, 37-75

Vos, M. de, 1993: Camillo Paderni, la tradizione antiquaria romana e i collezionisti inglesi, in: Franchi dell'Orto 1993, 99-116

Waarsenburg, D.J., 1991: Archeologisch Nieuws verzorgd door het Nederlands Instituut te Rome. De Schedel van Plinius Maior, *Hermeneus* 63, 39-43

Wachsmann, S., 1990: Una barca nel Mare di Galilea, *Archeologia Viva* IX, N.S. Nr. 11, 10-17

Waele, J. de, 1980A: Der Entwurf der dorischen Tempel von Akragas, *AA*, 180-241

Waele, J. de, 1980B: Der Entwurf der dorischen Tempel von Paestum, *AA*, 367-400

Waele, J. de, 1984: Der römische Fuß in Pompeji: der Tempel des Juppiter Capitolinus, *BABesch* 59, 1-8

Waele, J. de, 1988: Die Maße der Werkstatt des Pheidias in Olympia, in: Büsing, H., Hiller, F., *Bathron. Beiträge zur Architektur und verwandten Künsten. Für Heinrich Drerup zu seinem 80. Geburtstag* (Saarbrücker Studien zur Archäologie und Alten Geschichte, Bd. 3), Saarbrücken, 387-406

Waele, J. de, 1990A: Review of D. Mertens, Der Tempel von Segesta und die dorische Tempelbaukunst des griechischen Westens in klassischer Zeit (Mainz 1984), *Gnomon* 62, 248-264

Waele, J. de, 1990B: *The Propylaia of the Akropolis in Athens. The Project of Mnesikles*, Amsterdam (Publications of the Netherlands Institute at Athens, I)

Waldstein, Ch., Shoobridge, L., 1908: *Herculaneum, Past, Present and Future*, London

Wallace-Hadrill, A., 1994: *Houses and Society in Pompeii and Herculaneum*, Princeton

Walthew, C.V., 1978: Property-Boundaries and the Sizes of Building Plots in Roman Towns, *Britannia* IX, 335-350

Walthew, C.V., 1987: Length-Units in House-Planning at Silchester and Caerwent, *Britannia* XVIII, 201-231

Ward-Perkins, J.B., 1979: Note di topografia e urbanistica, in: Zevi, F. (ed.), *Pompei 79*, Napoli, 25-39

Watts, C.M., 1990: *A Pattern Language for Houses at Pompeii, Herculaneum and Ostia*, Ann Arbor (diss. Austin 1987)

Weber, E., 1976: *Tabula Peutingeriana. Codex Vindobonensis 324*, Graz

Wehrli, F. (ed.), 1969: *Die Schule des Aristoteles. Texte und Kommentar. IX. Phainias von Eresos*, Basel[2]

Widemann, F., 1986: Les effets économiques de l'éruption de 79. Nouvelles données et nouvelle approche, in: Albore Livadie 1986, 107-112

Winckelmann, J.J., 1762: *Sendschreiben von den Herculanischen Entdeckungen an dem Hochgebohrnen Herrn, Herrn Heinrich Reichsgrafen von Brühl*, Dresden

Winckelmann, J.J., 1764: *Nachrichten von den neuesten Herculanischen Entdeckungen an Herrn Heinrich Füssli aus Zürich*, Dresden

Wojcik, M.R., 1986: *La Villa dei Papiri ad Ercolano*, Roma (Monografie SAP, 1)

Zanker, P., 1981: Das Bildnis des M. Holconius Rufus, *AA*, 349-361

Zanker, P., 1983: Zur Bildnisrepräsentation führender Männer in mittelitalienischen und campanischen Städten zur Zeit der späten Republik und der iulisch-claudischen Kaiser, in: *Les 'bourgeoisies' municipales italiennes aux IIe et Ie siècles av. J.-C. (congress Napoli 1981)*, Paris-Naples, 251-266

Zevi, F., 1982: L'attività archeologica nelle province di Napoli e Caserta, in: *Atti del XXI. Convegno di studi sulla Magna Grecia (Taranto 1981)*, Taranto, 325-358

Zevi, F., Maggi, G., 1978: L'attività archeologica nelle province di Napoli e Caserta, in: *Atti del XVII. Convegno di studi sulla Magna Grecia (Taranto 1977)*, Napoli, 325-343

Zimmer, G., 1984: Maßstäbe römischer Architekten, in: Bauplanung 1984, 265-276

APPENDICES

Notes to the appendices

The numbers listed under the heading *Room* refer to the room numbers on the plans of the houses; wherever the total length of a house could be measured, it is listed under number 0.

The heading *Where?* shows which wall of the room is meant. If a measurement has not been taken along a wall, but across the room (lengthways or widthways), it is referred to as 'length' or 'width'. The measurements giving the dimensions of an impluvium and its distance from the sides of the atrium are marked as 'impl(l)' and 'impl(w)'.

A measurement can consist of several parts. The *kind* of measurement is reflected as 't' for total measurement and 'p' for partial measurement.

The measurements *in cm* are accurate to the nearest 0.5 cm, whereas the estimated measurements in *Oscan* or *Roman feet* are rounded to the nearest 0.25 ft.

The *ideal* measurement (in cm) is the product of the foot unit used and the estimated measurement in feet.

Casa dell'Albergo (III 1-2, 18-19) Lot III A

Room	where?	kind	in cm	O.ft (27.55)	ideal
32	west	t	561.0	20.25	557.9
32	west	p	47.0	1.75	48.2
32	west	p	289.5	10.50	289.3
32	west	p	224.5	8.25	227.3
32	north	t	827.5	30.00	826.5
32	south	t	827.5	30.00	826.5
32	south	p	106.5	3.75	103.3
32	south	p	721.0	26.25	723.2
32	east	t	557.5	20.25	557.9
32	east	p	60.5	2.25	62.0
32	east	p	87.0	3.25	89.5
32	east	p	412.0	15.00	413.3
33	west	t	555.5	20.25	557.9
33	west	p	57.5	2.00	55.1
33	west	p	80.5	3.00	82.7
33	west	p	407.5	14.75	406.4
33	north	t	282.0	10.25	282.4
33	south	t	268.0	9.75	268.6
33	east	t	553.0	20.00	551.0
34	west	t	399.0	14.50	399.5
34	north	t	374.0	13.50	371.9
34	north	p	249.0	9.00	248.0
34	north	p	125.0	4.50	124.0
34	south	t	368.0	13.25	365.0
34	east	p	81.0	3.00	82.7
34	east	p	282.0	10.25	282.4
34	east	p	34.0	1.25	34.4
34	east	t	397.0	14.50	399.5
35	west	t	551.0	20.00	551.0
35	north	t	408.0	14.75	406.4
35	south	t	411.5	15.00	413.3
35	south	p	211.5	7.75	213.5
35	south	p	161.5	5.75	158.4
35	south	p	38.5	1.50	41.3
35	east	t	549.0	20.00	551.0
36	west	t	164.5	6.00	165.3
36	north	t	373.0	13.50	371.9
36	south	t	374.0	13.50	371.9
36	east	t	160.0	5.75	158.4

Casa dell'Albergo (III 1-2, 18-19) Lot III K

Room	where?	kind	in cm	O.ft (27.55)	ideal	R.ft (29.45)	ideal
37	width	t	271.0	9.75	269.6	9.25	272.4
37	west	t	336.0	12.25	338.7	11.50	338.7
37	west	p	96.0	3.50	96.8	3.25	95.7
37	west	p	97.5	3.50	96.8	3.25	95.7
37	west	p	34.5	1.25	34.6	1.25	36.8
37	west	p	108.0	4.00	110.6	3.75	110.4
37	north	t	831.0	30.00	829.5	28.25	832.0
37	north	p	76.0	2.75	76.0	2.50	73.6
37	north	p	250.5	9.00	248.9	8.50	250.3
37	north	p	252.5	9.25	255.8	8.50	250.3
37	north	p	159.0	5.75	159.0	5.50	162.0
37	north	p	93.0	3.25	89.9	3.25	95.7
37	south	t	836.0	30.25	836.4	28.50	839.3
37	east	t	216.0	7.75	214.3	7.25	213.5
38	west	t	245.0	8.75	241.9	8.25	243.0
38	north	t	169.0	6.00	165.9	5.75	169.3
38	south	t	168.0	6.00	165.9	5.75	169.3
38	east	t	337.0	12.25	338.7	11.50	338.7
39	width	t	242.0	8.75	241.9	8.25	243.0
39	west	t	185.0	6.75	186.6	6.25	184.1
39	west	p	102.0	3.75	103.7	3.50	103.1
39	west	p	73.0	2.75	76.0	2.50	73.6
39	north	t	669.0	24.25	670.5	22.75	670.0
39	south	t	663.0	24.00	663.6	22.50	662.6
39	south	p	158.0	5.75	159.0	5.25	154.6
39	south	p	244.0	8.75	241.9	8.25	243.0
39	south	p	166.0	6.00	165.9	5.75	169.3
39	south	p	95.0	3.50	96.8	3.25	95.7
39	east	t	241.0	8.75	241.9	8.25	243.0
40	west	t	194.0	7.00	193.6	6.50	191.4
40	west	p	54.5	2.00	55.3	1.75	51.5
40	west	p	90.5	3.25	89.9	3.00	88.4
40	west	p	49.0	1.75	48.4	1.75	51.5
40	north	t	281.0	10.25	283.4	9.50	279.8
40	south	t	271.0	9.75	269.6	9.25	272.4
40	east	t	192.0	7.00	193.6	6.50	191.4
40	east	p	111.0	4.00	110.6	3.75	110.4
40	east	p	81.0	3.00	83.0	2.75	81.0
41	length	t	274.0	10.00	276.5	9.25	272.4
41	west	t	334.0	12.00	331.8	11.25	331.3
41	west	p	21.5	0.75	20.7	0.75	22.1
41	west	p	104.5	3.75	103.7	3.50	103.1
41	west	p	115.0	4.25	117.5	4.00	117.8

Casa dell'Albergo (III 1-2, 18-19) Lot III K

Room	where?	kind	in cm	O.ft (27.55)	ideal	R.ft (29.45)	ideal
41	west	p	93.0	3.25	89.9	3.25	95.7
41	west	p	93.0	3.25	89.9	3.25	95.7
41	north	t	332.0	12.00	331.8	11.25	331.3
41	south	t	273.0	9.75	269.6	9.25	272.4
41	east	t	334.0	12.00	331.8	11.25	331.3
41	east	p	100.0	3.50	96.8	3.50	103.1
41	east	p	97.0	3.50	96.8	3.25	95.7
41	east	p	37.0	1.25	34.6	1.25	36.8
41	east	p	100.0	3.50	96.8	3.50	103.1
42	west	t	396.5	14.25	394.0	13.50	397.6
42	west	p	136.0	5.00	138.3	4.50	132.5
42	west	p	131.0	4.75	131.3	4.50	132.5
42	west	p	129.5	4.75	131.3	4.50	132.5
42	north	t	275.0	10.00	276.5	9.25	272.4
42	south	t	283.0	10.25	283.4	9.50	279.8
42	south	p	37.5	1.25	34.6	1.25	36.8
42	south	p	61.0	2.25	62.2	2.00	58.9
42	south	p	184.5	6.75	186.6	6.25	184.1
42	east	t	390.0	14.00	387.1	13.25	390.2
42	east	p	68.5	2.50	69.1	2.25	66.3
42	east	p	96.5	3.50	96.8	3.25	95.7
42	east	p	77.0	2.75	76.0	2.50	73.6
42	east	p	89.5	3.25	89.9	3.00	88.4
42	east	p	58.5	2.00	55.3	2.00	58.9
43	length	t	478.0	17.25	477.0	16.25	478.6
43	west	t	382.0	13.75	380.2	13.00	382.9
43	north	t	472.5	17.00	470.1	16.00	471.2
43	south	t	477.0	17.25	477.0	16.25	478.6
43	east	t	385.0	14.00	387.1	13.00	382.9
43	east	p	127.5	4.50	124.4	4.25	125.2
43	east	p	130.5	4.75	131.3	4.50	132.5
43	east	p	127.0	4.50	124.4	4.25	125.2
44	west	t	131.0	4.75	131.3	4.50	132.5
44	north	t	795.0	28.75	794.9	27.00	795.2
44	north	p	36.0	1.25	34.6	1.25	36.8
44	north	p	63.0	2.25	62.2	2.25	66.3
44	north	p	64.0	2.25	62.2	2.25	66.3
44	north	p	632.0	22.75	629.0	21.50	633.2
44	south	t	800.0	29.00	801.9	27.25	802.5
44	south	p	74.5	2.75	76.0	2.50	73.6
44	south	p	725.5	26.25	725.8	24.75	728.9
44	east	t	138.0	5.00	138.3	4.75	139.9

Casa dell'Albergo (III 1-2, 18-19)   **Peristyle and terrace**

Room	where?	kind	in cm	O.ft (27.4)	ideal	R.ft (29.3)	ideal
1	west	t	454.0	16.50	452.1	15.50	454.2
1	north	t	938.0	34.25	938.5	32.00	937.6
1	south	t	937.0	34.25	938.5	32.00	937.6
1	south	p	804.0	29.25	801.5	27.50	805.8
1	south	p	133.0	4.75	130.2	4.50	131.9
1	east	t	415.0	15.25	417.9	14.25	417.5
2	length	t	345.5	12.50	342.5	11.75	344.3
2	west	t	356.5	13.00	356.2	12.25	358.9
2	west	p	106.0	3.75	102.8	3.50	102.6
2	west	p	250.5	9.25	253.5	8.50	249.1
2	north	t	342.5	12.50	342.5	11.75	344.3
2	east	t	357.5	13.00	356.2	12.25	358.9
3	west	t	539.0	19.75	541.2	18.50	542.1
3	north	t	317.0	11.50	315.1	10.75	315.0
3	south	t	318.0	11.50	315.1	10.75	315.0
3	east	t	542.0	19.75	541.2	18.50	542.1
3	east	p	374.5	13.75	376.8	12.75	373.6
3	east	p	98.5	3.50	95.9	3.25	95.2
3	east	p	69.0	2.50	68.5	2.25	65.9
4	west	t	457.5	16.75	459.0	15.50	454.2
4	north	t	379.0	13.75	376.8	13.00	380.9
4	south	t	379.0	13.75	376.8	13.00	380.9
4	east	t	435.0	16.00	438.4	14.75	432.2
5	width	t	251.0	9.25	253.5	8.50	249.1
5	length	t	360.5	13.25	363.1	12.25	358.9
5	west	t	248.5	9.00	246.6	8.50	249.1
5	north	t	360.0	13.25	363.1	12.25	358.9
5	north	p	93.0	3.50	95.9	3.25	95.2
5	north	p	267.0	9.75	267.2	9.00	263.7
5	south	t	402.5	14.75	404.2	13.75	402.9
6	width	t	155.0	5.75	157.6	5.25	153.8
6	west	t	157.0	5.75	157.6	5.25	153.8
6	north	t	358.0	13.00	356.2	12.25	358.9
6	south	t	360.0	13.25	363.1	12.25	358.9
6	south	p	93.0	3.50	95.9	3.25	95.2
6	south	p	267.0	9.75	267.2	9.00	263.7
7	length	t	219.5	8.00	219.2	7.50	219.8
7	west	t	449.5	16.50	452.1	15.25	446.8
7	west	p	91.5	3.25	89.1	3.00	87.9
7	west	p	358.0	13.00	356.2	12.25	358.9
7	north	t	219.0	8.00	219.2	7.50	219.8
7	east	t	449.0	16.50	452.1	15.25	446.8
7	east	p	87.0	3.25	89.1	3.00	87.9

Casa dell'Albergo (III 1-2, 18-19)   Peristyle and terrace

Room	where?	kind	in cm	O.ft (27.4)	ideal	R.ft (29.3)	ideal
7	east	p	362.0	13.25	363.1	12.25	358.9
8	length	t	302.0	11.00	301.4	10.25	300.3
8	west	t	454.0	16.50	452.1	15.50	454.2
8	west	p	90.5	3.25	89.1	3.00	87.9
8	west	p	363.5	13.25	363.1	12.50	366.3
8	north	t	305.0	11.25	308.3	10.50	307.7
8	east	t	453.0	16.50	452.1	15.50	454.2
9	west	p	153.5	5.50	150.7	5.25	153.8
9	west	t	552.0	20.25	554.9	18.75	549.4
9	west	p	398.5	14.50	397.3	13.50	395.6
9	north	t	243.0	8.75	239.8	8.25	241.7
9	north	p	86.0	3.25	89.1	3.00	87.9
9	north	p	66.0	2.50	68.5	2.25	65.9
9	north	p	91.0	3.25	89.1	3.00	87.9
9	south	t	235.0	8.50	232.9	8.00	234.4
9	east	t	558.0	20.25	554.9	19.00	556.7
10	west	t	355.0	13.00	356.2	12.00	351.6
10	north	t	151.0	5.50	150.7	5.25	153.8
10	south	t	148.0	5.50	150.7	5.00	146.5
10	east	t	356.0	13.00	356.2	12.25	358.9
10	east	p	207.0	7.50	205.5	7.00	205.1
10	east	p	110.0	4.00	109.6	3.75	109.9
10	east	p	80.0	3.00	82.2	2.75	80.6
11	west	t	335.0	12.25	335.7	11.50	337.0
11	north	t	145.0	5.25	143.9	5.00	146.5
11	south	t	152.0	5.50	150.7	5.25	153.8
11	south	p	89.0	3.25	89.1	3.00	87.9
11	south	p	63.0	2.25	61.7	2.25	65.9
11	east	t	340.0	12.50	342.5	11.50	337.0
12	width	t	416.5	15.25	417.9	14.25	417.5
12	west	t	456.0	16.75	459.0	15.50	454.2
12	west	p	382.0	14.00	383.6	13.00	380.9
12	west	p	74.0	2.75	75.4	2.50	73.3
12	north	t	324.0	11.75	322.0	11.00	322.3
12	south	t	326.0	12.00	328.8	11.25	329.6
12	east	t	412.0	15.00	411.0	14.00	410.2
13	west	t	417.0	15.25	417.9	14.25	417.5
13	west	p	112.0	4.00	109.6	3.75	109.9
13	west	p	305.0	11.25	308.3	10.50	307.7
13	north	t	326.0	12.00	328.8	11.25	329.6
13	south	t	329.0	12.00	328.8	11.25	329.6
13	east	t	415.0	15.25	417.9	14.25	417.5
13	east	p	345.0	12.50	342.5	11.75	344.3

Casa dell'Albergo (III 1-2, 18-19)   Peristyle and terrace

Room	where?	kind	in cm	O.ft (27.4)	ideal	R.ft (29.3)	ideal
13	east	p	70.0	2.50	68.5	2.50	73.3
14	width	t	637.0	23.25	637.1	21.75	637.3
14	width	p	12.0	0.50	13.7	0.50	14.7
14	width	p	491.0	18.00	493.2	16.75	490.8
14	width	p	122.0	4.50	123.3	4.25	124.5
14	width	t	635.0	23.25	637.1	21.75	637.3
14	width	p	101.0	3.75	102.8	3.50	102.6
14	width	p	408.0	15.00	411.0	14.00	410.2
14	width	p	128.0	4.75	130.2	4.25	124.5
14	west	t	409.0	15.00	411.0	14.00	410.2
14	north	t	402.0	14.75	404.2	13.75	402.9
14	north	p	109.0	4.00	109.6	3.75	109.9
14	north	p	189.0	7.00	191.8	6.50	190.5
14	north	p	104.0	3.75	102.8	3.50	102.6
14	south	t	396.0	14.50	397.3	13.50	395.6
14	south	p	85.0	3.00	82.2	3.00	87.9
14	south	p	216.0	8.00	219.2	7.25	212.4
14	south	p	95.0	3.50	95.9	3.25	95.2
14	east	t	509.5	18.50	506.9	17.50	512.8
15	west	t	106.5	4.00	109.6	3.75	109.9
15	north	t	413.0	15.00	411.0	14.00	410.2
15	north	p	329.0	12.00	328.8	11.25	329.6
15	north	p	84.0	3.00	82.2	2.75	80.6
15	south	t	413.0	15.00	411.0	14.00	410.2
15	south	p	75.0	2.75	75.4	2.50	73.3
15	south	p	338.0	12.25	335.7	11.50	337.0
15	east	t	73.0	2.75	75.4	2.50	73.3
16	west	t	310.5	11.25	308.3	10.50	307.7
16	west	p	149.0	5.50	150.7	5.00	146.5
16	west	p	161.5	6.00	164.4	5.50	161.2
16	north	t	415.0	15.25	417.9	14.25	417.5
16	north	p	212.0	7.75	212.4	7.25	212.4
16	north	p	203.0	7.50	205.5	7.00	205.1
16	south	t	407.0	14.75	404.2	14.00	410.2
16	south	p	207.0	7.50	205.5	7.00	205.1
16	south	p	117.0	4.25	116.5	4.00	117.2
16	south	p	83.0	3.00	82.2	2.75	80.6
16	east	t	311.0	11.25	308.3	10.50	307.7
17	west	t	252.0	9.25	253.5	8.50	249.1
17	north	t	98.0	3.50	95.9	3.25	95.2
17	south	t	53.0	2.00	54.8	1.75	51.3
17	east	t	252.0	9.25	253.5	8.50	249.1
17	east	p	131.0	4.75	130.2	4.50	131.9

Casa dell'Albergo (III 1-2, 18-19)   **Peristyle and terrace**

Room	where?	kind	in cm	O.ft (27.4)	ideal	R.ft (29.3)	ideal
17	east	p	121.0	4.50	123.3	4.25	124.5
18	west	t	118.0	4.25	116.5	4.00	117.2
18	north	t	362.0	13.25	363.1	12.25	358.9
18	north	p	152.0	5.50	150.7	5.25	153.8
18	north	p	210.0	7.75	212.4	7.25	212.4
18	south	t	362.0	13.25	363.1	12.25	358.9
18	south	p	154.0	5.50	150.7	5.25	153.8
18	south	p	120.0	4.50	123.3	4.00	117.2
18	south	p	88.0	3.25	89.1	3.00	87.9
18	east	t	118.0	4.25	116.5	4.00	117.2
19	west	t	327.5	12.00	328.8	11.25	329.6
19	north	t	551.0	20.00	548.0	18.75	549.4
19	south	t	555.0	20.25	554.9	19.00	556.7
19	south	p	213.0	7.75	212.4	7.25	212.4
19	south	p	93.0	3.50	95.9	3.25	95.2
19	south	p	249.0	9.00	246.6	8.50	249.1
19	east	t	320.0	11.75	322.0	11.00	322.3
20	west	t	307.0	11.25	308.3	10.50	307.7
20	north	t	328.0	12.00	328.8	11.25	329.6
20	south	t	320.0	11.75	322.0	11.00	322.3
20	south	p	83.0	3.00	82.2	2.75	80.6
20	south	p	237.0	8.75	239.8	8.00	234.4
20	east	t	328.0	12.00	328.8	11.25	329.6
21	west	t	396.0	14.50	397.3	13.50	395.6
21	north	t	355.5	13.00	356.2	12.25	358.9
21	north	p	237.0	8.75	239.8	8.00	234.4
21	north	p	88.0	3.25	89.1	3.00	87.9
21	north	p	30.5	1.00	27.4	1.00	29.3
21	south	t	363.0	13.25	363.1	12.50	366.3
21	east	t	394.0	14.50	397.3	13.50	395.6
22	west	t	416.0	15.25	417.9	14.25	417.5
22	west	p	296.5	10.75	294.6	10.00	293.0
22	west	p	89.5	3.25	89.1	3.00	87.9
22	west	p	30.0	1.00	27.4	1.00	29.3
22	north	t	353.0	13.00	356.2	12.00	351.6
22	north	p	228.0	8.25	226.1	7.75	227.1
22	north	p	74.0	2.75	75.4	2.50	73.3
22	north	p	51.0	1.75	48.0	1.75	51.3
22	south	t	353.0	13.00	356.2	12.00	351.6
22	south	p	256.5	9.25	253.5	8.75	256.4
22	south	p	66.5	2.50	68.5	2.25	65.9
22	south	p	30.0	1.00	27.4	1.00	29.3
22	east	t	430.0	15.75	431.6	14.75	432.2

Casa dell'Albergo (III 1-2, 18-19)   Peristyle and terrace

Room	where?	kind	in cm	O.ft (27.4)	ideal	R.ft (29.3)	ideal
22	east	p	75.0	2.75	75.4	2.50	73.3
22	east	p	355.0	13.00	356.2	12.00	351.6
23	length	t	593.0	21.75	596.0	20.25	593.3
23	length	p	61.0	2.25	61.7	2.00	58.6
23	length	p	474.5	17.25	472.7	16.25	476.1
23	length	p	57.5	2.00	54.8	2.00	58.6
23	west	t	983.0	36.00	986.4	33.50	981.6
23	west	p	589.5	21.50	589.1	20.00	586.0
23	west	p	393.5	14.25	390.5	13.50	395.6
23	north	t	592.0	21.50	589.1	20.25	593.3
23	north	p	91.0	3.25	89.1	3.00	87.9
23	north	p	413.5	15.00	411.0	14.00	410.2
23	north	p	87.5	3.25	89.1	3.00	87.9
23	south	t	474.0	17.25	472.7	16.25	476.1
23	south	p	93.5	3.50	95.9	3.25	95.2
23	south	p	380.5	14.00	383.6	13.00	380.9
23	east	t	981.0	35.75	979.6	33.50	981.6
23	east	p	591.5	21.50	589.1	20.25	593.3
23	east	p	389.5	14.25	390.5	13.25	388.2
24	west	t	627.0	23.00	630.2	21.50	630.0
24	north	t	362.5	13.25	363.1	12.25	358.9
24	north	p	251.5	9.25	253.5	8.50	249.1
24	north	p	111.0	4.00	109.6	3.75	109.9
24	south	t	363.5	13.25	363.1	12.50	366.3
24	south	p	252.5	9.25	253.5	8.50	249.1
24	south	p	111.0	4.00	109.6	3.75	109.9
24	east	t	530.5	19.25	527.5	18.00	527.4
25	west	t	543.0	19.75	541.2	18.50	542.1
25	north	t	569.0	20.75	568.6	19.50	571.4
25	north	p	87.0	3.25	89.1	3.00	87.9
25	north	p	338.0	12.25	335.7	11.50	337.0
25	north	p	144.0	5.25	143.9	5.00	146.5
25	south	t	545.0	20.00	548.0	18.50	542.1
25	south	p	87.0	3.25	89.1	3.00	87.9
25	south	p	367.0	13.50	369.9	12.50	366.3
25	south	p	91.0	3.25	89.1	3.00	87.9
25	east	t	541.0	19.75	541.2	18.50	542.1
26	west	t	585.0	21.25	582.3	20.00	586.0
26	north	t	395.0	14.50	397.3	13.50	395.6
26	north	p	74.0	2.75	75.4	2.50	73.3
26	north	p	251.0	9.25	253.5	8.50	249.1
26	north	p	70.0	2.50	68.5	2.50	73.3
26	south	t	398.5	14.50	397.3	13.50	395.6

Casa dell'Albergo (III 1-2, 18-19) Peristyle and terrace

Room	where?	kind	in cm	O.ft (27.4)	ideal	R.ft (29.3)	ideal
26	east	t	579.5	21.25	582.3	19.75	578.7
27	width	t	536.0	19.50	534.3	18.25	534.7
27	north	t	291.5	10.75	294.6	10.00	293.0
27	north	p	120.0	4.50	123.3	4.00	117.2
27	north	p	171.5	6.25	171.3	5.75	168.5
27	south	t	319.0	11.75	322.0	11.00	322.3
27	south	p	217.0	8.00	219.2	7.50	219.8
27	south	p	102.0	3.75	102.8	3.50	102.6
27	east	t	532.0	19.50	534.3	18.25	534.7
27	east	p	315.0	11.50	315.1	10.75	315.0
27	east	p	171.0	6.25	171.3	5.75	168.5
27	east	p	46.0	1.75	48.0	1.50	44.0
28	width	t	277.0	10.00	274.0	9.50	278.4
28	north	t	319.0	11.75	322.0	11.00	322.3
28	north	p	217.0	8.00	219.2	7.50	219.8
28	north	p	102.0	3.75	102.8	3.50	102.6
28	south	t	328.0	12.00	328.8	11.25	329.6
28	east	t	246.0	9.00	246.6	8.50	249.1
29	north	t	340.0	12.50	342.5	11.50	337.0
29	south	t	386.0	14.00	383.6	13.25	388.2
29	east	t	251.0	9.25	253.5	8.50	249.1
29	east	p	114.0	4.25	116.5	4.00	117.2
29	east	p	137.0	5.00	137.0	4.75	139.2
30	north	t	352.0	12.75	349.4	12.00	351.6
30	south	t	372.0	13.50	369.9	12.75	373.6
30	east	t	271.0	10.00	274.0	9.25	271.0
45	west	t	665.0	24.25	664.5	22.75	666.6
45	west	p	75.0	2.75	75.4	2.50	73.3
45	west	p	590.0	21.50	589.1	20.25	593.3
45	north	t	911.5	33.25	911.1	31.00	908.3
45	north	p	212.0	7.75	212.4	7.25	212.4
45	north	p	95.0	3.50	95.9	3.25	95.2
45	north	p	285.5	10.50	287.7	9.75	285.7
45	north	p	85.0	3.00	82.2	3.00	87.9
45	north	p	234.0	8.50	232.9	8.00	234.4
45	south	t	908.0	33.25	911.1	31.00	908.3
45	south	p	117.0	4.25	116.5	4.00	117.2
45	south	p	791.0	28.75	787.8	27.00	791.1
45	east	t	650.0	23.75	650.8	22.25	651.9
46	west	t	128.0	4.75	130.2	4.25	124.5
46	south	t	492.0	18.00	493.2	16.75	490.8
46	east	t	144.0	5.25	143.9	5.00	146.5
47	width	t	509.0	18.50	506.9	17.25	505.4

233

Casa dell'Albergo (III 1-2, 18-19)   **Peristyle and terrace**

Room	where?	kind	in cm	O.ft (27.4)	ideal	R.ft (29.3)	ideal
47	width	p	120.0	4.50	123.3	4.00	117.2
47	width	p	389.0	14.25	390.5	13.25	388.2
47	width	t	598.0	21.75	596.0	20.50	600.7
47	width	p	83.0	3.00	82.2	2.75	80.6
47	width	p	516.0	18.75	513.8	17.50	512.8
47	length	t	571.0	20.75	568.6	19.50	571.4
47	length	t	324.0	11.75	322.0	11.00	322.3
47	length	p	243.0	8.75	239.8	8.25	241.7
47	length	p	81.0	3.00	82.2	2.75	80.6
47	west	t	389.0	14.25	390.5	13.25	388.2
47	north	t	672.0	24.50	671.3	23.00	673.9
47	south	t	247.0	9.00	246.6	8.50	249.1
47	east	t	591.0	21.50	589.1	20.25	593.3
47	east	p	107.0	4.00	109.6	3.75	109.9
47	east	p	153.0	5.50	150.7	5.25	153.8
47	east	p	203.0	7.50	205.5	7.00	205.1
47	east	p	128.0	4.75	130.2	4.25	124.5
48	length	t	149.5	5.50	150.7	5.00	146.5
48	west	t	1091.0	39.75	1089.2	37.25	1091.4
48	north	t	117.0	4.25	116.5	4.00	117.2
48	south	t	150.5	5.50	150.7	5.25	153.8
49	width	t	491.0	18.00	493.2	16.75	490.8
49	west	t	489.0	17.75	486.4	16.75	490.8
49	west	p	142.0	5.25	143.9	4.75	139.2
49	west	p	262.0	9.50	260.3	9.00	263.7
49	west	p	85.0	3.00	82.2	3.00	87.9
49	north	t	394.5	14.50	397.3	13.50	395.6
49	north	p	150.5	5.50	150.7	5.25	153.8
49	north	p	244.0	9.00	246.6	8.25	241.7
49	south	t	398.5	14.50	397.3	13.50	395.6
49	south	p	144.0	5.25	143.9	5.00	146.5
49	south	p	254.5	9.25	253.5	8.75	256.4
50	west	t	244.0	9.00	246.6	8.25	241.7
50	north	t	144.0	5.25	143.9	5.00	146.5
50	south	t	143.5	5.25	143.9	5.00	146.5
51	width	t	646.0	23.50	643.9	22.00	644.6
51	width	p	178.0	6.50	178.1	6.00	175.8
51	width	p	290.0	10.50	287.7	10.00	293.0
51	width	p	178.0	6.50	178.1	6.00	175.8
51	width	t	645.0	23.50	643.9	22.00	644.6
51	width	p	177.0	6.50	178.1	6.00	175.8
51	width	p	290.0	10.50	287.7	10.00	293.0
51	width	p	178.0	6.50	178.1	6.00	175.8

Casa dell'Albergo (III 1-2, 18-19)   Peristyle and terrace

Room	where?	kind	in cm	O.ft (27.4)	ideal	R.ft (29.3)	ideal
51	length	p	521.5	19.00	520.6	17.75	520.1
51	length	p	179.5	6.50	178.1	6.25	183.1
51	length	t	875.5	32.00	876.8	30.00	879.0
51	west	t	640.5	23.50	643.9	21.75	637.3
51	west	p	208.5	7.50	205.5	7.00	205.1
51	west	p	432.0	15.75	431.6	14.75	432.2
51	north	t	875.0	32.00	876.8	29.75	871.7
51	east	t	644.0	23.50	643.9	22.00	644.6
51	east	p	119.0	4.25	116.5	4.00	117.2
51	east	p	181.0	6.50	178.1	6.25	183.1
51	east	p	263.0	9.50	260.3	9.00	263.7
51	east	p	81.0	3.00	82.2	2.75	80.6
52	west	t	119.0	4.25	116.5	4.00	117.2
52	north	t	252.0	9.25	253.5	8.50	249.1
52	east	t	118.0	4.25	116.5	4.00	117.2
53	west	t	1883.5	68.75	1883.8	64.25	1882.5
53	west	p	471.0	17.25	472.7	16.00	468.8
53	west	p	191.0	7.00	191.8	6.50	190.5
53	west	p	410.0	15.00	411.0	14.00	410.2
53	west	p	101.0	3.75	102.8	3.50	102.6
53	west	p	710.5	26.00	712.4	24.25	710.5
53	north	t	148.0	5.50	150.7	5.00	146.5
53	south	t	143.0	5.25	143.9	5.00	146.5
53	east	t	1575.0	57.50	1575.5	53.75	1574.9
53	east	p	529.5	19.25	527.5	18.00	527.4
53	east	p	158.0	5.75	157.6	5.50	161.2
53	east	p	243.0	8.75	239.8	8.25	241.7
53	east	p	152.0	5.50	150.7	5.25	153.8
53	east	p	493.0	18.00	493.2	16.75	490.8
54	west	t	152.0	5.50	150.7	5.25	153.8
54	north	t	177.5	6.50	178.1	6.00	175.8
54	north	p	10.0	0.25	6.9	0.25	7.3
54	north	p	130.5	4.75	130.2	4.50	131.9
54	north	p	37.0	1.25	34.3	1.25	36.6
54	south	t	179.5	6.50	178.1	6.25	183.1
54	east	t	152.0	5.50	150.7	5.25	153.8
54	east	p	21.0	0.75	20.6	0.75	22.0
54	east	p	112.0	4.00	109.6	3.75	109.9
54	east	p	19.0	0.75	20.6	0.75	22.0
55	west	t	183.0	6.75	185.0	6.25	183.1
55	west	p	50.5	1.75	48.0	1.75	51.3
55	west	p	113.0	4.00	109.6	3.75	109.9
55	west	p	19.5	0.75	20.6	0.75	22.0

Casa dell'Albergo (III 1-2, 18-19)   Peristyle and terrace

Room	where?	kind	in cm	O.ft (27.4)	ideal	R.ft (29.3)	ideal
55	north	t	128.0	4.75	130.2	4.25	124.5
55	south	t	127.0	4.75	130.2	4.25	124.5
55	east	t	249.0	9.00	246.6	8.50	249.1
56	west	t	174.0	6.25	171.3	6.00	175.8
56	north	t	298.5	11.00	301.4	10.25	300.3
56	north	p	127.5	4.75	130.2	4.25	124.5
56	north	p	171.0	6.25	171.3	5.75	168.5
56	east	t	104.0	3.75	102.8	3.50	102.6
57	west	t	158.0	5.75	157.6	5.50	161.2
57	north	t	952.0	34.75	952.2	32.50	952.3
57	south	t	1163.0	42.50	1164.5	39.75	1164.7
57	south	p	609.0	22.25	609.7	20.75	608.0
57	south	p	117.0	4.25	116.5	4.00	117.2
57	south	p	436.5	16.00	438.4	15.00	439.5
57	east	t	152.0	5.50	150.7	5.25	153.8
58	west	t	491.0	18.00	493.2	16.75	490.8
58	west	p	94.0	3.50	95.9	3.25	95.2
58	west	p	397.0	14.50	397.3	13.50	395.6
58	north	t	115.5	4.25	116.5	4.00	117.2
58	south	t	111.5	4.00	109.6	3.75	109.9
58	east	t	489.0	17.75	486.4	16.75	490.8
58	east	p	91.5	3.25	89.1	3.00	87.9
58	east	p	397.5	14.50	397.3	13.50	395.6
59	west	t	114.0	4.25	116.5	4.00	117.2
59	north	t	406.0	14.75	404.2	13.75	402.9
59	south	t	414.5	15.25	417.9	14.25	417.5
59	south	p	36.5	1.25	34.3	1.25	36.6
59	south	p	378.0	13.75	376.8	13.00	380.9
59	east	t	133.0	4.75	130.2	4.50	131.9
60	west	t	123.0	4.50	123.3	4.25	124.5
60	north	t	510.5	18.75	513.8	17.50	512.8
60	north	p	95.0	3.50	95.9	3.25	95.2
60	north	p	415.5	15.25	417.9	14.25	417.5
60	south	t	505.0	18.50	506.9	17.25	505.4
60	south	p	21.0	0.75	20.6	0.75	22.0
60	south	p	102.0	3.75	102.8	3.50	102.6
60	south	p	382.0	14.00	383.6	13.00	380.9
60	east	t	125.0	4.50	123.3	4.25	124.5
61	width	t	1432.5	52.25	1431.7	49.00	1435.7
61	width	p	94.5	3.50	95.9	3.25	95.2
61	width	p	159.5	5.75	157.6	5.50	161.2
61	width	p	87.0	3.25	89.1	3.00	87.9
61	width	p	169.5	6.25	171.3	5.75	168.5

Casa dell'Albergo (III 1-2, 18-19)   **Peristyle and terrace**

Room	where?	kind	in cm	O.ft (27.4)	ideal	R.ft (29.3)	ideal
61	width	p	91.0	3.25	89.1	3.00	87.9
61	width	p	162.0	6.00	164.4	5.50	161.2
61	width	p	92.5	3.50	95.9	3.25	95.2
61	width	p	191.5	7.00	191.8	6.50	190.5
61	width	p	93.0	3.50	95.9	3.25	95.2
61	width	p	292.0	10.75	294.6	10.00	293.0
61	width	t	383.0	14.00	383.6	13.00	380.9
61	width	p	91.0	3.25	89.1	3.00	87.9
61	width	p	292.0	10.75	294.6	10.00	293.0
61	width	t	2202.0	80.25	2198.9	75.25	2204.8
61	width	p	91.0	3.25	89.1	3.00	87.9
61	width	p	1729.0	63.00	1726.2	59.00	1728.7
61	width	p	91.5	3.25	89.1	3.00	87.9
61	width	p	290.5	10.50	287.7	10.00	293.0
61	width	t	2185.0	79.75	2185.2	74.50	2182.9
61	width	p	90.0	3.25	89.1	3.00	87.9
61	width	p	191.5	7.00	191.8	6.50	190.5
61	width	p	92.0	3.25	89.1	3.25	95.2
61	width	p	154.0	5.50	150.7	5.25	153.8
61	width	p	90.5	3.25	89.1	3.00	87.9
61	width	p	158.0	5.75	157.6	5.50	161.2
61	width	p	93.0	3.50	95.9	3.25	95.2
61	width	p	157.5	5.75	157.6	5.50	161.2
61	width	p	90.5	3.25	89.1	3.00	87.9
61	width	p	160.5	5.75	157.6	5.50	161.2
61	width	p	91.5	3.25	89.1	3.00	87.9
61	width	p	157.5	5.75	157.6	5.50	161.2
61	width	p	92.5	3.50	95.9	3.25	95.2
61	width	p	188.5	7.00	191.8	6.50	190.5
61	width	p	92.5	3.50	95.9	3.25	95.2
61	width	p	285.0	10.50	287.7	9.75	285.7
61	length	t	1431.0	52.25	1431.7	48.75	1428.4
61	length	p	202.0	7.25	198.7	7.00	205.1
61	length	p	93.0	3.50	95.9	3.25	95.2
61	length	p	183.5	6.75	185.0	6.25	183.1
61	length	p	93.0	3.50	95.9	3.25	95.2
61	length	p	293.5	10.75	294.6	10.00	293.0
61	length	p	94.0	3.50	95.9	3.25	95.2
61	length	p	181.0	6.50	178.1	6.25	183.1
61	length	p	95.0	3.50	95.9	3.25	95.2
61	length	p	196.0	7.25	198.7	6.75	197.8
61	length	t	1425.5	52.00	1424.8	48.75	1428.4
61	length	p	200.0	7.25	198.7	6.75	197.8

Casa dell'Albergo (III 1-2, 18-19)   Peristyle and terrace

Room	where?	kind	in cm	O.ft (27.4)	ideal	R.ft (29.3)	ideal
61	length	p	90.5	3.25	89.1	3.00	87.9
61	length	p	846.5	31.00	849.4	29.00	849.7
61	length	p	91.5	3.25	89.1	3.00	87.9
61	length	p	197.0	7.25	198.7	6.75	197.8
61	length	t	1426.0	52.00	1424.8	48.75	1428.4
61	length	p	200.0	7.25	198.7	6.75	197.8
61	length	p	93.0	3.50	95.9	3.25	95.2
61	length	p	845.5	30.75	842.6	28.75	842.4
61	length	p	92.0	3.25	89.1	3.25	95.2
61	length	p	195.5	7.25	198.7	6.75	197.8
61	length	t	1423.5	52.00	1424.8	48.50	1421.1
61	length	p	198.5	7.25	198.7	6.75	197.8
61	length	p	90.5	3.25	89.1	3.00	87.9
61	length	p	845.5	30.75	842.6	28.75	842.4
61	length	p	92.5	3.50	95.9	3.25	95.2
61	length	p	196.5	7.25	198.7	6.75	197.8
61	length	t	1421.5	52.00	1424.8	48.50	1421.1
61	length	p	199.5	7.25	198.7	6.75	197.8
61	length	p	91.0	3.25	89.1	3.00	87.9
61	length	p	843.0	30.75	842.6	28.75	842.4
61	length	p	92.5	3.50	95.9	3.25	95.2
61	length	p	195.5	7.25	198.7	6.75	197.8
61	west	t	1424.0	52.00	1424.8	48.50	1421.1
61	west	p	333.0	12.25	335.7	11.25	329.6
61	west	p	117.0	4.25	116.5	4.00	117.2
61	west	p	759.5	27.75	760.4	26.00	761.8
61	west	p	169.5	6.25	171.3	5.75	168.5
61	west	p	45.0	1.75	48.0	1.50	44.0
61	north	t	1445.5	52.75	1445.4	49.25	1443.0
61	north	p	305.0	11.25	308.3	10.50	307.7
61	north	p	110.0	4.00	109.6	3.75	109.9
61	north	p	134.0	5.00	137.0	4.50	131.9
61	north	p	266.5	9.75	267.2	9.00	263.7
61	north	p	238.5	8.75	239.8	8.25	241.7
61	north	p	108.5	4.00	109.6	3.75	109.9
61	north	p	283.0	10.25	280.9	9.75	285.7
61	east	t	2150.0	78.50	2150.9	73.50	2153.6
61	east	p	1585.0	57.75	1582.4	54.00	1582.2
61	east	p	123.0	4.50	123.3	4.25	124.5
61	east	p	442.0	16.25	445.3	15.00	439.5
62	north	t	99.0	3.50	95.9	3.50	102.6
62	south	t	120.0	4.50	123.3	4.00	117.2
62	east	t	670.0	24.50	671.3	22.75	666.6

238

Casa dell'Albergo (III 1-2, 18-19)   **Peristyle and terrace**

Room	where?	kind	in cm	O.ft (27.4)	ideal	R.ft (29.3)	ideal
63	west	t	648.0	23.75	650.8	22.00	644.6
63	north	t	111.5	4.00	109.6	3.75	109.9
63	south	t	108.5	4.00	109.6	3.75	109.9
63	east	t	647.0	23.50	643.9	22.00	644.6
64	west	t	423.0	15.50	424.7	14.50	424.9
64	north	t	2020.0	73.75	2020.8	69.00	2021.7
64	north	p	508.0	18.50	506.9	17.25	505.4
64	north	p	256.0	9.25	253.5	8.75	256.4
64	north	p	1214.0	44.25	1212.5	41.50	1216.0
64	north	p	42.0	1.50	41.1	1.50	44.0
64	south	t	2692.0	98.25	2692.1	92.00	2695.6
64	south	p	439.0	16.00	438.4	15.00	439.5
64	south	p	413.0	15.00	411.0	14.00	410.2
64	south	p	368.0	13.50	369.9	12.50	366.3
64	south	p	112.0	4.00	109.6	3.75	109.9
64	south	p	135.5	5.00	137.0	4.50	131.9
64	south	p	335.5	12.25	335.7	11.50	337.0
64	south	p	194.0	7.00	191.8	6.50	190.5
64	south	p	107.0	4.00	109.6	3.75	109.9
64	south	p	115.0	4.25	116.5	4.00	117.2
64	south	p	249.5	9.00	246.6	8.50	249.1
64	south	p	124.5	4.50	123.3	4.25	124.5
64	south	p	99.0	3.50	95.9	3.50	102.6
64	east	t	444.0	16.25	445.3	15.25	446.8
65	west	t	2603.0	95.00	2603.0	88.75	2600.4
65	west	p	188.0	6.75	185.0	6.50	190.5
65	west	p	231.0	8.50	232.9	8.00	234.4
65	west	p	241.0	8.75	239.8	8.25	241.7
65	west	p	240.0	8.75	239.8	8.25	241.7
65	west	p	246.0	9.00	246.6	8.50	249.1
65	west	p	249.0	9.00	246.6	8.50	249.1
65	west	p	242.0	8.75	239.8	8.25	241.7
65	west	p	238.0	8.75	239.8	8.00	234.4
65	west	p	241.0	8.75	239.8	8.25	241.7
65	west	p	240.0	8.75	239.8	8.25	241.7
65	west	p	247.0	9.00	246.6	8.50	249.1
65	north	t	340.0	12.50	342.5	11.50	337.0
65	south	t	344.0	12.50	342.5	11.75	344.3
65	east	t	3399.0	124.00	3397.6	116.00	3398.8
65	east	p	609.0	22.25	609.7	20.75	608.0
65	east	p	209.0	7.75	212.4	7.25	212.4
65	east	p	2452.5	89.50	2452.3	83.75	2453.9
65	east	p	91.0	3.25	89.1	3.00	87.9

Casa dell'Albergo (III 1-2, 18-19)   Peristyle and terrace

Room	where?	kind	in cm	O.ft (27.4)	ideal	R.ft (29.3)	ideal
65	east	p	37.5	1.25	34.3	1.25	36.6
66	width	t	330.0	12.00	328.8	11.25	329.6
66	west	t	335.0	12.25	335.7	11.50	337.0
66	north	t	2687.0	98.00	2685.2	91.75	2688.3
66	north	p	1132.0	41.25	1130.3	38.75	1135.4
66	north	p	368.0	13.50	369.9	12.50	366.3
66	north	p	1074.0	39.25	1075.5	36.75	1076.8
66	north	p	113.0	4.00	109.6	3.75	109.9
66	south	t	2007.0	73.25	2007.1	68.50	2007.1
66	south	p	250.0	9.00	246.6	8.50	249.1
66	south	p	253.0	9.25	253.5	8.75	256.4
66	south	p	252.0	9.25	253.5	8.50	249.1
66	south	p	252.0	9.25	253.5	8.50	249.1
66	south	p	249.0	9.00	246.6	8.50	249.1
66	south	p	250.0	9.00	246.6	8.50	249.1
66	south	p	251.0	9.25	253.5	8.50	249.1
66	south	p	250.0	9.00	246.6	8.50	249.1
66	east	t	350.0	12.75	349.4	12.00	351.6
67	west	t	3374.0	123.25	3377.1	115.25	3376.8
67	north	t	340.0	12.50	342.5	11.50	337.0
67	south	t	323.0	11.75	322.0	11.00	322.3
67	east	t	2626.0	95.75	2623.6	89.50	2622.4
67	east	p	306.0	11.25	308.3	10.50	307.7
67	east	p	334.0	12.25	335.7	11.50	337.0
67	east	p	242.0	8.75	239.8	8.25	241.7
67	east	p	239.0	8.75	239.8	8.25	241.7
67	east	p	244.0	9.00	246.6	8.25	241.7
67	east	p	238.0	8.75	239.8	8.00	234.4
67	east	p	244.0	9.00	246.6	8.25	241.7
67	east	p	243.0	8.75	239.8	8.25	241.7
67	east	p	241.0	8.75	239.8	8.25	241.7
67	east	p	243.0	8.75	239.8	8.25	241.7
68	west	t	2626.0	95.75	2623.6	89.50	2622.4
68	north	t	2007.0	73.25	2007.1	68.50	2007.1
68	south	t	2020.0	73.75	2020.8	69.00	2021.7
68	east	t	2603.0	95.00	2603.0	88.75	2600.4

Casa dello Scheletro (III 3) Lot III B

Room	where?	kind	in cm	O.ft (27.5)	ideal	R.ft (29.3)	ideal
0	length	t	2065.0	75.00	2062.5	70.50	2065.7
0	west	t	556.0	20.25	556.9	19.00	556.7
0	east	t	558.5	20.25	556.9	19.00	556.7
11	west	t	635.5	23.00	632.5	21.75	637.3
11	north	t	89.0	3.25	89.4	3.00	87.9
11	south	t	107.0	4.00	110.0	3.75	109.9
11	east	t	637.0	23.25	639.4	21.75	637.3
12	west	t	400.5	14.50	398.8	13.75	402.9
12	north	t	478.0	17.50	481.3	16.25	476.1
12	south	t	473.5	17.25	474.4	16.25	476.1
12	east	t	331.5	12.00	330.0	11.25	329.6
12	east	p	233.0	8.50	233.8	8.00	234.4
12	east	p	98.5	3.50	96.3	3.25	95.2
13	west	t	147.5	5.25	144.4	5.00	146.5
13	north	t	834.0	30.25	831.9	28.50	835.1
13	south	t	833.0	30.25	831.9	28.50	835.1
13	east	t	185.5	6.75	185.6	6.25	183.1
13	east	p	105.5	3.75	103.1	3.50	102.6
13	east	p	80.0	3.00	82.5	2.75	80.6
14	west	t	375.0	13.75	378.1	12.75	373.6
14	north	t	323.0	11.75	323.1	11.00	322.3
14	north	p	148.0	5.50	151.3	5.00	146.5
14	north	p	100.0	3.75	103.1	3.50	102.6
14	north	p	77.5	2.75	75.6	2.75	80.6
14	south	t	323.5	11.75	323.1	11.00	322.3
14	east	t	381.5	13.75	378.1	13.00	380.9
14	east	p	91.0	3.25	89.4	3.00	87.9
14	east	p	27.0	1.00	27.5	1.00	29.3
14	east	p	109.0	4.00	110.0	3.75	109.9
14	east	p	43.0	1.50	41.3	1.50	44.0
14	east	p	111.5	4.00	110.0	3.75	109.9
15	width	t	216.0	7.75	213.1	7.25	212.4
15	length	t	283.0	10.25	281.9	9.75	285.7
15	west	t	224.0	8.25	226.9	7.75	227.1
15	west	p	79.5	3.00	82.5	2.75	80.6
15	west	p	105.5	3.75	103.1	3.50	102.6
15	west	p	39.0	1.50	41.3	1.25	36.6
15	north	t	272.0	10.00	275.0	9.25	271.0
15	north	p	147.0	5.25	144.4	5.00	146.5
15	north	p	125.0	4.50	123.8	4.25	124.5
15	south	t	282.0	10.25	281.9	9.50	278.4
15	east	t	203.5	7.50	206.3	7.00	205.1
16	west	t	203.5	7.50	206.3	7.00	205.1

Casa dello Scheletro (III 3) Lot III B

Room	where?	kind	in cm	O.ft (27.5)	ideal	R.ft (29.3)	ideal
16	north	t	278.5	10.25	281.9	9.50	278.4
16	north	p	172.0	6.25	171.9	5.75	168.5
16	south	t	276.5	10.00	275.0	9.50	278.4
16	south	p	160.0	5.75	158.1	5.50	161.2
16	east	t	205.0	7.50	206.3	7.00	205.1
17	width	t	503.0	18.25	501.9	17.25	505.4
17	width	p	298.0	10.75	295.6	10.25	300.3
17	width	p	205.0	7.50	206.3	7.00	205.1
17	west	t	280.0	10.25	281.9	9.50	278.4
17	north	t	491.0	17.75	488.1	16.75	490.8
17	south	t	494.0	18.00	495.0	16.75	490.8
17	south	p	192.5	7.00	192.5	6.50	190.5
17	south	p	173.5	6.25	171.9	6.00	175.8
17	south	p	102.5	3.75	103.1	3.50	102.6
17	south	p	25.5	1.00	27.5	0.75	22.0
17	south	p	301.5	11.00	302.5	10.25	300.3
17	east	t	281.5	10.25	281.9	9.50	278.4
18	west	t	248.0	9.00	247.5	8.50	249.1
18	north	t	280.5	10.25	281.9	9.50	278.4
18	north	p	130.0	4.75	130.6	4.50	131.9
18	north	p	105.5	3.75	103.1	3.50	102.6
18	north	p	50.5	1.75	48.1	1.75	51.3
18	south	t	269.0	9.75	268.1	9.25	271.0
18	south	p	132.5	4.75	130.6	4.50	131.9
18	south	p	136.5	5.00	137.5	4.75	139.2
18	east	t	247.5	9.00	247.5	8.50	249.1
18	east	p	80.0	3.00	82.5	2.75	80.6
18	east	p	84.0	3.00	82.5	2.75	80.6
18	east	p	83.5	3.00	82.5	2.75	80.6
19	west	t	366.5	13.25	364.4	12.50	366.3
19	west	p	165.0	6.00	165.0	5.75	168.5
19	west	p	92.5	3.25	89.4	3.25	95.2
19	west	p	109.5	4.00	110.0	3.75	109.9
19	north	t	308.5	11.25	309.4	10.50	307.7
19	south	t	303.5	11.00	302.5	10.25	300.3
19	south	p	110.5	4.00	110.0	3.75	109.9
19	south	p	89.5	3.25	89.4	3.00	87.9
19	south	p	103.5	3.75	103.1	3.50	102.6
19	east	t	366.5	13.25	364.4	12.50	366.3
20	west	t	165.5	6.00	165.0	5.75	168.5
20	west	p	85.5	3.00	82.5	3.00	87.9
20	west	p	80.0	3.00	82.5	2.75	80.6
20	north	t	291.0	10.50	288.8	10.00	293.0

Casa dello Scheletro (III 3) Lot III B

Room	where?	kind	in cm	O.ft (27.5)	ideal	R.ft (29.3)	ideal
20	north	p	92.0	3.25	89.4	3.25	95.2
20	north	p	90.0	3.25	89.4	3.00	87.9
20	north	p	109.0	4.00	110.0	3.75	109.9
20	south	t	291.5	10.50	288.8	10.00	293.0
20	east	t	157.5	5.75	158.1	5.50	161.2
21	west	t	239.0	8.75	240.6	8.25	241.7
21	north	t	193.0	7.00	192.5	6.50	190.5
21	south	t	210.0	7.75	213.1	7.25	212.4
21	east	t	247.5	9.00	247.5	8.50	249.1
22	west	t	96.0	3.50	96.3	3.25	95.2
22	north	p	206.0	7.50	206.3	7.00	205.1
22	north	p	109.5	4.00	110.0	3.75	109.9
22	north	t	315.5	11.50	316.3	10.75	315.0
22	south	p	188.5	6.75	185.6	6.50	190.5
22	south	p	125.0	4.50	123.8	4.25	124.5
22	south	t	313.5	11.50	316.3	10.75	315.0
22	east	t	82.5	3.00	82.5	2.75	80.6

243

Casa dello Scheletro (III 3) Lot III C

Room	where?	kind	in cm	O.ft (27.75)	ideal	R.ft (29.3)	ideal
1	west	t	152.5	5.50	152.6	5.25	155.4
1	north	t	507.0	18.25	506.4	17.25	510.6
1	north	p	261.0	9.50	263.6	8.75	259.0
1	north	p	97.0	3.50	97.1	3.25	96.2
1	north	p	149.0	5.25	145.7	5.00	148.0
1	south	t	512.0	18.50	513.4	17.25	510.6
1	cast	t	146.0	5.25	145.7	5.00	148.0
2	west	t	223.5	8.00	222.0	7.50	222.0
2	north	t	287.0	10.25	284.4	9.75	288.6
2	south	t	291.0	10.50	291.4	9.75	288.6
2	south	p	214.0	7.75	215.1	7.25	214.6
2	south	p	77.0	2.75	76.3	2.50	74.0
2	east	t	241.5	8.75	242.8	8.25	244.2
3	west	t	224.5	8.00	222.0	7.50	222.0
3	north	t	89.0	3.25	90.2	3.00	88.8
3	south	t	96.0	3.50	97.1	3.25	96.2
3	east	t	226.0	8.25	228.9	7.75	229.4
3	east	p	107.5	3.75	104.1	3.75	111.0
3	east	p	106.0	3.75	104.1	3.50	103.6
3	east	p	12.5	0.50	13.9	0.50	14.8
4	west	t	585.0	21.00	582.8	19.75	584.6
4	north	t	412.5	14.75	409.3	14.00	414.4
4	south	t	413.0	15.00	416.3	14.00	414.4
4	east	t	580.0	21.00	582.8	19.50	577.2
4	east	p	11.0	0.50	13.9	0.25	7.4
4	east	p	116.5	4.25	117.9	4.00	118.4
4	east	p	452.5	16.25	450.9	15.25	451.4
5	west	t	318.0	11.50	319.1	10.75	318.2
5	north	t	252.5	9.00	249.8	8.50	251.6
5	north	p	74.0	2.75	76.3	2.50	74.0
5	north	p	96.0	3.50	97.1	3.25	96.2
5	north	p	82.5	3.00	83.3	2.75	81.4
5	south	t	252.5	9.00	249.8	8.50	251.6
5	east	t	320.0	11.50	319.1	10.75	318.2
7	west	t	370.5	13.25	367.7	12.50	370.0
7	west	p	50.5	1.75	48.6	1.75	51.8
7	west	p	270.5	9.75	270.6	9.25	273.8
7	west	p	49.5	1.75	48.6	1.75	51.8
7	north	t	254.0	9.25	256.7	8.50	251.6
7	south	t	254.0	9.25	256.7	8.50	251.6
7	east	t	372.0	13.50	374.6	12.50	370.0
7	east	p	98.0	3.50	97.1	3.25	96.2
7	east	p	173.0	6.25	173.4	5.75	170.2

Casa dello Scheletro (III 3) Lot III C

Room	where?	kind	in cm	O.ft (27.75)	ideal	R.ft (29.3)	ideal
7	east	p	83.0	3.00	83.3	2.75	81.4
8	west	t	361.0	13.00	360.8	12.25	362.6
8	west	p	43.5	1.50	41.6	1.50	44.4
8	west	p	30.5	1.00	27.8	1.00	29.6
8	west	p	149.0	5.25	145.7	5.00	148.0
8	west	p	138.5	5.00	138.8	4.75	140.6
8	north	t	202.0	7.25	201.2	6.75	199.8
8	south	t	202.5	7.25	201.2	6.75	199.8
8	east	t	366.0	13.25	367.7	12.25	362.6
8	east	p	44.5	1.50	41.6	1.50	44.4
8	east	p	33.0	1.25	34.7	1.00	29.6
8	east	p	181.5	6.50	180.4	6.25	185.0
8	east	p	107.0	3.75	104.1	3.50	103.6
9	west	t	312.5	11.25	312.2	10.50	310.8
9	north	t	267.5	9.75	270.6	9.00	266.4
9	south	t	270.5	9.75	270.6	9.25	273.8
9	east	t	311.5	11.25	312.2	10.50	310.8
9	east	p	32.0	1.25	34.7	1.00	29.6
9	east	p	147.0	5.25	145.7	5.00	148.0
9	east	p	132.5	4.75	131.8	4.50	133.2
10	width	t	672.0	24.25	672.9	22.75	673.4
10	width	p	81.0	3.00	83.3	2.75	81.4
10	width	p	591.0	21.25	589.7	20.00	592.0
10	west	t	583.5	21.00	582.8	19.75	584.6
10	west	p	148.0	5.25	145.7	5.00	148.0
10	west	p	170.0	6.25	173.4	5.75	170.2
10	west	p	145.0	5.25	145.7	5.00	148.0
10	west	p	111.0	4.00	111.0	3.75	111.0
10	west	p	9.5	0.25	6.9	0.25	7.4
10	north	t	434.0	15.75	437.1	14.75	436.6
10	north	p	61.0	2.25	62.4	2.00	59.2
10	north	p	317.0	11.50	319.1	10.75	318.2
10	north	p	56.0	2.00	55.5	2.00	59.2
10	south	t	444.5	16.00	444.0	15.00	444.0
10	south	p	118.5	4.25	117.9	4.00	118.4
10	south	p	234.0	8.50	235.9	8.00	236.8
10	south	p	92.0	3.25	90.2	3.00	88.8
10	east	t	593.0	21.25	589.7	20.00	592.0
23	width	t	687.5	24.75	686.8	23.25	688.2
23	length	t	771.0	27.75	770.1	26.00	769.6
23	west	t	692.0	25.00	693.8	23.50	695.6
23	west	p	103.0	3.75	104.1	3.50	103.6
23	west	p	103.5	3.75	104.1	3.50	103.6

Casa dello Scheletro (III 3) Lot III C

Room	where?	kind	in cm	O.ft (27.75)	ideal	R.ft (29.3)	ideal
23	west	p	64.5	2.25	62.4	2.25	66.6
23	west	p	146.0	5.25	145.7	5.00	148.0
23	west	p	67.0	2.50	69.4	2.25	66.6
23	west	p	117.0	4.25	117.9	4.00	118.4
23	west	p	94.0	3.50	97.1	3.25	96.2
23	west	p	273.0	9.75	270.6	9.25	273.8
23	west	p	278.0	10.00	277.5	9.50	281.2
23	north	t	764.0	27.50	763.1	25.75	762.2
23	south	t	775.5	28.00	777.0	26.25	777.0
23	east	t	693.0	25.00	693.8	23.50	695.6
23	east	p	115.0	4.25	117.9	4.00	118.4
23	east	p	96.0	3.50	97.1	3.25	96.2
23	east	p	211.0	7.50	208.1	7.25	214.6
23	east	p	90.0	3.25	90.2	3.00	88.8
23	east	p	120.0	4.25	117.9	4.00	118.4
23	east	p	272.0	9.75	270.6	9.25	273.8
23	east	p	210.0	7.50	208.1	7.00	207.2
24	west	t	361.5	13.00	360.8	12.25	362.6
24	north	t	89.0	3.25	90.2	3.00	88.8
24	south	t	85.5	3.00	83.3	3.00	88.8
24	east	t	363.5	13.00	360.8	12.25	362.6
24	east	p	50.0	1.75	48.6	1.75	51.8
24	east	p	313.5	11.25	312.2	10.50	310.8
25	west	t	113.5	4.00	111.0	3.75	111.0
25	south	t	273.0	9.75	270.6	9.25	273.8
25	east	t	118.0	4.25	117.9	4.00	118.4
26	west	t	120.0	4.25	117.9	4.00	118.4
26	north	t	339.5	12.25	339.9	11.50	340.4
26	east	t	111.0	4.00	111.0	3.75	111.0
27	west	t	319.0	11.50	319.1	10.75	318.2
27	west	p	19.5	0.75	20.8	0.75	22.2
27	west	p	192.5	7.00	194.3	6.50	192.4
27	west	p	107.5	3.75	104.1	3.75	111.0
27	north	t	449.0	16.25	450.9	15.25	451.4
27	north	p	117.0	4.25	117.9	4.00	118.4
27	north	p	234.5	8.50	235.9	8.00	236.8
27	north	p	97.5	3.50	97.1	3.25	96.2
27	south	t	446.0	16.00	444.0	15.00	444.0
27	south	p	120.5	4.25	117.9	4.00	118.4
27	south	p	108.5	4.00	111.0	3.75	111.0
27	south	p	89.5	3.25	90.2	3.00	88.8
27	south	p	127.5	4.50	124.9	4.25	125.8
27	east	t	320.5	11.50	319.1	10.75	318.2

Casa dello Scheletro (III 3) Lot III C

Room	where?	kind	in cm	O.ft (27.75)	ideal	R.ft (29.3)	ideal
27	east	p	107.5	3.75	104.1	3.75	111.0
27	east	p	212.5	7.75	215.1	7.25	214.6

Casa dello Scheletro (III 3) Lot III D

Room	where?	kind	in cm	R.ft (29.4)	ideal
6	west	t	501.5	17.00	499.8
6	north	t	640.5	21.75	639.5
6	south	t	655.5	22.25	654.2
6	south	p	548.0	18.75	551.3
6	south	p	107.5	3.75	110.3
6	east	t	527.5	18.00	529.2
6	east	p	150.5	5.00	147.0
6	east	p	226.5	7.75	227.9
6	east	p	150.5	5.00	147.0
28	west	t	519.5	17.75	521.9
28	west	p	144.0	5.00	147.0
28	west	p	227.0	7.75	227.9
28	west	p	148.5	5.00	147.0
28	north	t	215.0	7.25	213.2
28	south	t	203.5	7.00	205.8
28	south	p	36.5	1.25	36.8
28	south	p	100.5	3.50	102.9
28	south	p	66.0	2.25	66.2
28	east	t	526.5	18.00	529.2
28	east	p	136.0	4.75	139.7
28	east	p	235.5	8.00	235.2
28	east	p	155.0	5.25	154.4
29	west	t	531.5	18.00	529.2
29	north	t	446.5	15.25	448.4
29	north	p	109.5	3.75	110.3
29	north	p	17.5	0.50	14.7
29	north	p	319.5	10.75	316.1
29	south	t	456.0	15.50	455.7
29	south	p	112.5	3.75	110.3
29	south	p	29.5	1.00	29.4
29	south	p	314.5	10.75	316.1
29	east	t	537.5	18.25	536.6
29	east	p	169.5	5.75	169.1
29	east	p	184.5	6.25	183.8
29	east	p	183.5	6.25	183.8

Casa del Tramezzo di Legno (III 4-12)

Room	where?	kind	in cm	O.ft (27.4)	ideal	R.ft (29.45)	ideal
1	west	t	300.0	11.00	301.4	10.25	301.9
1	north	t	387.0	14.00	383.6	13.25	390.2
1	south	t	383.5	14.00	383.6	13.00	382.9
1	east	t	236.0	8.50	232.9	8.00	235.6
2	west	t	278.5	10.25	280.9	9.50	279.8
2	west	p	9.0	0.25	6.9	0.25	7.4
2	west	p	113.0	4.00	109.6	3.75	110.4
2	west	p	165.5	6.00	164.4	5.50	162.0
2	north	t	385.0	14.00	383.6	13.00	382.9
2	south	t	389.0	14.25	390.5	13.25	390.2
2	east	t	286.0	10.50	287.7	9.75	287.1
3	west	t	294.5	10.75	294.6	10.00	294.5
3	north	t	300.0	11.00	301.4	10.25	301.9
3	north	p	112.5	4.00	109.6	3.75	110.4
3	north	p	114.5	4.25	116.5	4.00	117.8
3	north	p	73.0	2.75	75.4	2.50	73.6
3	south	t	301.0	11.00	301.4	10.25	301.9
3	east	t	295.5	10.75	294.6	10.00	294.5
4	west	t	293.0	10.75	294.6	10.00	294.5
4	north	t	299.0	11.00	301.4	10.25	301.9
4	north	p	57.0	2.00	54.8	2.00	58.9
4	north	p	114.0	4.25	116.5	3.75	110.4
4	north	p	128.0	4.75	130.2	4.25	125.2
4	south	t	298.0	11.00	301.4	10.00	294.5
4	east	t	295.0	10.75	294.6	10.00	294.5
5	west	t	332.0	12.00	328.8	11.25	331.3
5	west	p	287.0	10.50	287.7	9.75	287.1
5	west	p	45.0	1.75	48.0	1.50	44.2
5	north	t	291.0	10.50	287.7	10.00	294.5
5	south	t	293.0	10.75	294.6	10.00	294.5
5	east	t	341.0	12.50	342.5	11.50	338.7
5	east	p	300.0	11.00	301.4	10.25	301.9
5	east	p	41.0	1.50	41.1	1.50	44.2
6	west	t	464.0	17.00	465.8	15.75	463.8
6	north	t	587.0	21.50	589.1	20.00	589.0
6	north	p	433.5	15.75	431.6	14.75	434.4
6	north	p	136.5	5.00	137.0	4.75	139.9
6	north	p	17.0	0.50	13.7	0.50	14.7
6	south	t	577.0	21.00	575.4	19.50	574.3
6	east	t	458.5	16.75	459.0	15.50	456.5
6	east	p	332.0	12.00	328.8	11.25	331.3
6	east	p	112.5	4.00	109.6	3.75	110.4
6	east	p	11.5	0.50	13.7	0.50	14.7

Casa del Tramezzo di Legno (III 4-12)

Room	where?	kind	in cm	O.ft (27.4)	ideal	R.ft (29.45)	ideal
7	length	t	336.5	12.25	335.7	11.50	338.7
7	length	t	338.0	12.25	335.7	11.50	338.7
7	west	t	486.0	17.75	486.4	16.50	485.9
7	west	p	54.5	2.00	54.8	1.75	51.5
7	west	p	341.0	12.50	342.5	11.50	338.7
7	west	p	90.5	3.25	89.1	3.00	88.4
7	north	t	337.0	12.25	335.7	11.50	338.7
7	south	t	335.0	12.25	335.7	11.50	338.7
7	east	t	488.5	17.75	486.4	16.50	485.9
8	length	t	227.0	8.25	226.1	7.75	228.2
8	west	t	659.0	24.00	657.6	22.50	662.6
8	west	p	429.0	15.75	431.6	14.50	427.0
8	west	p	230.0	8.50	232.9	7.75	228.2
8	north	t	262.0	9.50	260.3	9.00	265.1
8	north	p	107.0	4.00	109.6	3.75	110.4
8	north	p	154.5	5.75	157.6	5.25	154.6
8	south	t	251.5	9.25	253.5	8.50	250.3
8	south	p	12.0	0.50	13.7	0.50	14.7
8	south	p	136.0	5.00	137.0	4.50	132.5
8	south	p	103.5	3.75	102.8	3.50	103.1
8	east	t	659.5	24.00	657.6	22.50	662.6
8	east	p	58.5	2.25	61.7	2.00	58.9
8	east	p	343.0	12.50	342.5	11.75	346.0
8	east	p	132.0	4.75	130.2	4.50	132.5
8	east	p	126.0	4.50	123.3	4.25	125.2
9	west	t	298.0	11.00	301.4	10.00	294.5
9	north	t	329.0	12.00	328.8	11.25	331.3
9	south	t	326.0	12.00	328.8	11.00	324.0
9	south	p	38.5	1.50	41.1	1.25	36.8
9	south	p	84.5	3.00	82.2	2.75	81.0
9	south	p	183.0	6.75	185.0	6.25	184.1
9	east	t	309.5	11.25	308.3	10.50	309.2
10	west	t	272.5	10.00	274.0	9.25	272.4
10	north	t	417.0	15.25	417.9	14.25	419.7
10	south	t	413.5	15.00	411.0	14.00	412.3
10	south	p	36.5	1.25	34.3	1.25	36.8
10	south	p	104.0	3.75	102.8	3.50	103.1
10	south	p	273.0	10.00	274.0	9.25	272.4
10	east	t	299.0	11.00	301.4	10.25	301.9
11	width	t	361.5	13.25	363.1	12.25	360.8
11	west	t	364.5	13.25	363.1	12.50	368.1
11	north	t	490.5	18.00	493.2	16.75	493.3
11	south	t	490.5	18.00	493.2	16.75	493.3

Casa del Tramezzo di Legno (III 4-12)

Room	where?	kind	in cm	O.ft (27.4)	ideal	R.ft (29.45)	ideal
11	south	p	420.5	15.25	417.9	14.25	419.7
11	south	p	70.0	2.50	68.5	2.50	73.6
11	east	t	387.0	14.00	383.6	13.25	390.2
11	east	p	85.5	3.00	82.2	3.00	88.4
11	east	p	268.5	9.75	267.2	9.00	265.1
11	east	p	38.5	1.50	41.1	1.25	36.8
12	west	t	280.0	10.25	280.9	9.50	279.8
12	north	t	313.5	11.50	315.1	10.75	316.6
12	north	p	68.0	2.50	68.5	2.25	66.3
12	north	p	253.5	9.25	253.5	8.50	250.3
12	south	t	308.0	11.25	308.3	10.50	309.2
12	east	t	269.0	9.75	267.2	9.25	272.4
12	east	p	149.0	5.50	150.7	5.00	147.3
12	east	p	120.0	4.50	123.3	4.00	117.8
13	west	t	355.5	13.00	356.2	12.00	353.4
13	west	p	275.0	10.00	274.0	9.25	272.4
13	west	p	80.5	3.00	82.2	2.75	81.0
13	north	t	495.0	18.00	493.2	16.75	493.3
13	north	p	261.0	9.50	260.3	8.75	257.7
13	north	p	80.0	3.00	82.2	2.75	81.0
13	north	p	154.0	5.50	150.7	5.25	154.6
13	south	t	491.5	18.00	493.2	16.75	493.3
13	east	t	362.0	13.25	363.1	12.25	360.8
13	east	p	208.0	7.50	205.5	7.00	206.2
13	east	p	88.0	3.25	89.1	3.00	88.4
13	east	p	66.0	2.50	68.5	2.25	66.3
14	west	t	257.0	9.50	260.3	8.75	257.7
14	west	p	98.0	3.50	95.9	3.25	95.7
14	west	p	37.0	1.25	34.3	1.25	36.8
14	west	p	122.0	4.50	123.3	4.25	125.2
14	north	t	493.5	18.00	493.2	16.75	493.3
14	south	t	494.5	18.00	493.2	16.75	493.3
14	south	p	155.0	5.75	157.6	5.25	154.6
14	south	p	78.5	2.75	75.4	2.75	81.0
14	south	p	260.5	9.50	260.3	8.75	257.7
14	east	t	286.0	10.50	287.7	9.75	287.1
15	length	t	467.0	17.00	465.8	15.75	463.8
15	length	p	199.5	7.25	198.7	6.75	198.8
15	length	p	61.0	2.25	61.7	2.00	58.9
15	length	p	207.5	7.50	205.5	7.00	206.2
15	west	t	616.0	22.50	616.5	21.00	618.5
15	north	t	473.0	17.25	472.7	16.00	471.2
15	south	t	199.0	7.25	198.7	6.75	198.8

Casa del Tramezzo di Legno (III 4-12)

Room	where?	kind	in cm	O.ft (27.4)	ideal	R.ft (29.45)	ideal
15	south	t	234.5	8.50	232.9	8.00	235.6
15	east	t	638.5	23.25	637.1	21.75	640.5
15	east	p	275.5	10.00	274.0	9.25	272.4
15	east	p	82.0	3.00	82.2	2.75	81.0
15	east	p	280.5	10.25	280.9	9.50	279.8
16	west	t	534.5	19.50	534.3	18.25	537.5
16	west	p	335.0	12.25	335.7	11.50	338.7
16	west	p	183.0	6.75	185.0	6.25	184.1
16	west	p	16.5	0.50	13.7	0.50	14.7
16	north	t	468.5	17.00	465.8	16.00	471.2
16	north	p	310.5	11.25	308.3	10.50	309.2
16	north	p	75.0	2.75	75.4	2.50	73.6
16	north	p	83.0	3.00	82.2	2.75	81.0
16	south	t	348.0	12.75	349.4	11.75	346.0
16	east	t	413.0	15.00	411.0	14.00	412.3
16	east	p	258.0	9.50	260.3	8.75	257.7
16	east	p	79.0	3.00	82.2	2.75	81.0
16	east	p	76.0	2.75	75.4	2.50	73.6
17	west	t	413.5	15.00	411.0	14.00	412.3
17	west	p	281.5	10.25	280.9	9.50	279.8
17	west	p	132.5	4.75	130.2	4.50	132.5
17	north	t	260.0	9.50	260.3	8.75	257.7
17	north	p	174.5	6.25	171.3	6.00	176.7
17	north	p	85.5	3.00	82.2	3.00	88.4
17	south	t	260.5	9.50	260.3	8.75	257.7
17	east	t	279.0	10.25	280.9	9.50	279.8
18	west	t	288.0	10.50	287.7	9.75	287.1
18	north	t	386.0	14.00	383.6	13.00	382.9
18	north	p	210.0	7.75	212.4	7.25	213.5
18	north	p	176.0	6.50	178.1	6.00	176.7
18	south	t	396.0	14.50	397.3	13.50	397.6
18	east	t	380.0	13.75	376.8	13.00	382.9
18	east	p	116.0	4.25	116.5	4.00	117.8
18	east	p	172.0	6.25	171.3	5.75	169.3
18	east	p	92.0	3.25	89.1	3.00	88.4
19	west	t	192.0	7.00	191.8	6.50	191.4
19	north	t	476.5	17.50	479.5	16.25	478.6
19	south	t	474.5	17.25	472.7	16.00	471.2
19	south	p	43.0	1.50	41.1	1.50	44.2
19	south	p	87.5	3.25	89.1	3.00	88.4
19	south	p	344.0	12.50	342.5	11.75	346.0
19	east	t	195.0	7.00	191.8	6.50	191.4
20	impl(w)	t	827.5	30.25	828.9	28.00	824.6

252

Casa del Tramezzo di Legno (III 4-12)

Room	where?	kind	in cm	O.ft (27.4)	ideal	R.ft (29.45)	ideal
20	impl(w)	p	301.5	11.00	301.4	10.25	301.9
20	impl(w)	p	227.0	8.25	226.1	7.75	228.2
20	impl(w)	p	39.0	1.50	41.1	1.25	36.8
20	impl(w)	p	151.5	5.50	150.7	5.25	154.6
20	impl(w)	p	36.5	1.25	34.3	1.25	36.8
20	impl(w)	p	299.0	11.00	301.4	10.25	301.9
20	impl(w)	t	816.0	29.75	815.2	27.75	817.2
20	impl(w)	p	296.5	10.75	294.6	10.00	294.5
20	impl(w)	p	224.5	8.25	226.1	7.50	220.9
20	impl(w)	p	295.0	10.75	294.6	10.00	294.5
20	impl(w)	t	821.5	30.00	822.0	28.00	824.6
20	impl(w)	p	296.0	10.75	294.6	10.00	294.5
20	impl(w)	p	225.0	8.25	226.1	7.75	228.2
20	impl(w)	p	300.5	11.00	301.4	10.25	301.9
20	impl(w)	t	154.0	5.50	150.7	5.25	154.6
20	impl(w)	p	23.0	0.75	20.6	0.75	22.1
20	impl(w)	p	110.0	4.00	109.6	3.75	110.4
20	impl(w)	p	21.0	0.75	20.6	0.75	22.1
20	impl(w)	t	153.5	5.50	150.7	5.25	154.6
20	impl(w)	p	21.5	0.75	20.6	0.75	22.1
20	impl(w)	p	109.0	4.00	109.6	3.75	110.4
20	impl(w)	p	23.0	0.75	20.6	0.75	22.1
20	impl(w)	t	154.0	5.50	150.7	5.25	154.6
20	impl(w)	p	22.5	0.75	20.6	0.75	22.1
20	impl(w)	p	44.0	1.50	41.1	1.50	44.2
20	impl(w)	p	21.5	0.75	20.6	0.75	22.1
20	impl(w)	p	43.0	1.50	41.1	1.50	44.2
20	impl(w)	p	23.0	0.75	20.6	0.75	22.1
20	impl(l)	t	956.0	35.00	959.0	32.50	957.1
20	impl(l)	p	341.0	12.50	342.5	11.50	338.7
20	impl(l)	p	260.0	9.50	260.3	8.75	257.7
20	impl(l)	p	36.0	1.25	34.3	1.25	36.8
20	impl(l)	p	187.0	6.75	185.0	6.25	184.1
20	impl(l)	p	37.0	1.25	34.3	1.25	36.8
20	impl(l)	p	355.0	13.00	356.2	12.00	353.4
20	impl(l)	t	952.0	34.75	952.2	32.25	949.8
20	impl(l)	p	339.0	12.25	335.7	11.50	338.7
20	impl(l)	p	263.0	9.50	260.3	9.00	265.1
20	impl(l)	p	38.0	1.50	41.1	1.25	36.8
20	impl(l)	p	188.0	6.75	185.0	6.50	191.4
20	impl(l)	p	37.0	1.25	34.3	1.25	36.8
20	impl(l)	p	350.0	12.75	349.4	12.00	353.4
20	impl(l)	t	186.5	6.75	185.0	6.25	184.1

Casa del Tramezzo di Legno (III 4-12)

Room	where?	kind	in cm	O.ft (27.4)	ideal	R.ft (29.45)	ideal
20	impl(l)	t	188.0	6.75	185.0	6.50	191.4
20	impl(l)	t	152.5	5.50	150.7	5.25	154.6
20	impl(l)	p	23.0	0.75	20.6	0.75	22.1
20	impl(l)	p	111.0	4.00	109.6	3.75	110.4
20	impl(l)	p	21.0	0.75	20.6	0.75	22.1
20	impl(l)	t	152.5	5.50	150.7	5.25	154.6
20	impl(l)	p	19.5	0.75	20.6	0.75	22.1
20	impl(l)	p	112.5	4.00	109.6	3.75	110.4
20	impl(l)	p	20.5	0.75	20.6	0.75	22.1
20	impl(l)	t	151.5	5.50	150.7	5.25	154.6
20	impl(l)	p	19.5	0.75	20.6	0.75	22.1
20	impl(l)	p	43.5	1.50	41.1	1.50	44.2
20	impl(l)	p	22.0	0.75	20.6	0.75	22.1
20	impl(l)	p	45.5	1.75	48.0	1.50	44.2
20	impl(l)	p	21.5	0.75	20.6	0.75	22.1
20	west	t	827.5	30.25	828.9	28.00	824.6
20	west	p	111.0	4.00	109.6	3.75	110.4
20	west	p	58.5	2.25	61.7	2.00	58.9
20	west	p	488.5	17.75	486.4	16.50	485.9
20	west	p	54.0	2.00	54.8	1.75	51.5
20	west	p	115.5	4.25	116.5	4.00	117.8
20	north	t	954.5	34.75	952.2	32.50	957.1
20	north	p	751.0	27.50	753.5	25.50	751.0
20	north	p	111.5	4.00	109.6	3.75	110.4
20	north	p	92.0	3.25	89.1	3.00	88.4
20	south	t	957.5	35.00	959.0	32.50	957.1
20	south	p	113.5	4.25	116.5	3.75	110.4
20	south	p	112.5	4.00	109.6	3.75	110.4
20	south	p	163.5	6.00	164.4	5.50	162.0
20	south	p	114.5	4.25	116.5	4.00	117.8
20	south	p	162.5	6.00	164.4	5.50	162.0
20	south	p	291.0	10.50	287.7	10.00	294.5
20	east	t	827.5	30.25	828.9	28.00	824.6
20	east	p	325.0	11.75	322.0	11.00	324.0
20	east	p	192.0	7.00	191.8	6.50	191.4
20	east	p	37.0	1.25	34.3	1.25	36.8
20	east	p	117.0	4.25	116.5	4.00	117.8
20	east	p	156.5	5.75	157.6	5.25	154.6
21	west	t	126.0	4.50	123.3	4.25	125.2
21	north	t	382.5	14.00	383.6	13.00	382.9
21	south	t	380.0	13.75	376.8	13.00	382.9
21	east	t	115.5	4.25	116.5	4.00	117.8
22	width	t	234.0	8.50	232.9	8.00	235.6

Casa del Tramezzo di Legno (III 4-12)

Room	where?	kind	in cm	O.ft (27.4)	ideal	R.ft (29.45)	ideal
22	west	t	235.0	8.50	232.9	8.00	235.6
22	north	t	991.0	36.25	993.3	33.75	993.9
22	north	p	230.0	8.50	232.9	7.75	228.2
22	north	p	106.5	4.00	109.6	3.50	103.1
22	north	p	266.5	9.75	267.2	9.00	265.1
22	north	p	108.0	4.00	109.6	3.75	110.4
22	north	p	280.0	10.25	280.9	9.50	279.8
22	south	t	760.0	27.75	760.4	25.75	758.3
22	south	p	42.0	1.50	41.1	1.50	44.2
22	south	p	104.0	3.75	102.8	3.50	103.1
22	south	p	52.0	2.00	54.8	1.75	51.5
22	south	p	132.0	4.75	130.2	4.50	132.5
22	south	p	54.0	2.00	54.8	1.75	51.5
22	south	p	132.5	4.75	130.2	4.50	132.5
22	south	p	55.5	2.00	54.8	2.00	58.9
22	south	p	135.0	5.00	137.0	4.50	132.5
22	south	p	53.0	2.00	54.8	1.75	51.5
22	east	t	229.5	8.50	232.9	7.75	228.2
23	length	t	726.5	26.50	726.1	24.75	728.9
23	length	p	683.0	25.00	685.0	23.25	684.7
23	length	p	43.5	1.50	41.1	1.50	44.2
23	length	t	741.5	27.00	739.8	25.25	743.6
23	length	p	696.0	25.50	698.7	23.75	699.4
23	length	p	45.5	1.75	48.0	1.50	44.2
23	west	t	678.0	24.75	678.2	23.00	677.4
23	west	p	151.0	5.50	150.7	5.25	154.6
23	west	p	50.5	1.75	48.0	1.75	51.5
23	west	p	249.5	9.00	246.6	8.50	250.3
23	west	p	50.5	1.75	48.0	1.75	51.5
23	west	p	132.5	4.75	130.2	4.50	132.5
23	west	p	44.0	1.50	41.1	1.50	44.2
23	north	t	718.0	26.25	719.3	24.50	721.5
23	north	p	103.0	3.75	102.8	3.50	103.1
23	north	p	54.0	2.00	54.8	1.75	51.5
23	north	p	132.0	4.75	130.2	4.50	132.5
23	north	p	55.0	2.00	54.8	1.75	51.5
23	north	p	130.0	4.75	130.2	4.50	132.5
23	north	p	56.5	2.00	54.8	2.00	58.9
23	north	p	134.5	5.00	137.0	4.50	132.5
23	north	p	53.0	2.00	54.8	1.75	51.5
23	south	t	731.0	26.75	733.0	24.75	728.9
23	south	p	681.0	24.75	678.2	23.00	677.4
23	south	p	50.0	1.75	48.0	1.75	51.5

Casa del Tramezzo di Legno (III 4-12)

Room	where?	kind	in cm	O.ft (27.4)	ideal	R.ft (29.45)	ideal
23	east	t	662.0	24.25	664.5	22.50	662.6
23	east	p	242.0	8.75	239.8	8.25	243.0
23	east	p	26.0	1.00	27.4	1.00	29.5
23	east	p	318.0	11.50	315.1	10.75	316.6
23	east	p	24.5	1.00	27.4	0.75	22.1
23	east	p	51.5	2.00	54.8	1.75	51.5
24	width	t	914.5	33.50	917.9	31.00	913.0
24	width	t	917.0	33.50	917.9	31.25	920.3
24	length	t	227.5	8.25	226.1	7.75	228.2
24	west	t	914.0	33.25	911.1	31.00	913.0
24	west	p	118.0	4.25	116.5	4.00	117.8
24	west	p	80.0	3.00	82.2	2.75	81.0
24	west	p	268.5	9.75	267.2	9.00	265.1
24	west	p	287.5	10.50	287.7	9.75	287.1
24	west	p	92.5	3.50	95.9	3.25	95.7
24	west	p	67.5	2.50	68.5	2.25	66.3
24	north	t	232.0	8.50	232.9	8.00	235.6
24	south	t	230.0	8.50	232.9	7.75	228.2
24	south	p	75.0	2.75	75.4	2.50	73.6
24	south	p	70.0	2.50	68.5	2.50	73.6
24	south	p	95.0	3.50	95.9	3.25	95.7
24	east	t	673.0	24.50	671.3	22.75	670.0
24	east	p	8.5	0.25	6.9	0.25	7.4
24	east	p	133.5	4.75	130.2	4.50	132.5
24	east	p	53.0	2.00	54.8	1.75	51.5
24	east	p	250.0	9.00	246.6	8.50	250.3
24	east	p	54.0	2.00	54.8	1.75	51.5
24	east	p	130.5	4.75	130.2	4.50	132.5
24	east	p	54.5	2.00	54.8	1.75	51.5
25	west	t	130.0	4.75	130.2	4.50	132.5
25	north	t	955.5	34.75	952.2	32.50	957.1
25	north	p	731.0	26.75	733.0	24.75	728.9
25	north	p	75.0	2.75	75.4	2.50	73.6
25	north	p	71.0	2.50	68.5	2.50	73.6
25	north	p	78.0	2.75	75.4	2.75	81.0
25	south	t	961.5	35.00	959.0	32.75	964.5
25	east	t	122.0	4.50	123.3	4.25	125.2
26	west	t	326.0	12.00	328.8	11.00	324.0
26	north	t	97.5	3.50	95.9	3.25	95.7
26	south	t	103.0	3.75	102.8	3.50	103.1
26	east	t	337.0	12.25	335.7	11.50	338.7
27	west	t	330.0	12.00	328.8	11.25	331.3
27	north	t	880.0	32.00	876.8	30.00	883.5

Casa del Tramezzo di Legno (III 4-12)

Room	where?	kind	in cm	O.ft (27.4)	ideal	R.ft (29.45)	ideal
27	north	p	72.0	2.75	75.4	2.50	73.6
27	north	p	337.5	12.25	335.7	11.50	338.7
27	north	p	62.5	2.25	61.7	2.00	58.9
27	north	p	339.5	12.50	342.5	11.50	338.7
27	north	p	68.5	2.50	68.5	2.25	66.3
27	south	t	881.0	32.25	883.7	30.00	883.5
27	south	p	29.0	1.00	27.4	1.00	29.5
27	south	p	116.0	4.25	116.5	4.00	117.8
27	south	p	476.0	17.25	472.7	16.25	478.6
27	south	p	107.0	4.00	109.6	3.75	110.4
27	south	p	156.0	5.75	157.6	5.25	154.6
27	east	t	387.0	14.00	383.6	13.25	390.2
27	east	p	168.0	6.25	171.3	5.75	169.3
27	east	p	219.0	8.00	219.2	7.50	220.9
28	west	t	437.0	16.00	438.4	14.75	434.4
28	west	p	222.0	8.00	219.2	7.50	220.9
28	west	p	215.0	7.75	212.4	7.25	213.5
28	north	t	380.5	14.00	383.6	13.00	382.9
28	north	p	271.0	10.00	274.0	9.25	272.4
28	north	p	109.5	4.00	109.6	3.75	110.4
28	south	t	398.0	14.50	397.3	13.50	397.6
28	east	t	425.0	15.50	424.7	14.50	427.0
28	east	p	100.5	3.75	102.8	3.50	103.1
28	east	p	81.5	3.00	82.2	2.75	81.0
28	east	p	243.0	8.75	239.8	8.25	243.0
29	west	t	430.0	15.75	431.6	14.50	427.0
29	west	p	102.5	3.75	102.8	3.50	103.1
29	west	p	82.5	3.00	82.2	2.75	81.0
29	west	p	88.0	3.25	89.1	3.00	88.4
29	west	p	157.0	5.75	157.6	5.25	154.6
29	north	t	185.0	6.75	185.0	6.25	184.1
29	south	t	147.5	5.50	150.7	5.00	147.3
29	east	t	453.5	16.50	452.1	15.50	456.5
29	east	p	282.5	10.25	280.9	9.50	279.8
29	east	p	171.0	6.25	171.3	5.75	169.3
30	west	t	463.0	17.00	465.8	15.75	463.8
30	north	t	472.0	17.25	472.7	16.00	471.2
30	north	p	68.0	2.50	68.5	2.25	66.3
30	north	p	263.0	9.50	260.3	9.00	265.1
30	north	p	141.0	5.25	143.9	4.75	139.9
30	south	t	479.0	17.50	479.5	16.25	478.6
30	south	p	305.5	11.25	308.3	10.25	301.9
30	south	p	173.5	6.25	171.3	6.00	176.7

Casa del Tramezzo di Legno (III 4-12)

Room	where?	kind	in cm	O.ft (27.4)	ideal	R.ft (29.45)	ideal
30	east	t	487.0	17.75	486.4	16.50	485.9
31	west	t	114.5	4.25	116.5	4.00	117.8
31	south	t	519.5	19.00	520.6	17.75	522.7
32	west	t	117.0	4.25	116.5	4.00	117.8
32	north	t	251.0	9.25	253.5	8.50	250.3
32	south	t	251.0	9.25	253.5	8.50	250.3
32	east	t	86.0	3.25	89.1	3.00	88.4

Casa a Graticcio (III 13-15) Ground floor

Room	where?	kind	in cm	O.ft (27.5)	ideal	R.ft (29.6)	ideal
1	west	t	214.0	7.75	213.1	7.25	214.6
1	north	t	274.0	10.00	275.0	9.25	273.8
1	north	p	212.0	7.75	213.1	7.25	214.6
1	south	t	274.0	10.00	275.0	9.25	273.8
1	east	t	211.0	7.75	213.1	7.25	214.6
1	east	p	112.5	4.00	110.0	3.75	111.0
1	east	p	98.5	3.50	96.3	3.25	96.2
2	west	t	210.0	7.75	213.1	7.00	207.2
2	north	t	333.0	12.00	330.0	11.25	333.0
2	north	p	288.5	10.50	288.8	9.75	288.6
2	north	p	44.5	1.50	41.3	1.50	44.4
2	south	t	334.0	12.25	336.9	11.25	333.0
2	south	p	225.0	8.25	226.9	7.50	222.0
2	south	p	97.0	3.50	96.3	3.25	96.2
2	south	p	12.0	0.50	13.8	0.50	14.8
2	east	t	213.0	7.75	213.1	7.25	214.6
3	west	t	388.0	14.00	385.0	13.00	384.8
3	west	p	342.0	12.50	343.8	11.50	340.4
3	west	p	46.0	1.75	48.1	1.50	44.4
3	north	t	227.0	8.25	226.9	7.75	229.4
3	south	t	220.0	8.00	220.0	7.50	222.0
3	south	p	135.0	5.00	137.5	4.50	133.2
3	south	p	85.0	3.00	82.5	2.75	81.4
3	east	t	383.5	14.00	385.0	13.00	384.8
3	east	p	169.0	6.25	171.9	5.75	170.2
3	east	p	22.0	0.75	20.6	0.75	22.2
3	east	p	148.0	5.50	151.3	5.00	148.0
3	east	p	44.5	1.50	41.3	1.50	44.4
4	length	t	334.0	12.25	336.9	11.25	333.0
4	length	p	295.0	10.75	295.6	10.00	296.0
4	length	p	39.0	1.50	41.3	1.25	37.0
4	west	t	251.0	9.25	254.4	8.50	251.6
4	west	p	32.0	1.25	34.4	1.00	29.6
4	west	p	219.0	8.00	220.0	7.50	222.0
4	north	t	331.0	12.00	330.0	11.25	333.0
4	north	p	157.0	5.75	158.1	5.25	155.4
4	north	p	85.0	3.00	82.5	2.75	81.4
4	north	p	89.0	3.25	89.4	3.00	88.8
4	south	t	326.0	11.75	323.1	11.00	325.6
4	south	p	68.0	2.50	68.8	2.25	66.6
4	south	p	223.0	8.00	220.0	7.50	222.0
4	south	p	35.0	1.25	34.4	1.25	37.0
4	east	t	235.0	8.50	233.8	8.00	236.8

Casa a Graticcio (III 13-15) Ground floor

Room	where?	kind	in cm	O.ft (27.5)	ideal	R.ft (29.6)	ideal
4	east	p	37.0	1.25	34.4	1.25	37.0
4	east	p	198.0	7.25	199.4	6.75	199.8
5	west	t	298.0	10.75	295.6	10.00	296.0
5	west	p	251.5	9.25	254.4	8.50	251.6
5	west	p	46.5	1.75	48.1	1.50	44.4
5	north	t	281.0	10.25	281.9	9.50	281.2
5	south	t	273.0	10.00	275.0	9.25	273.8
5	east	t	301.0	11.00	302.5	10.25	303.4
5	east	p	69.5	2.50	68.8	2.25	66.6
5	east	p	186.5	6.75	185.6	6.25	185.0
5	east	p	45.0	1.75	48.1	1.50	44.4
6	west	t	292.0	10.50	288.8	9.75	288.6
6	west	p	75.0	2.75	75.6	2.50	74.0
6	west	p	85.0	3.00	82.5	2.75	81.4
6	west	p	132.0	4.75	130.6	4.50	133.2
6	north	t	269.0	9.75	268.1	9.00	266.4
6	south	t	271.0	9.75	268.1	9.25	273.8
6	east	t	289.0	10.50	288.8	9.75	288.6
6	east	p	222.0	8.00	220.0	7.50	222.0
6	east	p	67.0	2.50	68.8	2.25	66.6
7	west	t	332.5	12.00	330.0	11.25	333.0
7	west	p	224.0	8.25	226.9	7.50	222.0
7	west	p	68.0	2.50	68.8	2.25	66.6
7	west	p	40.5	1.50	41.3	1.25	37.0
7	north	t	335.0	12.25	336.9	11.25	333.0
7	north	p	75.5	2.75	75.6	2.50	74.0
7	north	p	183.5	6.75	185.6	6.25	185.0
7	north	p	76.0	2.75	75.6	2.50	74.0
7	south	t	333.0	12.00	330.0	11.25	333.0
7	east	t	331.5	12.00	330.0	11.25	333.0
7	east	p	48.5	1.75	48.1	1.75	51.8
7	east	p	239.5	8.75	240.6	8.00	236.8
7	east	p	43.5	1.50	41.3	1.50	44.4
8	west	t	362.0	13.25	364.4	12.25	362.6
8	west	p	48.0	1.75	48.1	1.50	44.4
8	west	p	238.0	8.75	240.6	8.00	236.8
8	west	p	76.0	2.75	75.6	2.50	74.0
8	north	t	222.0	8.00	220.0	7.50	222.0
8	south	t	217.0	8.00	220.0	7.25	214.6
8	east	t	359.0	13.00	357.5	12.25	362.6
8	east	p	54.0	2.00	55.0	1.75	51.8
8	east	p	248.0	9.00	247.5	8.50	251.6
8	east	p	57.0	2.00	55.0	2.00	59.2

Casa a Graticcio (III 13-15) Ground floor

Room	where?	kind	in cm	O.ft (27.5)	ideal	R.ft (29.6)	ideal
9	west	t	349.5	12.75	350.6	11.75	347.8
9	west	p	231.5	8.50	233.8	7.75	229.4
9	west	p	63.0	2.25	61.9	2.25	66.6
9	west	p	54.5	2.00	55.0	1.75	51.8
9	north	t	287.0	10.50	288.8	9.75	288.6
9	south	t	288.0	10.50	288.8	9.75	288.6
9	east	t	349.5	12.75	350.6	11.75	347.8
9	east	p	91.5	3.25	89.4	3.00	88.8
9	east	p	196.5	7.25	199.4	6.75	199.8
9	east	p	61.5	2.25	61.9	2.00	59.2
10	west	t	351.5	12.75	350.6	12.00	355.2
10	west	p	97.5	3.50	96.3	3.25	96.2
10	west	p	194.5	7.00	192.5	6.50	192.4
10	west	p	59.5	2.25	61.9	2.00	59.2
10	north	t	272.0	10.00	275.0	9.25	273.8
10	south	t	272.0	10.00	275.0	9.25	273.8
10	east	t	364.0	13.25	364.4	12.25	362.6
10	east	p	63.5	2.25	61.9	2.25	66.6
10	east	p	238.5	8.75	240.6	8.00	236.8
10	east	p	62.0	2.25	61.9	2.00	59.2
11	west	t	623.0	22.75	625.6	21.00	621.6
11	north	t	392.5	14.25	391.9	13.25	392.2
11	south	t	387.0	14.00	385.0	13.00	384.8
11	east	t	620.0	22.50	618.8	21.00	621.6
11	east	p	72.0	2.50	68.8	2.50	74.0
11	east	p	84.0	3.00	82.5	2.75	81.4
11	east	p	364.0	13.25	364.4	12.25	362.6
11	east	p	99.0	3.50	96.3	3.25	96.2
12	west	t	329.0	12.00	330.0	11.00	325.6
12	west	p	281.0	10.25	281.9	9.50	281.2
12	west	p	48.0	1.75	48.1	1.50	44.4
12	north	t	200.0	7.25	199.4	6.75	199.8
12	south	t	197.0	7.25	199.4	6.75	199.8
12	east	t	337.0	12.25	336.9	11.50	340.4
13	width	t	290.5	10.50	288.8	9.75	288.6
13	west	t	558.0	20.25	556.9	18.75	555.0
13	north	t	521.0	19.00	522.5	17.50	518.0
13	south	t	522.0	19.00	522.5	17.75	525.4
13	south	t	296.0	10.75	295.6	10.00	296.0
13	south	p	168.0	6.00	165.0	5.75	170.2
13	south	p	128.0	4.75	130.6	4.25	125.8
13	east	t	567.0	20.50	563.8	19.25	569.8
13	east	p	230.0	8.25	226.9	7.75	229.4

Casa a Graticcio (III 13-15) Ground floor

Room	where?	kind	in cm	O.ft (27.5)	ideal	R.ft (29.6)	ideal
14	west	t	169.0	6.25	171.9	5.75	170.2
14	north	t	685.0	25.00	687.5	23.25	688.2
14	north	p	39.0	1.50	41.3	1.25	37.0
14	north	p	81.0	3.00	82.5	2.75	81.4
14	north	p	463.0	16.75	460.6	15.75	466.2
14	north	p	89.0	3.25	89.4	3.00	88.8
14	north	p	13.0	0.50	13.8	0.50	14.8
14	south	t	689.0	25.00	687.5	23.25	688.2
14	south	p	38.0	1.50	41.3	1.25	37.0
14	south	p	273.0	10.00	275.0	9.25	273.8
14	south	p	46.0	1.75	48.1	1.50	44.4
14	south	p	286.0	10.50	288.8	9.75	288.6
14	south	p	45.0	1.75	48.1	1.50	44.4
14	east	t	149.0	5.50	151.3	5.00	148.0
15	west	t	83.0	3.00	82.5	2.75	81.4
15	north	t	1127.0	41.00	1127.5	38.00	1124.8
15	south	t	1122.0	40.75	1120.6	38.00	1124.8
15	south	p	650.0	23.75	653.1	22.00	651.2
15	south	p	472.0	17.25	474.4	16.00	473.6
15	east	t	146.0	5.25	144.4	5.00	148.0

Casa a Graticcio (III 13-15) Upper Storey

Room	where?	kind	in cm	O.ft (27.5)	ideal	R.ft (29.6)	ideal
1	width	t	209.0	7.50	206.3	7.00	207.2
1	north	t	282.5	10.25	281.9	9.50	281.2
1	north	p	91.5	3.25	89.4	3.00	88.8
1	north	p	191.0	7.00	192.5	6.50	192.4
1	south	t	278.0	10.00	275.0	9.50	281.2
1	east	t	218.0	8.00	220.0	7.25	214.6
2	west	t	366.5	13.25	364.4	12.50	370.0
2	west	p	131.0	4.75	130.6	4.50	133.2
2	west	p	230.0	8.25	226.9	7.75	229.4
2	north	t	332.5	12.00	330.0	11.25	333.0
2	north	p	165.5	6.00	165.0	5.50	162.8
2	north	p	78.0	2.75	75.6	2.75	81.4
2	north	p	89.0	3.25	89.4	3.00	88.8
2	south	t	359.5	13.00	357.5	12.25	362.6
2	east	t	342.5	12.50	343.8	11.50	340.4
2	east	p	38.5	1.50	41.3	1.25	37.0
2	east	p	250.0	9.00	247.5	8.50	251.6
2	east	p	54.0	2.00	55.0	1.75	51.8
3	west	t	417.0	15.25	419.4	14.00	414.4
3	west	p	60.0	2.25	61.9	2.00	59.2
3	west	p	55.5	2.00	55.0	2.00	59.2
3	west	p	251.0	9.25	254.4	8.50	251.6
3	west	p	50.5	1.75	48.1	1.75	51.8
3	north	t	248.0	9.00	247.5	8.50	251.6
3	north	p	74.5	2.75	75.6	2.50	74.0
3	north	p	173.5	6.25	171.9	5.75	170.2
3	south	t	245.0	9.00	247.5	8.25	244.2
3	south	p	10.0	0.25	6.9	0.25	7.4
3	south	p	216.0	7.75	213.1	7.25	214.6
3	south	p	19.0	0.75	20.6	0.75	22.2
3	east	t	426.0	15.50	426.3	14.50	429.2
3	east	p	121.0	4.50	123.8	4.00	118.4
3	east	p	257.0	9.25	254.4	8.75	259.0
3	east	p	48.0	1.75	48.1	1.50	44.4
4	west	t	362.5	13.25	364.4	12.25	362.6
4	west	p	52.0	2.00	55.0	1.75	51.8
4	west	p	259.5	9.50	261.3	8.75	259.0
4	west	p	51.0	1.75	48.1	1.75	51.8
4	north	t	292.5	10.75	295.6	10.00	296.0
4	north	p	85.0	3.00	82.5	2.75	81.4
4	north	p	207.5	7.50	206.3	7.00	207.2
4	south	t	286.0	10.50	288.8	9.75	288.6
4	east	t	358.5	13.00	357.5	12.00	355.2

Casa a Graticcio (III 13-15) Upper Storey

Room	where?	kind	in cm	O.ft (27.5)	ideal	R.ft (29.6)	ideal
4	east	p	63.5	2.25	61.9	2.25	66.6
4	east	p	255.0	9.25	254.4	8.50	251.6
4	east	p	47.0	1.75	48.1	1.50	44.4
5	west	t	420.0	15.25	419.4	14.25	421.8
5	west	p	64.0	2.25	61.9	2.25	66.6
5	west	p	57.0	2.00	55.0	2.00	59.2
5	west	p	258.0	9.50	261.3	8.75	259.0
5	west	p	41.0	1.50	41.3	1.50	44.4
5	north	t	317.0	11.50	316.3	10.75	318.2
5	south	t	288.0	10.50	288.8	9.75	288.6
5	east	t	418.0	15.25	419.4	14.00	414.4
5	east	p	149.0	5.50	151.3	5.00	148.0
5	east	p	102.0	3.75	103.1	3.50	103.6
5	east	p	167.0	6.00	165.0	5.75	170.2
6	west	t	218.0	8.00	220.0	7.25	214.6
6	north	t	220.0	8.00	220.0	7.50	222.0
6	south	t	225.0	8.25	226.9	7.50	222.0
6	south	p	87.5	3.25	89.4	3.00	88.8
6	south	p	81.0	3.00	82.5	2.75	81.4
6	south	p	56.5	2.00	55.0	2.00	59.2
6	east	t	213.0	7.75	213.1	7.25	214.6
7	west	t	426.0	15.50	426.3	14.50	429.2
7	west	p	164.0	6.00	165.0	5.50	162.8
7	west	p	102.5	3.75	103.1	3.50	103.6
7	west	p	159.5	5.75	158.1	5.50	162.8
7	north	t	175.0	6.25	171.9	6.00	177.6
7	south	t	186.0	6.75	185.6	6.25	185.0
7	east	t	521.0	19.00	522.5	17.50	518.0
8	west	t	85.5	3.00	82.5	3.00	88.8
8	north	t	508.0	18.50	508.8	17.25	510.6
8	north	p	88.0	3.25	89.4	3.00	88.8
8	north	p	81.0	3.00	82.5	2.75	81.4
8	north	p	164.0	6.00	165.0	5.50	162.8
8	north	p	66.0	2.50	68.8	2.25	66.6
8	north	p	109.0	4.00	110.0	3.75	111.0
8	south	t	341.0	12.50	343.8	11.50	340.4
8	east	t	94.0	3.50	96.3	3.25	96.2
9	west	t	105.0	3.75	103.1	3.50	103.6
9	north	t	246.5	9.00	247.5	8.25	244.2
9	south	t	250.0	9.00	247.5	8.50	251.6
9	south	p	91.0	3.25	89.4	3.00	88.8
9	south	p	66.0	2.50	68.8	2.25	66.6
9	south	p	93.0	3.50	96.3	3.25	96.2

Casa a Graticcio (III 13-15) Upper Storey

Room	where?	kind	in cm	O.ft (27.5)	ideal	R.ft (29.6)	ideal
9	east	t	92.5	3.25	89.4	3.25	96.2
10	length	t	175.0	6.25	171.9	6.00	177.6
10	west	t	285.0	10.25	281.9	9.75	288.6
10	west	p	120.0	4.25	116.9	4.00	118.4
10	west	p	103.0	3.75	103.1	3.50	103.6
10	west	p	62.0	2.25	61.9	2.00	59.2
10	north	t	171.0	6.25	171.9	5.75	170.2
10	east	t	283.5	10.25	281.9	9.50	281.2
10	east	p	120.5	4.50	123.8	4.00	118.4
10	east	p	85.0	3.00	82.5	2.75	81.4
10	east	p	77.5	2.75	75.6	2.50	74.0
11	west	t	96.0	3.50	96.3	3.25	96.2
11	north	t	412.0	15.00	412.5	14.00	414.4
11	north	p	178.0	6.50	178.8	6.00	177.6
11	north	p	78.5	2.75	75.6	2.75	81.4
11	north	p	155.5	5.75	158.1	5.25	155.4
11	south	t	409.0	14.75	405.6	13.75	407.0
11	south	p	173.5	6.25	171.9	5.75	170.2
11	south	p	78.0	2.75	75.6	2.75	81.4
11	south	p	157.5	5.75	158.1	5.25	155.4
11	east	t	103.0	3.75	103.1	3.50	103.6
12	west	t	216.5	7.75	213.1	7.25	214.6
12	west	p	84.5	3.00	82.5	2.75	81.4
12	west	p	74.0	2.75	75.6	2.50	74.0
12	west	p	58.0	2.00	55.0	2.00	59.2
12	north	t	263.5	9.50	261.3	9.00	266.4
12	south	t	257.5	9.25	254.4	8.75	259.0
12	south	p	78.5	2.75	75.6	2.75	81.4
12	south	p	179.0	6.50	178.8	6.00	177.6
12	east	t	227.5	8.25	226.9	7.75	229.4
12	east	p	87.0	3.25	89.4	3.00	88.8
12	east	p	140.5	5.00	137.5	4.75	140.6
13	west	t	77.5	2.75	75.6	2.50	74.0
13	north	t	305.0	11.00	302.5	10.25	303.4
13	north	p	110.0	4.00	110.0	3.75	111.0
13	north	p	163.0	6.00	165.0	5.50	162.8
13	north	p	32.0	1.25	34.4	1.00	29.6
13	south	t	303.0	11.00	302.5	10.25	303.4
13	south	p	215.0	7.75	213.1	7.25	214.6
13	south	p	88.0	3.25	89.4	3.00	88.8
13	east	t	70.0	2.50	68.8	2.25	66.6
14	width	t	274.0	10.00	275.0	9.25	273.8
14	length	t	196.0	7.25	199.4	6.50	192.4

265

Casa a Graticcio (III 13-15) Upper Storey

Room	where?	kind	in cm	O.ft (27.5)	ideal	R.ft (29.6)	ideal
14	length	p	20.0	0.75	20.6	0.75	22.2
14	length	p	151.0	5.50	151.3	5.00	148.0
14	length	p	25.0	1.00	27.5	0.75	22.2
14	west	t	243.0	8.75	240.6	8.25	244.2
14	north	t	146.5	5.25	144.4	5.00	148.0
14	north	p	35.5	1.25	34.4	1.25	37.0
14	north	p	75.0	2.75	75.6	2.50	74.0
14	north	p	36.0	1.25	34.4	1.25	37.0
14	south	t	163.0	6.00	165.0	5.50	162.8
14	east	t	279.0	10.25	281.9	9.50	281.2
14	east	p	38.0	1.50	41.3	1.25	37.0
14	east	p	241.0	8.75	240.6	8.25	244.2
14	east	p	55.0	2.00	55.0	1.75	51.8

Casa dell'Erma di Bronzo (III 16)

Room	where?	kind	in cm	O.ft (27.55)	ideal
0	south	t	2021.0	73.25	2018.0
1	west	t	168.0	6.00	165.3
1	north	t	360.0	13.00	358.2
1	south	t	359.0	13.00	358.2
1	east	t	162.0	6.00	165.3
2	west	t	218.0	8.00	220.4
2	north	t	278.0	10.00	275.5
2	north	p	104.0	3.75	103.3
2	north	p	174.0	6.25	172.2
2	south	t	273.5	10.00	275.5
2	east	t	216.0	7.75	213.5
3	west	t	310.0	11.25	309.9
3	west	p	221.0	8.00	220.4
3	west	p	89.0	3.25	89.5
3	north	t	273.0	10.00	275.5
3	south	t	273.0	10.00	275.5
3	east	t	320.0	11.50	316.8
4	west	t	359.5	13.00	358.2
4	west	p	94.0	3.50	96.4
4	west	p	169.5	6.25	172.2
4	west	p	96.0	3.50	96.4
4	north	t	384.5	14.00	385.7
4	south	t	347.0	12.50	344.4
4	east	t	355.5	13.00	358.2
4	east	p	66.5	2.50	68.9
4	east	p	289.0	10.50	289.3
5	west	t	205.0	7.50	206.6
5	north	t	596.0	21.75	599.2
5	south	t	598.0	21.75	599.2
5	east	t	236.0	8.50	234.2
5	east	p	130.5	4.75	130.9
5	east	t	203.0	7.25	199.7
6	west	t	118.0	4.25	117.1
6	north	t	674.5	24.50	675.0
6	north	p	415.0	15.00	413.3
6	north	p	91.0	3.25	89.5
6	north	p	168.5	6.00	165.3
6	south	t	666.5	24.25	668.1
6	east	t	114.0	4.25	117.1
7	west	t	363.0	13.25	365.0
7	north	t	221.0	8.00	220.4
7	south	t	220.0	8.00	220.4
7	south	p	89.0	3.25	89.5

Casa dell'Erma di Bronzo (III 16)

Room	where?	kind	in cm	O.ft (27.55)	ideal
7	south	p	131.0	4.75	130.9
7	east	t	401.5	14.50	399.5
7	east	p	136.5	5.00	137.8
7	east	p	165.0	6.00	165.3
7	east	p	100.0	3.75	103.3
8	west	t	751.0	27.25	750.7
8	north	t	418.0	15.25	420.1
8	south	t	406.0	14.75	406.4
8	east	t	749.0	27.25	750.7
9	impl(w)	t	756.0	27.50	757.6
9	impl(w)	p	259.0	9.50	261.7
9	impl(w)	p	43.0	1.50	41.3
9	impl(w)	p	145.0	5.25	144.6
9	impl(w)	p	47.0	1.75	48.2
9	impl(w)	p	235.0	8.50	234.2
9	impl(w)	p	262.0	9.50	261.7
9	impl(w)	t	753.0	27.25	750.7
9	impl(w)	p	260.0	9.50	261.7
9	impl(w)	p	40.5	1.50	41.3
9	impl(w)	p	144.5	5.25	144.6
9	impl(w)	p	48.0	1.75	48.2
9	impl(w)	p	233.0	8.50	234.2
9	impl(w)	p	260.0	9.50	261.7
9	impl(l)	t	578.0	21.00	578.6
9	impl(l)	p	169.5	6.25	172.2
9	impl(l)	p	44.0	1.50	41.3
9	impl(l)	p	46.5	1.75	48.2
9	impl(l)	p	236.0	8.50	234.2
9	impl(l)	p	172.5	6.25	172.2
9	impl(l)	t	576.0	21.00	578.6
9	impl(l)	p	163.0	6.00	165.3
9	impl(l)	p	45.0	1.75	48.2
9	impl(l)	p	148.0	5.25	144.6
9	impl(l)	p	46.0	1.75	48.2
9	impl(l)	p	239.0	8.75	241.1
9	impl(l)	p	174.0	6.25	172.2
9	west	t	753.0	27.25	750.7
9	west	p	114.0	4.25	117.1
9	west	p	109.0	4.00	110.2
9	west	p	294.0	10.75	296.2
9	west	p	105.5	3.75	103.3
9	west	p	130.5	4.75	130.9
9	east	t	752.0	27.25	750.7

Casa dell'Erma di Bronzo (III 16)

Room	where?	kind	in cm	O.ft (27.55)	ideal
9	east	p	4.0	0.25	6.9
9	east	p	78.0	2.75	75.8
9	east	p	165.0	6.00	165.3
9	east	p	168.0	6.00	165.3
9	east	p	249.0	9.00	248.0
9	east	p	89.0	3.25	89.5

Casa dell'Ara Laterizia (III 17)

Room	where?	kind	in cm	O.ft (27.5)	ideal
0	length	t	2019.0	73.50	2021.3
0	west	t	562.0	20.50	563.8
0	east	t	555.0	20.25	556.9
1	west	t	391.0	14.25	391.9
1	west	p	106.0	3.75	103.1
1	west	p	285.0	10.25	281.9
1	north	t	321.5	11.75	323.1
1	south	t	322.0	11.75	323.1
1	east	t	382.0	14.00	385.0
2	west	t	213.0	7.75	213.1
2	north	t	277.0	10.00	275.0
2	south	t	281.0	10.25	281.9
2	east	t	205.0	7.50	206.3
2	east	p	100.0	3.75	103.1
2	east	p	105.0	3.75	103.1
3	west	t	196.0	7.25	199.4
3	north	t	275.0	10.00	275.0
3	north	p	154.0	5.50	151.3
3	north	p	121.0	4.50	123.8
3	south	t	279.5	10.25	281.9
3	east	t	189.0	6.75	185.6
4	west	t	180.5	6.50	178.8
4	north	t	281.0	10.25	281.9
4	north	p	121.0	4.50	123.8
4	north	p	160.0	5.75	158.1
4	south	t	285.0	10.25	281.9
4	east	t	187.0	6.75	185.6
5	west	t	276.0	10.00	275.0
5	north	t	358.0	13.00	357.5
5	south	t	371.0	13.50	371.3
5	east	t	282.0	10.25	281.9
5	east	p	60.0	2.25	61.9
5	east	p	222.0	8.00	220.0
6	length	t	88.0	3.25	89.4
6	west	t	221.0	8.00	220.0
7	width	t	342.0	12.50	343.8
7	length	p	413.0	15.00	412.5
7	length	t	781.0	28.50	783.8
7	length	p	365.0	13.25	364.4
7	west	t	255.0	9.25	254.4
7	west	p	70.0	2.50	68.8
7	west	p	90.0	3.25	89.4
7	west	p	95.0	3.50	96.3

Casa dell'Ara Laterizia (III 17)

Room	where?	kind	in cm	O.ft (27.5)	ideal
7	north	t	400.0	14.50	398.8
7	north	p	162.0	6.00	165.0
7	north	p	74.0	2.75	75.6
7	north	p	79.0	2.75	75.6
7	north	p	85.0	3.00	82.5
7	south	t	782.0	28.50	783.8
7	east	t	341.0	12.50	343.8
7	east	p	250.0	9.00	247.5
7	east	p	82.0	3.00	82.5
7	east	p	9.0	0.25	6.9
8	west	t	88.5	3.25	89.4
8	north	t	364.0	13.25	364.4
8	north	p	322.0	11.75	323.1
8	north	p	42.0	1.50	41.3
8	south	t	368.0	13.50	371.3
8	south	p	324.0	11.75	323.1
8	south	p	44.0	1.50	41.3
8	east	t	103.0	3.75	103.1
9	west	t	550.0	20.00	550.0
9	west	p	100.0	3.75	103.1
9	west	p	95.5	3.50	96.3
9	west	p	39.5	1.50	41.3
9	west	p	103.0	3.75	103.1
9	west	p	42.0	1.50	41.3
9	west	p	88.0	3.25	89.4
9	west	p	82.0	3.00	82.5
9	north	t	467.0	17.00	467.5
9	south	t	464.0	16.75	460.6
9	east	t	555.0	20.25	556.9
9	east	p	135.0	5.00	137.5
9	east	p	41.5	1.50	41.3
9	east	p	93.5	3.50	96.3
9	east	p	134.0	4.75	130.6
9	east	p	56.0	2.00	55.0
9	east	p	95.0	3.50	96.3
10	west	t	135.0	5.00	137.5
10	north	t	404.0	14.75	405.6
10	east	t	146.5	5.25	144.4

Casa dell'Atrio a Mosaico (IV 1-2) Lot IV A

Room	where?	kind	in cm	O.ft (27.5)	ideal
0	length	t	2130.5	77.50	2131.3
0	south	t	2087.0	76.00	2090.0
1	width	t	224.0	8.25	226.9
1	west	t	178.0	6.50	178.8
1	north	t	520.5	19.00	522.5
1	north	p	44.0	1.50	41.3
1	north	p	99.0	3.50	96.3
1	north	p	332.0	12.00	330.0
1	north	p	45.5	1.75	48.1
1	south	t	527.5	19.25	529.4
1	south	p	44.0	1.50	41.3
1	south	p	83.0	3.00	82.5
1	south	p	354.5	13.00	357.5
1	south	p	44.0	1.50	41.3
1	east	t	188.5	6.75	185.6
2	width	t	215.0	7.75	213.1
2	west	t	255.0	9.25	254.4
2	north	t	422.0	15.25	419.4
2	north	p	109.0	4.00	110.0
2	north	p	313.0	11.50	316.3
2	south	t	428.0	15.50	426.3
2	south	p	101.5	3.75	103.1
2	south	p	326.5	11.75	323.1
2	east	t	219.0	8.00	220.0
3	width	t	310.0	11.25	309.4
3	west	t	383.0	14.00	385.0
3	north	t	437.5	16.00	440.0
3	north	p	84.0	3.00	82.5
3	north	p	353.5	12.75	350.6
3	south	t	448.0	16.25	446.9
3	east	t	300.0	11.00	302.5
3	east	p	176.0	6.50	178.8
3	east	p	90.0	3.25	89.4
3	east	p	34.0	1.25	34.4
4	impl(w)	t	828.0	30.00	825.0
4	impl(w)	p	288.0	10.50	288.8
4	impl(w)	p	248.0	9.00	247.5
4	impl(w)	p	50.0	1.75	48.1
4	impl(w)	p	159.0	5.75	158.1
4	impl(w)	p	39.0	1.50	41.3
4	impl(w)	p	292.0	10.50	288.8
4	impl(w)	t	824.0	30.00	825.0
4	impl(w)	p	295.0	10.75	295.6

Casa dell'Atrio a Mosaico (IV 1-2) Lot IV A

Room	where?	kind	in cm	O.ft (27.5)	ideal
4	impl(w)	p	248.0	9.00	247.5
4	impl(w)	p	39.5	1.50	41.3
4	impl(w)	p	167.5	6.00	165.0
4	impl(w)	p	41.0	1.50	41.3
4	impl(w)	p	281.0	10.25	281.9
4	impl(l)	t	875.5	31.75	873.1
4	impl(l)	p	308.5	11.25	309.4
4	impl(l)	p	271.5	9.75	268.1
4	impl(l)	p	38.0	1.50	41.3
4	impl(l)	p	194.5	7.00	192.5
4	impl(l)	p	39.0	1.50	41.3
4	impl(l)	p	294.5	10.75	295.6
4	impl(l)	t	874.5	31.75	873.1
4	impl(l)	p	302.5	11.00	302.5
4	impl(l)	p	272.0	10.00	275.0
4	impl(l)	p	36.0	1.25	34.4
4	impl(l)	p	198.0	7.25	199.4
4	impl(l)	p	38.0	1.50	41.3
4	impl(l)	p	300.0	11.00	302.5
4	west	t	860.0	31.25	859.4
4	west	p	280.0	10.25	281.9
4	west	p	186.0	6.75	185.6
4	west	p	230.0	8.25	226.9
4	west	p	90.0	3.25	89.4
4	west	p	74.0	2.75	75.6
4	north	t	871.5	31.75	873.1
4	south	t	873.0	31.75	873.1
4	south	p	150.5	5.50	151.3
4	south	p	234.0	8.50	233.8
4	south	p	148.5	5.50	151.3
4	south	p	340.0	12.25	336.9
4	east	t	835.5	30.50	838.8
4	east	p	35.0	1.25	34.4
4	east	p	88.0	3.25	89.4
4	east	p	157.5	5.75	158.1
4	east	p	285.5	10.50	288.8
4	east	p	179.0	6.50	178.8
4	east	p	85.0	3.00	82.5
4	east	p	37.0	1.25	34.4
5	width	t	823.0	30.00	825.0
5	width	p	137.0	5.00	137.5
5	width	p	35.5	1.25	34.4
5	width	p	482.5	17.50	481.3

Casa dell'Atrio a Mosaico (IV 1-2) Lot IV A

Room	where?	kind	in cm	O.ft (27.5)	ideal
5	width	p	38.0	1.50	41.3
5	width	p	130.0	4.75	130.6
5	width	t	827.0	30.00	825.0
5	width	p	142.5	5.25	144.4
5	width	p	34.5	1.25	34.4
5	width	p	478.0	17.50	481.3
5	width	p	36.0	1 25	34.4
5	width	p	136.0	5.00	137.5
5	length	t	680.5	24.75	680.6
5	length	p	27.5	1.00	27.5
5	length	p	173.5	6.25	171.9
5	length	p	44.0	1.50	41.3
5	length	p	182.0	6.50	178.8
5	length	p	46.5	1.75	48.1
5	length	p	176.5	6.50	178.8
5	length	p	30.0	1.00	27.5
5	length	t	697.0	25.25	694.4
5	length	p	30.0	1.00	27.5
5	length	p	188.0	6.75	185.6
5	length	p	42.5	1.50	41.3
5	length	p	181.5	6.50	178.8
5	length	p	44.0	1.50	41.3
5	length	p	180.5	6.50	178.8
5	length	p	31.0	1.25	34.4
5	west	t	829.0	30.25	831.9
5	west	p	32.0	1.25	34.4
5	west	p	85.5	3.00	82.5
5	west	p	20.0	0.75	20.6
5	west	p	40.0	1.50	41.3
5	west	p	106.0	3.75	103.1
5	west	p	284.5	10.25	281.9
5	west	p	92.0	3.25	89.4
5	west	p	40.5	1.50	41.3
5	west	p	12.0	0.50	13.8
5	west	p	84.0	3.00	82.5
5	west	p	32.0	1.25	34.4
5	north	t	699.0	25.50	701.3
5	south	t	677.0	24.50	673.8
5	south	p	128.5	4.75	130.6
5	south	p	110.5	4.00	110.0
5	south	p	318.5	11.50	316.3
5	south	p	119.5	4.25	116.9
5	east	t	864.0	31.50	866.3

Casa dell'Atrio a Mosaico (IV 1-2) Lot IV A

Room	where?	kind	in cm	O.ft (27.5)	ideal
5	east	p	135.5	5.00	137.5
5	east	p	39.5	1.50	41.3
5	east	p	474.0	17.25	474.4
5	east	p	40.5	1.50	41.3
5	east	p	174.5	6.25	171.9

Casa dell'Atrio a Mosaico (IV 1-2) Garden and terrace

Room	where?	kind	in cm	O.ft (27.4)	ideal	R.ft (29.8)	ideal
6	width	t	422.0	15.50	424.7	14.25	424.7
6	west	p	135.0	5.00	137.0	4.50	134.1
6	west	p	129.5	4.75	130.2	4.25	126.7
6	north	t	366.0	13.25	363.1	12.25	365.1
6	south	t	364.5	13.25	363.1	12.25	365.1
6	south	p	89.0	3.25	89.1	3.00	89.4
6	south	p	275.5	10.00	274.0	9.25	275.7
6	east	t	428.5	15.75	431.6	14.50	432.1
7	width	t	413.0	15.00	411.0	13.75	409.8
7	west	t	416.5	15.25	417.9	14.00	417.2
7	north	t	366.5	13.50	369.9	12.25	365.1
7	north	p	91.0	3.25	89.1	3.00	89.4
7	north	p	275.5	10.00	274.0	9.25	275.7
7	south	t	364.5	13.25	363.1	12.25	365.1
7	south	p	292.0	10.75	294.6	9.75	290.6
7	south	p	72.5	2.75	75.4	2.50	74.5
8	west	t	110.0	4.00	109.6	3.75	111.8
8	north	t	397.5	14.50	397.3	13.25	394.9
8	south	t	392.0	14.25	390.5	13.25	394.9
8	east	t	117.0	4.25	116.5	4.00	119.2
9	width	t	520.0	19.00	520.6	17.50	521.5
9	length	t	505.0	18.50	506.9	17.00	506.6
9	west	t	589.0	21.50	589.1	19.75	588.6
9	west	p	161.0	6.00	164.4	5.50	163.9
9	west	p	266.0	9.75	267.2	9.00	268.2
9	west	p	162.0	6.00	164.4	5.50	163.9
9	north	t	503.0	18.25	500.1	17.00	506.6
9	north	p	115.0	4.25	116.5	3.75	111.8
9	north	p	388.0	14.25	390.5	13.00	387.4
9	south	t	500.0	18.25	500.1	16.75	499.2
9	south	p	103.5	3.75	102.8	3.50	104.3
9	south	p	396.5	14.50	397.3	13.25	394.9
9	east	t	512.5	18.75	513.8	17.25	514.1
10	west	t	347.5	12.75	349.4	11.75	350.2
10	west	p	72.5	2.75	75.4	2.50	74.5
10	west	p	62.0	2.25	61.7	2.00	59.6
10	west	p	131.0	4.75	130.2	4.50	134.1
10	west	p	82.0	3.00	82.2	2.75	82.0
10	north	t	359.5	13.00	356.2	12.00	357.6
10	south	t	361.5	13.25	363.1	12.25	365.1
10	south	p	78.5	2.75	75.4	2.75	82.0
10	south	p	283.0	10.25	280.9	9.50	283.1
10	east	t	346.0	12.75	349.4	11.50	342.7

Casa dell'Atrio a Mosaico (IV 1-2) Garden and terrace

Room	where?	kind	in cm	O.ft (27.4)	ideal	R.ft (29.8)	ideal
11	west	t	392.5	14.25	390.5	13.25	394.9
11	west	p	195.0	7.00	191.8	6.50	193.7
11	west	p	130.0	4.75	130.2	4.25	126.7
11	west	p	67.5	2.50	68.5	2.25	67.1
11	north	t	365.5	13.25	363.1	12.25	365.1
11	north	p	79.5	3.00	82.2	2.75	82.0
11	north	p	286.0	10.50	287.7	9.50	283.1
11	south	t	363.0	13.25	363.1	12.25	365.1
11	east	t	363.5	13.25	363.1	12.25	365.1
12	west	t	890.0	32.50	890.5	29.75	886.6
12	west	p	32.0	1.25	34.3	1.00	29.8
12	west	p	108.5	4.00	109.6	3.75	111.8
12	west	p	497.5	18.25	500.1	16.75	499.2
12	west	p	177.5	6.50	178.1	6.00	178.8
12	west	p	74.5	2.75	75.4	2.50	74.5
12	north	t	748.5	27.25	746.7	25.00	745.0
12	north	p	220.0	8.00	219.2	7.50	223.5
12	north	p	297.5	10.75	294.6	10.00	298.0
12	north	p	231.0	8.50	232.9	7.75	231.0
12	south	t	735.0	26.75	733.0	24.75	737.6
12	south	p	176.0	6.50	178.1	6.00	178.8
12	south	p	359.0	13.00	356.2	12.00	357.6
12	south	p	200.0	7.25	198.7	6.75	201.2
12	east	t	876.0	32.00	876.8	29.50	879.1
12	east	p	717.0	26.25	719.3	24.00	715.2
12	east	p	105.0	3.75	102.8	3.50	104.3
12	east	p	54.0	2.00	54.8	1.75	52.2
13	west	t	377.0	13.75	376.8	12.75	380.0
13	north	t	428.5	15.75	431.6	14.50	432.1
13	north	p	131.5	4.75	130.2	4.50	134.1
13	north	p	164.0	6.00	164.4	5.50	163.9
13	north	p	133.0	4.75	130.2	4.50	134.1
13	south	t	425.5	15.50	424.7	14.25	424.7
13	south	p	339.5	12.50	342.5	11.50	342.7
13	south	p	86.0	3.25	89.1	3.00	89.4
13	east	t	386.0	14.00	383.6	13.00	387.4
14	width	t	464.0	17.00	465.8	15.50	461.9
14	length	t	425.0	15.50	424.7	14.25	424.7
14	west	t	475.5	17.25	472.7	16.00	476.8
14	west	p	312.0	11.50	315.1	10.50	312.9
14	west	p	97.0	3.50	95.9	3.25	96.9
14	west	p	65.5	2.50	68.5	2.25	67.1
14	north	t	426.5	15.50	424.7	14.25	424.7

Casa dell'Atrio a Mosaico (IV 1-2) Garden and terrace

Room	where?	kind	in cm	O.ft (27.4)	ideal	R.ft (29.8)	ideal
14	north	p	341.5	12.50	342.5	11.50	342.7
14	north	p	85.5	3.00	82.2	2.75	82.0
14	south	t	425.5	15.50	424.7	14.25	424.7
14	south	p	66.5	2.50	68.5	2.25	67.1
14	south	p	178.5	6.50	178.1	6.00	178.8
14	south	p	180.5	6.50	178.1	6.00	178.8
14	east	t	452.5	16.50	452.1	15.25	454.5
14	east	p	304.0	11.00	301.4	10.25	305.5
14	east	p	89.0	3.25	89.1	3.00	89.4
14	east	p	59.5	2.25	61.7	2.00	59.6
15	length	t	343.0	12.50	342.5	11.50	342.7
15	length	p	183.5	6.75	185.0	6.25	186.3
15	length	p	159.5	5.75	157.6	5.25	156.5
15	west	t	794.5	29.00	794.6	26.75	797.2
15	west	p	110.0	4.00	109.6	3.75	111.8
15	west	p	684.5	25.00	685.0	23.00	685.4
15	north	t	331.0	12.00	328.8	11.00	327.8
15	south	t	133.0	4.75	130.2	4.50	134.1
15	east	t	796.0	29.00	794.6	26.75	797.2
16	width	t	360.0	13.25	363.1	12.00	357.6
16	width	p	133.0	4.75	130.2	4.50	134.1
16	width	p	227.0	8.25	226.1	7.50	223.5
16	length	t	112.5	4.00	109.6	3.75	111.8
16	west	t	367.0	13.50	369.9	12.25	365.1
16	west	p	249.0	9.00	246.6	8.25	245.9
16	west	p	53.0	2.00	54.8	1.75	52.2
16	west	p	90.0	3.25	89.1	3.00	89.4
16	west	p	106.0	3.75	102.8	3.50	104.3
16	west	p	118.0	4.25	116.5	4.00	119.2
16	north	t	132.0	4.75	130.2	4.50	134.1
16	south	t	349.5	12.75	349.4	11.75	350.2
16	east	t	362.0	13.25	363.1	12.25	365.1
17	west	t	684.0	25.00	685.0	23.00	685.4
17	west	p	521.0	19.00	520.6	17.50	521.5
17	west	p	101.0	3.75	102.8	3.50	104.3
17	west	p	62.0	2.25	61.7	2.00	59.6
17	north	t	240.0	8.75	239.8	8.00	238.4
17	north	p	72.0	2.75	75.4	2.50	74.5
17	north	p	101.0	3.75	102.8	3.50	104.3
17	north	p	67.0	2.50	68.5	2.25	67.1
17	south	t	280.0	10.25	280.9	9.50	283.1
17	south	p	45.0	1.75	48.0	1.50	44.7
17	south	p	175.0	6.50	178.1	5.75	171.4

Casa dell'Atrio a Mosaico (IV 1-2) Garden and terrace

Room	where?	kind	in cm	O.ft (27.4)	ideal	R.ft (29.8)	ideal
17	south	p	62.0	2.25	61.7	2.00	59.6
17	east	t	683.5	25.00	685.0	23.00	685.4
17	east	p	433.5	15.75	431.6	14.50	432.1
17	east	p	177.0	6.50	178.1	6.00	178.8
17	east	p	73.0	2.75	75.4	2.50	74.5
18	west	t	685.0	25.00	685.0	23.00	685.4
18	north	t	371.0	13.50	369.9	12.50	372.5
18	south	t	379.0	13.75	376.8	12.75	380.0
18	south	p	114.0	4.25	116.5	3.75	111.8
18	south	p	174.0	6.25	171.3	5.75	171.4
18	south	p	91.0	3.25	89.1	3.00	89.4
18	east	t	686.5	25.00	685.0	23.00	685.4
18	east	p	520.5	19.00	520.6	17.50	521.5
18	east	p	102.0	3.75	102.8	3.50	104.3
18	east	p	64.0	2.25	61.7	2.25	67.1
19	length	p	148.5	5.50	150.7	5.00	149.0
19	length	t	321.0	11.75	322.0	10.75	320.4
19	length	p	172.5	6.25	171.3	5.75	171.4
19	west	t	1120.5	41.00	1123.4	37.50	1117.5
19	north	t	110.0	4.00	109.6	3.75	111.8
19	south	t	326.0	12.00	328.8	11.00	327.8
19	east	t	1063.0	38.75	1061.8	35.75	1065.4
19	east	p	770.0	28.00	767.2	25.75	767.4
19	east	p	148.0	5.50	150.7	5.00	149.0
19	east	p	145.0	5.25	143.9	4.75	141.6
20	west	t	148.0	5.50	150.7	5.00	149.0
20	north	t	658.0	24.00	657.6	22.00	655.6
20	north	p	47.0	1.75	48.0	1.50	44.7
20	north	p	71.0	2.50	68.5	2.50	74.5
20	north	p	398.0	14.50	397.3	13.25	394.9
20	north	p	142.0	5.25	143.9	4.75	141.6
20	south	t	677.0	24.75	678.2	22.75	678.0
20	south	p	512.5	18.75	513.8	17.25	514.1
20	south	p	94.5	3.50	95.9	3.25	96.9
20	south	p	70.0	2.50	68.5	2.25	67.1
20	east	t	137.0	5.00	137.0	4.50	134.1
20	east	p	108.0	4.00	109.6	3.50	104.3
20	east	p	29.0	1.00	27.4	1.00	29.8
21	length	t	1680.0	61.25	1678.3	56.50	1683.7
21	west	t	337.0	12.25	335.7	11.25	335.3
21	west	p	155.0	5.75	157.6	5.25	156.5
21	west	p	59.0	2.25	61.7	2.00	59.6
21	west	p	95.0	3.50	95.9	3.25	96.9

Casa dell'Atrio a Mosaico (IV 1-2) Garden and terrace

Room	where?	kind	in cm	O.ft (27.4)	ideal	R.ft (29.8)	ideal
21	west	p	28.0	1.00	27.4	1.00	29.8
21	north	t	1672.0	61.00	1671.4	56.00	1668.8
21	north	p	170.0	6.25	171.3	5.75	171.4
21	north	p	181.0	6.50	178.1	6.00	178.8
21	north	p	175.0	6.50	178.1	5.75	171.4
21	north	p	290.0	10.50	287.7	9.75	290.6
21	north	p	357.0	13.00	356.2	12.00	357.6
21	north	p	325.0	11.75	322.0	11.00	327.8
21	north	p	174.0	6.25	171.3	5.75	171.4
21	south	t	1704.0	62.25	1705.7	57.25	1706.1
21	south	p	306.0	11.25	308.3	10.25	305.5
21	south	p	281.0	10.25	280.9	9.50	283.1
21	south	p	216.0	8.00	219.2	7.25	216.1
21	south	p	32.0	1.25	34.3	1.00	29.8
21	south	p	400.0	14.50	397.3	13.50	402.3
21	south	p	36.0	1.25	34.3	1.25	37.3
21	south	p	247.0	9.00	246.6	8.25	245.9
21	south	p	186.0	6.75	185.0	6.25	186.3
21	east	t	331.5	12.00	328.8	11.00	327.8
21	east	p	112.5	4.00	109.6	3.75	111.8
21	east	p	69.0	2.50	68.5	2.25	67.1
21	east	p	95.0	3.50	95.9	3.25	96.9
21	east	p	55.0	2.00	54.8	1.75	52.2
22	width	t	280.5	10.25	280.9	9.50	283.1
22	length	p	338.0	12.25	335.7	11.25	335.3
22	west	t	308.0	11.25	308.3	10.25	305.5
22	west	p	48.0	1.75	48.0	1.50	44.7
22	west	p	85.0	3.00	82.2	2.75	82.0
22	west	p	100.5	3.75	102.8	3.25	96.9
22	west	p	74.5	2.75	75.4	2.50	74.5
22	north	t	1704.0	62.25	1705.7	57.25	1706.1
22	south	t	2460.0	89.75	2459.2	82.50	2458.5
22	south	p	38.0	1.50	41.1	1.25	37.3
22	south	p	2397.0	87.50	2397.5	80.50	2398.9
22	south	p	25.0	1.00	27.4	0.75	22.4
22	east	t	283.5	10.25	280.9	9.50	283.1
22	east	p	37.5	1.25	34.3	1.25	37.3
22	east	p	81.0	3.00	82.2	2.75	82.0
22	east	p	52.0	2.00	54.8	1.75	52.2
22	east	p	113.0	4.00	109.6	3.75	111.8
23	west	t	312.0	11.50	315.1	10.50	312.9
23	west	p	28.5	1.00	27.4	1.00	29.8
23	west	p	92.5	3.50	95.9	3.00	89.4

Casa dell'Atrio a Mosaico (IV 1-2) Garden and terrace

Room	where?	kind	in cm	O.ft (27.4)	ideal	R.ft (29.8)	ideal
23	west	p	91.0	3.25	89.1	3.00	89.4
23	west	p	86.0	3.25	89.1	3.00	89.4
23	west	p	14.0	0.50	13.7	0.50	14.9
23	north	t	307.0	11.25	308.3	10.25	305.5
23	south	t	289.0	10.50	287.7	9.75	290.6
23	south	p	112.0	4.00	109.6	3.75	111.8
23	south	p	123.5	4.50	123.3	4.25	126.7
23	south	p	53.5	2.00	54.8	1.75	52.2
23	east	t	313.0	11.50	315.1	10.50	312.9
24	length	t	368.5	13.50	369.9	12.25	365.1
24	length	t	353.0	13.00	356.2	11.75	350.2
24	west	t	326.0	12.00	328.8	11.00	327.8
24	north	t	292.0	10.75	294.6	9.75	290.6
24	south	t	317.0	11.50	315.1	10.75	320.4
24	south	p	64.0	2.25	61.7	2.25	67.1
24	south	p	121.0	4.50	123.3	4.00	119.2
24	south	p	132.0	4.75	130.2	4.50	134.1
24	east	t	340.0	12.50	342.5	11.50	342.7
24	east	p	20.5	0.75	20.6	0.75	22.4
24	east	p	95.5	3.50	95.9	3.25	96.9
24	east	p	72.0	2.75	75.4	2.50	74.5
24	east	p	88.0	3.25	89.1	3.00	89.4
24	east	p	64.0	2.25	61.7	2.25	67.1
25	west	t	315.0	11.50	315.1	10.50	312.9
25	north	t	1681.5	61.25	1678.3	56.50	1683.7
25	north	p	492.0	18.00	493.2	16.50	491.7
25	north	p	151.5	5.50	150.7	5.00	149.0
25	north	p	235.5	8.50	232.9	8.00	238.4
25	north	p	147.5	5.50	150.7	5.00	149.0
25	north	p	515.5	18.75	513.8	17.25	514.1
25	north	p	110.0	4.00	109.6	3.75	111.8
25	north	p	29.0	1.00	27.4	1.00	29.8
25	south	t	1248.0	45.50	1246.7	42.00	1251.6
25	south	p	41.0	1.50	41.1	1.50	44.7
25	south	p	241.0	8.75	239.8	8.00	238.4
25	south	p	229.0	8.25	226.1	7.75	231.0
25	south	p	249.0	9.00	246.6	8.25	245.9
25	south	p	278.0	10.25	280.9	9.25	275.7
25	south	p	210.0	7.75	212.4	7.00	208.6
25	east	t	311.0	11.25	308.3	10.50	312.9
26	west	t	2813.0	102.75	2815.4	94.50	2816.1
26	north	t	315.0	11.50	315.1	10.50	312.9
26	south	t	328.0	12.00	328.8	11.00	327.8

Casa dell'Atrio a Mosaico (IV 1-2) Garden and terrace

Room	where?	kind	in cm	O.ft (27.4)	ideal	R.ft (29.8)	ideal
26	east	t	1929.0	70.50	1931.7	64.75	1929.6
26	east	p	333.0	12.25	335.7	11.25	335.3
26	east	p	321.0	11.75	322.0	10.75	320.4
26	east	p	324.0	11.75	322.0	10.75	320.4
26	east	p	327.5	12.00	328.8	11.00	327.8
26	east	p	310.0	11.25	308.3	10.50	312.9
26	east	p	313.5	11.50	315.1	10.50	312.9
27	width	t	422.0	15.50	424.7	14.25	424.7
27	width	t	408.0	15.00	411.0	13.75	409.8
27	west	t	489.0	17.75	486.4	16.50	491.7
27	north	t	1290.0	47.00	1287.8	43.25	1288.9
27	north	p	452.0	16.50	452.1	15.25	454.5
27	north	p	432.0	15.75	431.6	14.50	432.1
27	north	p	406.0	14.75	404.2	13.50	402.3
27	south	t	1743.0	63.50	1739.9	58.50	1743.3
27	south	p	69.5	2.50	68.5	2.25	67.1
27	south	p	298.5	11.00	301.4	10.00	298.0
27	south	p	87.0	3.25	89.1	3.00	89.4
27	south	p	135.0	5.00	137.0	4.50	134.1
27	south	p	277.0	10.00	274.0	9.25	275.7
27	south	p	294.0	10.75	294.6	9.75	290.6
27	south	p	424.0	15.50	424.7	14.25	424.7
27	south	p	158.0	5.75	157.6	5.25	156.5
27	east	t	376.5	13.75	376.8	12.75	380.0
28	west	t	699.0	25.50	698.7	23.50	700.3
28	north	t	124.0	4.50	123.3	4.25	126.7
28	south	t	115.0	4.25	116.5	3.75	111.8
28	east	t	1014.0	37.00	1013.8	34.00	1013.2
28	east	p	132.0	4.75	130.2	4.50	134.1
28	east	p	132.0	4.75	130.2	4.50	134.1
28	east	p	309.5	11.25	308.3	10.50	312.9
28	east	p	132.5	4.75	130.2	4.50	134.1
28	east	p	198.0	7.25	198.7	6.75	201.2
28	east	p	110.0	4.00	109.6	3.75	111.8
29	west	t	578.0	21.00	575.4	19.50	581.1
29	north	t	103.5	3.75	102.8	3.50	104.3
29	south	t	107.0	4.00	109.6	3.50	104.3
29	east	t	978.0	35.75	979.6	32.75	976.0
29	east	p	166.0	6.00	164.4	5.50	163.9
29	east	p	133.0	4.75	130.2	4.50	134.1
29	east	p	324.0	11.75	322.0	10.75	320.4
29	east	p	132.0	4.75	130.2	4.50	134.1
29	east	p	119.0	4.25	116.5	4.00	119.2

Casa dell'Atrio a Mosaico (IV 1-2) Garden and terrace

Room	where?	kind	in cm	O.ft (27.4)	ideal	R.ft (29.8)	ideal
29	east	p	104.0	3.75	102.8	3.50	104.3
30	width	p	427.0	15.50	424.7	14.25	424.7
30	width	p	425.0	15.50	424.7	14.25	424.7
30	length	t	1202.0	43.75	1198.8	40.25	1199.5
30	length	p	557.0	20.25	554.9	18.75	558.8
30	length	p	173.0	6.25	171.3	5.75	171.4
30	length	p	326.0	12.00	328.8	11.00	327.8
30	length	p	146.0	5.25	143.9	5.00	149.0
30	length	t	1211.0	44.25	1212.5	40.75	1214.4
30	length	p	575.0	21.00	575.4	19.25	573.7
30	length	p	169.0	6.25	171.3	5.75	171.4
30	length	p	319.0	11.75	322.0	10.75	320.4
30	length	p	148.0	5.50	150.7	5.00	149.0

Casa dell'Alcova (IV 3-4) Lot IV B

Room	where?	kind	in cm	O.ft (27.5)	ideal	R.ft (29.5)	ideal
17	west	t	783.5	28.50	783.8	26.50	781.8
17	west	p	84.0	3.00	82.5	2.75	81.1
17	west	p	126.0	4.50	123.8	4.25	125.4
17	west	p	197.0	7.25	199.4	6.75	199.1
17	west	p	294.0	10.75	295.6	10.00	295.0
17	west	p	82.5	3.00	82.5	2.75	81.1
17	north	t	427.0	15.50	426.3	14.50	427.8
17	north	p	114.5	4.25	116.9	4.00	118.0
17	north	p	190.0	7.00	192.5	6.50	191.8
17	north	p	95.5	3.50	96.3	3.25	95.9
17	south	t	423.0	15.50	426.3	14.25	420.4
17	east	t	773.0	28.00	770.0	26.25	774.4
17	east	p	152.0	5.50	151.3	5.25	154.9
17	east	p	284.0	10.25	281.9	9.75	287.6
17	east	p	189.0	6.75	185.6	6.50	191.8
17	east	p	148.0	5.50	151.3	5.00	147.5
18	west	t	291.0	10.50	288.8	9.75	287.6
18	west	p	44.5	1.50	41.3	1.50	44.3
18	west	p	55.5	2.00	55.0	2.00	59.0
18	west	p	86.0	3.25	89.4	3.00	88.5
18	west	p	56.5	2.00	55.0	2.00	59.0
18	west	p	48.5	1.75	48.1	1.75	51.6
18	north	t	455.0	16.50	453.8	15.50	457.3
18	south	t	461.5	16.75	460.6	15.75	464.6
18	south	p	343.0	12.50	343.8	11.75	346.6
18	south	p	97.0	3.50	96.3	3.25	95.9
18	south	p	21.5	0.75	20.6	0.75	22.1
18	east	t	295.0	10.75	295.6	10.00	295.0
18	east	p	89.5	3.25	89.4	3.00	88.5
18	east	p	119.5	4.25	116.9	4.00	118.0
18	east	p	86.0	3.25	89.4	3.00	88.5
19	west	t	450.0	16.25	446.9	15.25	449.9
19	west	p	70.0	2.50	68.8	2.25	66.4
19	west	p	90.0	3.25	89.4	3.00	88.5
19	west	p	130.5	4.75	130.6	4.50	132.8
19	west	p	81.5	3.00	82.5	2.75	81.1
19	west	p	78.0	2.75	75.6	2.75	81.1
19	north	t	457.5	16.75	460.6	15.50	457.3
19	north	p	339.5	12.25	336.9	11.50	339.3
19	north	p	95.5	3.50	96.3	3.25	95.9
19	north	p	22.5	0.75	20.6	0.75	22.1
19	south	t	468.5	17.00	467.5	16.00	472.0
19	east	t	453.5	16.50	453.8	15.25	449.9

Casa dell'Alcova (IV 3-4) Lot IV B

Room	where?	kind	in cm	O.ft (27.5)	ideal	R.ft (29.5)	ideal
19	east	p	85.0	3.00	82.5	3.00	88.5
19	east	p	284.0	10.25	281.9	9.75	287.6
19	east	p	84.5	3.00	82.5	2.75	81.1
20	west	t	591.0	21.50	591.3	20.00	590.0
20	west	p	157.0	5.75	158.1	5.25	154.9
20	west	p	285.0	10.25	281.9	9.75	287.6
20	west	p	149.0	5.50	151.3	5.00	147.5
20	north	t	850.0	31.00	852.5	28.75	848.1
20	south	t	858.0	31.25	859.4	29.00	855.5
20	south	p	63.0	2.25	61.9	2.25	66.4
20	south	p	131.5	4.75	130.6	4.50	132.8
20	south	p	663.5	24.25	666.9	22.50	663.8
20	east	t	592.0	21.50	591.3	20.00	590.0
21	west	t	148.0	5.50	151.3	5.00	147.5
21	north	t	1497.0	54.50	1498.8	50.75	1497.1
21	north	p	102.0	3.75	103.1	3.50	103.3
21	north	p	131.5	4.75	130.6	4.50	132.8
21	north	p	663.5	24.25	666.9	22.50	663.8
21	north	p	68.0	2.50	68.8	2.25	66.4
21	north	p	105.5	3.75	103.1	3.50	103.3
21	north	p	28.5	1.00	27.5	1.00	29.5
21	north	p	108.0	4.00	110.0	3.75	110.6
21	north	p	28.5	1.00	27.5	1.00	29.5
21	north	p	105.0	3.75	103.1	3.50	103.3
21	north	p	23.5	0.75	20.6	0.75	22.1
21	north	p	133.0	4.75	130.6	4.50	132.8
21	south	t	1498.5	54.50	1498.8	50.75	1497.1
21	east	t	132.0	4.75	130.6	4.50	132.8
22	width	t	136.5	5.00	137.5	4.75	140.1
22	west	t	238.0	8.75	240.6	8.00	236.0
22	north	t	563.0	20.50	563.8	19.00	560.5
22	north	p	43.0	1.50	41.3	1.50	44.3
22	north	p	287.0	10.50	288.8	9.75	287.6
22	north	p	69.0	2.50	68.8	2.25	66.4
22	north	p	41.0	1.50	41.3	1.50	44.3
22	north	p	131.0	4.75	130.6	4.50	132.8
22	south	t	558.0	20.25	556.9	19.00	560.5
22	south	p	28.5	1.00	27.5	1.00	29.5
22	south	p	105.0	3.75	103.1	3.50	103.3
22	south	p	29.0	1.00	27.5	1.00	29.5
22	south	p	109.0	4.00	110.0	3.75	110.6
22	south	p	27.5	1.00	27.5	1.00	29.5
22	south	p	105.5	3.75	103.1	3.50	103.3

Casa dell'Alcova (IV 3-4) Lot IV B

Room	where?	kind	in cm	O.ft (27.5)	ideal	R.ft (29.5)	ideal
22	south	p	24.5	1.00	27.5	0.75	22.1
22	south	p	129.0	4.75	130.6	4.25	125.4
22	east	t	265.5	9.75	268.1	9.00	265.5
22	east	p	125.0	4.50	123.8	4.25	125.4
22	east	p	26.5	1.00	27.5	1.00	29.5
22	east	p	90.0	3.25	89.4	3.00	88.5
22	east	p	24.0	0.75	20.6	0.75	22.1
23	length	t	307.5	11.25	309.4	10.50	309.8
23	west	t	342.0	12.50	343.8	11.50	339.3
23	west	p	261.5	9.50	261.3	8.75	258.1
23	west	p	80.5	3.00	82.5	2.75	81.1
23	north	t	306.0	11.25	309.4	10.25	302.4
23	south	p	92.5	3.25	89.4	3.25	95.9
23	south	p	178.0	6.50	178.8	6.00	177.0
23	south	t	306.5	11.25	309.4	10.50	309.8
23	south	p	36.5	1.25	34.4	1.25	36.9
23	east	t	335.5	12.25	336.9	11.25	331.9
24	width	t	441.0	16.00	440.0	15.00	442.5
24	length	t	361.5	13.25	364.4	12.25	361.4
24	west	t	340.5	12.50	343.8	11.50	339.3
24	north	t	359.0	13.00	357.5	12.25	361.4
24	south	p	68.0	2.50	68.8	2.25	66.4
24	south	p	233.0	8.50	233.8	8.00	236.0
24	south	t	369.0	13.50	371.3	12.50	368.8
24	east	t	344.0	12.50	343.8	11.75	346.6
24	east	p	263.0	9.50	261.3	9.00	265.5
24	east	p	81.0	3.00	82.5	2.75	81.1

Casa dell'Alcova (IV 3-4) Lot IV C

Room	where?	kind	in cm	O.ft (27.5)	ideal
1	west	t	270.5	9.75	268.1
1	west	p	109.0	4.00	110.0
1	west	p	45.0	1.75	48.1
1	west	p	116.5	4.25	116.9
1	north	t	205.0	7.50	206.3
1	south	t	200.0	7.25	199.4
1	south	p	105.0	3.75	103.1
1	south	p	95.0	3.50	96.3
1	east	t	271.0	9.75	268.1
1	east	p	197.0	7.25	199.4
1	east	p	74.0	2.75	75.6
2	west	t	265.0	9.75	268.1
2	west	p	120.0	4.25	116.9
2	west	p	145.0	5.25	144.4
2	north	t	245.0	9.00	247.5
2	north	p	135.0	5.00	137.5
2	north	p	72.0	2.50	68.8
2	north	p	38.0	1.50	41.3
2	south	t	195.0	7.00	192.5
2	east	t	277.0	10.00	275.0
3	length	t	291.0	10.50	288.8
3	west	t	782.5	28.50	783.8
3	west	p	165.0	6.00	165.0
3	west	p	108.0	4.00	110.0
3	west	p	35.5	1.25	34.4
3	west	p	154.5	5.50	151.3
3	west	p	169.5	6.25	171.9
3	west	p	150.0	5.50	151.3
3	north	t	281.0	10.25	281.9
3	south	p	44.0	1.50	41.3
3	south	p	190.0	7.00	192.5
3	east	t	789.0	28.75	790.6
3	east	p	71.0	2.50	68.8
3	east	p	126.0	4.50	123.8
3	east	p	128.0	4.75	130.6
3	east	p	207.0	7.50	206.3
3	east	p	206.0	7.50	206.3
3	east	p	51.0	1.75	48.1
4	length	t	282.0	10.25	281.9
4	west	t	277.5	10.00	275.0
4	north	t	284.5	10.25	281.9
4	south	t	326.5	11.75	323.1
4	east	t	272.0	10.00	275.0

Casa dell'Alcova (IV 3-4) Lot IV C

Room	where?	kind	in cm	O.ft (27.5)	ideal
4	east	p	171.0	6.25	171.9
4	east	p	101.0	3.75	103.1
5	length	t	313.0	11.50	316.3
5	west	t	276.5	10.00	275.0
5	north	t	308.5	11.25	309.4
5	east	t	286.0	10.50	288.8
5	east	p	139.5	5.00	137.5
5	east	p	146.5	5.25	144.4
6	west	t	324.0	11.75	323.1
6	west	p	72.0	2.50	68.8
6	west	p	125.5	4.50	123.8
6	west	p	71.5	2.50	68.8
6	west	p	55.0	2.00	55.0
6	north	t	478.0	17.50	481.3
6	south	t	484.0	17.50	481.3
6	east	t	312.5	11.25	309.4
6	east	p	106.5	3.75	103.1
6	east	p	96.0	3.50	96.3
6	east	p	110.0	4.00	110.0
7	width	t	473.5	17.25	474.4
7	west	t	483.0	17.50	481.3
7	west	p	15.0	0.50	13.8
7	west	p	153.5	5.50	151.3
7	west	p	314.5	11.50	316.3
7	north	t	682.0	24.75	680.6
7	north	p	28.0	1.00	27.5
7	north	p	119.5	4.25	116.9
7	north	p	325.5	11.75	323.1
7	north	p	84.5	3.00	82.5
7	north	p	45.5	1.75	48.1
7	north	p	79.0	2.75	75.6
7	south	t	680.5	24.75	680.6
7	east	t	451.0	16.50	453.8
7	east	p	103.5	3.75	103.1
7	east	p	96.5	3.50	96.3
7	east	p	69.0	2.50	68.8
7	east	p	182.5	6.75	185.6
8	west	t	262.5	9.50	261.3
8	west	p	109.0	4.00	110.0
8	west	p	96.5	3.50	96.3
8	west	p	57.0	2.00	55.0
8	north	t	434.0	15.75	433.1
8	south	t	434.5	15.75	433.1

Casa dell'Alcova (IV 3-4) Lot IV C

Room	where?	kind	in cm	O.ft (27.5)	ideal
8	south	p	26.0	1.00	27.5
8	south	p	120.0	4.25	116.9
8	south	p	288.5	10.50	288.8
8	east	t	269.0	9.75	268.1
9	width	t	270.5	9.75	268.1
9	west	t	302.0	11.00	302.5
9	north	t	214.5	7.75	213.1
9	south	t	209.0	7.50	206.3
9	south	p	85.0	3.00	82.5
9	south	p	45.0	1.75	48.1
9	south	p	79.0	2.75	75.6
9	east	t	324.0	11.75	323.1
10	west	t	286.5	10.50	288.8
10	west	p	32.5	1.25	34.4
10	west	p	72.0	2.50	68.8
10	west	p	181.0	6.50	178.8
10	north	t	217.0	8.00	220.0
10	south	t	225.5	8.25	226.9
10	east	t	294.0	10.75	295.6
11	west	t	162.0	6.00	165.0
11	north	t	798.0	29.00	797.5
11	north	p	165.5	6.00	165.0
11	north	p	110.0	4.00	110.0
11	north	p	83.5	3.00	82.5
11	north	p	115.0	4.25	116.9
11	north	p	81.5	3.00	82.5
11	north	p	87.0	3.25	89.4
11	north	p	52.0	2.00	55.0
11	north	p	68.5	2.50	68.8
11	north	p	35.0	1.25	34.4
11	south	t	591.0	21.50	591.3
11	south	p	271.5	9.75	268.1
11	south	p	256.5	9.25	254.4
11	south	p	63.0	2.25	61.9
11	east	t	152.0	5.50	151.3
12	west	t	300.0	11.00	302.5
12	north	t	302.0	11.00	302.5
12	north	p	20.0	0.75	20.6
12	north	p	257.0	9.25	254.4
12	north	p	25.0	1.00	27.5
12	south	t	304.5	11.00	302.5
12	east	t	302.0	11.00	302.5
13	west	t	268.0	9.75	268.1

Casa dell'Alcova (IV 3-4) Lot IV C

Room	where?	kind	in cm	O.ft (27.5)	ideal
13	north	t	327.0	12.00	330.0
13	south	t	327.0	12.00	330.0
13	south	p	162.0	6.00	165.0
13	south	p	111.0	4.00	110.0
13	south	p	54.0	2.00	55.0
13	east	t	268.5	9.75	268.1
14	west	t	301.5	11.00	302.5
14	north	t	276.5	10.00	275.0
14	south	t	280.5	10.25	281.9
14	south	p	110.0	4.00	110.0
14	south	p	83.0	3.00	82.5
14	south	p	87.5	3.25	89.4
14	east	t	300.0	11.00	302.5
15	west	t	268.5	9.75	268.1
15	north	t	127.5	4.75	130.6
15	south	t	126.0	4.50	123.8
15	south	p	37.0	1.25	34.4
15	south	p	67.0	2.50	68.8
15	south	p	22.0	0.75	20.6
15	east	t	269.5	9.75	268.1
16	west	t	422.5	15.25	419.4
16	west	p	249.0	9.00	247.5
16	west	p	141.0	5.25	144.4
16	west	p	32.5	1.25	34.4
16	north	t	472.0	17.25	474.4
16	south	t	481.0	17.50	481.3
16	east	t	417.0	15.25	419.4
25	west	t	168.5	6.25	171.9
25	north	t	618.0	22.50	618.8
25	north	p	155.0	5.75	158.1
25	north	p	94.5	3.50	96.3
25	north	p	368.5	13.50	371.3
25	south	t	628.0	22.75	625.6
25	south	p	135.5	5.00	137.5
25	south	p	67.5	2.50	68.8
25	south	p	425.0	15.50	426.3
25	east	t	158.5	5.75	158.1
26	west	t	457.5	16.75	460.6
26	west	p	207.0	7.50	206.3
26	west	p	208.0	7.50	206.3
26	west	p	42.5	1.50	41.3
26	north	t	470.0	17.00	467.5
26	south	t	459.0	16.75	460.6

Casa dell'Alcova (IV 3-4) Lot IV C

Room	where?	kind	in cm	O.ft (27.5)	ideal
26	east	t	470.0	17.00	467.5
26	east	p	154.5	5.50	151.3
26	east	p	315.5	11.50	316.3
27	length	t	202.0	7.25	199.4
27	length	p	166.5	6.00	165.0
27	length	p	35.5	1.25	34.4
27	west	t	339.0	12.25	336.9
27	west	p	29.0	1.00	27.5
27	west	p	244.0	8.75	240.6
27	west	p	66.0	2.50	68.8
27	north	t	204.0	7.50	206.3
27	south	t	170.0	6.25	171.9
27	east	t	491.5	17.75	488.1
27	east	p	39.5	1.50	41.3
27	east	p	143.0	5.25	144.4
27	east	p	73.0	2.75	75.6
27	east	p	236.0	8.50	233.8

Casa della Fullonica (IV 5-7)

Room	where?	kind	in cm	O.ft (27.55)	ideal	R.ft (29.5)	ideal
0	south	t	2618.5	95.00	2617.3	88.75	2618.1
1	west	t	478.0	17.25	475.2	16.25	479.4
1	west	p	361.0	13.00	358.2	12.25	361.4
1	west	p	117.0	4.25	117.1	4.00	118.0
1	north	t	297.0	10.75	296.2	10.00	295.0
1	south	t	298.0	10.75	296.2	10.00	295.0
1	east	t	486.0	17.75	489.0	16.50	486.8
2	west	t	133.5	4.75	130.9	4.50	132.8
2	north	t	319.0	11.50	316.8	10.75	317.1
2	north	p	38.5	1.50	41.3	1.25	36.9
2	north	p	280.5	10.25	282.4	9.50	280.3
2	south	t	322.0	11.75	323.7	11.00	324.5
2	east	t	136.5	5.00	137.8	4.75	140.1
3	west	t	97.5	3.50	96.4	3.25	95.9
3	north	t	369.0	13.50	371.9	12.50	368.8
3	north	p	334.5	12.25	337.5	11.25	331.9
3	north	p	34.5	1.25	34.4	1.25	36.9
3	east	t	103.0	3.75	103.3	3.50	103.3
4	west	t	264.0	9.50	261.7	9.00	265.5
4	north	t	328.0	12.00	330.6	11.00	324.5
4	south	t	333.0	12.00	330.6	11.25	331.9
4	east	t	277.5	10.00	275.5	9.50	280.3
5	west	t	233.5	8.50	234.2	8.00	236.0
5	north	t	524.0	19.00	523.5	17.75	523.6
5	south	t	524.0	19.00	523.5	17.75	523.6
5	south	p	288.5	10.50	289.3	9.75	287.6
5	south	p	100.5	3.75	103.3	3.50	103.3
5	south	p	135.0	5.00	137.8	4.50	132.8
5	east	t	242.5	8.75	241.1	8.25	243.4
6	length	t	475.0	17.25	475.2	16.00	472.0
6	west	t	410.0	15.00	413.3	14.00	413.0
6	west	p	298.5	10.75	296.2	10.00	295.0
6	west	p	111.5	4.00	110.2	3.75	110.6
6	north	t	474.5	17.25	475.2	16.00	472.0
6	south	t	516.0	18.75	516.6	17.50	516.3
6	east	t	425.0	15.50	427.0	14.50	427.8
7	length	t	523.0	19.00	523.5	17.75	523.6
7	west	t	341.5	12.50	344.4	11.50	339.3
7	west	p	123.5	4.50	124.0	4.25	125.4
7	west	p	108.0	4.00	110.2	3.75	110.6
7	west	p	110.0	4.00	110.2	3.75	110.6
7	north	t	475.0	17.25	475.2	16.00	472.0
7	south	t	494.5	18.00	495.9	16.75	494.1

Casa della Fullonica (IV 5-7)

Room	where?	kind	in cm	O.ft (27.55)	ideal	R.ft (29.5)	ideal
7	east	t	332.5	12.00	330.6	11.25	331.9
8	impl(w)	t	505.0	18.25	502.8	17.00	501.5
8	impl(w)	p	139.0	5.00	137.8	4.75	140.1
8	impl(w)	p	147.0	5.25	144.6	5.00	147.5
8	impl(w)	p	219.0	8.00	220.4	7.50	221.3
8	impl(w)	t	511.5	18.50	509.7	17.25	508.9
8	impl(w)	p	140.0	5.00	137.8	4.75	140.1
8	impl(w)	p	148.0	5.25	144.6	5.00	147.5
8	impl(w)	p	223.5	8.00	220.4	7.50	221.3
8	impl(l)	t	876.0	31.75	874.7	29.75	877.6
8	impl(l)	p	648.5	23.50	647.4	22.00	649.0
8	impl(l)	p	227.5	8.25	227.3	7.75	228.6
8	impl(l)	t	870.0	31.50	867.8	29.50	870.3
8	impl(l)	p	422.0	15.25	420.1	14.25	420.4
8	impl(l)	p	224.0	8.25	227.3	7.50	221.3
8	impl(l)	p	224.0	8.25	227.3	7.50	221.3
8	west	t	506.0	18.25	502.8	17.25	508.9
8	west	p	403.0	14.75	406.4	13.75	405.6
8	west	p	103.0	3.75	103.3	3.50	103.3
8	north	t	880.0	32.00	881.6	29.75	877.6
8	north	p	330.5	12.00	330.6	11.25	331.9
8	north	p	157.5	5.75	158.4	5.25	154.9
8	north	p	101.0	3.75	103.3	3.50	103.3
8	north	p	291.0	10.50	289.3	9.75	287.6
8	south	t	867.0	31.50	867.8	29.50	870.3
8	east	t	513.0	18.50	509.7	17.50	516.3
8	east	p	130.0	4.75	130.9	4.50	132.8
8	east	p	162.5	6.00	165.3	5.50	162.3
8	east	p	103.5	3.75	103.3	3.50	103.3
8	east	p	117.0	4.25	117.1	4.00	118.0
9	length	t	467.0	17.00	468.4	15.75	464.6
9	length	t	467.5	17.00	468.4	15.75	464.6
9	west	t	788.5	28.50	785.2	26.75	789.1
9	west	p	102.0	3.75	103.3	3.50	103.3
9	west	p	139.5	5.00	137.8	4.75	140.1
9	west	p	74.5	2.75	75.8	2.50	73.8
9	west	p	160.0	5.75	158.4	5.50	162.3
9	west	p	61.5	2.25	62.0	2.00	59.0
9	west	p	251.0	9.00	248.0	8.50	250.8
9	north	t	467.0	17.00	468.4	15.75	464.6
9	south	t	470.0	17.00	468.4	16.00	472.0
9	east	t	785.5	28.50	785.2	26.75	789.1
9	east	p	36.5	1.25	34.4	1.25	36.9

Casa della Fullonica (IV 5-7)

Room	where?	kind	in cm	O.ft (27.55)	ideal	R.ft (29.5)	ideal
9	east	p	96.0	3.50	96.4	3.25	95.9
9	east	p	397.5	14.50	399.5	13.50	398.3
9	east	p	158.0	5.75	158.4	5.25	154.9
9	east	p	97.5	3.50	96.4	3.25	95.9
10	west	t	280.0	10.25	282.4	9.50	280.3
10	north	t	326.0	11.75	323.7	11.00	324.5
10	south	t	331.5	12.00	330.6	11.25	331.9
10	east	t	283.5	10.25	282.4	9.50	280.3
11	west	t	166.0	6.00	165.3	5.75	169.6
11	north	t	375.5	13.75	378.8	12.75	376.1
11	south	t	381.0	13.75	378.8	13.00	383.5
11	east	t	160.0	5.75	158.4	5.50	162.3
12	west	t	283.0	10.25	282.4	9.50	280.3
12	west	p	179.0	6.50	179.1	6.00	177.0
12	west	p	104.0	3.75	103.3	3.50	103.3
12	north	t	295.0	10.75	296.2	10.00	295.0
12	south	t	350.0	12.75	351.3	11.75	346.6
12	south	p	39.5	1.50	41.3	1.25	36.9
12	south	p	310.5	11.25	309.9	10.50	309.8
12	east	t	274.5	10.00	275.5	9.25	272.9
12	east	p	255.0	9.25	254.8	8.75	258.1
12	east	p	19.5	0.75	20.7	0.75	22.1

Casa del Papiro Dipinto (IV 8-9)

Room	where?	kind	in cm	O.ft (27.85)	ideal	R.ft (29.5)	ideal
0	south	t	2063.0	74.00	2060.9	70.00	2065.0
1	west	t	242.0	8.75	243.7	8.25	243.4
1	north	t	276.0	10.00	278.5	9.25	272.9
1	south	t	278.0	10.00	278.5	9.50	280.3
1	east	t	278.5	10.00	278.5	9.50	280.3
2	west	t	369.5	13.25	369.0	12.50	368.8
2	west	p	75.0	2.75	76.6	2.50	73.8
2	west	p	294.5	10.50	292.4	10.00	295.0
2	north	t	203.0	7.25	201.9	7.00	206.5
2	south	t	200.0	7.25	201.9	6.75	199.1
2	east	t	383.0	13.75	382.9	13.00	383.5
2	east	p	154.0	5.50	153.2	5.25	154.9
2	east	p	29.0	1.00	27.9	1.00	29.5
2	east	p	200.0	7.25	201.9	6.75	199.1
3	width	t	348.5	12.50	348.1	11.75	346.6
3	width	p	87.0	3.00	83.6	3.00	88.5
3	width	p	261.5	9.50	264.6	8.75	258.1
3	length	t	375.0	13.50	376.0	12.75	376.1
3	length	p	253.0	9.00	250.7	8.50	250.8
3	length	p	29.0	1.00	27.9	1.00	29.5
3	length	p	93.0	3.25	90.5	3.25	95.9
3	west	t	390.5	14.00	389.9	13.25	390.9
3	north	t	378.0	13.50	376.0	12.75	376.1
3	south	t	380.0	13.75	382.9	13.00	383.5
3	south	p	245.0	8.75	243.7	8.25	243.4
3	south	p	28.0	1.00	27.9	1.00	29.5
3	south	p	107.0	3.75	104.4	3.75	110.6
3	east	t	350.5	12.50	348.1	12.00	354.0
4	west	t	358.0	12.75	355.1	12.25	361.4
4	north	t	348.0	12.50	348.1	11.75	346.6
4	south	t	340.0	12.25	341.2	11.50	339.3
4	east	t	399.5	14.25	396.9	13.50	398.3
4	east	p	126.0	4.50	125.3	4.25	125.4
4	east	p	97.0	3.50	97.5	3.25	95.9
4	east	p	176.5	6.25	174.1	6.00	177.0
5	west	t	283.0	10.25	285.5	9.50	280.3
5	west	p	126.5	4.50	125.3	4.25	125.4
5	west	p	97.5	3.50	97.5	3.25	95.9
5	west	p	59.0	2.00	55.7	2.00	59.0
5	north	t	236.0	8.50	236.7	8.00	236.0
5	south	t	249.5	9.00	250.7	8.50	250.8
5	south	p	33.0	1.25	34.8	1.00	29.5
5	south	p	178.0	6.50	181.0	6.00	177.0

Casa del Papiro Dipinto (IV 8-9)

Room	where?	kind	in cm	O.ft (27.85)	ideal	R.ft (29.5)	ideal
5	south	p	38.5	1.50	41.8	1.25	36.9
5	east	t	289.0	10.50	292.4	9.75	287.6
6	west	t	527.0	19.00	529.2	17.75	523.6
6	north	t	408.0	14.75	410.8	13.75	405.6
6	south	t	413.0	14.75	410.8	14.00	413.0
6	east	t	526.0	19.00	529.2	17.75	523.6
7	length	t	239.5	8.50	236.7	8.00	236.0
7	west	t	212.5	7.75	215.8	7.25	213.9
7	west	p	82.0	3.00	83.6	2.75	81.1
7	west	p	130.5	4.75	132.3	4.50	132.8
7	north	t	244.5	8.75	243.7	8.25	243.4
7	north	p	31.0	1.00	27.9	1.00	29.5
7	north	p	173.0	6.25	174.1	5.75	169.6
7	north	p	100.5	3.50	97.5	3.50	103.3
7	east	t	204.5	7.25	201.9	7.00	206.5
7	east	p	55.5	2.00	55.7	2.00	59.0
7	east	p	149.0	5.25	146.2	5.00	147.5
8	width	t	134.5	4.75	132.3	4.50	132.8
8	west	t	143.0	5.25	146.2	4.75	140.1
8	north	t	837.0	30.00	835.5	28.25	833.4
8	north	p	39.5	1.50	41.8	1.25	36.9
8	north	p	152.5	5.50	153.2	5.25	154.9
8	north	p	482.0	17.25	480.4	16.25	479.4
8	north	p	126.0	4.50	125.3	4.25	125.4
8	north	p	37.0	1.25	34.8	1.25	36.9
8	east	t	130.5	4.75	132.3	4.50	132.8
9	west	t	151.0	5.50	153.2	5.00	147.5
9	north	t	556.0	20.00	557.0	18.75	553.1
9	north	p	252.0	9.00	250.7	8.50	250.8
9	north	p	66.0	2.25	62.7	2.25	66.4
9	north	p	38.0	1.25	34.8	1.25	36.9
9	north	p	200.0	7.25	201.9	6.75	199.1
9	east	t	151.5	5.50	153.2	5.25	154.9
10	west	t	89.5	3.25	90.5	3.00	88.5
10	south	t	321.0	11.50	320.3	11.00	324.5
10	south	p	42.0	1.50	41.8	1.50	44.3
10	south	p	279.0	10.00	278.5	9.50	280.3
10	east	t	75.0	2.75	76.6	2.50	73.8

Bottega (IV 10-11)

Room	where?	kind	in cm	O.ft (27.85)	ideal	R.ft (29.45)	ideal
0	north	t	2106.0	75.50	2102.7	71.50	2105.7
1	width	t	509.0	18.25	508.3	17.25	508.0
1	width	p	182.0	6.50	181.0	6.25	184.1
1	width	p	327.0	11.75	327.2	11.00	324.0
1	length	t	552.0	19.75	550.0	18.75	552.2
1	length	p	257.0	9.25	257.6	8.75	257.7
1	length	p	108.0	4.00	111.4	3.75	110.4
1	length	p	68.0	2.50	69.6	2.25	66.3
1	length	p	119.0	4.25	118.4	4.00	117.8
1	west	t	501.0	18.00	501.3	17.00	500.7
1	north	t	513.0	18.50	515.2	17.50	515.4
1	north	p	233.0	8.25	229.8	8.00	235.6
1	north	p	280.0	10.00	278.5	9.50	279.8
1	south	t	255.0	9.25	257.6	8.75	257.7
1	east	t	336.0	12.00	334.2	11.50	338.7
1	east	p	72.0	2.50	69.6	2.50	73.6
1	east	p	264.0	9.50	264.6	9.00	265.1
2	west	t	151.0	5.50	153.2	5.25	154.6
2	north	t	226.0	8.00	222.8	7.75	228.2
2	south	t	236.0	8.50	236.7	8.00	235.6
2	east	t	160.0	5.75	160.1	5.50	162.0
3	length	t	481.5	17.25	480.4	16.25	478.6
3	length	p	419.0	15.00	417.8	14.25	419.7
3	length	p	62.5	2.25	62.7	2.00	58.9
3	west	t	517.0	18.50	515.2	17.50	515.4
3	west	p	177.0	6.25	174.1	6.00	176.7
3	west	p	73.0	2.50	69.6	2.50	73.6
3	west	p	267.0	9.50	264.6	9.00	265.1
3	north	t	487.0	17.50	487.4	16.50	485.9
3	south	t	444.0	16.00	445.6	15.00	441.8
3	east	t	530.0	19.00	529.2	18.00	530.1
3	east	p	81.0	3.00	83.6	2.75	81.0
3	east	p	60.0	2.25	62.7	2.00	58.9
3	east	p	389.0	14.00	389.9	13.25	390.2
4	west	t	343.0	12.25	341.2	11.75	346.0
4	north	t	226.0	8.00	222.8	7.75	228.2
4	south	t	228.5	8.25	229.8	7.75	228.2
4	south	p	72.5	2.50	69.6	2.50	73.6
4	south	p	88.0	3.25	90.5	3.00	88.4
4	south	p	68.0	2.50	69.6	2.25	66.3
4	east	t	346.0	12.50	348.1	11.75	346.0
5	west	t	141.0	5.00	139.3	4.75	139.9
5	north	t	307.5	11.00	306.4	10.50	309.2

Bottega (IV 10-11)

Room	where?	kind	in cm	O.ft (27.85)	ideal	R.ft (29.45)	ideal
5	north	p	118.5	4.25	118.4	4.00	117.8
5	north	p	88.0	3.25	90.5	3.00	88.4
5	north	p	101.0	3.75	104.4	3.50	103.1
5	south	t	328.5	11.75	327.2	11.25	331.3
5	east	t	152.0	5.50	153.2	5.25	154.6
6	west	t	542.0	19.50	543.1	18.50	544.8
6	west	p	152.0	5.50	153.2	5.25	154.6
6	west	p	390.0	14.00	389.9	13.25	390.2
6	north	t	131.0	4.75	132.3	4.50	132.5
6	south	t	154.5	5.50	153.2	5.25	154.6
6	east	t	541.0	19.50	543.1	18.25	537.5
6	east	p	45.5	1.75	48.7	1.50	44.2
6	east	p	171.5	6.25	174.1	5.75	169.3
6	east	p	217.5	7.75	215.8	7.50	220.9
6	east	p	106.5	3.75	104.4	3.50	103.1
7	west	t	106.5	3.75	104.4	3.50	103.1
7	north	t	541.0	19.50	543.1	18.25	537.5
7	south	t	522.0	18.75	522.2	17.75	522.7
7	east	t	106.0	3.75	104.4	3.50	103.1
8	west	t	402.0	14.50	403.8	13.75	404.9
8	west	p	46.5	1.75	48.7	1.50	44.2
8	west	p	167.0	6.00	167.1	5.75	169.3
8	west	p	188.5	6.75	188.0	6.50	191.4
8	north	t	492.0	17.75	494.3	16.75	493.3
8	south	t	491.5	17.75	494.3	16.75	493.3
8	east	t	421.0	15.00	417.8	14.25	419.7

Grande Taberna (IV 12-13, 15-16); Taberna Vasaria (IV 14)

Room	where?	kind	in cm	O.ft (27.5)	ideal	R.ft (29.5)	ideal
0	north	t	2257.0	82.00	2255.0	76.50	2256.8
0	north	t	2246.5	81.75	2248.1	76.25	2249.4
1	west	t	241.0	8.75	240.6	8.25	243.4
1	north	t	241.0	8.75	240.6	8.25	243.4
1	south	t	254.0	9.25	254.4	8.50	250.8
1	east	t	253.0	9.25	254.4	8.50	250.8
1	east	p	90.0	3.25	89.4	3.00	88.5
1	east	p	163.0	6.00	165.0	5.50	162.3
2	west	t	247.0	9.00	247.5	8.25	243.4
2	north	t	274.0	10.00	275.0	9.25	272.9
2	north	p	240.5	8.75	240.6	8.25	243.4
2	north	p	32.0	1.25	34.4	1.00	29.5
2	south	t	244.0	8.75	240.6	8.25	243.4
2	east	t	237.0	8.50	233.8	8.00	236.0
2	east	p	148.0	5.50	151.3	5.00	147.5
2	east	p	89.0	3.25	89.4	3.00	88.5
3	length	t	762.0	27.75	763.1	25.75	759.6
3	west	t	542.0	19.75	543.1	18.25	538.4
3	west	p	65.5	2.50	68.8	2.25	66.4
3	west	p	176.5	6.50	178.8	6.00	177.0
3	west	p	155.0	5.75	158.1	5.25	154.9
3	west	p	145.0	5.25	144.4	5.00	147.5
3	south	t	758.0	27.50	756.3	25.75	759.6
3	east	t	542.0	19.75	543.1	18.25	538.4
3	east	p	117.0	4.25	116.9	4.00	118.0
3	east	p	165.0	6.00	165.0	5.50	162.3
3	east	p	111.0	4.00	110.0	3.75	110.6
3	east	p	149.0	5.50	151.3	5.00	147.5
4	width	t	261.0	9.50	261.3	8.75	258.1
4	west	t	264.0	9.50	261.3	9.00	265.5
4	north	t	526.0	19.25	529.4	17.75	523.6
4	south	t	536.5	19.50	536.3	18.25	538.4
4	east	t	256.0	9.25	254.4	8.75	258.1
4	east	p	63.5	2.25	61.9	2.25	66.4
4	east	p	176.5	6.50	178.8	6.00	177.0
4	east	p	16.0	0.50	13.8	0.50	14.8
5	west	t	363.0	13.25	364.4	12.25	361.4
5	west	p	118.0	4.25	116.9	4.00	118.0
5	west	p	165.0	6.00	165.0	5.50	162.3
5	west	p	80.0	3.00	82.5	2.75	81.1
5	north	t	299.5	11.00	302.5	10.25	302.4
5	north	p	200.0	7.25	199.4	6.75	199.1
5	north	p	99.5	3.50	96.3	3.25	95.9

Grande Taberna (IV 12-13, 15-16); Taberna Vasaria (IV 14)

Room	where?	kind	in cm	O.ft (27.5)	ideal	R.ft (29.5)	ideal
5	south	t	305.0	11.00	302.5	10.25	302.4
5	east	t	365.0	13.25	364.4	12.25	361.4
6	west	t	521.0	19.00	522.5	17.75	523.6
6	west	p	106.5	3.75	103.1	3.50	103.3
6	west	p	415.5	15.00	412.5	14.00	413.0
6	north	t	195.0	7.00	192.5	6.50	191.8
6	south	t	194.0	7.00	192.5	6.50	191.8
6	east	t	533.0	19.50	536.3	18.00	531.0
6	east	p	399.0	14.50	398.8	13.50	398.3
6	east	p	134.0	4.75	130.6	4.50	132.8
7	west	t	522.0	19.00	522.5	17.75	523.6
7	north	t	340.0	12.25	336.9	11.50	339.3
7	south	t	358.0	13.00	357.5	12.25	361.4
7	east	t	520.5	19.00	522.5	17.75	523.6
7	east	p	100.0	3.75	103.1	3.50	103.3
7	east	p	420.5	15.25	419.4	14.25	420.4
8	west	t	208.0	7.50	206.3	7.00	206.5
8	west	p	66.0	2.50	68.8	2.25	66.4
8	west	p	125.0	4.50	123.8	4.25	125.4
8	west	p	17.0	0.50	13.8	0.50	14.8
8	north	t	552.0	20.00	550.0	18.75	553.1
8	north	p	62.0	2.25	61.9	2.00	59.0
8	north	p	91.5	3.25	89.4	3.00	88.5
8	north	p	57.0	2.00	55.0	2.00	59.0
8	north	p	60.0	2.25	61.9	2.00	59.0
8	north	p	288.5	10.50	288.8	9.75	287.6
8	south	t	552.0	20.00	550.0	18.75	553.1
8	south	p	63.0	2.25	61.9	2.25	66.4
8	south	p	128.0	4.75	130.6	4.25	125.4
8	south	p	361.0	13.25	364.4	12.25	361.4
8	east	t	207.0	7.50	206.3	7.00	206.5
9	west	t	287.0	10.50	288.8	9.75	287.6
9	north	t	551.5	20.00	550.0	18.75	553.1
9	north	p	63.5	2.25	61.9	2.25	66.4
9	north	p	127.0	4.50	123.8	4.25	125.4
9	north	p	361.0	13.25	364.4	12.25	361.4
9	south	t	538.5	19.50	536.3	18.25	538.4
9	south	p	249.5	9.00	247.5	8.50	250.8
9	south	p	62.0	2.25	61.9	2.00	59.0
9	south	p	227.0	8.25	226.9	7.75	228.6
9	east	t	289.0	10.50	288.8	9.75	287.6
10	width	t	236.0	8.50	233.8	8.00	236.0
10	west	t	853.0	31.00	852.5	29.00	855.5

Grande Taberna (IV 12-13, 15-16); Taberna Vasaria (IV 14)

Room	where?	kind	in cm	O.ft (27.5)	ideal	R.ft (29.5)	ideal
10	west	p	147.5	5.25	144.4	5.00	147.5
10	west	p	89.0	3.25	89.4	3.00	88.5
10	west	p	40.5	1.50	41.3	1.25	36.9
10	west	p	87.0	3.25	89.4	3.00	88.5
10	west	p	197.0	7.25	199.4	6.75	199.1
10	west	p	91.0	3.25	89.4	3.00	88.5
10	west	p	201.0	7.25	199.4	6.75	199.1
10	north	t	241.5	8.75	240.6	8.25	243.4
10	north	p	132.5	4.75	130.6	4.50	132.8
10	north	p	109.0	4.00	110.0	3.75	110.6
10	south	t	249.0	9.00	247.5	8.50	250.8
10	east	t	810.0	29.50	811.3	27.50	811.3
10	east	p	93.0	3.50	96.3	3.25	95.9
10	east	p	146.0	5.25	144.4	5.00	147.5
10	east	p	571.0	20.75	570.6	19.25	567.9
11	west	t	149.0	5.50	151.3	5.00	147.5
11	south	t	341.5	12.50	343.8	11.50	339.3
11	south	p	242.0	8.75	240.6	8.25	243.4
11	south	p	99.5	3.50	96.3	3.25	95.9
11	east	t	130.0	4.75	130.6	4.50	132.8
12	west	t	293.0	10.75	295.6	10.00	295.0
12	north	t	226.0	8.25	226.9	7.75	228.6
12	south	t	239.0	8.75	240.6	8.00	236.0
12	east	t	293.0	10.75	295.6	10.00	295.0
12	east	p	92.0	3.25	89.4	3.00	88.5
12	east	p	163.0	6.00	165.0	5.50	162.3
12	east	p	38.0	1.50	41.3	1.25	36.9
13	width	t	539.0	19.50	536.3	18.25	538.4
13	west	p	127.5	4.75	130.6	4.25	125.4
13	west	p	398.5	14.50	398.8	13.50	398.3
13	west	t	526.0	19.25	529.4	17.75	523.6
13	north	t	622.5	22.75	625.6	21.00	619.5
13	north	p	75.5	2.75	75.6	2.50	73.8
13	north	p	408.0	14.75	405.6	13.75	405.6
13	north	p	139.0	5.00	137.5	4.75	140.1
13	south	t	592.0	21.50	591.3	20.00	590.0
13	south	p	102.0	3.75	103.1	3.50	103.3
13	south	p	87.0	3.25	89.4	3.00	88.5
13	south	p	58.0	2.00	55.0	2.00	59.0
13	south	p	75.0	2.75	75.6	2.50	73.8
13	south	p	270.0	9.75	268.1	9.25	272.9
13	east	t	544.0	19.75	543.1	18.50	545.8
13	east	p	140.5	5.00	137.5	4.75	140.1

Grande Taberna (IV 12-13, 15-16); Taberna Vasaria (IV 14)

Room	where?	kind	in cm	O.ft (27.5)	ideal	R.ft (29.5)	ideal
13	east	p	264.0	9.50	261.3	9.00	265.5
13	east	p	139.5	5.00	137.5	4.75	140.1
14	length	t	90.0	3.25	89.4	3.00	88.5
14	west	t	533.0	19.50	536.3	18.00	531.0
14	west	p	101.0	3.75	103.1	3.50	103.3
14	west	p	40.0	1.50	41.3	1.25	36.9
14	west	p	392.0	14.25	391.9	13.25	390.9
14	north	t	421.0	15.25	419.4	14.25	420.4
14	north	p	70.0	2.50	68.8	2.25	66.4
14	north	p	273.0	10.00	275.0	9.25	272.9
14	north	p	78.0	2.75	75.6	2.75	81.1
14	south	t	426.0	15.50	426.3	14.50	427.8
14	east	t	531.0	19.25	529.4	18.00	531.0

Taberna (IV 17-18)

Room	where?	kind	in cm	O.ft (27.4)	ideal	R.ft (29.45)	ideal
1	west	t	314.0	11.50	315.1	10.75	316.6
1	west	p	226.5	8.25	226.1	7.75	228.2
1	west	p	87.5	3.25	89.1	3.00	88.4
1	north	t	458.0	16.75	459.0	15.50	456.5
1	north	p	93.0	3.50	95.9	3.25	95.7
1	north	p	75.5	2.75	75.4	2.50	73.6
1	north	p	289.0	10.50	287.7	9.75	287.1
1	south	t	471.0	17.25	472.7	16.00	471.2
1	east	t	297.0	10.75	294.6	10.00	294.5
2	west	t	313.0	11.50	315.1	10.75	316.6
2	north	t	227.5	8.25	226.1	7.75	228.2
2	north	p	101.0	3.75	102.8	3.50	103.1
2	north	p	126.5	4.50	123.3	4.25	125.2
2	south	t	222.0	8.00	219.2	7.50	220.9
2	east	t	310.0	11.25	308.3	10.50	309.2
3	west	t	314.0	11.50	315.1	10.75	316.6
3	north	t	293.5	10.75	294.6	10.00	294.5
3	north	p	102.5	3.75	102.8	3.50	103.1
3	north	p	191.0	7.00	191.8	6.50	191.4
3	south	t	295.0	10.75	294.6	10.00	294.5
3	east	t	307.0	11.25	308.3	10.50	309.2
4	west	t	312.0	11.50	315.1	10.50	309.2
4	north	t	292.5	10.75	294.6	10.00	294.5
4	north	p	101.5	3.75	102.8	3.50	103.1
4	north	p	191.0	7.00	191.8	6.50	191.4
4	south	t	294.0	10.75	294.6	10.00	294.5
4	east	t	310.5	11.25	308.3	10.50	309.2
5	west	t	256.0	9.25	253.5	8.75	257.7
5	north	t	302.0	11.00	301.4	10.25	301.9
5	south	t	299.5	11.00	301.4	10.25	301.9
5	east	t	235.0	8.50	232.9	8.00	235.6
5	east	p	92.0	3.25	89.1	3.00	88.4
5	east	p	143.0	5.25	143.9	4.75	139.9
6	length	t	301.0	11.00	301.4	10.25	301.9
6	west	t	496.0	18.00	493.2	16.75	493.3
6	north	t	298.0	11.00	301.4	10.00	294.5
6	south	t	302.0	11.00	301.4	10.25	301.9
6	east	t	507.0	18.50	506.9	17.25	508.0
6	east	p	106.5	4.00	109.6	3.50	103.1
6	east	p	400.5	14.50	397.3	13.50	397.6
7	west	t	385.5	14.00	383.6	13.00	382.9
7	north	t	318.0	11.50	315.1	10.75	316.6
7	south	t	316.0	11.50	315.1	10.75	316.6

Taberna (IV 17-18)

Room	where?	kind	in cm	O.ft (27.4)	ideal	R.ft (29.45)	ideal
7	south	p	101.0	3.75	102.8	3.50	103.1
7	south	p	215.0	7.75	212.4	7.25	213.5
7	east	t	374.0	13.75	376.8	12.75	375.5
8	west	t	371.5	13.50	369.9	12.50	368.1
8	north	t	248.5	9.00	246.6	8.50	250.3
8	south	t	247.0	9.00	246.6	8.50	250.3
8	south	p	96.0	3.50	95.9	3.25	95.7
8	south	p	151.0	5.50	150.7	5.25	154.6
8	east	t	371.0	13.50	369.9	12.50	368.1
9	west	t	606.5	22.25	609.7	20.50	603.7
9	west	p	159.0	5.75	157.6	5.50	162.0
9	west	p	145.5	5.25	143.9	5.00	147.3
9	west	p	302.0	11.00	301.4	10.25	301.9
9	north	t	227.0	8.25	226.1	7.75	228.2
9	south	t	232.0	8.50	232.9	8.00	235.6
9	east	t	608.5	22.25	609.7	20.75	611.1
9	east	p	157.5	5.75	157.6	5.25	154.6
9	east	p	152.0	5.50	150.7	5.25	154.6
9	east	p	188.5	7.00	191.8	6.50	191.4
9	east	p	110.0	4.00	109.6	3.75	110.4
10	west	t	371.5	13.50	369.9	12.50	368.1
10	west	p	73.5	2.75	75.4	2.50	73.6
10	west	p	162.0	6.00	164.4	5.50	162.0
10	west	p	136.0	5.00	137.0	4.50	132.5
10	north	t	474.0	17.25	472.7	16.00	471.2
10	south	t	470.0	17.25	472.7	16.00	471.2
10	east	t	365.0	13.25	363.1	12.50	368.1
11	width	t	206.5	7.50	205.5	7.00	206.2
11	length	t	465.0	17.00	465.8	15.75	463.8
11	west	t	200.0	7.25	198.7	6.75	198.8
11	west	p	123.0	4.50	123.3	4.25	125.2
11	west	p	77.0	2.75	75.4	2.50	73.6
11	north	t	471.0	17.25	472.7	16.00	471.2
11	east	t	217.0	8.00	219.2	7.25	213.5
11	east	p	140.5	5.25	143.9	4.75	139.9
11	east	p	76.5	2.75	75.4	2.50	73.6
12	west	t	137.5	5.00	137.0	4.75	139.9
12	north	t	308.0	11.25	308.3	10.50	309.2
12	east	t	123.0	4.50	123.3	4.25	125.2
13	width	t	606.5	22.25	609.7	20.50	603.7
13	width	p	162.5	6.00	164.4	5.50	162.0
13	width	p	290.0	10.50	287.7	9.75	287.1
13	width	p	154.0	5.50	150.7	5.25	154.6

Taberna (IV 17-18)

Room	where?	kind	in cm	O.ft (27.4)	ideal	R.ft (29.45)	ideal
13	width	t	615.0	22.50	616.5	21.00	618.5
13	width	p	155.5	5.75	157.6	5.25	154.6
13	width	p	294.5	10.75	294.6	10.00	294.5
13	width	p	165.0	6.00	164.4	5.50	162.0
13	length	t	623.5	22.75	623.4	21.25	625.8
13	length	p	146.0	5.25	143.9	5.00	147.3
13	length	p	302.0	11.00	301.4	10.25	301.9
13	length	p	175.5	6.50	178.1	6.00	176.7
13	length	t	603.5	22.00	602.8	20.50	603.7
13	length	p	147.0	5.25	143.9	5.00	147.3
13	length	p	282.0	10.25	280.9	9.50	279.8
13	length	p	153.0	5.50	150.7	5.25	154.6
13	west	t	607.5	22.25	609.7	20.75	611.1
13	west	p	205.0	7.50	205.5	7.00	206.2
13	west	p	37.0	1.25	34.3	1.25	36.8
13	west	p	89.0	3.25	89.1	3.00	88.4
13	west	p	96.5	3.50	95.9	3.25	95.7
13	west	p	180.0	6.50	178.1	6.00	176.7
13	north	t	603.0	22.00	602.8	20.50	603.7
13	north	p	94.0	3.50	95.9	3.25	95.7
13	north	p	195.0	7.00	191.8	6.50	191.4
13	north	p	100.0	3.75	102.8	3.50	103.1
13	north	p	214.5	7.75	212.4	7.25	213.5
13	east	t	611.0	22.25	609.7	20.75	611.1
13	east	p	137.5	5.00	137.0	4.75	139.9
13	east	p	193.5	7.00	191.8	6.50	191.4
13	east	p	144.0	5.25	143.9	5.00	147.3
13	east	p	136.0	5.00	137.0	4.50	132.5
14	length	t	259.0	9.50	260.3	8.75	257.7
14	length	p	40.0	1.50	41.1	1.25	36.8
14	length	p	182.0	6.75	185.0	6.25	184.1
14	length	p	37.0	1.25	34.3	1.25	36.8
14	length	t	260.0	9.50	260.3	8.75	257.7
14	length	p	41.0	1.50	41.1	1.50	44.2
14	length	p	182.0	6.75	185.0	6.25	184.1
14	length	p	37.0	1.25	34.3	1.25	36.8
14	west	t	218.0	8.00	219.2	7.50	220.9
14	west	p	34.0	1.25	34.3	1.25	36.8
14	west	p	147.0	5.25	143.9	5.00	147.3
14	west	p	37.0	1.25	34.3	1.25	36.8
14	north	t	221.5	8.00	219.2	7.50	220.9
14	south	t	225.5	8.25	226.1	7.75	228.2
14	east	t	217.5	8.00	219.2	7.50	220.9

Taberna (IV 17-18)

Room	where?	kind	in cm	O.ft (27.4)	ideal	R.ft (29.45)	ideal
14	east	p	40.0	1.50	41.1	1.25	36.8
14	east	p	142.0	5.25	143.9	4.75	139.9
14	east	p	35.5	1.25	34.3	1.25	36.8
15	west	t	382.0	14.00	383.6	13.00	382.9
15	west	p	12.0	0.50	13.7	0.50	14.7
15	west	p	71.0	2.50	68.5	2.50	73.6
15	west	p	116.0	4.25	116.5	4.00	117.8
15	west	p	141.0	5.25	143.9	4.75	139.9
15	west	p	42.0	1.50	41.1	1.50	44.2
15	north	t	482.0	17.50	479.5	16.25	478.6
15	south	t	477.0	17.50	479.5	16.25	478.6
15	east	t	377.0	13.75	376.8	12.75	375.5
15	east	p	20.0	0.75	20.6	0.75	22.1
15	east	p	203.0	7.50	205.5	7.00	206.2
15	east	p	154.0	5.50	150.7	5.25	154.6

Casa della Stoffa (IV 19-20)

Room	where?	kind	in cm	O.ft (27.55)	ideal	R.ft (29.45)	ideal
1	length	t	479.5	17.50	482.1	16.25	478.6
1	west	t	545.5	19.75	544.1	18.50	544.8
1	west	p	241.5	8.75	241.1	8.25	243.0
1	west	p	113.0	4.00	110.2	3.75	110.4
1	west	p	88.0	3.25	89.5	3.00	88.4
1	west	p	103.0	3.75	103.3	3.50	103.1
1	north	t	477.0	17.25	475.2	16.25	478.6
1	north	p	31.0	1.25	34.4	1.00	29.5
1	north	p	135.0	5.00	137.8	4.50	132.5
1	north	p	311.0	11.25	309.9	10.50	309.2
1	south	t	485.0	17.50	482.1	16.50	485.9
1	east	t	555.0	20.25	557.9	18.75	552.2
1	east	p	130.5	4.75	130.9	4.50	132.5
1	east	p	139.0	5.00	137.8	4.75	139.9
1	east	p	145.5	5.25	144.6	5.00	147.3
1	east	p	140.0	5.00	137.8	4.75	139.9
2	west	t	414.0	15.00	413.3	14.00	412.3
2	north	t	652.0	23.75	654.3	22.25	655.3
2	south	t	654.0	23.75	654.3	22.25	655.3
2	south	p	32.0	1.25	34.4	1.00	29.5
2	south	p	131.5	4.75	130.9	4.50	132.5
2	south	p	491.5	17.75	489.0	16.75	493.3
2	east	t	414.0	15.00	413.3	14.00	412.3
3	west	t	407.0	14.75	406.4	13.75	404.9
3	north	t	235.0	8.50	234.2	8.00	235.6
3	south	t	236.0	8.50	234.2	8.00	235.6
3	east	t	410.0	15.00	413.3	14.00	412.3
3	east	p	229.5	8.25	227.3	7.75	228.2
3	east	p	129.0	4.75	130.9	4.50	132.5
3	east	p	51.0	1.75	48.2	1.75	51.5
4	west	t	414.0	15.00	413.3	14.00	412.3
4	north	t	213.0	7.75	213.5	7.25	213.5
4	south	t	212.5	7.75	213.5	7.25	213.5
4	south	p	65.5	2.50	68.9	2.25	66.3
4	south	p	83.0	3.00	82.7	2.75	81.0
4	south	p	64.0	2.25	62.0	2.25	66.3
4	east	t	414.5	15.00	413.3	14.00	412.3
5	west	t	287.0	10.50	289.3	9.75	287.1
5	north	t	294.0	10.75	296.2	10.00	294.5
5	north	p	168.5	6.00	165.3	5.75	169.3
5	north	p	104.0	3.75	103.3	3.50	103.1
5	north	p	21.0	0.75	20.7	0.75	22.1
5	south	t	292.0	10.50	289.3	10.00	294.5

Casa della Stoffa (IV 19-20)

Room	where?	kind	in cm	O.ft (27.55)	ideal	R.ft (29.45)	ideal
5	east	t	291.0	10.50	289.3	10.00	294.5
6	west	t	289.5	10.50	289.3	9.75	287.1
6	north	t	296.5	10.75	296.2	10.00	294.5
6	north	p	75.0	2.75	75.8	2.50	73.6
6	north	p	221.5	8.00	220.4	7.50	220.9
6	south	t	293.0	10.75	296.2	10.00	294.5
6	east	t	289.5	10.50	289.3	9.75	287.1
7	length	t	68.0	2.50	68.9	2.25	66.3
7	west	t	217.0	8.00	220.4	7.25	213.5
7	north	t	226.5	8.25	227.3	7.75	228.2
7	south	t	255.0	9.25	254.8	8.75	257.7
7	south	p	78.0	2.75	75.8	2.75	81.0
7	south	p	177.0	6.50	179.1	6.00	176.7
7	east	t	225.0	8.25	227.3	7.75	228.2
7	east	p	109.5	4.00	110.2	3.75	110.4
7	east	p	115.5	4.25	117.1	4.00	117.8
8	west	t	221.0	8.00	220.4	7.50	220.9
8	west	p	110.5	4.00	110.2	3.75	110.4
8	west	p	110.5	4.00	110.2	3.75	110.4
8	south	t	296.5	10.75	296.2	10.00	294.5
8	south	p	22.5	0.75	20.7	0.75	22.1
8	south	p	105.5	3.75	103.3	3.50	103.1
8	south	p	168.5	6.00	165.3	5.75	169.3
8	east	t	208.0	7.50	206.6	7.00	206.2
8	east	p	109.0	4.00	110.2	3.75	110.4
8	east	p	99.0	3.50	96.4	3.25	95.7
9	west	t	99.0	3.50	96.4	3.25	95.7
9	south	t	311.0	11.25	309.9	10.50	309.2
9	east	t	103.0	3.75	103.3	3.50	103.1

Casa dei Cervi (IV 21) Lot IV K

Room	where?	kind	in cm	O.ft (27.5)	ideal	R.ft (29.4)	ideal
0	north	t	2309.0	84.00	2310.0	78.50	2307.9
1	west	t	169.5	6.25	171.9	5.75	169.1
1	north	t	353.0	12.75	350.6	12.00	352.8
1	north	p	59.5	2.25	61.9	2.00	58.8
1	north	p	74.0	2.75	75.6	2.50	73.5
1	north	p	219.5	8.00	220.0	7.50	220.5
1	east	t	159.0	5.75	158.1	5.50	161.7
2	west	t	297.0	10.75	295.6	10.00	294.0
2	north	t	287.0	10.50	288.8	9.75	286.7
2	north	p	60.0	2.25	61.9	2.00	58.8
2	north	p	227.0	8.25	226.9	7.75	227.9
2	south	t	277.0	10.00	275.0	9.50	279.3
2	east	t	260.0	9.50	261.3	8.75	257.3
3	width	t	257.5	9.25	254.4	8.75	257.3
3	west	t	296.0	10.75	295.6	10.00	294.0
3	north	t	434.5	15.75	433.1	14.75	433.7
3	south	t	425.0	15.50	426.3	14.50	426.3
3	south	p	230.0	8.25	226.9	7.75	227.9
3	south	p	60.0	2.25	61.9	2.00	58.8
3	south	p	45.0	1.75	48.1	1.50	44.1
3	south	p	90.0	3.25	89.4	3.00	88.2
3	east	t	258.5	9.50	261.3	8.75	257.3
4	west	t	257.0	9.25	254.4	8.75	257.3
4	north	t	233.0	8.50	233.8	8.00	235.2
4	south	t	232.5	8.50	233.8	8.00	235.2
4	south	p	14.0	0.50	13.8	0.50	14.7
4	south	p	91.5	3.25	89.4	3.00	88.2
4	south	p	127.0	4.50	123.8	4.25	125.0
4	east	t	256.0	9.25	254.4	8.75	257.3
5	length	t	558.5	20.25	556.9	19.00	558.6
5	west	t	696.0	25.25	694.4	23.75	698.3
5	west	p	555.0	20.25	556.9	19.00	558.6
5	west	p	122.0	4.50	123.8	4.25	125.0
5	west	p	19.0	0.75	20.6	0.75	22.1
5	north	t	601.5	21.75	598.1	20.50	602.7
5	south	t	556.5	20.25	556.9	19.00	558.6
5	south	p	134.5	5.00	137.5	4.50	132.3
5	south	p	309.0	11.25	309.4	10.50	308.7
5	south	p	113.0	4.00	110.0	3.75	110.3
5	east	t	694.0	25.25	694.4	23.50	690.9
5	east	p	72.5	2.75	75.6	2.50	73.5
5	east	p	482.5	17.50	481.3	16.50	485.1
5	east	p	120.5	4.50	123.8	4.00	117.6

Casa dei Cervi (IV 21) Lot IV K

Room	where?	kind	in cm	O.ft (27.5)	ideal	R.ft (29.4)	ideal
5	east	p	18.5	0.75	20.6	0.75	22.1
6	west	t	277.0	10.00	275.0	9.50	279.3
6	west	p	134.5	5.00	137.5	4.50	132.3
6	west	p	123.5	4.50	123.8	4.25	125.0
6	west	p	19.0	0.75	20.6	0.75	22.1
6	north	t	263.5	9.50	261.3	9.00	264.6
6	north	p	91.0	3.25	89.4	3.00	88.2
6	north	p	120.0	4.25	116.9	4.00	117.6
6	north	p	52.5	2.00	55.0	1.75	51.5
6	south	t	267.5	9.75	268.1	9.00	264.6
6	east	t	276.0	10.00	275.0	9.50	279.3
7	west	t	479.5	17.50	481.3	16.25	477.8
7	north	t	377.0	13.75	378.1	12.75	374.9
7	south	t	376.0	13.75	378.1	12.75	374.9
7	south	p	98.0	3.50	96.3	3.25	95.6
7	south	p	177.5	6.50	178.8	6.00	176.4
7	south	p	100.5	3.75	103.1	3.50	102.9
7	east	t	482.5	17.50	481.3	16.50	485.1
7	east	p	340.0	12.25	336.9	11.50	338.1
7	east	p	127.0	4.50	123.8	4.25	125.0
7	east	p	15.5	0.50	13.8	0.50	14.7
8	west	t	178.0	6.50	178.8	6.00	176.4
8	north	t	217.0	8.00	220.0	7.50	220.5
8	south	t	225.0	8.25	226.9	7.75	227.9
8	south	p	53.0	2.00	55.0	1.75	51.5
8	south	p	122.5	4.50	123.8	4.25	125.0
8	south	p	49.5	1.75	48.1	1.75	51.5
8	east	t	177.0	6.50	178.8	6.00	176.4
9	length	t	207.5	7.50	206.3	7.00	205.8
9	west	t	316.0	11.50	316.3	10.75	316.1
9	west	p	91.5	3.25	89.4	3.00	88.2
9	west	p	224.5	8.25	226.9	7.75	227.9
9	north	t	263.5	9.50	261.3	9.00	264.6
9	south	t	253.0	9.25	254.4	8.50	249.9
9	east	t	316.5	11.50	316.3	10.75	316.1
9	east	p	100.0	3.75	103.1	3.50	102.9
9	east	p	128.0	4.75	130.6	4.25	125.0
9	east	p	88.5	3.25	89.4	3.00	88.2
10	length	t	379.5	13.75	378.1	13.00	382.2
10	west	t	312.5	11.25	309.4	10.75	316.1
10	north	t	383.0	14.00	385.0	13.00	382.2
10	south	t	374.5	13.50	371.3	12.75	374.9
10	east	t	308.5	11.25	309.4	10.50	308.7

Casa dei Cervi (IV 21) Lot IV K

Room	where?	kind	in cm	O.ft (27.5)	ideal	R.ft (29.4)	ideal
10	east	p	93.0	3.50	96.3	3.25	95.6
10	east	p	215.5	7.75	213.1	7.25	213.2
11	west	t	102.0	3.75	103.1	3.50	102.9
11	north	t	265.5	9.75	268.1	9.00	264.6
11	south	t	434.0	15.75	433.1	14.75	433.7
11	south	p	322.0	11.75	323.1	11.00	323.4
11	south	p	102.0	3.75	103.1	3.50	102.9
11	east	t	110.0	4.00	110.0	3.75	110.3
12	length	t	235.0	8.50	233.8	8.00	235.2
12	west	t	258.0	9.50	261.3	8.75	257.3
12	north	t	266.5	9.75	268.1	9.00	264.6
12	south	t	229.0	8.25	226.9	7.75	227.9
12	east	t	253.5	9.25	254.4	8.50	249.9
12	east	p	180.5	6.50	178.8	6.25	183.8
12	east	p	73.0	2.75	75.6	2.50	73.5
13	width	t	374.0	13.50	371.3	12.75	374.9
13	length	t	201.0	7.25	199.4	6.75	198.5
13	west	t	340.0	12.25	336.9	11.50	338.1
13	west	p	221.0	8.00	220.0	7.50	220.5
13	west	p	119.0	4.25	116.9	4.00	117.6
13	north	t	305.0	11.00	302.5	10.25	301.4
13	south	t	180.0	6.50	178.8	6.00	176.4
13	south	p	116.5	4.25	116.9	4.00	117.6
13	south	p	64.0	2.25	61.9	2.25	66.2
13	east	t	182.0	6.50	178.8	6.25	183.8
14	west	t	145.0	5.25	144.4	5.00	147.0
14	north	t	158.0	5.75	158.1	5.25	154.4
14	south	t	156.0	5.75	158.1	5.25	154.4
14	south	p	73.0	2.75	75.6	2.50	73.5
14	south	p	83.0	3.00	82.5	2.75	80.9
14	east	t	104.0	3.75	103.1	3.50	102.9
24	width	t	550.5	20.00	550.0	18.75	551.3
24	length	t	506.5	18.50	508.8	17.25	507.2
24	west	t	618.0	22.50	618.8	21.00	617.4
24	west	p	477.0	17.25	474.4	16.25	477.8
24	west	p	120.0	4.25	116.9	4.00	117.6
24	west	p	21.0	0.75	20.6	0.75	22.1
24	north	t	508.5	18.50	508.8	17.25	507.2
24	north	p	90.5	3.25	89.4	3.00	88.2
24	north	p	52.5	2.00	55.0	1.75	51.5
24	north	p	92.0	3.25	89.4	3.25	95.6
24	north	p	169.0	6.25	171.9	5.75	169.1
24	north	p	104.5	3.75	103.1	3.50	102.9

Casa dei Cervi (IV 21) Lot IV K

Room	where?	kind	in cm	O.ft (27.5)	ideal	R.ft (29.4)	ideal
24	east	t	587.5	21.25	584.4	20.00	588.0
24	east	p	291.0	10.50	288.8	10.00	294.0
24	east	p	89.5	3.25	89.4	3.00	88.2
24	east	p	38.0	1.50	41.3	1.25	36.8
24	east	p	169.0	6.25	171.9	5.75	169.1
25	west	t	223.5	8.25	226.9	7.50	220.5
25	west	p	78.5	2.75	75.6	2.75	80.9
25	west	p	45.0	1.75	48.1	1.50	44.1
25	west	p	100.0	3.75	103.1	3.50	102.9
25	north	t	105.5	3.75	103.1	3.50	102.9
25	south	t	102.5	3.75	103.1	3.50	102.9
25	east	t	299.5	11.00	302.5	10.25	301.4
26	west	t	97.0	3.50	96.3	3.25	95.6
26	north	t	721.0	26.25	721.9	24.50	720.3
26	south	t	644.5	23.50	646.3	22.00	646.8
26	east	t	100.5	3.75	103.1	3.50	102.9
27	west	t	843.5	30.75	845.6	28.75	845.3
27	west	p	104.5	3.75	103.1	3.50	102.9
27	west	p	126.5	4.50	123.8	4.25	125.0
27	west	p	87.5	3.25	89.4	3.00	88.2
27	west	p	249.0	9.00	247.5	8.50	249.9
27	west	p	276.0	10.00	275.0	9.50	279.3
27	north	t	102.5	3.75	103.1	3.50	102.9
27	south	t	130.0	4.75	130.6	4.50	132.3
27	south	p	15.0	0.50	13.8	0.50	14.7
27	south	p	115.0	4.25	116.9	4.00	117.6
27	east	t	752.0	27.25	749.4	25.50	749.7
27	east	p	603.5	22.00	605.0	20.50	602.7
27	east	p	118.5	4.25	116.9	4.00	117.6
27	east	p	22.0	0.75	20.6	0.75	22.1
28	west	t	282.0	10.25	281.9	9.50	279.3
28	west	p	75.0	2.75	75.6	2.50	73.5
28	west	p	207.0	7.50	206.3	7.00	205.8
28	north	t	177.5	6.50	178.8	6.00	176.4
28	north	p	66.0	2.50	68.8	2.25	66.2
28	north	p	45.5	1.75	48.1	1.50	44.1
28	north	p	66.0	2.50	68.8	2.25	66.2
28	south	t	171.5	6.25	171.9	5.75	169.1
28	east	t	396.0	14.50	398.8	13.50	396.9

Casa dei Cervi (IV 21) Garden and terrace

Room	where?	kind	in cm	R.ft (29.4)	ideal
15	west	t	1070.0	36.50	1073.1
15	west	p	68.0	2.25	66.2
15	west	p	83.5	2.75	80.9
15	west	p	120.5	4.00	117.6
15	west	p	97.0	3.25	95.6
15	west	p	701.0	23.75	698.3
15	north	t	703.5	24.00	705.6
15	north	p	54.0	1.75	51.5
15	north	p	89.5	3.00	88.2
15	north	p	58.0	2.00	58.8
15	north	p	289.0	9.75	286.7
15	north	p	66.0	2.25	66.2
15	north	p	86.0	3.00	88.2
15	north	p	61.0	2.00	58.8
15	south	t	704.0	24.00	705.6
15	south	p	50.0	1.75	51.5
15	south	p	101.0	3.50	102.9
15	south	p	53.0	1.75	51.5
15	south	p	295.0	10.00	294.0
15	south	p	50.0	1.75	51.5
15	south	p	104.0	3.50	102.9
15	south	p	51.0	1.75	51.5
15	east	t	1073.5	36.50	1073.1
15	east	p	67.0	2.25	66.2
15	east	p	90.5	3.00	88.2
15	east	p	117.0	4.00	117.6
15	east	p	96.5	3.25	95.6
15	east	p	702.5	24.00	705.6
16	west	t	579.0	19.75	580.7
16	west	p	456.5	15.50	455.7
16	west	p	79.0	2.75	80.9
16	west	p	43.5	1.50	44.1
16	north	t	460.0	15.75	463.1
16	north	p	164.0	5.50	161.7
16	north	p	123.0	4.25	125.0
16	north	p	173.0	6.00	176.4
16	south	t	447.5	15.25	448.4
16	south	p	144.5	5.00	147.0
16	south	p	154.5	5.25	154.4
16	south	p	148.5	5.00	147.0
16	east	t	582.5	19.75	580.7
17	west	t	579.5	19.75	580.7
17	north	t	438.5	15.00	441.0

Casa dei Cervi (IV 21) Garden and terrace

Room	where?	kind	in cm	R.ft (29.4)	ideal
17	north	p	170.0	5.75	169.1
17	north	p	99.5	3.50	102.9
17	north	p	169.0	5.75	169.1
17	south	t	431.0	14.75	433.7
17	south	p	132.5	4.50	132.3
17	south	p	145.0	5.00	147.0
17	south	p	153.5	5.25	154.4
17	east	t	581.5	19.75	580.7
17	east	p	431.5	14.75	433.7
17	east	p	105.0	3.50	102.9
17	east	p	45.0	1.50	44.1
18	width	t	370.0	12.50	367.5
18	width	p	78.0	2.75	80.9
18	width	p	216.0	7.25	213.2
18	width	p	76.0	2.50	73.5
18	width	t	366.0	12.50	367.5
18	width	p	78.0	2.75	80.9
18	width	p	211.0	7.25	213.2
18	width	p	77.0	2.50	73.5
18	length	t	496.0	16.75	492.5
18	length	p	78.0	2.75	80.9
18	length	p	340.0	11.50	338.1
18	length	p	78.0	2.75	80.9
18	length	t	506.0	17.25	507.2
18	length	p	83.0	2.75	80.9
18	length	p	343.0	11.75	345.5
18	length	p	80.0	2.75	80.9
18	west	t	371.5	12.75	374.9
18	west	p	77.5	2.75	80.9
18	west	p	221.0	7.50	220.5
18	west	p	73.0	2.50	73.5
18	north	t	492.0	16.75	492.5
18	north	p	77.0	2.50	73.5
18	north	p	341.0	11.50	338.1
18	north	p	74.0	2.50	73.5
18	south	t	503.0	17.00	499.8
18	south	p	81.0	2.75	80.9
18	south	p	343.0	11.75	345.5
18	south	p	79.0	2.75	80.9
18	east	t	371.0	12.50	367.5
18	east	p	79.0	2.75	80.9
18	east	p	206.0	7.00	205.8
18	east	p	86.0	3.00	88.2

Casa dei Cervi (IV 21) Garden and terrace

Room	where?	kind	in cm	R.ft (29.4)	ideal
19	west	t	296.0	10.00	294.0
19	west	p	78.5	2.75	80.9
19	west	p	117.0	4.00	117.6
19	west	p	100.5	3.50	102.9
19	north	t	127.0	4.25	125.0
19	south	t	135.0	4.50	132.3
19	east	t	294.0	10.00	294.0
20	west	t	296.0	10.00	294.0
20	west	p	109.0	3.75	110.3
20	west	p	74.0	2.50	73.5
20	west	p	113.0	3.75	110.3
20	north	t	135.0	4.50	132.3
20	south	t	136.0	4.75	139.7
20	east	t	292.0	10.00	294.0
21	west	t	332.5	11.25	330.8
21	west	p	41.0	1.50	44.1
21	west	p	89.0	3.00	88.2
21	west	p	202.5	7.00	205.8
21	north	t	132.0	4.50	132.3
21	south	t	134.0	4.50	132.3
21	east	t	332.5	11.25	330.8
22	west	t	348.5	11.75	345.5
22	west	p	152.0	5.25	154.4
22	west	p	102.0	3.50	102.9
22	west	p	94.5	3.25	95.6
22	north	t	207.0	7.00	205.8
22	south	t	210.0	7.25	213.2
22	east	t	345.0	11.75	345.5
23	west	t	321.0	11.00	323.4
23	north	t	285.0	9.75	286.7
23	north	p	77.0	2.50	73.5
23	north	p	106.0	3.50	102.9
23	north	p	102.0	3.50	102.9
23	south	t	285.0	9.75	286.7
23	south	p	94.0	3.25	95.6
23	south	p	147.0	5.00	147.0
23	south	p	44.0	1.50	44.1
23	east	t	333.5	11.25	330.8
23	east	p	158.0	5.25	154.4
23	east	p	110.0	3.75	110.3
23	east	p	65.5	2.25	66.2
29	west	t	265.0	9.00	264.6
29	north	t	2277.5	77.50	2278.5

Casa dei Cervi (IV 21) Garden and terrace

Room	where?	kind	in cm	R.ft (29.4)	ideal
29	north	p	112.5	3.75	110.3
29	north	p	176.0	6.00	176.4
29	north	p	403.0	13.75	404.3
29	north	p	114.5	4.00	117.6
29	north	p	175.0	6.00	176.4
29	north	p	308.0	10.50	308.7
29	north	p	465.5	15.75	463.1
29	north	p	117.0	4.00	117.6
29	north	p	406.5	13.75	404.3
29	south	t	1743.0	59.25	1742.0
29	south	p	113.5	3.75	110.3
29	south	p	97.0	3.25	95.6
29	south	p	253.0	8.50	249.9
29	south	p	96.5	3.25	95.6
29	south	p	161.0	5.50	161.7
29	south	p	316.5	10.75	316.1
29	south	p	463.0	15.75	463.1
29	south	p	119.5	4.00	117.6
29	south	p	123.5	4.25	125.0
29	east	t	268.5	9.25	272.0
30	west	t	2460.0	83.75	2462.3
30	west	p	731.5	25.00	735.0
30	west	p	94.0	3.25	95.6
30	west	p	84.5	2.75	80.9
30	west	p	97.0	3.25	95.6
30	west	p	443.5	15.00	441.0
30	west	p	94.0	3.25	95.6
30	west	p	526.0	18.00	529.2
30	west	p	103.5	3.50	102.9
30	west	p	85.5	3.00	88.2
30	north	t	267.5	9.00	264.6
30	south	t	268.0	9.00	264.6
30	east	t	3081.5	104.75	3079.7
30	east	p	2168.5	73.75	2168.3
30	east	p	116.0	4.00	117.6
30	east	p	245.0	8.25	242.6
30	east	p	70.0	2.50	73.5
30	east	p	196.5	6.75	198.5
30	east	p	79.5	2.75	80.9
30	east	p	206.0	7.00	205.8
31	west	t	355.0	12.00	352.8
31	north	t	1733.5	59.00	1734.6
31	north	p	187.0	6.25	183.8

Casa dei Cervi (IV 21) Garden and terrace

Room	where?	kind	in cm	R.ft (29.4)	ideal
31	north	p	151.5	5.25	154.4
31	north	p	243.0	8.25	242.6
31	north	p	102.0	3.50	102.9
31	north	p	50.5	1.75	51.5
31	north	p	295.5	10.00	294.0
31	north	p	51.5	1.75	51.5
31	north	p	101.0	3.50	102.9
31	north	p	228.0	7.75	227.9
31	north	p	145.5	5.00	147.0
31	north	p	178.0	6.00	176.4
31	south	t	2245.5	76.50	2249.1
31	south	p	80.5	2.75	80.9
31	south	p	102.0	3.50	102.9
31	south	p	276.0	9.50	279.3
31	south	p	131.5	4.50	132.3
31	south	p	180.0	6.00	176.4
31	south	p	105.0	3.50	102.9
31	south	p	90.5	3.00	88.2
31	south	p	321.0	11.00	323.4
31	south	p	89.0	3.00	88.2
31	south	p	104.0	3.50	102.9
31	south	p	179.0	6.00	176.4
31	south	p	132.0	4.50	132.3
31	south	p	278.0	9.50	279.3
31	south	p	126.0	4.25	125.0
31	south	p	51.0	1.75	51.5
31	east	t	356.0	12.00	352.8
32	west	t	3088.0	105.00	3087.0
32	north	t	267.0	9.00	264.6
32	south	t	253.5	8.50	249.9
32	east	t	2481.5	84.50	2484.3
32	east	p	96.5	3.25	95.6
32	east	p	81.0	2.75	80.9
32	east	p	546.0	18.50	543.9
32	east	p	94.5	3.25	95.6
32	east	p	636.5	21.75	639.5
32	east	p	89.5	3.00	88.2
32	east	p	743.0	25.25	742.4
32	east	p	95.0	3.25	95.6
32	east	p	90.0	3.00	88.2
33	width	t	1258.0	42.75	1256.9
33	width	t	1265.5	43.00	1264.2
33	length	t	1661.0	56.50	1661.1

Casa dei Cervi (IV 21) Garden and terrace

Room	where?	kind	in cm	R.ft (29.4)	ideal
33	length	p	125.5	4.25	125.0
33	length	p	1536.5	52.25	1536.2
33	west	t	1782.0	60.50	1778.7
33	west	p	1219.0	41.50	1220.1
33	west	p	563.0	19.25	566.0
33	north	t	1664.5	56.50	1661.1
33	north	p	662.5	22.50	661.5
33	north	p	316.0	10.75	316.1
33	north	p	686.0	23.25	683.6
33	south	t	1554.5	52.75	1550.9
33	south	p	326.5	11.00	323.4
33	south	p	788.0	26.75	786.5
33	south	p	102.0	3.50	102.9
33	south	p	87.0	3.00	88.2
33	south	p	61.5	2.00	58.8
33	south	p	292.0	10.00	294.0
33	south	p	61.0	2.00	58.8
33	south	p	86.0	3.00	88.2
33	south	p	99.0	3.25	95.6
33	south	p	306.0	10.50	308.7
33	south	p	32.5	1.00	29.4
33	south	p	101.0	3.50	102.9
33	east	t	1050.0	35.75	1051.1
34	west	t	563.0	19.25	566.0
34	west	p	153.0	5.25	154.4
34	west	p	410.0	14.00	411.6
34	north	t	439.5	15.00	441.0
34	north	p	306.0	10.50	308.7
34	north	p	32.5	1.00	29.4
34	north	p	91.0	3.00	88.2
34	south	t	463.0	15.75	463.1
34	east	t	513.5	17.50	514.5
35	length	t	319.5	10.75	316.1
35	west	t	509.0	17.25	507.2
35	north	t	326.5	11.00	323.4
35	south	t	444.0	15.00	441.0
35	south	p	159.0	5.50	161.7
35	south	p	107.0	3.75	110.3
35	south	p	178.0	6.00	176.4
35	east	t	728.5	24.75	727.7
35	east	p	153.0	5.25	154.4
35	east	p	575.5	19.50	573.3
36	west	t	543.0	18.50	543.9

Casa dei Cervi (IV 21) Garden and terrace

Room	where?	kind	in cm	R.ft (29.4)	ideal
36	north	t	130.0	4.50	132.3
36	south	t	92.5	3.25	95.6
36	east	t	689.0	23.50	690.9
36	east	p	90.0	3.00	88.2
36	east	p	599.0	20.25	595.4

INDEX

Venuti, Rudolfino de · 57
versus · 4; 24; 75; 76; 77
vestibule · 91; 115; 185
vestibulum · *See* vestibule
Vesuvius · 3; 18; 19; 22; 27; 28; 29; 30; 31; 32; 33; 35; 37
Victor Emmanuel II, king of Italy · 43
Virgil · 22
viridarium · 107; 135; 136; 180 *See also* garden
Vitruvius · 95; 115; 118; 185; 186
vorsus · *See versus*

W

Waldstein, Charles · 17; 44; 45; 51
wall construction · 91; 99; 106; 115; 124; 128; 132; 140; 147; 152; 156; 160; 166; 172; 177 *See also* wall structures
wall mosaic · 100; 178
wall painting
   decorations with architectural elements · 107; 133; 141; 147; 152; 156; 160; 166; 172; 178
figured scenes · 56; 134; 166; 178
First Style · 146; 147; 148; 201
Fourth Style · 92; 100; 107; 116; 133; 141; 147; 156; 160; 166; 178
landscape paintings · 124; 160
monochrome walls · 116
mythical scenes · 134
panel decorations · 92; 100; 107; 116; 124; 141; 152; 160; 172; 178
sacro-idyllic scenes · 124
Second Style · 11; 91; 92; 94; 109; 143; 202
Third Style · 54; 107; 110; 116; 118; 124; 125; 162; 172
wall structures · 4; 9; 11; 53; 65; 89; 90; 91; 94; 98; 99; 102; 123; 130; 132; 153; 160; 162; 163; 166; 191
washbasins · 91; 99
Weber, Karl · 38; 39; 40; 41
wheat · 155; 156; 162
Winckelmann, Johann Joachim · 40; 41
windlass · 117; 159; 162
writing tablets · 162; 167

ILLUSTRATIONS

List of figures

1. Plan of Herculaneum, indicating the periods in the history of the excavations.
2. Proposal for the reconstruction of the complete plan of Herculaneum.
3. The original size of the *insulae* III and IV.
4. Diagram of the division in lots in the *insulae* III, IV, V, and VI, indicating the total lengths and widths of the *insulae* (in feet and cm.).
5. Diagram of the division in lots in *insula* III, indicating the lengths and widths of the lots (in feet).
6. Diagram of the division in lots in *insula* IV, indicating the lengths and widths of the lots (in feet).
7. Central part of *insula* IV (around Casa della Fullonica).
8. Reconstruction of the back wall of the large *nymphaeum* (room 29) in the Casa dello Scheletro.
9. Proposal for the reconstruction of lot III E (rear part of the Casa del Tramezzo di Legno).
10. Proposal for the reconstruction of lot III H (ground floor of the Casa a Graticcio).
11. Examples of the various types of houses in Herculaneum:
    1) Casa del Bicentenario (V 13-18)
    2) Casa dell'Atrio Corinzio (V 30)
    3) Casa dell'Erma di Bronzo (III 16)
    4) Casa dell'Ara Laterizia (III 17)
    5) Casa del Papiro Dipinto (IV 8-9)
    6) Casa dell'Alcova (IV 3-4)
    7) Casa dell'Atrio a Mosaico (IV 1-2)
    8) Casa della Stoffa (IV 19-20).

List of plates

NB: Where possible the measurements of the rooms are given in feet (between dashes). The rules show the measurements in meters only approximately.
Figs. 7, 9-11: author; other illustrations: E.J. Ponten (Fig. 7: after Maiuri 1958; figs. 1, 3: after De Franciscis 1974).

Fig. 1. Plan of Herculaneum.

‑‑‑‑‑‑‑‑‑ = excavated area *before* the campaign by A. Maiuri

.... = excavated area *after* the campaign by A. Maiuri

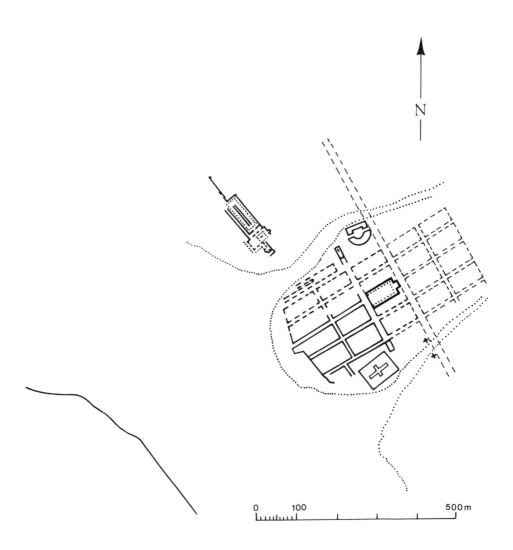

N

0   100   500m

Fig. 2. Proposal for the reconstruction of the complete plan of Herculaneum.

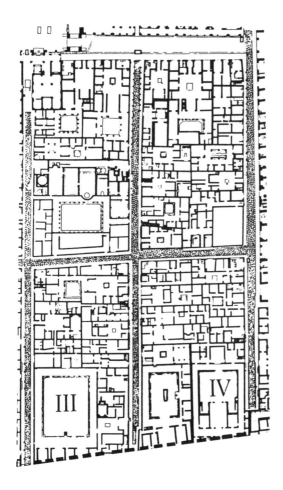

Fig. 3. The original size of the *insulae* III and IV.

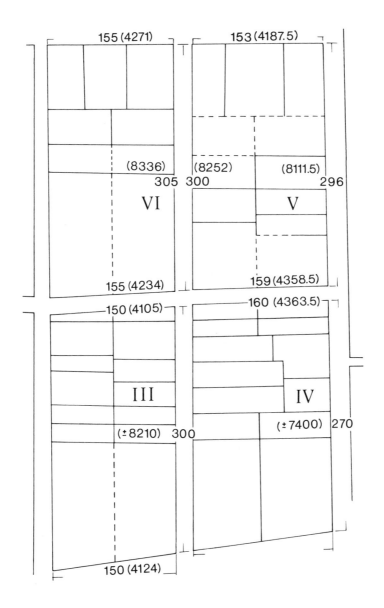

Fig. 4. Diagram of the division in lots in the *insulae* III, IV, V, and VI.

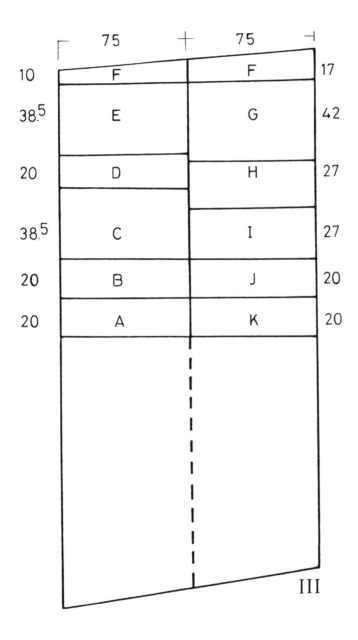

Fig. 5. Diagram of the division in lots in *insula* III

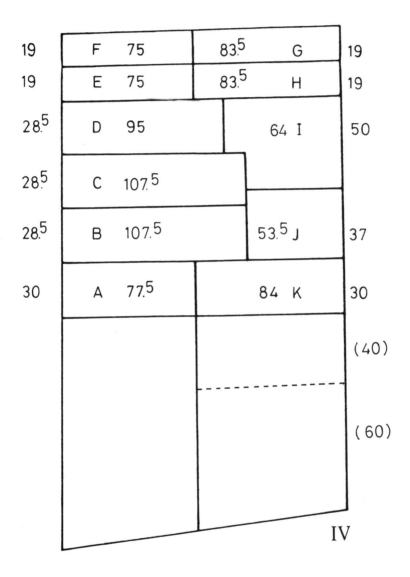

Fig. 6. Diagram of the division in lots in *insula* IV

Fig. 7. Central part of *insula* IV.

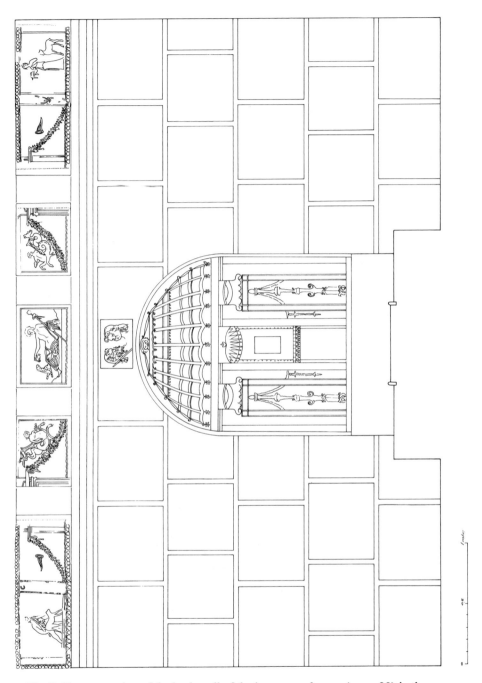

Fig. 8. Reconstruction of the back wall of the large *nymphaeum* (room 29) in the
Casa dello Scheletro.

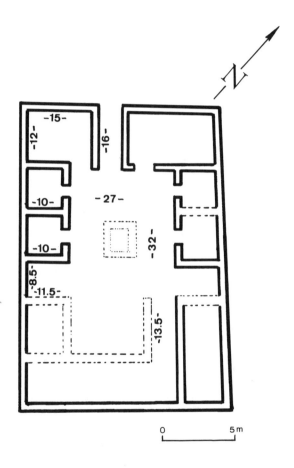

Fig. 9. Proposal for the reconstruction of lot III E (rear part of the Casa del
Tramezzo di Legno).

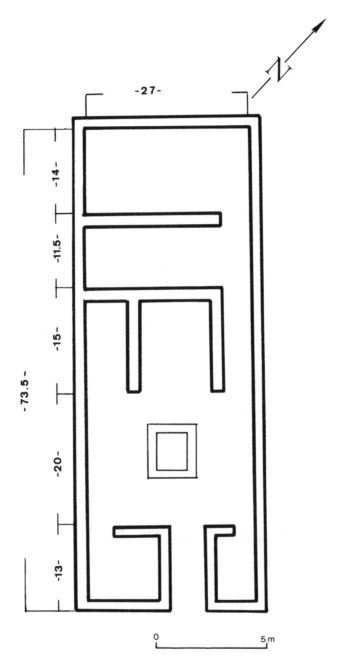

Fig.10. Proposal for the reconstruction of lot III H (ground floor of the Casa a Graticcio).

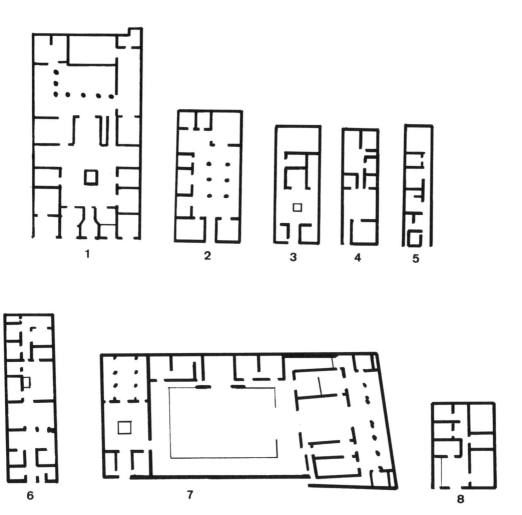

Fig.11. Examples of the various types of houses in Herculaneum:
1) Casa del Bicentenario (V 13-18)
2) Casa dell'Atrio Corinzio (V 30)
3) Casa dell'Erma di Bronzo (III 16)
4) Casa dell'Ara Laterizia (III 17)
5) Casa del Papiro Dipinto (IV 8-9)
6) Casa dell'Alcova (IV 3-4)
7) Casa dell'Atrio a Mosaico (IV 1-2)
8) Casa della Stoffa (IV 19-20).

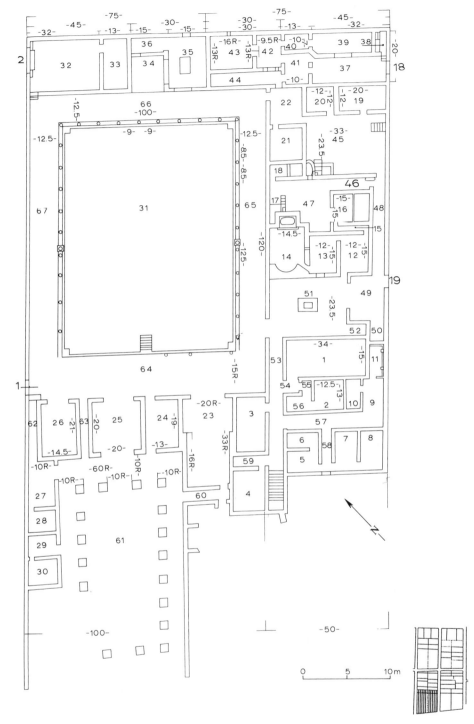

I. Casa dell'Albergo (III 1-2, 18-19)

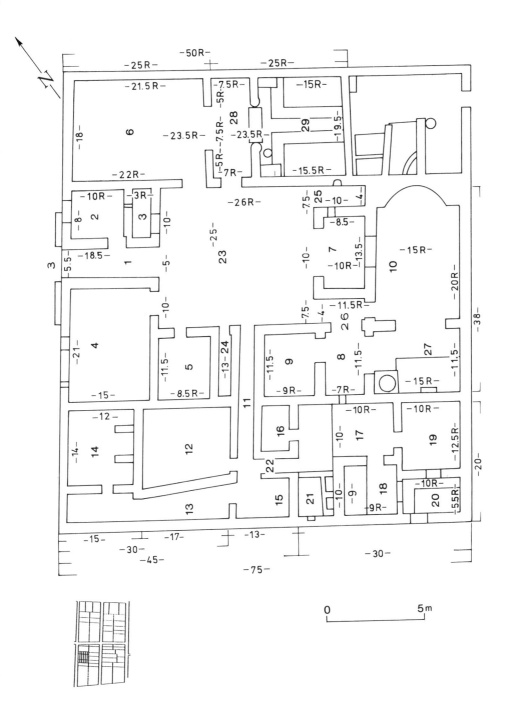

II. Casa dello Scheletro (III 3)

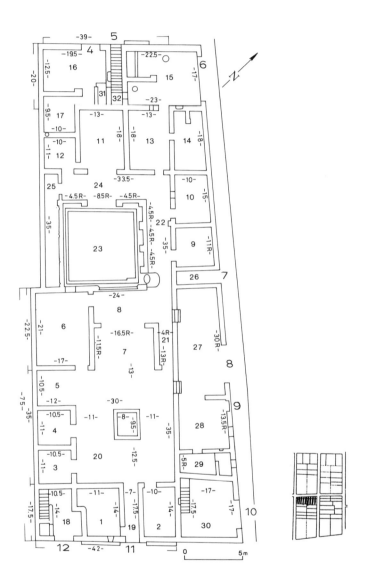

III. Casa del Tramezzo di Legno (III 4-12)

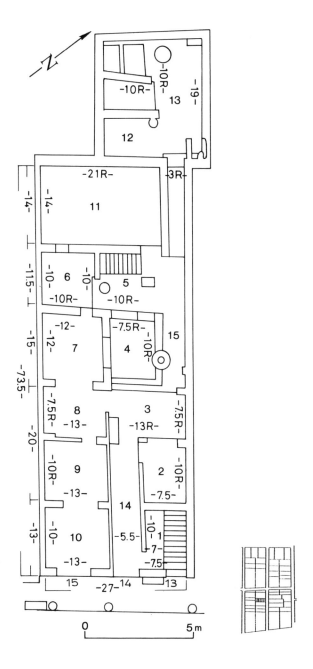

IV.   Casa a Graticcio (III 13-15) - ground floor

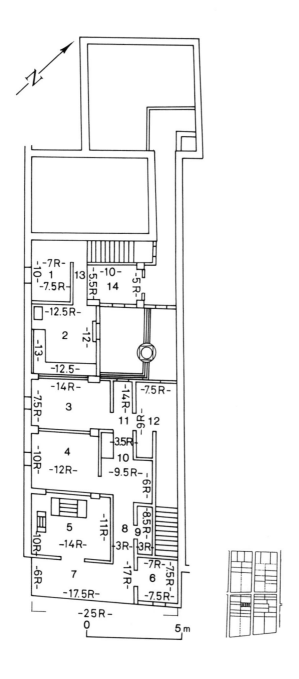

V. Casa a Graticcio (III 13-15) - upper storey

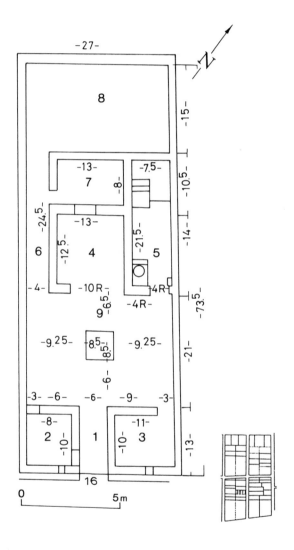

VI. Casa dell'Erma di Bronzo (III 16)

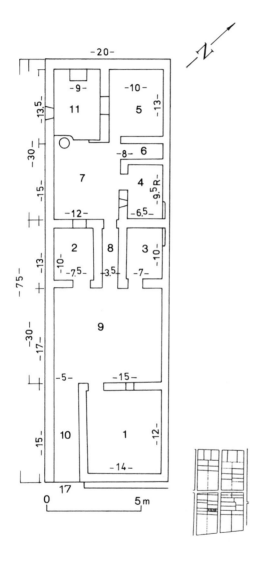

VII. Casa dell'Ara Laterizia (III 17)

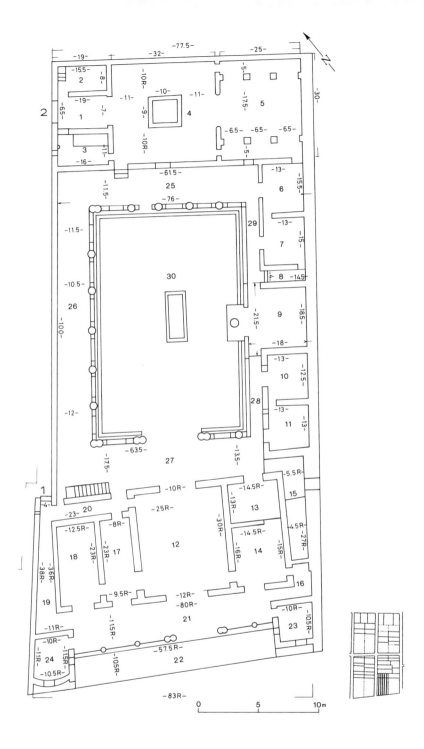

VIII. Casa dell'Atrio a Mosaico (IV 1-2)

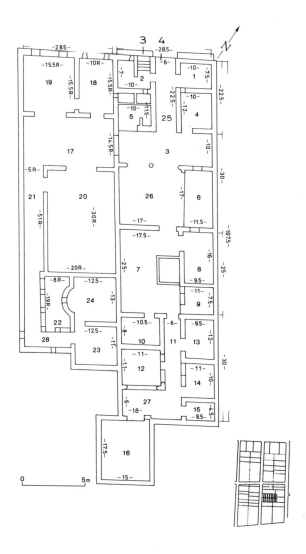

IX.   Casa dell'Alcova (IV 3-4)

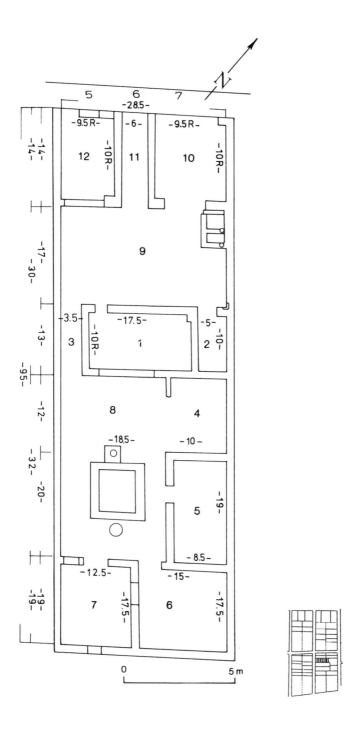

X. Casa della Fullonica (IV 5-7)

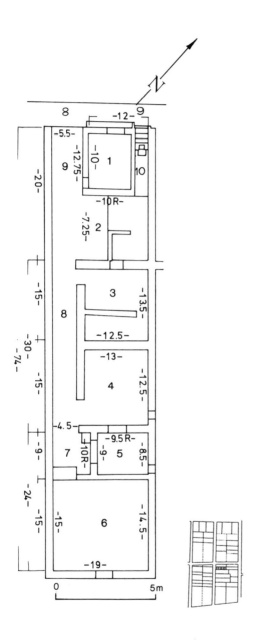

XI. Casa del Papiro Dipinto (IV 8-9)

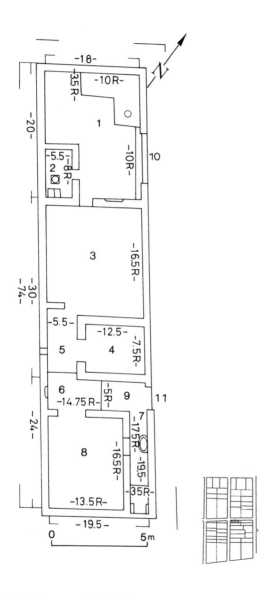

XII. Bottega (IV 10-11)

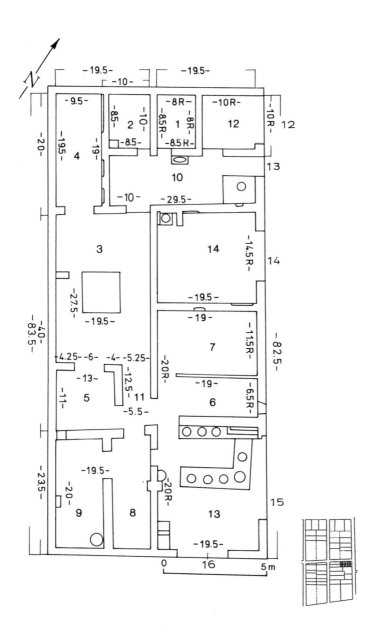

XIII. Grande Taberna (IV 12-13, 15-16); Taberna Vasaria (IV 14)

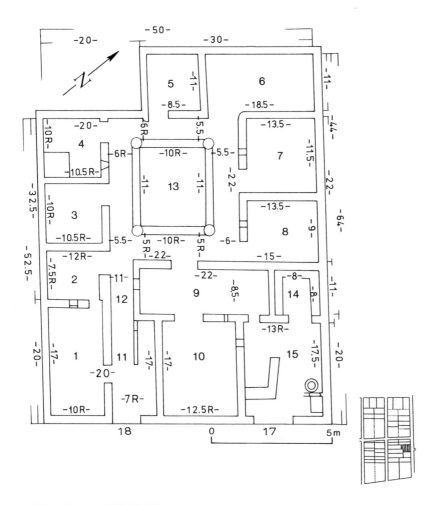

XIV. Taberna (IV 17-18)

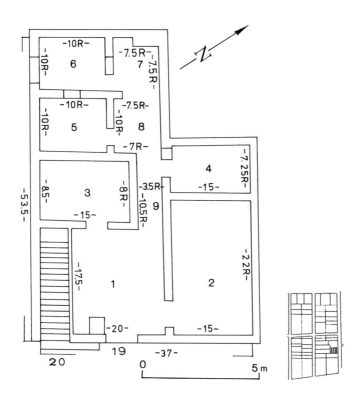

XV. Casa della Stoffa (IV 19-20)

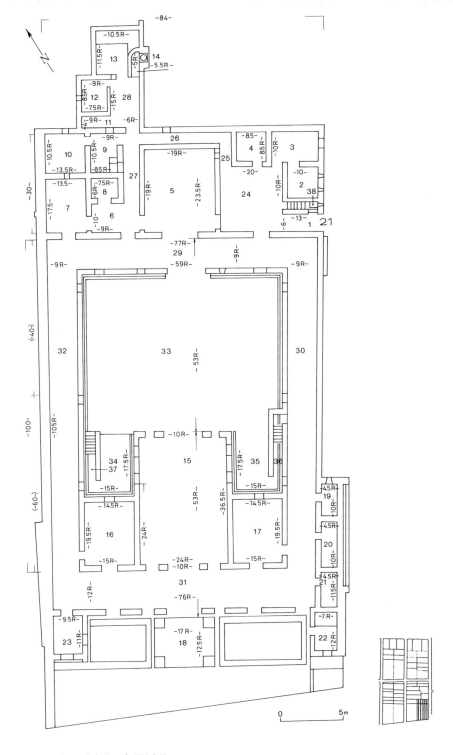

XVI. Casa dei Cervi (IV 21)